Classical Indian Philosophy of Mind

CLASSICAL INDIAN PHILOSOPHY OF MIND

The Nyāya Dualist Tradition

Kisor Kumar Chakrabarti

State University of New York Press

Published by
State University of New York Press, Albany

Printed in the United States of America

For information, address State University of New York Press, State University Plaza, Albany, N.Y., 12246

Production by Diane Ganeles
Marketing by Nancy Farrell

Library of Congress Cataloging-in-Publication Data

Chakrabarti, Kisor Kumar.
Classical indian philosophy of mind : the Nyāya dualist tradition / by Kisor Kumar Chakrabarti.
p. cm.
Includes bibliographical references and index.
ISBN 0-7914-4171-7 (alk. paper). — ISBN 0-7914-4172-5 (pbk. : alk. paper)
1. Nyaya. 2. Ātman. I. Title
B132.N8C35 1999
181′.43—dc21 98-47027
CIP

10 9 8 7 6 5 4 3 2 1

Contents

5. The Existence and Permanence of the Self 55

Six signs of the self offered by Gotama 55, the Buddhist no-self theory 57, the argument from memory and how each of the six signs involves memory as shown by Vatsyayana 58, personal identity cannot be grounded in a flowing stream of causally connected states: the arguments of Uddyotakara and Vacaspati Misra 60, the Humean view 66, objection to the Humean view 66, the neo-Humean view of Shoemaker and its refutation 68, Parfit's view and its refutation 69, the James-Flanagan view and its critique 71.

6. The Self as a Substance 79

Vatsyayana's argument for the self as a substance 79, the Buddhist aggregate theory and objections to the category of substance 81, reply to Buddhist objections and additional arguments for substance 82, the two stage argument for the self 86, Vacaspati Misra's reformulation of the argument in the exclusion mood 88, Uddyotakara's argument in the exclusion mood 89.

7. The Self and the External Sense Organs 93

Arguments of Gotama and Vatsyayana to show that the self is not identical with the external sense organs 94, further remarks on the argument from memory 97, the argument from the persistence of consciousness 101.

8. The Self and the Inner Sense 103

Grounds for the admission of the inner sense 103, arguments of Gotama and Vatsyayana to show that the self is not identical with the inner sense 106, Uddyotakara's argument from the intentional nature of cognitive states 109, the argument from the capability of self control and its application against the theory that the self (or the mind) is the brain 110.

9. The Self and the Body 115

Gotama's and Vatsyayana's argument from the lack of consciousness in a dead body to show that the self is not the body 117, comparison with Kripke's argument for the mental-physical contrast 122, the argument that if consciousness belonged to the body, there would have been many cognizers

Preface

There are many books in English and other European languages in which classical Indian views of the self (*ātman*) are discussed. But in none of them these views are presented in such a way that a reader who is not familiar with the original sources can see for himself that Indian philosophers have thoroughly and rigorously dealt with a wide range of issues in the philosophy of mind. Our work is the first attempt to fill this gap although in a very limited way. It is not a comprehensive work seeking to cover all major classical Indian philosophies of mind. Rather it is mainly devoted to selected topics pertaining to the Nyāya-Vaiśeṣika (Nyāya for short) philosophy of mind. Besides the Nyāya, we have discussed the Cārvāka, Buddhist, Sāṃkhya, Advaita, and Cartesian views and offered criticisms of each of these from the Nyāya point of view. There are also references to some recent physicalist, functionalist and neo-Humean views and brief critiques of them. In the appendix we have provided an annotated translation of selected passages of Udayana's masterpiece entitled *Ātmatattvaviveka*, which is devoted to some key issues in the Nyāya philosophy of mind.

All the translations in this work are our own though we are not fully satisfied with them. Partly because of the great expressive power of Sanskrit and partly because we are dealing with great thinkers who have compressed a lot of thought into a very short space, the translation of Sanskrit philosophical works is often an enormously difficult task. A more thorough job would have involved adding alternative translations and more comments. But that would have required much more space than was available.

We should add a word about diacritical marks. We have used diacritical marks for Sanskrit words, titles of Sanskrit texts, and names of Sanskrit philosophical schools. But we have left them out of names of individuals, for some to whose names they would have been applicable, do not like them.

Our aim in this work is not that of using classical Indian sources to develop an original theory of mind or self. Nor is it our aim to provide a purely historical research in philosophy. Accordingly, we are not concerned to compare different interpretations of historical texts or to trace historical developments. Our aim is partly historical. We seek to utilize fully the original source literature in Sanskrit, let the Indian theorists speak for themselves as far as practicable and with the help of our comments and interpretations provide our readers with access to Indian theories of the mind or self with the focus on the Nyāya dualist tradition. Our aim is to present the views of a major Indian school of philosophy in a clear and compelling way that should make it easy for a student of philosophy to understand and appreciate them. Our presentation should help our readers to situate the Indian accounts with respect to the relevant theories of Western philosophers. The Indian views are interesting in themselves and quite pertinent to Western philosophy, including contemporary discussions of mind and cognition. The Nyāya school in particular has worked out distinctive theories with original features, and these can contribute to current discussions. Our aim is to make this clear with the hope that this may motivate a future scholar to make more progress. Our aim is also to show that the Nyāya position is viable and defensible. This does not imply that the Nyāya is always right nor that it is immune to objection. However, this does imply that the Nyāya view is plausible and that it can be argued for. But we do not rule out that there are other viewpoints that are plausible and can be argued for. In fact, Vacaspati Misra, one of the greatest Indian philosophers, has written sympathetically and extensively on several different schools of Indian philosophy. If we get to write book length works on some other views, we shall try, within our limitations, to emulate that to some extent.

In the course of discussing classical Nyaya dualism we have drawn attention to two logical principles. The first is that of general acceptability of inductive examples (GAIE). According to it, all examples brought in support or critique of an empirical generalization should be acceptable to both sides in a philosophical or scientific debate. This is formulated by Gotama, the founder of Indian logic, but is not explicitly mentioned by Aristotle, Bacon or Mill, the three main sources of European inductive logic. In certain areas of the study of induction Indian logic has been ahead of European logic. For example, the problem of induction is not discussed explicitly in Europe before Hume, but Indians have been discussing it for many centuries before that, as we have shown in *Definition and Induction*, (University of Hawaii Press, 1995). So the mere fact that GAIE is not well known in the European tradition should not be a ground for disregarding it. GAIE may be challenged just as even classical formal logical principles like the law of excluded middle may be challenged. However, more often than not something like GAIE is honored by empirical scientists who require independent verification of observations and experiments (whether confirming or disconfirming) offered in support of general claims that go beyond observation. GAIE is not toothless and can be effectively used by a dualist to build his case, as we have shown. A physicalist or a functionalist may not like this. But this should be a matter of interest to a physicalist or a functionalist, particularly if the latter happens to be pro-science. A logical principle which seems to work well for empirical sciences but seems to cause problems for a physicalist or a functionalist should make would-be physicalists or functionalists wonder if the principle is objectionable or irrelevant or if physicalism or functionalism are in need of reexamination.

It should not be thought that GAIE can be utilized only by a dualist and not by a physicalist. On the contrary, GAIE is a logical principle and can be utilized by both sides in a philosophical debate. We illustrate this below.

A dualist may offer the following argument: All colored things are unconscious; all living bodies are colored; so all living bodies are unconscious. If the conclusion is acceptable, it shows that consciousness does not belong to the body; a dualist may then with the help of other arguments press for the admission of a non-physical self as the conscious being. But whether the conclusion is acceptable depends on whether the general premise that all colored things are unconscious is acceptable. This premise is supported by examples like bricks and stones acceptable to both the dualist and the physicalist. The physicalist may offer living bodies as counterexamples. But living bodies are the subject of the conclusion and part of the bone of contention. So, given GAIE, living bodies do not qualify as counterexamples. The said premise thus becomes acceptable and GAIE is useful for that.

However, a physicalist may offer the following counter argument: All physical states are caused by physical causal conditions; all bodily states are physical states; hence all bodily states are caused by physical causal conditions. This counter argument is designed to forestall the dualist claim that bodily states like redness of the face can be caused by non-physical states like anger. But whether the conclusion is acceptable depends on whether the general premise that all physical states are caused by physical causal conditions is acceptable. This premise is supported by examples like the color of a mango changed by temperature that are acceptable to both the dualist and the physicalist. The dualist may offer bodily states like redness of the face or the clenching of fists caused by anger (which in the dualist view is a non-physical state) as counterexamples. But a physicalist may claim that anger is a bodily state and reject all such counterexamples. So, given GAIE, the said premise becomes acceptable and thus GAIE can be useful for a physicalist as well.

Accordingly, a philosophical dispute cannot be settled by GAIE alone. But other considerations can be brought in on a case by case basis to tilt the balance on one side. If confronted by the above counter argument, the dualist may try to show that the counter argument is not an equal match to the dualist argument. If the counter argument were an equal match to the dualist argument, the result would be a stalemate which would frustrate the dualist's purpose. So a dualist may try to weaken the counter argument. One possible objection is that the conclusion that all bodily states are caused by physical causal conditions is acceptable to a dualist. The latter too accepts that for all bodily states physical causal conditions are necessary. The disagreement is over whether all the causal conditions of bodily states are exclusively physical. So the physicalist needs to show that all bodily states are caused by only physical causal conditions. For this to follow logically the first premise in the counter argument should be reformulated as that all physical states are caused by only physical causal conditions. Now the premise states the usual closure assumption of a physicalist.

A dualist may challenge the reformulated premise by suggesting that there is a divine being which is non-physical and conscious and a causal condition of all non-eternal things. If this is so, it is no longer true that physical states are caused by only physical causal conditions. Of course, a physicalist is likely to object to the suggestion that God exists. Proving the existence of God is also extremely controversial. (A proof is discussed in a later chapter.) Still the suggestion shows that the physicalist assumption that physical states have only physical causal conditions is open to challenge and needs to be argued for and not merely taken for granted.

A physicalist may retort that if a dualist throws in God to challenge the reformulated premise a physicalist may also suppose for the sake of argument that everything is conscious. Then the dualist would be robbed of supporting examples for his premise that all colored things are unconscious. The dualist has offered examples like bricks and stones to support the induction. But if bricks and so on are conscious, no undisputable examples can be found.

Such a retort, however, does not really help a physicalist. The latter is committed to the position that there are physical things and that at least some of them are unconscious. To suppose that even bricks and stones are conscious contradicts the physicalist thesis. This invites the ground of defeat called *pratijna-virodha* or contradicting the thesis. But the supposition of the existence of God is not inconsistent with the dualist position. So by throwing in that suggestion the dualist is not guilty of contradicting his thesis.

Besides the suggestion of the existence of God the dualist may argue that space and time are among the causal conditions of all physical states. But if space and time are infinite and continuous quantities and lack any specific quale that are externally perceptible, neither space nor time are physical in the usual Nyaya sense (explained in the first chapter) that all that is physical possesses an externally perceptible specific quale. Accordingly, the physicalist assumption that physical states have only physical causal conditions is questionable on that ground.

A physicalist may disagree and argue either that space and time are not causal conditions or argue that they are physical. But such claims are controversial and may be challenged by the dualist. Until some progress is made in resolving the debate over the nature of space and time and the concept of the physical, the dualist remains entitled to point out that the assumption that physical states have only physical causal conditions is questionable. This weakens the counter argument and prevents it from being an equal match of the dualist argument.

Even in the unlikely scenario that a physicalist is able to quash the objections from the suggestions that God or space or time are non-physical causal conditions of physical states, it is unclear how a physicalist can justify the claim that nothing non-physical is or can be a causal condition of something physical. This negation is contained in the assumption that physical states have only physical causal conditions. Until the negation is justified, the counter argument cannot be an equal match of the dualist argument. Thus not GAIE alone but GAIE combined with other suitable arguments and methods can help to tilt the balance in favor of the dualist. GAIE is an important methodological principle and may be used to build the case for a wide range of philosophical theories. Still a Nyāya dualist is able to take full advantage of it primarily because the Nyāya is a fully developed philosopical system. It is the greatness of that system that speaks volumes for Nyāya dualism.

The other logical principle alluded to above may be called the flaw of uniqueness. This implies that a unique property of an inferential subject (*paksa*) is logically (from the viewpoint of observational co-relation) inadequate (the issue is not one of merely formal validity) to prove that something else is true or false of that subject. Recent physicalists and functionalists have argued that although no other physical states are subject to privileged access the brain states are so because of their greater and unique complexity. We have pointed out that, irrespective of whether brain states are uniquely more complex than any other physical states, this argument may have a flawed inductive structure. There is room for deep disagreement over these logical principles (which go beyond the controversy over dualism) and this, we hope, will mean an invitation to all concerned to think.

Acknowledgments

I happily acknowledge my debt to the anonymous readers appointed by the publisher for valuable comments. I am also grateful to John Kearns, Michael Ferejohn, Owen Flanagan, William Lycan, Jay Rosenberg, Adam Constaberas, Tushar Sarkar, Sukharanjan Saha and Jay Garfield for reading parts of the manuscript and giving useful suggestions. My homage goes to my teachers of Indian philosophy: late Pt. Madhusudana Nyayacharya, late Pt. Pancanana Sastri, late Pt. Narmada Tarkatirtha, Pt. Visvabandhu Tarkatirtha, late Gopinath Bhattacharya, Narayana Chandra Goswami and Ashoke Kumar Gangopadhyaya. I thank Sukanya (daughter) and most of all Chandana (wife) for drawing attention to unclarities and offering sympathetic criticisms. I also thank Nancy Ellegate, Diane Ganeles, Nancy Farrell, and the anonymous copyeditor of SUNY Press for help with the publication of this work.

Abbreviations

AD	*Advaiasiddhi* of Madhusudana Sarasvati
AN	*Avacchedakatvanirukti* of Raghunatha Siromani
ATV	*Ātmatattvaviveka* of Udayana
BH	*Bhāmatī* of Vacaspati Misra
BP	*Bhāṣāpariccheda* of Visvanatha
BU	*Bṛhadāraṇyaka Upaniṣad*
BT	Bhagiratha Thakkura's Commentary on ATV
CD	*Cārvākadarśana* of Pancanana Sastri
CPM	*A Companion to the Philosophy of Mind*, ed. S. Guttenplan
CR	*Consciousness Reconsidered* by Owen Flanagan
DI	*Definition and Induction* by Kisor K. Chakrabarti
DT	Dinanatha Tripathi's Commentary on ATV
ER	*The Engine of Reason*, by Paul M. Churchland
GB	*Gauḍabrahmānandī* of Gaudabrahmananda
GD	*Gādādharī* of Gadadhara
GMS	Madhusudana Sarasvati's Commentary on the *Gītā*
NDFC	*Nyāyasūtra*, ed. A. L. Thakur
NDP	*Nyādarśana* of Phanibhusana Tarkavagisa
NK	*Nyāyakusumāñjali* of Udayana
NKD	*Nyāyakandalī* of Sridhara
NL	*Nyāyalīlāvatī* of Vallabha
NM	*Nyāyamañjarī* of Jayanta Bhatta
NOM	*The Nature of Mind*, ed. D. M. Rosenthal
NS	*Nyāyasūtra* of Gotama
NSB	*Nyāyasūtra* of Gotama with the *Bhāṣya* of Vatsyayana
NV	*Nyāyavārttika* of Uddyotakara
PDS	*Padārthadharmasaṁgraha* of Prasastapada
PTN	*Padārthatattvanirūpaṇa* of Raghunatha Siromani
RS	Raghunatha Siromani's Commentary on ATV
SK	*Sāṁkhyakārikā* of Isvarakrsna
SM	*Siddhāntamuktāvalī* of Visvanatha

SR	Samkara Misra's Commentary on ATV
SS	*Sāṃkhyasūtra* of Kapila
STK	*Sāṃkhyatattvakaumudī* of Vacaspati Misra
TC	*Tattvacintāmaṇi* of Gangesa
TP	*Tātparyatīkā* of Vacaspati Misra
TS	*Tarkasaṃgraha* of Annambhata, ed. Pancanana Sastri
TSD	*Tarkasaṃgrahadīpikā* of Annambhatta, ed. Gopinatha Bhattacharya
TSN	*Tarkasaṃgraha* of Annambhatta, ed. Narayana Chandra Goswami
UP	*Upaskāra* of Samkara Misra
VP	*Vedāntaparibhāṣā* of Dharmarajadhvarindra
VPS	*Vivaraṇaprameyasaṃgraha* of Vidyaranya Muni
VS	*Vaiśeṣikasūtra* of Kanada

CHAPTER 1

Introduction

Psychophysical dualism is the theory that mind and matter are ontologically different and are not reducible to each other. Such a theorist may hold that both material and mental entities are there for all the time. Or such a theorist may hold that either material or mental entities come first. In the currently popular scientific picture of the origin of the solar system our mother Earth was separated from the Sun in a distant past and was then devoid of all life and consciousness, for it was too hot and lacked the atmosphere requisite for the origin and sustenance of life. Gradually the Earth cooled down over millions of years and life evolved slowly from the humblest beginnings to the most complex found today in the form of human beings. This scientific account is compatible with dualism and, in particular, with the Nyāya-Vaiśeṣika dualism that is the subject of our study. The Nyāya-Vaiśeṣika holds that a living body is a necessary condition for the origin of conscious states. It follows therefrom that no conscious states can exist if there are no living bodies. It is worth noting that the Biblical and the Koranic accounts of genesis speak of relatively short periods of time spanning over several thousand years, which is at odds with the scientific estimate. But the Hindu accounts of genesis with which the Nyāya-Vaiśeṣika is familiar, usually speak of vast expanses of time to estimate the periods of creation (*sṛṣṭi*).[1] They also usually speak of states of dissolution (*pralaya*) when there is water and other kinds of matter but no animals or plants (and no conscious states belonging to any animals or plants). Since the Nyāya-Vaiśeṣika dualism fits such Hindu accounts of genesis that are not at odds with the current scientific account, the former is also not at odds with the latter.

For a study of this dualism we begin with a brief outline of Nyāya-Vaiśeṣika philosophy. According to the standard view (there are other views having a smaller following within the Nyāya-Vaiśeṣika tradition), there are seven kinds of reals called substance (*dravya*), qualia (*guṇa*), action (*karma*), universal (*sāmānya*), ultimate individuater (*viśeṣa*), inherence (*samavāya*), and negative entities (*abhāva*). A substance is the substratum (*āśraya*) of qualia and actions in the sense that it is something in which there cannot be any absolute absence (*atyantābhāva*) of the latter.[2] A substance is a continuant and different from its qualia and actions: it may remain the same even when its qualia or actions change. For example, a mango as a substance may remain the same even when its color (a quale) has changed from green to yellow or even when it starts to roll down (a kind of action) after being stationary before. Qualia and actions are often perceptible and if so, the substance to which they belong may also be perceptible. This differs from Locke's view that a substance is imperceptible. That is, in the Nyāya view, not only the yellow or green color of the mango but also the mango is perceived. However, it may be noted that though, in the Nyāya view, a substance may be perceptible if its qualia or actions are perceptible, it is not always so. For example, in the view of many Nyāya philosophers the self (*ātman*) is an imperceptible substance though it possesses perceptible qualia like cognition or desire.

The Nyāya admits five kinds of physical substance called earth, water, fire, air, and *ākāśa* (the substratum of sound).[3] These are physical (*bhautika*) substances in the sense that each possesses a specific quale that is externally perceivable (e.g., earth has smell).[4] Of these the first four are ultimately atomic (*aṇu*) and the last is non-atomic and pervasive (*vibhu*). The self is a spiritual (*cetana*) substance radically different from all of them, for it alone is the substratum of consciousness and lacks any externally perceivable features. Further, the self is both beginningless and endless. We shall later discuss the reasons for these views. But it may be noted that the admission of eternal, spiritual substances is not ruled out by the current scientific account of the origin of the species or of the planetary system. The scientific picture is not concerned with anything that is nonphysical or spiritual, does not either endorse or oppose it and is not interested in whether such entities, if they exist, are eternal or not. As already said, a dualist who holds that conscious states (which are ephemeral) do not exist except when there are living bodies does not contradict the scientific view.

There is also no inconsistency in holding that although the self is a spiritual substance, it can exist devoid of all consciousness. While the qualia depend on the substance, the reverse is not true (in the view of the Nyāya and many other pro-substance philosophers). Accordingly, although the conscious states are qualia and need the self as their support, the self can exist without them. Further, the radical difference between the self and the physical substances is not wiped out when the self is devoid of consciousness. It still remains true, as the Nyāya would argue, that there is absolute absence of consciousness in the physical substances but not in the self.

Besides the self and the five physical substances the Nyāya also admits three other kinds of substance. The first two of these are space (*dik*) and time, each of which is one, infinite, and continuous. These two do not possess any externally perceivable specific quale. So they are not 'physical' insofar as being physical is to be understood in terms of having some externally perceivable specific quale. They are both imperceptible. They are nevertheless inferred as two of the common (*sādhāraṇa*) causal conditions without which nothing non-eternal can come into being.[5]

The last remaining kind of substance is the inner sense (*manas*). The inner sense is imperceptible but is inferred to account for the direct awareness of internal states like pleasure.[6] It is also inferred to account for the fact that there are occasions when although two or more perceptions could arise at the same time only one does. The inner sense is an indispensable instrument (*karaṇa*) just as an external sense organ like the eye is an indispensable instrument. Accordingly, the inner sense is not the cognizer or the thinker that provides the ground of our personal identity. It is not the owner of the internal states; the latter belong only to the self. The inner sense too is not a 'physical' substance in the traditional Nyāya-Vaiśeṣika sense, for it too lacks any externally perceivable specific quale.[7]

Although space, time, and the inner sense are not physical, they are not spiritual either, for there is absolute absence of consciousness in them. This is why the self radically differs from these as well.

Qualia are features of a substance that do not primarily generate motion and are as particular as the substances to which they belong. Examples are color, smell, and the like. In the Nyāya view the particular red color of a particular mango is causally dependent on and inheres in that mango and cannot belong to anything else. Thus *guṇa* is always a particular though it instantiates universals. For example, the particular red color of a certain mango is an instance of the universal redness that is the common property of all particular red colors. The universal redness (*raktatva*) is ontologically different from particular red colors (*rakta-rūpa-vyakti*) that too are ontologically different from the substances. Since *guṇas* are non-repeatable features, we call them (for the lack of anything better) qualia (without implying that they are always mental) and not qualities or properties as they are sometimes called, for qualities or properties are repeatable features. Thus qualia are quality particulars and not quality universals. Among the qualia are cognition, desire, and so on, regarded as qualia of the self. These will be studied in chapters 3 and 4.

Actions are features of a substance that primarily generate motion (resulting in conjunction with or disjunction from other substances). Like qualia they are as particular as the substances to which they belong and for the same reason. That is, an action is causally dependent on and inheres in the particular substance to which it belongs and, therefore, cannot belong to any other substance.

All substances, qualia, and actions are particulars. But they possess recurrent properties that are shared by other substances, qualia, or actions. These recurrent properties shared by many particulars are the universals. Examples are cowness and greenness. Universals are not mere concepts or names. They are objective, independent of the particulars that share them and are, in fact, changeless and eternal. But unlike Platonic Ideas they are not in some sense transcendent exemplars that can only be grasped by the reason and that particulars can only approximate. In the Nyāya view the particulars are as real as the universals themselves. The latter are present in the former and (if the particular loci are perceptible) are perceptible as well. For example, cowness is perceptible as are individual cows and redness is perceptible as are particular red colors.

Sometimes two particulars cannot be found to be different in any recognizable way although they have already been accepted to be different on substantial grounds. Such may be the case with two atoms that may be indiscernible in every respect but that are known to be different on the very grounds that prove their existence. In these cases ultimate individuators (*viśeṣa*) are inferred to keep the eternal substances concerned distinct (the reasoning involves an application of Leibniz's law of identity of indiscernibles).

The relation between a universal and a particular is natural (*svābhāvika*) and the latter cannot exist without the former. For example, an individual cow cannot but be a cow as long as it exists and, in the Nyāya jargon, cowness is present in it from the moment of its birth till the moment of its death. Such intimate relation between two relata at least one of which cannot exist without the other is called *samavāya*, which for the lack of anything better we translate as "inherence." Inherence is also the relation between a quale or an action and its substance, between a substantial whole (*avayavin*) such as a pot and its parts (and between an eternal substance and its individuator).

Negative entities are objective counterparts of true negative judgments, such as there is no book on the table. In the Nyāya view such judgments are not covert affirmations and require the admission of negative entities such as the absence of the book on the table. Negative entities always have a locus (*anuyogin*) [the table being the locus in the above example] and a negatum (*pratiyogin*) [the book being the negatum in the same example].

It will take us very far afield if we discuss the many rigorous arguments produced by Nyāya philosophers in defense of the above ontology.[8] However, although we use this ontology throughout our work, much of it is not critically presupposed in the Nyāya-Vaiśeṣika philosophy of mind. For the latter the crucial claims are the following. The self is a kind of substance different from internal states like cognition, desire, or pleasure. The latter are qualia that belong only to the self and not to any physical substances. Thus the Nyāya is committed to both of what may be called qualia dualism and substance dualism. It holds that there are qualia of the self which are not reducible to qualia of any other kind of substance. It also holds that the self is a different kind of substance over and above the other substances. We discuss in later chapters some of the arguments for these views.

We have given above a brief outline of Nyāya ontology. Our discussion will be facilitated if it is clear which methodological principles governing philosophical disputes are employed in this work. For our study we adopt some ground rules of Nyāya epistemology that it may be thus useful to state at this point. At the very outset we offer, from the Nyāya point of view, a (mild) antiskeptical argument. The aim is not to show that some cognitions are reliable but to show that there are some cognitions that cannot be false (or doubtful). A cognition, in the Nyāya view, is false if what is featured as the qualifier (*prakāra*) is absent in the qualificand (*viśeṣya*). For example, the cognition of the flower being red is false if the qualifier, namely, the red color, is missing in the flower, the qualificand. It follows that only a cognition in which something is featured as a qualifier can be false. Now, the cognition of something as qualified by something must be preceded by the cognition of the qualifier. In the above example one cannot be aware of the flower being red unless one is already aware of the red color. The prior awareness of the qualifier may itself be an awareness of something qualified by still another qualifier. But this process cannot go on forever. That is, each and every awareness of a qualifier cannot be an awareness having yet another qualifier. That opens the door of a vicious infinite regress that cuts at the root of the very possibility of qualificative or judgmental awareness. This is unacceptable. So there must be some kind of an awareness of a qualifier in which nothing is featured as a qualifier. Such awareness is indeterminate or nonjudgmental (*nirvikalpaka*). (BPP 277) Since it is devoid of any qualifier, it cannot be false (or doubtful). This opens up the possibility that there are other cases of cognition too that are not false or doubtful. An all-engulfing skepticism is, the Nyāya claims, self-refuting. If one claims that no cognition is reliable, the question is: What about this very denial? Is it reliable or not? If it is reliable, it is false to say that no cognition is reliable. But if it is unreliable, there may be some cognition that is reliable. (NS 2.1.13)

In the Nyāya view perception, external or internal, is reliable unless countermanded by another perception or some other evidence. Even when we use some other evidence to undermine a given perception, some dependence on perception becomes inevitable. For example, when a person misperceives a rope as a snake and later learns from another person that the thing was actually a rope and realizes his mistake, he is relying on the testimony he heard of which at least the hearing part is a form of perceiving. This is merely illustrative. But it may suggest that a given perception cannot be disallowed without giving credence to some other perception, such as reading some letters, hearing some sounds, and so on. Dependence on perception is also unavoidable in other forms of cognizing, such as inferring fire from seeing smoke. Unless one can rely on seeing smoke, one cannot rely on the inference of fire either. So the Nyāya holds that a perceptual foundation is needed in all cases of inferences about matters of fact. A perceptual basis is further necessary in the two other forms of cognizing accepted by the Nyāya, namely, *upamāna* (which has an analogical component) and testimony. So the Nyāya philosophers disagree with those who reject perception as a source of reliable information. Perceptions are certainly corrigible. But we have to rely on some perception to correct the error in a given perception and we have to rely on some perception in other forms of cognizing as well. Accordingly, either we have to accept the credibility of perception or we land in skepticism. The Nyāya chooses the former (a thorough discussion of the reasons for not choosing skepticism is beyond the scope of this work) and advocates what may be called the principle of credibility of perception. We adopt this and hold that our perceptions, except when countermanded, provide a reliable basis for making philosophical claims.

The Nyāya also advocates what may be called the principle of credibility of induction (*vyāptigraha*). Inductions are specially useful, for when combined with observation reports or other inductions, they can serve as premises of a valid deduction about something unobserved. For example, the induction that all men are mortal, when combined with the observational premise that this is a man, validly yields the conclusion that this is mortal. Now, in an induction that all *a* is *b* the former is called the pervaded (*vyāpya*) and the latter, the pervader (*vyāpaka*). An induction is credible or reliable if it meets the conditions of observation (or awareness) of co-presence of the pervaded with the pervader or observation (or awareness) of co-absence of the pervaded with the pervader (or both) and the lack of any counter-example (which is the observation or awareness of the presence of the putative pervaded without the putative pervader). For example, smoke and fire are observed to be co-present in a kitchen and to be co-absent in a lake. There is also no known case of there being smoke without fire. So it is permissible to generalize that wherever there is smoke there is fire. On the other hand, it is false to generalize that wherever there is fire there is smoke. Fire and smoke are observed to be co-present in a kitchen and to be co-absent in a lake; still fire is observed to be present in an electric heater without smoke and this shows that they are not always together.

It may be noted that if an inductive premise that fulfils the above three conditions is available in support of a view upheld within a fully developed philosophical system (such as the Nyāya-Vaiśeṣika), it is no small gain. Assuming that no observational refutation is available, the epistemic value of such a premise may be (and, very likely, will be) sought to be neutralized by careful analysis by philosophical opponents. But this attempt will surely invite response from the proponent (as long as the latter has a fully developed system to fall back on). Such critical analysis and response may go on indefinitely: the probability of reaching an impartial judgment about who comes out ahead is not, if the history of philosophy is any lesson, very high. Under the circumstances, if an empirically confirmed and empirically unconfuted inductive premise is available in support of one's view, it is of significant weight.

Of course, the above three conditions do not tell the whole story. Besides them, Nyāya philosophers require investigating whether the connection between the (assumed) pervader and the (assumed) pervaded is dependent on an additional third factor (*upādhi*). They have offered a classification of such third factors and studied how an induction may be vitiated by them in different ways. They also consider whether the reasonableness of an induction is hindered by an unfavorable subjunctive argument (*pratikūla-tarka*) or bolstered by a favorable subjunctive argument (*anukūla-tarka*). They further explore whether the pervader or the pervaded is unsubstantiated (*aprasiddha*) and evaluate an induction by considerations of economy (*lāghava*). Without any doubt, the Nyāya account of induction, though old, is very advanced and contains important developments that are useful for current studies of induction. Since the space is limited and since we have already discussed the Nyāya view in an earlier work,[9] we do not explore in detail these additional dimensions here.

It may be pointed out that the evidence cited as observation (or awareness) of co-presence or of co-absence or of a counterexample should be acceptable to both sides in a philosophical (or scientific) debate. This may be called the principle of general acceptability of inductive examples (abbreviated as GAIE), which we utilize repeatedly in this work. It seems to work for empirical sciences where observations are checked and independently rechecked before any claims based on them are accepted. Nevertheless, there is room for disagreement over this principle (some philosophers tend to think that a plausible scenario that may not have broad support can still be a counterexample) and we do not propose to settle that here. However, we indicate some reasons why the principle is useful.

The principle is useful to avoid partiality and prevent either party from gaining undue advantage over the other as also frivolous acceptance or rejection of an induction. Without this principle either party could be in a position to make claims about co-presence or co-absence or deviation (which gives a counterexample) that appears to the other party to be quite absurd.

For example, suppose one generalizes that all swans are white after observing many white rats. One should be entitled to reject it as frivolous, for rats are not generally acceptable as swans. Again, suppose one generalizes that all swans are white after observing many white swans. Although this is false and can be disconfirmed by producing one black swan, this should not be allowed to be falsified merely by producing a black cat. If a black cat is ever offered as a counterexample, one who holds that all swans are white should be entitled to dismiss it as frivolous. Again, suppose one generalizes that all fish breathe under water after observing many fish that do so. Whether this is true or false, this should not be casually abandoned merely if one offers as counterexamples whales, which cannot breathe under water. One should be allowed to explore whether whales (which are mammals) are fish or not and until whales are shown to be fish, one should remain entitled to continue to claim that all fish breathe under water.

Since, in particular, a single counterexample suffices to refute a generalization confirmed by numerous examples, the counterexample should be a good one, be more than merely logically possible or plausible and should be generally acceptable or acceptable to both sides of an issue. At any rate, a counterexample should not be required to meet a standard lower than that of a confirming example but rather the same standard. In other words, the epistemic burden of both the proponent and the opponent of a thesis should be the same; the burden should not be allowed to become different (i.e., lower or higher) merely by switching sides on some issue. This implies that examples that are treated differently by different theories are not acceptable as either confirming or disconfirming examples; both confirmation and disconfirmation should proceed on the basis of examples that are undisputable by either side or generally acceptable.

One may say that so far as observation reports like whether something is a cat or a swan is concerned, one should let science (or common sense) tell the way it is and that one should have an open mind only about theories. But, unfortunately, it is far from clear where to draw the line between an observation report and a theory. A disagreement over whether something is a cat or a swan may seem to be trivial and irrelevant. If someone does claim a cat to be a swan, we may point out such things as that a cat does not fly while a swan does, that a cat is a mammal while a swan is not, that his claim does not fit with his behavior, that his claim to be accepted would require too far-reaching changes within our belief systems, and so on. It is also more than likely that near total agreement on whether something is a cat or a swan will be reached. But philosophical issues often involve disagreements over borderline or disputed cases where such near total agreement is hard to achieve. For example, consider the disagreement over whether a painting is obscene (where differences of opinions even among experts are galore) or whether a system of government is just (where communists and capitalists do not see eye to eye) or, more relevantly to our present concern, the disagreement over whether an internal state like cognition is physical or nonphysical. Some dualists may claim that we are directly acquainted with such a state and that it is more than obvious that it is nonphysical. Then this should suffice, some may suppose, as a counterexample to the materialist claim that everything is material. But a materialist would never agree to that. Where is the independent and impartial court of appeal to judge which party is playing fair or foul here?[10] Accordingly, both sides in a philosophical debate should have an equal right to accept or reject an observation report about co-presence, co-absence, or deviation and examples that are treated differently by different theories should be held in abeyance. This has the consequence that an induction based on observation of co-presence or co-absence (or both) acceptable to both parties but challenged by a counterexample acceptable to only one party but not to the other is still reliable. Such an induction, like other inductions, is of course corrigible and may be set aside by some counter evidence that is acceptable to both parties. But until that happens it is credible and a proper basis for philosophical claims.

A Nyāya philosopher says sometimes that an observation report is obviously true and that some sayings are to be ignored (*upekṣaṇīya*) as the ravings of someone insane (*unmatta*). Being commonly accepted (*loka-prasiddhi*) is sometimes cited as a distinctive advantage. A distinction is also drawn between what is not accepted by either side (*anyatarāsiddha*) and what is not accepted by both sides (*ubhayāsiddha*). Still it is implied in much Nyāya writing that all possible proponents or opponents of a philosophical thesis have the equal right to accept or reject an observation report of co-presence, co-absence, or deviation. This is implied in the famous dictum of Gotama that an example (*dṛṣṭānta*) is such that both commoners (*laukika*) and researchers (*parīkṣaka*) may agree on that (NS 1.2.25). There is no suggestion here that it suffices if the example is accepted by only the proponents or only the opponents. Rather the suggestion is that the example should be acceptable to all researchers, whether proponents or opponents. There is also no suggestion that the condition of general acceptibility applies only to confirming and not to disconfirming examples. Rather the suggestion is that it applies to both.

Gotama significantly imposes the condition that the example should be acceptable to common sense as well. This is an important epistemic commitment that implies a certain continuity between ordinary understanding and theoretical understanding and between ordinary language and theoretical language. The implication is not that common sense is a safe and incontrovertible touchstone. (In particular, there is no implication specially in the area of philosophy of mind that folk psychology could never in principle be replaced by neuroscience.) But the implication is clearly that a philosopher or a scientist does not have the liberty of dismissing common sense summarily (or even after it has served its purpose in providing the starting points of an inquiry as Aristotle sometimes says) when it comes to articulating the evidence for the general claims that philosophers (or scientists) are so fond of making. The evidence for generalization, Gotama requires, should be acceptable not only to researchers but also to common sense. That is, bridges should be built between philosophy, science, or theoretical enterprise on the one hand and common sense on the other when it comes to supporting general, factual claims. Whatever may be one's final judgment of this, it shows that the criterion is epistemic and not dialectical. The criterion might have been dialectical in a way if Gotama had required that examples should be acceptable only to researchers or only to common sense. But by requiring that examples should be acceptable to both researchers and commoners Gotama is in effect demanding that a generalization should have a broad and impartial base.

Why might the criterion have been dialectical in a way had Gotama required that examples should be acceptable only to researchers? The researchers after all are in a position to conduct a more thorough and systematic inquiry than the commoners. The answer may not be rooted in any deep epistemological reason but in practical considerations. Researchers sometimes get to enjoy substantial rewards for their contributions. The motivation for (financial or social or other) rewards may sometimes be too great to conduct an impartial inquiry. Or sometimes researchers may simply overlook something that is known to commoners. Hence Gotama may have felt it prudent to include the commoners too among the observers and take note of additional points of view. The other possible explanation is that Gotama does not share the rationalistic enthusiasm of uncovering through the "natural light of reason" (of which the wiser among us may be thought to have a greater or even exclusive share) the essences of things hidden behind the appearances of the senses. Perception for him is the chief source of knowing. Since both commoners and researchers rely on perception, there may not be sufficient epistemic justification for leaving the commoners out. Without any doubt the researchers can conduct the observation in an environment over which they have much greater control. While such control is an added value, it may also come at a price. Gotama was perhaps not convinced that the possibility of having to pay such a price can be ruled out.

That the said criterion is epistemic can also be gathered from the concepts of *sapakṣa* and *vipakṣa*. The former is a particular instance different from the inferential subject (*pakṣa*) where the pervader is certainly (*niścita*) present, while the latter is an instance where the pervader is certainly absent (TS 142). The certainty may sometimes be derived from perception or from common acceptance. But the requirement of certainty disqualifies something doubtful or debatable or questionable to the other party from being passed on as a confirming or disconfirming example. This is also evident from ruling out the inferential subject (*pakṣa*). Since the latter is a part of the bone of contention, it cannot be offered as a confirming or disconfirming example.

Besides perception, induction and deduction, the Nyāya advocates (and we accept) the credibility of testimony (*śabda*) which is a kind of indirect cognition (*parokṣa-jñāna*). One form of it is the reliability of what is commonly accepted (*loka-prasiddha*) except when there is overriding consideration to the contrary. Another form of it is that if the speaker or the author of the testimony is reliable, the testimony (unless there is counter evidence) is reliable.

In general, the Nyāya subscribes to a causal-reliabilist standpoint. If the sources are reliable, the information derived from the sources is also deemed to be reliable unless there is a reason for doubt or rejection. Accordingly, the Nyāya devotes a lot of attention to spelling out precisely what is the reliable method of perceiving, generalizing, inferring, and testifying. This viewpoint allows the Nyāya to have a vast network of reliable information and we adopt that for our study. In a particular application in the philosophy of mind this permits one to have a credible basis for information about other persons even from a dualist point of view. A dualist often holds (as does the Nyāya) that internal states are private. So one cannot directly know what somebody else is thinking or feeling. But since perceiving, generalizing, inferring, and testifying are all reliable except when there is counterevidence, one may gather that other people have internal experiences similar to one's own from the observation of their behavior or their testimony. That is, one is directly aware of one's own experience and observes one's own behavior attending such experience. Then when one observes other people behaving in a similar way, one may infer that other people have similar experiences or one may learn about their experiences from their testimony.

Finally, the Nyāya advocates (and we also accept) the credibility of the best available hypothesis (*prayojaka-kalpanā*) for an explanation of a problematic phenomenon. For example, if a person is fat but never eats during the day, one may form the hypothesis (*arthāpatti*) that the person eats at night. The Nyāya holds that the statement of the phenomenon requiring explanation or the explanandum should be validly deducible from the explanans, which includes the statement of a general law (*vyāpti*) and the statement or a set of statements describing the relevant circumstances applicable to the thing to be explained. Thus, in the above example, it should be possible to come up with a deduction like the following: Whoever is fat but does not eat during the day, eats at night, for example, X, and so on. This person is fat but does not eat during the day. So this person eats at night (BP 552). Moreover, the hypothesis should be economical (*laghu*). Three primary considerations of economy are economy with respect to constitution (*śarīra*), that with respect to presentation (*upasthiti*) and that with respect to relationship (*sambandha*).[11]

We have given an overview of Nyāya-Vaiśeṣika ontology and epistemology. We now give a brief survey of the names, dates, and works of some major Nyāya-Vaiśeṣika philosophers and other Indian philosophers cited in this work. The chronological data about ancient Indian philosophers are vague and different scholarly estimates of dates of ancient Indian philosophers vary widely. Some scholars prefer to assign the most recent date possible. This does not rule out that the former could be of an earlier date. But in some cases this method may produce misleading results particularly if there is evidence that the former could be of a significantly earlier date. In the same way assigning the earliest possible date may be misleading if there is evidence that it could be of a much later date. So instead of assigning the earliest possible or the latest possible date, we prefer to assign the date that is most likely based on our judgment of the best evidence we have. We avoid discussing the evidence here, for that requires a lot of space and we are not trying to determine the chronology of Indian philosophers in this work. We simply record what appear to us to be the most likely dates for various Indian philosophers.[12]

The Nyāya school was founded by Gotama, the author of the *Nyāyasūtra*. Gotama belongs to the sixth century BCE when the Vedic age comes to an end with the rise of Buddhism and Jainism after the Persians score major military victories over the Indians. The Vedic Hindus appear to have enjoyed a long period of relative peace and prosperity before the Persian aggression. The Persian victory probably led to some soul searching among Hindu thinkers, who, confronted with powerful Buddhist and Jain rivals, found it useful to present in an organized way the main currents of Hindu thought. Gotama's work and other *sūtra* works that provide the beginnings of the Hindu *darśanas* are the products of this effort. The basic ideas found in these works are often anticipated in the Vedic literature. The *sūtra* works present them in a systematic manner that paved the way for a fruitful dialogue and exchange of ideas among the competing points of view.

The *Nyāyasūtra* is a philosophical masterpiece covering a wide range of topics in a decisive, precise, and rigorous manner. It is extremely cryptic and is obviously intended to be supplemented by oral instructions of the teacher to the student. It was never intended to be studied on one's own (as some modern scholars try to do and, not surprisingly, miss a lot). The importance of the oral tradition that has existed without any real discontinuity from the antiquity to the present, can hardly be exaggerated for the Nyāya including the *Nyāyasūtra*. The only sensible approach is to study it first with the help of a pandit well versed in the oral tradition.

It may be noted that arguments for the self occupy a central position in the *Nyāyasūtra*. This is not surprising if we keep in mind that the self plays a pivotal role in Hinduism. In keeping with the Hindu tradition, Gotama has declared release (*apavarga*) from worldly bondage and suffering to be the ultimate goal of life (*parama-puruṣārtha*). This goal can be achieved only by removing false beliefs (*mithyajñāna*) about the primary (*mukhya*) knowables (*prameya*). Gotama has given a list of twelve primary knowables. The self is at the head of this list. The self is clearly the cornerstone of the fundamental Hindu doctrines of afterlife, rebirth, transmigration, karma, and God. So false views about the self (two typical examples of which from the Hindu point of view are (1) that the self does not exist [*nairātmya-vāda*] and (2) that the self is the body [*dehātma-vāda*]) are discussed and sought to be refuted.

The first available commentary on the *Nyāyasūtra* is the *Nyāya-bhāṣya* of Vatsyayana (2nd century BCE). It is invaluable for an understanding of the *Nyāyasūtra* and provides an amplified interpretation of Gotama's aphorisms that has become the standard interpretation. However, Vastsyayana is also an original thinker in his own right. He disagrees with Gotama on a number of points and introduces a large number of topics not directly mentioned by Gotama that too have become a part of the orthodox Nyāya. As an example drawn from the philosophy of mind, we mention that Gotama nowhere explicitly calls *manas* (translated by us as the inner sense) a sense organ (*indriya*). Vatsyayana does so without any hesitation, attributes this to Gotama himself, and this view has become a part of the Nyāya tradition.

Other leading Nyāya philosophers of the old school are Uddyotakara (6th century CE), the author of *Nyāyavārttika*, Bhasarvajna (9th century CE), the author of *Nyāyabhūṣaṇa*, Vacaspati Misra (9th century CE), the author of *Tātparyatīkā*, Jayanta Bhatta (10th century CE), the author of *Nyāyamañjarī* and Udayana (11th century CE), the author of *Pariśuddhi*, *Nyāyakusumāñjali*, and *Ātmatattvaviveka*.

Far-reaching changes were brought about within the Nyāya around the twelfth century CE with the rise of the so-called new Nyāya. The four most influential philosophers of the new school are Gangesa (13th century CE), the author of *Tattvacintāmaṇi*, Raghunatha Siromani (15th century CE), the author of *Dīdhiti* and *Padārthatattvanirūpaṇa*, Jagadisa (17th century CE), the author of *Jāgadīsī* and *Śabdaśaktiprakāśikā*, and Gadadhara (17th century CE), the author of *Gādādharī* and *Śaktivāda*.

The sister school of Nyāya, called the Vaiśeṣika, was founded by Kanada, the author of *Vaiśeṣikasūtra*. This is a philosophical masterpiece of similar antiquity as the *Nyāyasūtra* and written in a similar aphoristic but rigorous style. Some other leading philosophers of this school are Prasastapada (2nd century CE), the author of *Padārthadharmasaṃgraha*, Sridhara (10th century CE), the author of *Nyāyakandalī*, Udayana (11th century CE), the author of *Kiraṇāvalī*, Srivallabha (11th century CE), the author of *Nyāyalīlāvatī* and Samkara Misra (15th century CE), the author of *Upaskāra*.

Two syncretic works that combine the philosophies of the Nyāya and the Vaiśeṣika are the *Tarkasaṃgraha* with the *Dīpikā* of Annam Bhatta (18th century CE) and the *Bhāṣāpariccheda* with the *Siddhāntamuktāvalī* of Visvanatha (18th century CE).

Some leading philosophers of the Buddhist school are Nagarjuna (2nd century CE), the author of *Mūlamādhyamikakārikā* and *Vigrahavyāvartanī*, Vasubandhu (4th century CE), the author of *Vijñaptimātratāsiddhi* and *Tṛṁsikā*, Dignaga (5th century CE), the author of *Nyāyapraveśa* and *Ālambanaparikṣā*, Dharmakirti (7th century CE), the author of *Pramāṇavārttika* and *Nyāyabindu*, Santaraksita (8th century CE), the author of *Tattvasaṃgraha*, Kamalasila (8th century CE), the author of *Pañjikā*, and Ratnakirti (11th century CE), the author of *Apohasiddhi* and *Kṣaṇabhaṅgasiddhi*.

Carvaka (6th century BCE) is the founder of Indian materialism. Unfortunately, his writings are lost except for some fragments surviving in quotations by others. We have to rely on the philosophical opponents of the Carvaka, such as the Nyāya (as identified in later chapters), as sources for the Cārvāka position. The only available work of the Cārvāka school is the *Tattvopaplavasiṁha* of Jayarasi (7th century CE).

The Sāṃkhya school was founded by Kapila (7th century BCE), whose aphorisms are lost. Three of the most influential philosophers of this school whose writings are available are Isvarakrsna (2nd century CE), the author of *Sāṃkhyakārikā*, Vacaspati Misra (9th century CE), the author of *Tattvakaumudī*, and Vijnanabhiksu (15th century CE), the author of *Sāṃkhyapravacanabhāṣya*.

The roots of the Advaita school are clearly found in the Upaniṣads some of which, such as the *Vṛhadāraṇyaka*, date back to before the sixth century BCE. Three of the most influential philosophers of this school are Samkara (7th century CE), the author of *Śārīrakabhāṣya* and *Gītābhāṣya*, Vacaspati Misra (9th century CE), the author of *Bhāmatī*, and Madhusadana Sarasvati (16th century CE), the author of *Advaitasiddhi*.

The next chapter is devoted to clarifying some salient features of Nyāya dualism and distinguishing it from Cartesian dualism. The latter is beset with well-known difficulties over the mind-body interaction. These difficulties, we try to show, are avoided by a Nyāya dualist and why: this brings out some of the distinctive and important aspects of the Nyāya position. The third and the fourth chapters give an account of cognition and some other internal states. Since the self (in the Nyāya view) is the substratum of internal states, an account (of the Nyāya understanding) of them is needed. However, in the Nyāya view the self is a permanent substratum although the internal states are fleeting. (This is one main reason why the self is held to be ontologically different from its states.) So the fifth chapter provides a critique of the Buddhist and some neo-Humean views from the Nyāya standpoint and argues for the permanence of the self. The sixth chapter explains the rationale for the doctrine of the self as a substance. After thus discussing why the self is a permanent substance, the seventh, eighth and ninth chapters discuss why the self is immaterial as well. The tenth chapter is devoted to miscellaneous arguments, the eleventh, to proofs of the existence of God, the twelfth and the thirteenth, to the Nyāya critique of respectively the Sāṃkhya and the Advaita views and the fourteenth, to the conclusion. This is followed by an appendix containing an annotated translation of selected portions of Udayana's *Ātmatattvaviveka* so that one may get an overview of Udayana's main lines of reasoning. The upshot of the whole work is that the Nyāya-Vaiśeṣika view of the self as a permanent, immaterial substance that serves as the substratum of internal states such as cognition or desire, is a well-developed, well-argued, and coherent philosophical theory.

Chart of Indian Philosophers and Schools

Nyaya	Vaisesika	Bauddha	Samkhya	Carvaka	Advaita
Gotama	Kanada	Nagarjuna	Kapila	Carvaka	Samkara
6th century BCE	6th century BCE	2nd century CE	7th century BCE	6th century BCE	7th century CE
Vatsyayana	Prasastapada	Vasubandhu	Isvarakrsna	Jayarasi	Vacaspati Misra
2nd century BCE	2nd century CE	4th century CE	2nd century CE	7th century CE	9th century CE
Uddyotakara	Sridhara	Dignaga	Vacaspati Misra		Madhusudana
6th century CE	10th century CE	5th century CE	9th century CE		Sarasvati
Bhasarvajna	Udayana	Dharmakirti	Vijnabhiksu		16th century CE
9th century CE	11th century CE	7th century CE	15th century CE		
Vacaspati Misra	Srivallabha	Santaraksita			
9th century CE	11th century CE	8th century CE			
Jayanta Bhatta	Samkara Misra	Kamalasila			
10th century CE	15th century CE	8th century CE			
Udayana		Ratnakirti			
11th century CE	<u>Syncretic School</u>	11th century CE			
Gangesa	Annambhatta				
13th century CE	18th century CE				
Raghunatha	Visvanatha				
Siromani	18th century CE				
15th century CE					
Jagadisa					
17th century CE					
Gadadhara					
17th century CE					

CHAPTER 2

Understanding Nyāya-Vaiśeṣika Dualism

Nyāya-Vaiśeṣika philosophers hold that there are physical substances like bricks and stones. While such objects are available in plenty, it is not easy to make clear what precisely is meant by being physical. One possible view is that the physical is that which has causal powers or, at least, that the physical is that which can causally influence another physical object. This view may seem to underlie well-known physical laws such as the law of conservation of energy and of linear and angular momentum (and may seem to survive the partial blurring of the distinction between particle and wave in current physical theory). But in the context of the debate over psychophysical dualism such a conception of being physical is starkly question begging. For it would then follow that if something (putatively) mental causally interacts with something physical, the former is physical too.

Another possible view is that being physical necessarily implies being extended or being in space and vice versa. There is no doubt that physical objects such as bricks or stones are in space. But whether everything that is physical is in space in the same sense in which bricks or stones are in space is questionable. Bricks or stones occupy a limited region of space (*mūrta*) and offer resistance to other physical substances of limited magnitude from occupying that same space. Everything that is in space in this sense is physical in the Nyāya-Vaiśeṣika view. But everything physical is not in space in this precise sense from the Nyāya standpoint. Thus *ākāśa*, the substratum of sound, is extended and in space. But it does not occupy any limited region of space and prevent other physical (or nonphysical) substances from occupying that same space.

So a distinction should be drawn between two different senses of being extended or being in space. The first sense of occupying a particular region of space and preventing other measurable physical substances from being in that space (or being solid) is a sure sign of being physical, according to the Nyāya, and true of innumerable physical substances. But it is not true of all physical substances. There are physical substances that are extended in a different sense. The latter sense is that of being in contact with a substance (*saṃyogitva*). Something in contact with a measurable (or immeasurable) substance need not prevent other measurable (or immeasurable) substances from being in contact with that same thing. All physical substances, in the Nyāya view, are in space in either the first or the second sense. But these are two different senses and although the first implies the second, the second does not imply the first.

Is everything that is extended in either the first or the second sense physical? Not according to the Nyāya. Being extended in the sense of being in contact with another substance is true of all substances, physical or nonphysical, including the self. So the self turns out to be an extended, immaterial substance in the Nyāya view (virtually a contradiction from the Cartesian standpoint). We return to this soon.

It is thus clear that extension (*parimāṇa*) is not a defining property of being physical in the Nyāya view. What then is the defining property? As noted earlier, it is that of having a specific quale (*viśeṣa-guṇa*) that is externally perceivable (*vahirindriya-grāhya*) (BPP 121–22). That is, all physical substances have a specific quale that is externally perceivable and all that has a specific quale that is externally perceivable is physical. (For example, physical objects such as bricks or stones have externally perceivable qualia like color or smell.) This definition should not be thought to be an a priori, necessary truth. Rather it is an empirical generalization amply confirmed by innumerable observation reports and not challenged by any above-the-board counterexample. It is conceivable that a physical object may not have any externally perceivable specific quale. It is also possible to cook up thought experiments in which the above generalization does not hold. But none of these would detract from the credibility of an otherwise reliable, empirical generalization.

This view of matter may seem to conflict with that of Locke. Locke distinguished between primary qualities like extension and motion on the one hand and secondary qualities like color and smell on the other. One may interpret this to mean that while primary qualities really belong to the physical objects and are objective, the secondary qualities do not and are subjective.

While the interpretation of Locke's view is a matter of controversy, the Nyāya view does not imply that a physical object must have an externally perceived quale like color. When it is said that a physical substance has a specific quale that is externally perceivable, what the Nyāya claims is that a physical substance is the causal substratum (*samavāyi-kāraṇa*) of externally perceivable qualia like color.[1] A causal substratum is different from and independent of the effects supported by it. So in the Nyāya view matter is that without the support of which externally perceivable qualia such as color could not exist. This does not rule out that a physical substance can exist without any externally perceived quale.

The Nyāya view is also not incompatible with the view of some that physical science assigns only position in space and motion to matter. Even if the latter is a correct interpretation of physical theory, it does not rule out that matter can have other causal roles. In particular, it does not rule out that unless there were things in space with motion, qualia such as color could not exist. It is true that one kind of physical substance recognized by the Nyāya, namely, *ākāśa*, is immobile (because of being ubiquitous). But it is still a necessary causal condition for the motion of flying birds, falling bodies, and so forth. Thus whether the Nyāya view of matter is compatible with that of physical science largely depends on one's understanding of the Nyāya and of physics. This issue cannot be resolved in a short space. Irrespective of what may be one's final judgment on this, the Nyāya account of a physical substance as that which is the causal substratum of externally perceivable specific qualia is noncircular and offers a viable perspective for a philosophical study of the mind-body problem.[2]

In the Nyāya-Vaiśeṣika view, all positive noneternal things exist in a particular space and endure for a particular period of time. This is true of internal states such as pleasure as well. In other words, it is true of my pleasure that it arises within the limits (*avaccheda*) of my body and so also of other internal states.

Does this conflict with the view held by some traditional Western dualists that mental states such as pleasure exist only in time but not in space? Although this also is largely a matter of interpretation, the conflict, if there is one, may not be as great as it may first seem. The internal states arise within the limits of the body, but they do not belong to the body. They belong only to the self, which is an immaterial substance. However, unless the self were in contact with the particular body, the particular internal state would not come into being. So the contact with the body and, therefore, space is a necessary causal condition of the internal state.

Still, from the Nyāya-Vaiśeṣika point of view, the contact between the self and the body not only determines the spatial characteristic of an internal state but also its temporal characteristic. Time, like space, is one, infinite, and continuous. Its division into particular temporal periods is dependent on the existence of noneternal things like the body. So the contact between the self and the body also provides (in part) the ontological basis of the truth of the statement that my pleasure exists at this particular time. Thus both temporal and spatial predicates of an internal state, so to speak, sail in the same boat. If the traditional Western dualist view implies that temporal predicates are true of internal states such as pleasure but spatial predicates are not, that is not accepted by the Nyāya-Vaiśeṣika. The cogency of the latter view depends on that of the view that both space and time are one, infinite, and continuous and that spatial and temporal divisions are dependent on the existence of noneternal things. If this view of space and time is acceptable, the view that internal states have both temporal and spatial predicates is also reasonable and defensible. It also seems to be impossible to give an account of my pleasure, my perception, and so on, without reference to my body. If this is true, it may lend support to the view that both spatial and temporal predicates are true of internal states.

It may appear from the above that there are some notable differences between Nyāya-Vaiśeṣika dualism and Cartesian dualism. We have just noted that while internal states such as cognition and pleasure do not have extension and do not belong to the body, in the Nyāya-Vaiśeṣika view it is still true of them to say that they are here in my body. This is not the view of Descartes. Further, according to Cartesian dualism, only two kinds of substance exist: mind and matter. The former is spiritual and unextended and the latter is extended. Thus Descartes holds that while thinking is the essence of the self or the mind, extension is the essence of matter. Matter cannot be conscious; the mind cannot be extended. These views appear to be quite foundational in the Cartesian metaphysics. But the Nyāya-Vaiśeṣika does not espouse this (as already indicated) and does not formulate the basic issue in quite the same way. The crucial issue for the Nyāya-Vaiśeṣika is the following: Is it necessary to admit the existence of a separate kind of substance that alone is the substratum of consciousness and that lacks any externally perceivable specific quale? The Nyāya-Vaiśeṣika answers this question in the affirmative but rejects the Cartesian view that such a substance must be unextended. In fact, the Nyāya-Vaiśeṣika holds that the self, as remarked earlier, has extension (*parimāṇa*). (We take up this issue below.) The Nyāya also rejects the assumption that the physical-mental dichotomy is exhaustive and recognizes several kinds of substance that, as explained, are neither physical nor mental. Finally, the self is distinguished from the inner sense and these two are considered to be different kinds of substance. No such distinction is entertained in traditional Western philosophy and functions of the inner sense are usually attributed to the self.[3]

We have noted above that in the Nyāya view the immaterial self has extension. What is the evidence for it? It may be pointed out that other known substances have extension. For example, bricks and stones are substances and have extension (and this is acceptable to Nyāya dualists, Cartesian dualists, and physicalists alike if we bracket the possible disagreement over the category of substance). A Cartesian would claim that the immaterial self is an unextended substance and may offer this as a counterexample. But this is disputable (and would be rejected by the Nyāya), for there is no noncircular evidence to show that what is immaterial must be unextended. On the basis of undisputable supportive instances and from the lack of any undisputable counterexample it is permissible, given GAIE, to generalize that all substances have extension.

This generalization may also be supported by a subjunctive argument (*tarka*). Suppose that not all substances are extended. Then there is at least one unextended substance. But such an unextended substance cannot come into contact with another substance, for contact presupposes extension (explained below). Accordingly, it cannot fulfil the typical roles of a substance, such as that of providing support for another substance (as when the table supports the book on it) or that of being the causal substratum of another substance (as when the cloth is woven out of the threads), for all these require contact. Admitting such a substance would then not be useful.

[Nyāya philosophers usually offer subjunctive arguments to support a generalization. Subjunctive arguments may also be added in favor of many generalizations that we shall use as premises in later chapters. But we have avoided explaining those subjunctive arguments, for that would have significantly increased the size of this work.]

Now that the self has extension can be demonstrated by the following valid argument:

All substances have extension, for example, a brick.

All selves are substances.

Therefore, all selves have extension. (TSD 101)

Descartes himself would reject this argument as unsound, for he is a rationalist and has little faith in empirical generalization. (The Cartesian method of appealing to intuition and the natural light of reason while making crucial claims does not have a large following in this century.) But if the principles of generalization outlined in the introductory chapter and the subjunctive argument given above are acceptable, the above argument is defensible. There are more specimens of similar arguments and defensive strategies in chapters 10 and 11. They provide an understanding of how a Nyāya philosopher would defend an argument such as the above against possible objections. Needless to say, the above argument is not likely to face much challenge from physicalists in spite of the possible disagreement over the ontology of substance. A physicalist would eventually have to opt for some ontology of object or thing and so on. As long as the self (or whatever it is reduced to or replaced with) would fit that description, the argument, *mutatis mutandis*, would go through.

Although (in the Nyāya view) the self has extension, it is not solid and does not prevent other physical objects from occupying the same space. We have distinguished between two different senses of being extended. In the first sense an extended thing is solid and offers resistance to other measurable substances' occupying the same space. But in the second sense an extended thing is merely in contact with another substance and does not prevent other substances from being in contact with that same substance. This is true even though the self remains in contact with the body throughout the lifetime of an individual and pervades that body. However, since every other substance coming into contact with another substance is found to have extension and since the self is supposed to be different from the body (the reasons for which are discussed in later chapters) and still to be in contact with it, the self too is supposed to have extension.

What is contact? It is the conjunction of two substances that were previously not in conjunction (*aprāptayoḥ prāptiḥ*).[4] For example, one billiard ball while hitting another billiard ball comes into contact with it. The self becomes conjoined with the body immediately after it is conceived and, in normal cases, remains conjoined with it till the death of that body.[5] It thus appears that contact involves being together in space and this presupposes extension. (However, contact is a separable relation; that is, two substances in contact may be separated from each other. So in unusual circumstances the self may be separated from the body even before the death and another self be conjoined with that body or two or more selves may be associated with the same body, and so on, and all this may result in abnormal behavior.)

One serious problem in the Cartesian view may now be indicated. Descartes held that consciousness and extension are two fundamentally opposed attributes. Nothing conscious can be extended and nothing extended can be conscious. Still, according to Descartes, mind and matter interact. But how can something extended causally interact with something unextended? Descartes supposed that the interaction takes place in the pineal gland, which was regarded as the seat of the essentially conscious self or the soul. But since this is no more than an ad hoc assumption, it only highlights the difficulty in his position. Further, if there is such interaction, how does that fit in with the principle of conservation of energy? When the extended matter interacts with the unextended mind, should not some energy be lost in the process? How then can the total energy remain constant? (Whether the Nyāya dualist view offends the conservation laws is addressed in chapter 14.)

These puzzles forced Spinoza, a follower of Descartes in many ways, to reject the interaction of matter and mind and maintain that there is a parallelism between mental states and bodily states. That is, corresponding to any bodily state there is always a parallel mental state and corresponding to any mental state there is always a parallel bodily state but neither causes the other. However, parallelism is not a comfortable position either. For one thing, it appears to be counterintuitive. It seems to be obvious that when, for example, I want to get up and do get up, my desire influences my body and similarly when I am physically exhausted and unable to concentrate, my bodily condition influences my mental condition. For another, parallelism forces us to assume that whenever there is a bodily change there is a parallel mental change (and vice versa). Thus for every act of exhaling or inhaling, for every act of digestion or secretion, and so on, there must be each time a corresponding mental state although there is no such evidence. This shows that as a theory parallelism is grossly overburdened with unwarranted assumptions and is uneconomical. Thus both interactionism and parallelism are found to be beset with serious difficulties. This has worked against dualism. If dualism implies either interactionism (which makes it a mystery how an extended thing can interact with something unextended) or parallelism (which is overburdened with assumptions), why not give up dualism and look elsewhere?

One advantage of the Nyāya kind of dualism may be apparent now. A Nyāya dualist is not faced here with a difficult choice. The

Nyāya does not espouse parallelism. It accepts the causal interaction between bodily states and internal states as our everyday experience points to. But since the self is extended and conjoined with the body, there is no special problem in supposing that bodily states and internal states influence each other.

Further, the Nyāya critically examines and rejects the doctrine that the effect is preexistent (*satkārya*) in the cause and also rejects the doctrine of causal power (*śakti*) (BPP 20). It does not subscribe to the causal adequacy principle that since the cause determines the nature of the effect, the latter may have less but cannot have any more than what is in the cause. It also does not hold that there is in some sense an identity and continuity between the cause and the effect. If the cause is understood in the above ways (which have been influential in both Western and Indian philosophy) that the Nyāya rejects, there may be difficulty in accounting for causal interaction between bodily and internal states from a dualist point of view. Thus it is not at all clear in what sense a bodily state may be preexistent in the internal state that causes it or is identical or continuous with it or is causally adequate for it although the two are very different. (Such an understanding of causation may work for a physicalist or a mentalist espousing monism.) Since Descartes subscribes to the causal adequacy principle (and also holds that mind is unextended and matter, extended) the difficulty has been compounded for him.

But a dualist does not have to subscribe to such a view of causation (and does not have to deny that the self has extension or that internal states have location). A dualist may opt for a Hume-like view (which does not necessarily lead to skepticism or irrationalism) that a causal condition is a regular and contiguous antecedent. [Since the Cartesians subscribe to the causal adequacy principle, the Hume-like view of causation is not available to them.] For example, hydrogen and oxygen are causal conditions of water not in the sense that there is a continuity between the former and the latter (which does not appear to be the case, the former being gases and the latter being a liquid, so that the latter appears to be a different entity) but in the sense that the two gases regularly precede water where it is produced.

This is what the Nyāya has done.[6] According to the Nyāya account of causation, a causal condition is always present where the effect originates immediately before its production (TS 103). It is not our project here to discuss which view of causation is the most satisfactory although the Nyāya philosophers have responded to various objections to the Hume-like view of causation. But if this view of causation is acceptable, there is no difficulty in explaining the interaction between bodily and internal states. Such interaction is no different from that between two bodily states or two internal states. When a bodily state is said to be a causal condition of another bodily state, what is meant, for the Nyāya, is that the former invariably precedes the latter in the same body or the same complex of bodies. Similarly, when an internal state is said to be a causal condition of another internal state, what is meant is that the former invariably precedes the latter in the same self or the same complex of selves. In the same way an internal state that causally influences a bodily state is present where the bodily state is produced immediately before its production and similarly, *mutatis mutandis*, for a bodily state that causally influences an internal state, for the self and the body are in contact and together form the self-body complex.

To recapitulate: for Descartes the problem of mind-body interaction assumed enormous proportions because he assumed that anything extended must be physical and anything conscious must be unextended. It is perhaps safe to say that all physical things are extended. But it does not follow therefrom that all extended things are physical. At least the Nyāya philosophers saw clearly that these are different claims and rejected the latter while accepting the former. Again, Descartes assumes that location necessarily involves extension. But the Nyāya denies that. For the Nyāya internal states have location but not extension.[7] These powerful views, combined with a well-developed regularity theory of causation, help them to avoid one of the most frustrating problems confronting the Cartesian type of dualism.[8]

Another important difference is that, unlike Descartes, the Nyāya does not hold that consciousness is the essence of the self. In the Nyāya view the self alone is the substratum of consciousness; but consciousness or thought is an adventitious (*āgantuka*) quale and originates in the self only when other necessary causal conditions are available. For Descartes the self is a thinking substance and is never without consciousness. Being without consciousness is, for Descartes, tantamount to being material. But, as we have already said, the Nyāya does not accept the assumption that everything is either mental or physical and either essentially conscious or essentially extended. So far as consciousness is concerned, there is no empirical evidence that the self remains conscious in states of deep sleep, coma, and the like. Hence the view that consciousness is an adventitious quale of the self.

In the philosophy of Descartes, dualism is married to rationalism, essentialism, and necessitarianism. Many philosophers today are opposed to these latter views and may dislike dualism because of its historical links with these. But the Nyāya, while upholding dualism, espouses empiricism, fallibilism, and probabilism. This shows that dualism has no unbreakable links with rationalism, essentialism, or necessitarianism and that a dualist does not have to prove such claims as that the self is essentially conscious. From the Nyāya point of view what the dualist does need to prove is the weaker claim that the self (or the mind as long as we do not confuse it with the inner sense) alone is conscious. A major part of this is sought to be accomplished, as we shall see in the later chapters, in trying to prove that the self is not identifiable with the body, the external senses, or the inner sense.

Again, Descartes held that while the human self is a thinking substance, nonhuman animals are nothing more than unconscious automata.[9] This may put the materialist at an advantage. What Descartes has to show is that there is some radical difference between a human being and all other animals. This is surely not easy to prove, particularly in the light of our enhanced knowledge of animal behavior, which shows that at least the higher animals (which will generate a slippery slope) are capable of highly complex activities of learning, communication, and exploitation of the environment. For example, monkeys have been observed to use branches of trees as tools to dig up food from under the ground or break open hard shells with the help of stones. Dogs have been known to trace their masters even when separated by significant distance and to recognize them even after the lapse of significant time. Birds have been found to build multichambered nests and to provide for light by sticking fireflies to the walls. And so on. If animals are unconscious automata in spite of being capable of such activities, why not also the humans? All that the materialist has to do under the circumstances is shoot down the attempts on the part of a Cartesian to prove any radical difference between humans and other animals and demand that the same conclusions should apply to both. If all other animals are machines, so are the humans. The Nyāya has not offered any such opportunity to the opponent. In other words, a Cartesian dualist has not only (*a*) to make a case for psychophysical dualism but also (*b*) a case for the unique status of humans in the animal world. He can succeed only by making good both claims. But a Nyāya dualist does not carry the burden of making good the second claim.

The Nyāya, of course, may face a challenge from the materialist from the other direction that since the animals are machines and since the humans are not radically different from the animals, the humans are also machines. In other words, while Cartesian dualism may remain safe even if the materialist succeeds in showing that animals are machines, that would jeopardize the Nyāya kind of dualism. Needless to say, if there is such a challenge, the Nyāya would disagree and offer evidence to show that animals are not machines. The Nyāya, of course, is not precluded from accepting that the humans possess a higher level of conscious activity than other animals. In fact, the Nyāya position is that human consciousness is more developed than that of animals in many ways, but it is still a difference in degree and not in kind. This seems to be compatible with our current knowledge of human and animal behavior, which does not suggest that consciousness is the exclusive possession of humans.

CHAPTER 3

Cognition

In the Nyāya view the self is the substratum of internal states. An account of the latter is therefore useful for an understanding of the Nyāya and other Indian philosophies of self.

One important kind of internal state is cognition or awareness (*jñāna*, *buddhi*, *upalabdhi*, *cetanā*, etc.). It reveals something (*artha-prakāśanam*). In the Nyāya view cognition is a causal condition (*kāraṇa*, *hetu*) of deliberate actions (*vyavahāra*) (TS 94). The latter usually consists in avoiding (*hāna*) what is unpleasant and/or harmful or in acquiring (*upādāna*) what is pleasant or useful. Such actions do not occur unless there is cognition of something as pleasant/useful or unpleasant/harmful.

Eternal and Noneternal Cognition. In the Nyāya view, cognition is noneternal or eternal (TS 212–13). The former is the cognition of mortals and nonpervasive (*avyāpyavṛtti*). It arises in the self within the confines (*avaccheda*) of the body. It is a fleeting state and usually endures for only two moments. After that it may leave behind an impression (*saṃskāra*) or may be replaced by another similar or dissimilar internal state. On the other hand, the cognition of God is eternal and pervasive (*vyāpyavṛtti*).[1] It is always direct and everything is included as its object (*sarva-viṣayaka*).[2]

Determinate and Indeterminate Cognition. Cognition is determinate (*savikalpaka*) or indeterminate (*nirvikalpaka*). In the former the distinction and relation between a qualificand (*viśeṣya*) and a qualifier (*viśeṣaṇa*, *prakāra*) is cognized and something is cognized as something. For example, being aware of a rose as red is a determinate cognition. Here the rose is the qualificand, the red color is the qualifier and the latter is cognized as being inherent (*samaveta*) in the former.

The qualificand-qualifier distinction is relative and may vary depending on the nature of the cognition. If instead of the cognition that the rose is red, what is cognized is that the red color is in the rose, the red color becomes the qualificand and the rose or belonging to the rose, the qualifier. A situation may be described and cognized in two or five or ten or even more different ways and the distinction between the qualificand and the qualifier will vary accordingly. Such fluidity of the distinction is a chief reason for the privacy of cognitive states. The latter are private in the sense that only the cognizer knows what the content of the cognition is. Additionally, only that person knows what precisely is the qualificand and the qualifier. Even if a third person may make an intelligent guess about what roughly is the content, he may have no inkling of what exactly is the qualificand and the qualifier.

The cognitive fluidity also provides a serious obstacle to many antidualist theories of the mind. Those who hold that cognitive states are identical with brain states, for example, have singularly failed to show that there are actually ten different brain states corresponding to ten different descriptions and cognitions of a situation. In fact, the most advanced and detailed study of what is happening in the brain has yielded no clue as to what precisely is the qualificand or the qualifier of a particular cognition of a particular person at a particular time.

The explanatory gap does not appear to be similar to what happens when there is a gap between the explanandum and the explanas where both are physical. For example, some physicists thought that light is a wave and accordingly looked for a medium. When they found none, they hypostatized one called ether. Although the concept of ether was fraught with difficulties, they knew what it should be like in so far as it was to be a medium for the movement of light. Eventually it was found that the speed of light was constant and this did not fit with the required concept of a medium. So ether turned out to be ethereal and was abandoned. Here the physicists who supported ether, knew that there was an explanatory gap. But they also knew what could fill the gap and settle the issue in their favor. Similarly, the opponents of ether also knew what could decisively refute the theory.

But the situation appears to be different with respect to brain states and cognitive states. The closest scrutiny of brain states does not reveal anything like the fluid distinction between the qualifier and the qualificand. Rather a scrutiny seems to reveal a gap that is ever more yawning. Thus whatever is chosen for the qualifier or the qualificand within a brain state must be in some kind of a spatial relation with the other cognate. But it is quite unclear that it makes sense to say that the qualifier of my cognitive state is to the left (or right, etc.) of the qualificand. One can here metaphorically speak of logical or epistemic or conceptual space and imagine spatial relations of a sort for the qualifier and the qualificand as well. But that may serve no real purpose. The constituents of a brain state are not in logical or epistemic or conceptual space but in physical space. What may or may not transpire from such "thought experiments" may have no decisive bearing on the issue at hand. For there may remain the lurking suspicion that what transpires in logical or epistemic or conceptual space may not hold in physical space.

In the same way, whatever is chosen for the qualifier or the qualificand within a brain state must be in a temporal relation (of before or after or being at the same time) with the other cognate. But it is far from clear that we can legislate the same for the qualifier and the qualificand of my cognitive state, that is, it does not seem to follow that the qualifier must be before or after at the same time as the qualificand. One can again try to introduce logical or epistemic or conceptual time and grope for something like a temporal relation there. But there seems to be no reason to think that the talk about logical or epistemic or conceptual time will fare any better than that about logical or epistemic or conceptual space. Thus we seem to be left with no clue or evidence of how the ever yawning explanatory gap can be overcome and the precise mapping of brain states with cognitive states (by way of identifying within a brain state what is the qualifier and what is the qualificand) is to be carried out. The lack of evidence of precise mapping of brain states with cognitive states makes the above identity theory questionable. Further, when combined with the Nyāya arguments for dualism and objections to materialism to be introduced in the later chapters, it makes the identity theory appear less plausible.[3]

Not only is the distinction between and the qualificand and the qualifier fluid, but also both the qualificand and the qualifier may be subject to multilayered specifications. In the cognition 'the man with the red stick is slightly lame', the man is the qualificand. But it is further specified as the man with the stick and then specified even further as the man with the red stick. So the stick first becomes the specifier of the fact that the man is the qualificand. Such a specifier is called in the Nyāya terminology the specifier of the qualificandness (*viśeṣyatāvachhedaka*). Since the stick is further specified by being red, the red color is called the specifier of the specifier of qualificandness (*viśeṣyatāvachhedakatāvachhedaka*). More such specifiers may be needed depending on how exactly the qualificand is revealed in the cognition. Similarly, the qualifier may be subject to further specification which are called the specifier of qualifierness (*viśeṣaṇatāvachhedaka*), the specifier of the specifier of qualifierness (*viśeṣaṇatāvachhedakatāvachhedaka*) and so on, these being useful for showing exactly how the qualifier has become the content of cognition.

Such layeredness of cognition presents another problem for the identity theorist. No amount of the study of brain states gives any useful information about the layeredness of cognition. The layeredness is dependent on the distinction between the qualificand and the qualifier and since the latter is fluid, the former is fluid too. In the above example the content could also be presented to a different cognizer at the same time or to the same cognizer at a different time as that the slightly lame man has a red stick. Again, the study of brain states yields no reliable information about why such changes take place and gives no adequate basis for predicting them.

It may here be added that the qualificand-qualifier distinction is somewhat similar to the distinction between the subject and the predicate in Western logic and grammar; but it is not quite the same distinction.[4] Thus according to the highly influential view of Aristotle, the predicate must always be a universal. But in the Nyāya view the qualifier may be a universal or a particular. Thus in the cognition, 'the man carries a white stick', the particular white stick the man carries is considered to be the qualifier (and the particular man, the qualificand). A follower of Aristotle could argue that the carrying of the white stick is the actually intended qualifier and that it is possible to interpret this as a universal predicate true of many particulars. This is acceptable to the Nyāya up to a point. But the latter would insist that on a deeper analysis the carrying involves a relation of contact (*saṃyoga*) between two particular substances, namely, the man and the white stick and that the relation of contact is as particular as these substances themselves. The Nyāya is not opposed to regarding the innumerable different contacts as instances of the universal contactness (*saṃyogatva*). Still each contact is a non-repeated particular. Each particular contact is brought about by two particular substances, is causally dependent on them, and therefore, cannot exist apart from them. In fact, from the Nyāya standpoint the distinction between the qualificand and the qualifier and the distinction between the different layers of specification are epistemic distinctions and do not imply any fixed ontological stratification.[5]

Returning to the distinction between determinate and indeterminate cognition when a cognition is without any qualifier (*niṣpra-*

kāraka), it is indeterminate. Since the relation between the qualificand and the qualifier is not cognized in this case, nothing is cognized as something. It is a mere acquaintance with something with which there is sensory connection. Accordingly, only perception can be indeterminate.[6] But we can never "catch" any cognition that is indeterminate and introspect it. We can only introspect a determinate cognition. Further, indeterminate cognition cannot directly lead to deliberate activity, only derminate cognition can.

The distinction between determinate and indeterminate cognition poses another challenge to the theory that cognitive states are identical with brain states. If this theory were true, one would expect that the study of cerebral processes may contribute at least in part toward an understanding of this distinction. But it does not. This seems to reinforce the dualist view that the objective of neuroscience is not a philosophical study of cognition, which is what is crucial for the philosophy of mind. Of course, the determinate-indeterminate distinction may be challenged on philosophical grounds and set aside. But, again, neuroscience would not have anything important to contribute toward showing that the distinction is untenable.

Reproductive and Productive Cognition. From another point of view cognition is reproductive (*smṛti*) or productive (*anubhava*) (TS 97). The former is the kind of awareness that results from disposition (*saṃskāra*) alone, such as remembering a lost necklace. This should be distinguished from recognitive perception (*pratyavijñā*), for instance, that I saw this house a year ago. This latter requires disposition; but it also needs sensory connection with the perceived and recognized object at the time of cognition. It should be kept in mind, however, that in addition to disposition memory also requires, in the Nyāya view, the contact between the self and the inner sense (*ātma-manas-saṃyoga*) that is a causal condition of all cognitions. So when memory is said to arise from disposition alone, what is meant is that memory is not dependent on anything but disposition as its specific (*viśeṣa*) causal condition. Other kinds of cognition are invariably dependent on some other specific causal condition, for example, perception requires sensory connection. Hence this account of memory is precise enough. Accordingly, productive cognition, such as smelling an orange, may be explained as that kind of awareness which has some content that is not derived solely from disposition. We shall explore the nature of memory later.

Direct and Indirect Cognition. Productive cognition is direct (*pratyakṣa*) or indirect (*parokṣa*). In the view of Gotama, the founder of the Nyāya school, direct cognition or perception arises from sense-object connection (NS 1.1.4). For example, the perception of a pot arises from the sensory connection between the eye and the pot. However, if this is strictly construed as a definition of perception, it is too narrow: it fails to cover divine perception.[7] Divine knowledge is direct, in the Nyāya view. But it does not arise from sensory connection. God is bodiless and lacks any sense organs.

To avoid this Gangesa (13th century CE) has defined perception as that kind of awareness that does not arise with the help of any cognition serving as the instrument (*karaṇa*) (TC 552). In nonperceptual awareness some cognition invariably serves as the instrument. For example, in inferring that there is fire in the hill from seeing smoke, the awareness that smoke is pervaded by fire serves, according to one widely held Nyāya view, as the instrument (*karaṇa*). So this definition of perception is not too wide.[8] But it also applies to divine perception. The latter is unoriginated and so not originated with the help of some cognition functioning as the instrument.

The Nyāya is not mainly concerned with divine perception but with that of mortals. The latter is of two kinds: external (*vāhya*) and internal (*āntara*). The former is the perception of an external object with which there is sensory connection of an external sense organ, for example, the perception of a rose through its contact with the eye. The latter is the direct awareness of internal states such as pleasure and cognition with the help of the inner sense.

We now turn to memory, which plays an indispensable role in our cognitive enterprise. Gotama has listed the major causes of memory as follows: "Concentration, collection, practice, sign, distinctive feature, similarity, ownership, the support, the supported, relationship, succession, separation, having the same effect, rivalry, excellence, gain, gap, pleasure, pain, desire, aversion, fear, need, motion, attachment, merit and demerit: from [these] causal conditions [arises memory]" (NS 3.2.41). Vatsyayana comments:

> Concentration is a fixation of the inner sense from the desire to remember or repeated thinking of some sign of what is sought to be remembered: this is a causal condition of the remembrance of things. Collection is the citation of many things in the same work. Things included in the same work, whether serially or otherwise, become the causal condition of the remembrance of one another. . . . Practice is the repeated cognition of the same thing; the disposition resulting from practice is a quale of the self; this also is equally a causal condition of memory. . . . The sign is but that which is conjoined

> or that which is inherent or those which are co-inherent or that which is opposed, e.g., smoke of fire, the horn of the cow, the hand of the foot, color of touch and the future of the past. The distinctive mark on the body is a causal condition of remembering the clan. . . . Similarity, e.g., the image of Devadatta in a picture [reminds one of Devadatta]. Ownership: From the possession the possessor or from the possessor the possession is remembered. From the support: from the chief the subordinate is remembered. From the supported: from the subordinate [there is remembrance] of the chief. From relationship: the teacher is remembered from the student, the worshipper from the priest. From succession: things to be done [are remembered]. From separation: he who knows about the separation remembers keenly the one who separates. From the same effect: from the awareness of one agent another agent is remembered. From rivalry: of two rivals from the awareness of either the other is remembered. From excellence: he who has achieved excellence [is remembered]. From gain: that from whom one had gained or is likely to gain something is repeatedly remembered. From the gap: the sword is remembered from the shield, etc. From pleasure and pain: the causes of these are remembered. From desire and aversion: that which is desired or hated is remembered. From fear: that which is feared [is remembered]. From need: that which one needs, such as food or garment, is remembered. From motion: the charioteer is remembered from the chariot. From attachment: the woman to whom one is attached is repeatedly remembered. From merit: remembrance of previous lives and retention here of what is studied and heard. From demerit: [one] remembers the source of some previously encountered suffering. . . . This is illustrative and is not meant to be an exhaustive count of the causal conditions of memory. (NSB 3.2.41)

We add a few words to clarify some of the above cases. Concentration (*praṇidhāna*) is fixing the inner sense on what is sought to be remembered. This involves not to let the inner sense be distracted by other things and have it focused on the object of remembrance or some distinctive feature (*liṅga*) of the object sought to be remembered. Collection (*nibandha*) is the inclusion of various topics in the same work. Because of this association one topic helps one to be reminded of the next topic or some other topic in the same work. For example, Gotama has listed sixteen topics such as the source of knowing, the knowable, and so forth, in his work. Hence the source of knowing may remind one of the knowables or of some other topic, say, doubt. Practice often means the repeated awareness of the same thing. But here, as explained by Vatsyayana, it means the disposition left in the self; such disposition (*bhāvanā*) is a quale of the self and serves as a causal condition of memory.

For sign Vatayayana offers an explanation that accords with the view of Kanada, the founder of the Vaiśeṣika school. Smoke is a sign of fire by way of conjunction; unless smoke is conjoined with its source, it may deviate from fire and become a flawed sign. The horn is a sign of a cow by way of inherence. The horn is a part of the cow which is a substantial whole (*avayavin*). The whole is inherent (*samaveta*) in the parts. Co-inherence is two things being related by way of inherence to the same thing. The hand and the foot are both related by way of inherence to the same body: the latter is the substantial whole of which both the hand and the foot are parts. In a similar way, both color and touch are related by way of inherence to the same pot: the latter is the substance (*dravya*) that serves as the substratum of both color and touch, which are qualia (*guṇa*). Finally, of two opposed things one may remind one of the other. These four kinds of sign serve as grounds for inferring something unperceived; they also serve as the reasons for remembering that thing. The remaining cases are easy to decipher and may be left without further annotation.

The total number of grounds of memory cited by Gotama add up to seventeen. Vatsyayana remarks that this is not an exhaustive list, for such grounds are virtually innumerable. By listing the seventeen grounds Gotama has spelt out in some detail the associative laws of memory. The principal grounds recognized by him appear to be contiguity in time or space or both and similarity or dissimilarity. The list as a whole is impressive. It shows a careful attention paid to an internal state that provides, as we shall see, the basis for a major argument for the existence of the immaterial and permanent self. Gotama's crypticness and the habit of packing an enormous body of information into a few words in the form of an aphorism is legendary. The fact that his aphorism on memory is one his longest and most detailed aphorisms is a pointer to the crucial role memory has to play for supporting one of his pivotal doctrines—that of the self. Each of the seventeen grounds of memory gives credence to the thesis that the agent who remembers endures through the time of the past experience and that of its remembrance and also retains both continuity and identity. This is variously exploited by Gotama and other Nyāya philosophers to argue for not only the permanence of the self but also its preexistence and eternality.

A similar account of memory is given by Prasastapada, the great Vaisesika commentator. He says that remembrance arises from a particular kind of contact between the self and the inner sense and depends on awareness of the sign, desire, memory, and so on (i.e., awareness of the sign, etc., serve as the stimuli of remembrance) as well as impression. It pertains to what is already known through observation, inference, or testimony and, therefore, to something past. It serves as a causal condition of recognitive perception, inference, memory, desire, and aversion. The impression results from a cognition that is vivid (*patu*), frequently repeated (*abhyāsa*), or interesting (*ādara*) (PDS 625–26). Once again, the account is brief but does provide the essential information about memory in a clear and precise manner.

Regarding impression Prasastapada adds that it is weakened or destroyed by cognition (of other thing), addiction, suffering, and so on (PDS 647). He remarks that something strange, even if experienced infrequently or only once, may leave a firm impression. As an example, he cites a South Indian's encounter with a camel. (Although camels were commonly used in some parts of northwestern India, they were nonexistent in South India.) Similarly, a vivid experience may leave a firm impression as also frequent repetition of the experience. A firm impression may also result if the object is of special interest to the cognizer in which case the latter may wilfully focus the inner sense on that (PDS 656–57).

Another familiar cognitive state is doubt. Doubt, says Prasastapada, is a state of indecision (*vimarśa*) between two positions (*ubhayāvalambī*) of the form 'is it this or that'. It arises when the common (*sādhāraṇa*) and the distinctive (*viśeṣa*) features of two kinds of things are already known but only the common features happen to get noticed in something to the exclusion of the distinctive features. For example, one might doubt whether the thing in front is a man or a statue. This would happen if only the common features of a man and a statue, such as similar height, are noticed and distinctive features, such as movement of limbs, are unnoticed. (PDS 511–14). The doubt is resolved when a distinctive feature is noticed and the doubt is replaced by a belief (*nirṇaya*). For example, in the above doubt if the thing in front is noticed to move any limb, the doubt will make way for the belief that the thing is a man and not a statue. Since it is already known that a statue cannot move but a man can, the movement will rule out the possibility of the thing being a statue and give rise to the belief that it is a man (PDS 622).

It may be noticed that the distinction between a doubt and a belief is a commonplace theme that can, without any mystery, be understood and explained by incorporating (partly) introspective data from first person accounts. But a merely neuroscientific analysis talking about how nerve endings get fired or connected, and so on, would fail to throw much light on this distinction. This reduces the plausibility of the claim made by some thinkers that someday all folk psychological notions about internal, nonphysical states will make way for neuroscientific notions.

Many of our beliefs are of course erroneous. Errors (*viparyaya*), says Prasastapada, are either perceptual or inferential. (Prasastapada, following Kanada who is the founder of the Vaiśeṣika school, holds the view that all sources of reliable information are ultimately reducible to perception or inference.) Perceptual errors may be caused by some kind of physical impairment due to excess bile (*pitta*), cold (*kapha*), wind (*anila*), injury to the sense organ, or whatever, that leads to an improper (*ayathārtha*) sensory connection (*ālocana*). Due to such factors and demerit, which may cause inattention, and the contact between the self and the inner sense, there results erroneous perception of something that is not adjacent (*asannihita*). For this to happen the distinctive features (*viśeṣa*) of the misperceived thing must be already known. Later when that thing is not adjacent, the distinctive features of it are wrongly attributed to what is adjacent from the impression (*saṃskāra*) of such features (PDS 423). For example, a cow may be mistaken for a horse. This can happen only if one already knows about the features of a horse. Although the distinctive horse features are missing in a cow that is adjacent to the sense organ, the perceiver's impression of such features is revived. This together with the faulty sensory connection (which prevents the perceiver from noticing the distinctive features of a cow and allows him to notice only some horselike features, as Sridhara points out in NKD 424–25) due to some kind of physical impairment and some kind of demerit give rise to the misperception.

It may here be noted that Prabhakara and his followers have disputed the very existence of perceptual error. They have argued that no external perception can arise without the external sense organs. But the external sense organs never misrepresent the nature of things, for they merely function as the instruments of sensory connection and, if they reveal things, they reveal them as they are (NKD 430). It is true that the efficacy of an external organ may be impaired due to some defect. Then it may not be able to reveal a thing with which there is sensory connection. It follows that an external sense organ cannot function as the causal instrument (*karaṇa*) in the so-called illusions and hallucinations. And it follows therefrom that the latter cannot be perceptions, for, as already said, no external perception can arise without the instrumentality of an external organ. So a different account of what is misleadingly labeled as erroneous perception is called for.

In Prabhakara's view what really happens in a so-called illusion is that there is a lack of discrimination between a percept and a revived image. For example, a shell may be mistaken for silver. Here the eye, which is the instrument of sensory connection with the shell, fails to reveal the shell because of some defect. But the eye cannot reveal the silver, for there is no sensory connection with the silver. So the awareness of the silver must come from some other source. This source, according to Prabhakara, is memory. Although the eye has failed to grasp the shell, it may still suffice to grasp its brightness, whiteness, and such. This helps the revival of the image of some silver seen in the past that had similar features. (The image may also be composite and drawn from several different experiences. So the specific piece of silver or whatever is the content of an illusion need not be encountered before.) Thus the cognizer has two very different items presented to him: the percepts of brightness, and the like, and the reproduced image of the silver. He fails, perhaps due to carelessness or the expectancy of seeing silver, to distinguish between the two and behaves as if he has seen the silver. But no seeing of the silver has taken place, for there is not silver to be seen.

This account of misperception, though highly ingenious, is rejected by Nyāya-Vaiśeṣika philosophers. The latter's main objection is that a misperception is of the form 'this is that', such as 'this is silver'. So it is not merely a juxtaposition of two different cognitive items and a lack of discrimination between the two. It is more than lack of awareness of a distinction or some omission; it is a commission, for otherwise we would not have a single awareness. The revived image of the silver does have to play a crucial role, for we can be in error only about something that is at least partly familiar. But this is not a sufficient reason for refusing to regard an illusion as a perception. It is obvious that an illusion cannot be merely the remembrance of some previously seen thing, for then that thing would not be seen as being here and now but as being in the past. In other words, it could not then be apprehended as 'this' but only as 'that'. Further, when the person later realizes his mistake, he recalls that he saw the shell as silver. He does not recall that he remembered the silver. This reinforces the conclusion that the awareness was perceptual, albeit erroneous. It should accordingly be described as the mistaken perception of the shell as silver (NKD 431–32).

Like errors, dreams are also a kind of nonveridical cognition (*avidyā*). A dream, says Prasastapada, is an internal (*mānasa*) cognitive state that has the appearance (*ākāra*) of a perception (but is not a perception). A dream arises from the contact between the self and the inner sense when the external sense organs are largely inactive (*uparata*) and the person is tired and taking a rest. The impressions from previous experiences together with the ongoing vital processes help to generate the perception-like internal cognitions of things that are not there (*asat*) (PDS 436–37).

This happens sometimes, Prasastapada observes, if the impression is vivid and strong. The person may be filled with desire or anger and preoccupied with the thought of something or someone while going to sleep. Then he may dream of that. Sometimes the dream may be due to some disturbance of the bodily level of biles, wind, or cold. For example, a rise in the level of the bile may result in dreaming of fiery or hot things, a rise in the level of the cold may result in dreaming of watery things, and so on. Sometimes dreams may also have a snowball effect and generate further dreams (*svapnāntika*) (PDS 439–41).

While a waking experience may be veridical or nonveridical, dreaming is always nonveridical. But what reasons are there to separate dreaming from waking? Should we say that in a dream things appear to be different from what they are and hence dreaming is different from waking? Vallabha (12th century CE) argues that this is not a safe ground, for in a waking state also things may appear differently from what they are. Should we say that a dream is sublated (*bādha*) and hence is different from waking? But this too is not a sure ground, for the sublation itself may be a part of a dream. What about the regularity and coherence (*prabandha-saṃvāda*) that is found when we are awake and at best coherence by chance (*kākatalīya-saṃvāda*) in a dream? But even a chance coherence may lead to truth, as when something lost for a long time is suddenly rediscovered in an accidental way. On the other hand, regularity is not a sure ground for truth, for things like a circling firebrand that appear to move continuously and to be one are not really so. Should we say that while objects of waking are useful and get things done (*arthakriyā*), dream objects are not so? But even dream objects can be useful, for example, when a person becomes thirsty in a dream and his thirst is quenched by the water he dreams. Should we say that what we dream is found to be false when we are awake? But in the same way what we learn while awake may be found to be false when we are dreaming. Should we say that while waking experiences are mostly true, dreams are mostly false? But this does not work, for waking experiences also may be mostly false.

Vallabha resolves the issue by claiming that the difference between dreaming and waking is known from perception (*anubhava*) (which is reliable except when there is counterevidence). No arguments are called for here. But if this is not accepted on the strength of perception, like many other things we know from perception, such as that pleasure and pain are different, no amount of reasoning can prove that such is the case (NL 54–56). Vallabha seems to imply that the situation is different when a previous perception is countermanded by a later corrective perception. For example, when a person misperceives a rope as a snake and later perceives it as a rope and realizes his mistake, the previous perception is set aside on the strength of the subsequent counterevidence. But when a person is perceptually aware of being awake, there is no such counterevidence to set it aside. There is the possibility that he could be dreaming. But a mere possibility falls short of the counterevidence provided by an actual, corrective perception. The perception of being awake at a particular time and place is a specific perception that can be rebutted by another specific perception but not by a mere possibility. If a particular perception is labeled as untrustworthy merely because of the possibility that it could be wrong, the result would be a general skepticism and agnosticism that is unacceptable.

So far we have explored the distinction between eternal and noneternal cognition, determinate and indeterminate cognition, productive and reproductive cognition, direct and indirect cognition as well as the nature and grounds of memory, impression, and doubt and the distinction between sleeping and waking as expounded by Nyāya-Vaiśeṣika thinkers. We have also explained the distinction between the qualificand and the qualifier and their specifiers and pointed out the bearing of these concepts and distinctions on psychophysical dualism. Dualists are sometimes accused of being negligent in paying attention to relevant details needed for a fuller understanding of our internal lives. As even this brief account may help to show, such an accusation would not be justified against the Nyāya-Vaiśeṣika. Further examination of other internal states in the next chapter will throw more light on the subject.

CHAPTER 4

Other Internal States

After briefly discussing cognition we now look at some other internal states, first at pain and pleasure. Prasastapada says that pleasure is the experience of something favorable (*anugraha*). It arises from association (*sānnidhya*) with desirable (*abhipreta*) things. The contact between the self and the inner sense is a causal condition of pleasure that may bring about such bodily changes as brightness of the face (PDS 630–31). On the other hand, pain is the experience of something hurtful (*upaghāta*). It arises from association with undesirable (*anabhipreta*) things. The contact between the self and the inner sense is also a causal condition of pain that may bring about such bodily changes as darkness of the face (PDS 633).

Gotama says: "Pain is of the nature of suffering (*bādhanā*)" (NS 1.1.21). In this connection Vatsyayana remarks that all knowables, including pleasure and the sources of pleasure, are invariably mixed with suffering: "All these are contaminated with suffering" (NSB 1.1.21). This should not, Vaiśeṣika thinkers argue, lead one to think that pain and pleasure are really not different in the sense that pleasure eventually boils down to pain (but not pain to pleasure). Thus Kanada says: "Since what causes liking and what causes disliking are different and since there is opposition, pleasure and pain are different from each other" (VS 10.1). Samkara Misra comments:

> Pleasure and pain are different from each other. . . . Why? Because the causal conditions of liking and disliking are different. The garland, sandal, wife, etc., are liked. The snake, thorn, etc., are disliked. The causal conditions of such natures are different: if the causal conditions are of different kinds, the effects also must be of different kinds. Another

> ground of difference is mentioned: because of opposition which is of the nature of not belonging together. There is never the experience of both pleasure and pain in the same self at the same time. By the word 'and' [*ca* in VS 10.1 quoted above] is implied the difference of these on the ground that their effects are different. While being favorably disposed, a contented look, etc., are the effects of pleasure, sadness, darkness of the face, etc., are the effects of suffering—for this reason also these are different . . . . With regard to past garland, sandal, etc., this (pleasure or pain) arises from memory and with regard to the future, from desire. The lack of citation of pleasure in Gotama's aphorism is motivated by that considering even pleasure as pain is conducive to detachment. (UP 520-1)

So there are three grounds for the thesis that pleasure and pain are different internal states (of the self). First, their causal conditions are different. This does not mean that something that becomes a causal condition of pleasure or pain in someone will always have the same effect in that person as well as in other persons. It is only the totality (*sāmagrī*) of causal conditions that can bring about the effect. So if there is some change in the totality, in spite of the continuity of a given causal condition, the result may be different. However, it still remains true that what causes pleasure is usually different from what causes pain. For example, while gentle warmth may usually cause pleasure in cold weather, intense heat may cause pain. Since thus their causes are different and since effects are different if causes are different, pleasure and pain are different. Second, no one experiences pleasure and pain at the same time; this makes sense only if they are different. Third, their effects are different, such as that pain may bring about darkness of the face while pleasure may bring about brightness of the face. It is a commonplace in the Nyāya that if the effects are of different kinds, the causes should also be of different kinds. It should be noted that the above remarks about the role of the totality of causal conditions apply here as well.

Toward the end of the passage Samkara Misra, the commentator (who as the author of this work owes his allegiance to the Vaiśeṣika school though as the author of a different work may owe his allegiance to a different school as is not unusual in the Sanskrit tradition), willingly avoids a confrontation with Gotama, the founder of the Nyāya. Samkara Misra is commenting on Kanada, the founder of the Vaiśeṣika school. Kanada's own position is clearly and unambiguously that pleasure and pain are different internal states. But since Gotama does not mention pleasure in his list of knowables (NS 1.1.9) and mentions only pain, it could be interpreted to mean that in Gotama's view pleasure is not really different from pain but eventually reduces to pain. However, Samkara Misra suggests that the omission of pleasure and the inclusion of pain in that list does not imply that in Gotama's view pleasure and pain are the same. Rather the purpose of that list is to get one motivated toward detachment (*vairāgya*). If one considers every knowable, including pleasure and the sources of pleasure, to be painful, that helps one to move toward detachment. In fact, in the very next aphorism (NS 1.1.10) Gotama lists pleasure and pain separately among the signs of the self. So the mere omission of pleasure from one list should not be taken to mean that for Gotama pleasure and pain are nondifferent.

Granted that pleasure and pain are different, should they be subsumed under cognition? No, says Kanada: "Not being either a doubt or a belief (*nirṇaya*) is a ground for (holding that pleasure and pain) are different from cognition" (VS 10.2). Samkara Misra amplifies:

> If pleasure or pain were (the same as) cognition, are they of the nature of a doubt or of the nature of a belief? Not the first, for twofold positions are not featured. Not the second, for a onefold position is not featured. Thus there is negation of the genus on the ground of the negation of each species. Indeed, there are two species of cognition: doubt and belief. Since both are negated with reference to pleasure or pain (i.e., since neither pleasure nor pain is ever a doubt or a belief), being a cognition is also negated there. . . . Of pleasure and pain there is internal experience of the form 'I am happy' or 'I am sorry', but not of the form 'I cognize', 'I doubt' or 'I believe'. (UP 522)

So both pleasure and pain involve an awareness of pleasure or pain, but neither pleasure nor pain is merely a cognitive state. A cognitive state is either a doubt (*saṃśaya*) or a belief (*niścaya*). In the former there are two choices between which the cognizer is undecided. For example, there may be doubt as to whether the thing before you is a snake or a rope. Since doubt involves an indecision between two positions and neither pleasure nor pain involves that, the latter cannot be states of doubt.[1] The latter is also not a belief. In a belief there is acceptance of one position, such as that the thing before you is a rope. Since this is missing in pleasure or pain, the latter cannot be states of belief either. This exhausts all the possibilities for a cognitive state and thus it follows that pleasure or pain are not cognitive states. Incidentally, Samkara Misra explicitly states and reminds us of the logical law that if something is excluded from each species falling under a genus, it is also excluded from that genus. For example, if something lacks each of the seven kinds of color, it must also lack color. Samkara Misra adds that experientially pleasure and pain are different from cognition. Being happy or being sorry is clearly different from merely being aware of something.

Kanada adds a second argument: "Their origin is from perception or inference" (VS 10.3). Samkara Misra elaborates:

> Another ground of difference is stated. Their origin, i.e., the origin of doubt and belief is from perception or from signs. But neither pleasure nor pain arises from the [same] conditions as that of perception and not also from signs. Indeed, there are four kinds of pleasure: arising from objects, arising from the inner sense, arising from the ego and arising from practice. There [the last] three do not result from [external] sensory connection at all. It may be said that since the first arises from the connection between an [external] sense organ and an object, it is a cognitive state. But this is not acceptable, for merely sharing some of the causal conditions does not prove that the effect is of the same kind. If that were so, since space and time are common causal conditions, all effects would be of the same kind. Further, should pleasure arising from the sense-object connection be indeterminate or determinate? Not the first, for then [pleasure and pain] would have been imperceptible. Not the second, for [neither pleasure nor pain] involves the awareness of two items being related as the qualificand and the qualifier. Moreover, since pleasure and pain are invariably known, if cognition were also to be invariably known, an infinite regress would have resulted. [Pleasure and pain] arising from inference is in the same way as that arising from objects. (UP 523)

Thus our doubts and beliefs are based either on perception or on inference.[2] But pleasure and pain do not result exclusively from the conditions of perception or of inference. Hence pleasure and pain cannot be reduced to merely states of doubt or belief. Some pleasures and pains do arise from the sensory connection with external objects.

Perception too results from such sensory connection. Still it does not follow that some pleasures and pains are perceptual states. All that follows is that some pleasures and pains share some causal conditions with perception. Merely sharing some causal conditions does not prove that the two things are of the same kind. Further, if some pleasures or pains were merely perceptual states, they would be either determinate or indeterminate perceptions, for all perceptions are either determinate or indeterminate.[3] But pleasures and pains are not determinate states, for they do not exhibit two contents related as the qualificand and the qualifier as all determinate cognitions do. Pleasure and pain are not also indeterminate states, for unlike the latter, they are perceptible. So even those pleasures and pains that arise from sensory connection with objects cannot be merely perceptual states. Here also it is implied that if something is excluded from each species of a genus, it is excluded from that genus as well.

Again, pleasures and pains are invariably known, but cognitions are not. That is, in the Nyāya view, if one is happy or sorry, one is also invariably aware of the fact that one is happy or sorry, so that there is no pleasure or pain which goes unknown or unnoticed. But if one is aware of something, one is not necessarily aware of the fact of being aware of something.[4] For example, one may be totally preoccupied with the perception of some immediate danger, such as a tiger, and may not have the opportunity of paying attention to anything else including the awareness itself. Now, if pleasure and pain were nothing but cognition, some account would have to be given for allowing them to be invariably known. Then, given the externalist theory of knowing to which the Nyāya is committed, a vicious infinite regress would be inevitable. This shows that pleasure and pain cannot be subsumed under cognition if externalism is to be upheld. Similarly, some pleasures and pains may also result from inferences. But that too would fall short of proving that they are merely cognitive states for the same reasons that those pleasures and pains that arise from sensory connection with external objects are not classifiable as perceptions.

Kanada adds another argument: "Also applies to the past" (VS 10.4). Samkara Misra explains: "Another kind of difference of pleasure, etc., from inferential awareness is stated. . . . The word 'also' implies the inclusion of the future. Thus there was or will be fire in the hill—an inferential awareness is also found to be of the past, etc, variety. But pleasure or pain are not known to be such" (UP 524). In other words, pleasure or pain may be derived from some inference.

Still the former are not reducible to inference. If it were so, the former too could be of something past or future—which is not the case. Pleasure or pain always need a present stimulus and always involve a current enjoyment. These may be derived from some thought of the past or the future. But as occurrent states these always pertain to the present, unlike inference, which may also pertain to the past or the future.

Kanada supplies one more argument: "Since the effect is not observed in spite of the presence [of the causal conditions]" (VS 10.5). Samkara Misra elaborates:

> Another ground of difference is added. In spite of the availability of the sense-object connection [which is the instrumental causal condition of perception] and of the recognition of pervasion, etc., [which is the instrumental causal condition of inference], there is non-observation of pleasure or pain. Hence pleasure or pain are not merely perceptual or merely inferential states. . . . When there is the sense-object connection and perception of the garland, the sandal, etc., there is lack of experience of pleasure. . . . When there is inference of the sandal or of fire, there is lack of the experience of pleasure or pain. (UP 524–25)

If pleasure or pain were reducible to perception or inference, the grounds of perception or inference should also suffice as grounds of pleasure or pain. But this is not so. The causes of perception or inference do not always produce pleasure or pain when such causes lead to an act of perception or inference. So they are different.

Kanada mentions one final argument: "Since other causal conditions co-inherent in the same thing are found" (10.6). Samkara Misra elucidates:

> Another ground of difference [of pleasure or pain from cognition] is stated. . . . There are specific causal conditions of pleasure which are co-inherent (i.e., both pleasure and such a causal condition inhere in the self), viz., merit, liking, desire for what gives pleasure, the effort for acquiring that and cognition of the garland, the sandal, etc. For pain: demerit, cognition of unwelcome things like the thorn, etc. . . . But cognition, if it is indeterminate, does not require any specific causal condition which is co-inherent in the same thing. If determinate, it does require cognition of the qualifier

which is another [specific] causal condition [co-inherent in the same thing]; but this is not of a different kind. (UP 525)

Thus the specific causal conditions of pleasure or pain on the one hand and that of cognition on the other are not the same. The specific causal conditions of pleasure or pain include such factors as desire, aversion, and so on, which are co-inherent with pleasure or pain in the self but which are not of the same kind as pleasure or pain. (Pleasure, pain, desire, aversion, and so forth, are, according to the Nyāya-Vaiśeṣika, different kinds of internal qualia that all belong to the self.) However, there are no specific conditions of cognition that are co-inherent with cognition in the self and are not of the same kind as cognition. Cognition is either determinate or indeterminate. If it is indeterminate, no other *laukika* or ordinary[5] internal quale is involved as a specific causal condition. If cognition is determinate, the preceding indeterminate cognition is involved as a specific causal condition; but it is of the same kind for it too is a cognitive state. Because of this difference in the nature of their specific causal conditions, pleasure or pain cannot be reduced to cognition. If pleasure or pain were the same as cognition, their specific causal conditions should also have been the same as those of cognition.

We now move on to consider very briefly some other internal states. According to the Prasastapada, desire is the craving (*prārthanā*) for something unobtained for the sake of oneself or someone else (PDS 635). That is, one has desire for things that are useful or pleasing for oneself; one also has desire for things useful or pleasing for others.[6] The object of desire is something that is yet to be achieved or realized. When it is achieved or realized, the desire is replaced by satisfaction or contentment (*santoṣa*, *tṛpti*).[7] Like other internal states, desire arises from the contact of the self and the inner sense; but it depends on pleasure, and so on, or remembrance. (PDS 635). In other words, if something is found to be a source of pleasure, the awareness of that thing including its remembrance arouses desire for it.[8] Desire serves as a causal condition of effort, memory, demerit, and merit (PDS 635). Since the object of desire is yet to be obtained, the desire may lead to the volition (*prayatna*) to acquire it. Desire also helps the impression (*saṃskāra*) of the thing to be firmer by bringing it into the focus of one's attention and consciousness with greater frequency than otherwise and thus promotes the cause of its memory. Further, since voluntary actions may be meritorious or otherwise, desire, as a causal condition of volition, is also indirectly a source of such merit or demerit.[9]

The main kinds of desire are (1) sexual desire (*kāma*), (2) desire for food (*abhilāṣa*), (3) desire to experience something frequently and repeatedly (*rāga*), (4) desire to do or have something in the future (*saṃkalpa*), (5) compassion or desire to do something for relieving the suffering of someone else without regard to any personal gain (*kāruṇya*), (6) detachment or desire to give up something by realizing its fault (*vairāgya*), (7) desire to cheat someone else (*upadhā*), and (8) hidden desire (*bhāva*) (PDS 635–36). Here in the first two kinds desires are distinguished with reference to their objects. A wide range of subsidiary desires are included in the first two kinds. These two kinds are singled out first as being quite basic, for they often serve directly or indirectly as the fountainheads of many other desires, such as desire for money. In the third kind the distinctive feature is the frequency of the occurrence. Some desires of the first two kinds may also belong to the third kind. Thus the classification is not intended to be exclusive. There is also no claim that the classification is exhaustive. The aim rather is to gain an understanding of the complexity and variety of an internal state that contributes decisively to the unity and identity of a person or a self. So each kind recognizes an important feature of some desires that may or may not be found in some of the other kinds. Prasastapada observes that desires may also be distinguished with reference to the different actions involved, such as desire to do something, desire to steal, desire to go, and so forth (PDS 636).

Aversion (*dveṣa*), says Prasastapada, is what makes one feel as if one were being burnt. It arises from the contact between the self and the inner sense depending on the availability of the other conditions of suffering or remembrance. It gives rise to effort, memory, merit, and demerit. It is of the following kinds:[10] anger (*krodha*), which is of short and sudden duration and brings about visible bodily changes; enmity (*droha*), which does not bring about noticeable bodily changes but motivates one to inflict injury even in a distant future; sulking (*manyu*), which is the suppressed aversion of someone who has been harmed or belittled and is unable to return the favor; unforgivingness (*akṣamā*), which is aversion toward another person's excellence; and indignation (*amarśa*) which is aversion arising from one's defeat in spite of one's strength (PDS 637). Once again, the account is brief but clear and precise and shows a good understanding of human emotions.

The distinction between different kinds of desire and aversion illustrates the value and relevance of the introspective method favored by the dualists. For example, the distinction between unforgivingness and indignation or that between compassion and detachment are significant distinctions that an average adult can understand (partly) with the help of one's introspective data drawn from one's own rich, first person experiences. Similarly, the grounds of the distinction between pleasure and pain on the one hand and cognition on the other have been clearly spelt out by the Nyāya-Vaiśeṣika dualists. But a merely neuroscientific approach would not take one very far toward a proper understanding of these distinctions. For the most complete account of neurons and synapses sheds little light on unforgivingness or indignation or the distinction between the two. We have no clue about which kind of neural and synaptic connections or combinations should explain indignation rather than unforgivingness or which such connections or combinations should explain unforgivingness rather than indignation and so on. This reveals the explanatory gap. There is of course nothing mysterious about these concepts and distinctions and Prasastapada and Sridhara have spelt them out. But as long as the explanatory gap is there, these cannot be fully captured by the methods of neuroscience.

When an internal concept is not explicable in neuroscientific terms, some thinkers label it as mysterious and argue for its expulsion. But this is nothing more than a crude attempt to cover up the shortcomings of wrong applications of some (probably) right findings. A Nyāya-Vaiśeṣika dualist would wholeheartedly welcome and respect the findings of neuroscience where they belong but would refuse to accept that neuroscience tells the *whole* story of our internal lives. Calling something mysterious merely if it escapes neuroscientific analysis would from the Nyāya-Vaiśeṣika point of view reinforce the suspicion that neuroscience may not tell the *whole* story of our internal lives. The charge of mysterianism is particularly baseless in this context. If we take note of the discussion above, we can see that the Nyāya-Vaiśeṣika has offered what may loosely be called a functionalist account of various internal states. For example, pleasure has been explained as being caused by a certain state of contact between the self and the inner sense and as also being a state with a causal role for certain bodily states. There is nothing mysterious in the latter part of this explanation. It may be thought that there is something mysterious in the earlier part of this explanation because of the reference to the self. But this is not so, for the self (as an immaterial and extended substance) is introduced in a functionalist fashion with the express purpose of accounting for the kind of contact that has a causal role in the origin of a natural state like pleasure. (Why such a self should be introduced and why it is immaterial will be discussed later.) A functionalist account of internal states may of course be compatible with dualism.[11] The Nyāya-Vaiśeṣika insight of accommodating a functionalist account within dualism helps to dissipate the charge of mysterianism. Suffice it to say, as we move deeper into the case for psychophysical dualism in the subsequent chapters, that the survey of cognition and other internal states shows that the Nyāya-Vaiśeṣika has at its disposal the conceptual tools and resources for a sophisticated philosophical study of self hood and internality.

CHAPTER 5

The Existence and Permanence of the Self

The Nyāya-Vaiśeṣika thesis that the self is a permanent, immaterial substance is highly controversial. Accordingly, the arguments for this position occupy an important position in Gotama's *Nyayā-sūtra* and the commentarial literature thereon. To study this we first look at the following aphorism: "Desire, aversion, volition, pleasure, pain and cognition are the signs of the self" (NS 1.1.10).[1] A part of what Gotama means, as Uddyotakara points out, is that with the help of desire, and so forth, the self may be distinguished from everything else (NV 64). Desire and so on are unique characters of the self and are not possessed by anything else. In other words, only selves have desire and so on. Such unique characters are accepted by the Nyāya as identifying (*paricāyaka*) characters. For such identifying characters are not too wide and it can be truly claimed that if something has X, say desire, then it is Y, say a self. Thus desire and so forth are each an identifying character of the self and provides a ground for application of the concept of self.[2]

Another significance of desire and so forth being signs is that they provide the grounds from which the existence of an immaterial substance may be inferred. Vatsyayana explicitly says that the self is not perceived (NSB 1.1.10). So the grounds for the existence of the self become a natural concern. Uddyotakara does not say here that the self is imperceptible. He observes that the existence of the self is known from authoritative sources (*āgama*). By offering the signs Gotama has shown that its existence can also be proved through inference. Thus the self is knowable from more than one source (NV 64). Since Uddyotakara does not mention perception as a source of knowing the self and since he does not criticize Vatsyayana for holding that the self is imperceptible (he frequently mentions his disagreements with Vatsyayana), he may be said to have left here open the issue of whether the self is perceptible. However, in another polemical, aporetic passage (NV 341) he rejects the view that the self is imperceptible. Moreover, Vacaspati Misra interprets Vatsyayana's remark so as not to exclude the perceptibility of the self. He observes that the true import of Vatsyayana's remark that the self is imperceptible is that since the self is ascribed bodily attributes in such common perceptions as 'I am fair', the existence of the self as an immaterial substance cannot immediately be settled through perception (TP 210). Udayana sides with Vacaspati Misra (NDFC 368) and so do some later Nyāya philosophers. Thus in the view of many Nyāya philosophers not only the internal states such as pleasure but also the self becomes the object of internal perception. However, such perception does not show beyond a reasonable doubt that the self is an immaterial substance. That task must be left to the more arduous process of reasoning and argumentation (although the claim that the self becomes the content of internal perception may and will be utilized as a part of the argumentative process).

The task of arguing for the self is sought to be accomplished by the Nyāya philosophers in several stages. First they try to prove that the self is a permanent (*sthira*) entity. Then they try to show that this permanent entity is a substance (*dravya*). Finally, they try to prove that this permanent substance is immaterial. So we initially turn to a passage from Vatsyayana arguing for the permanence of the self. In the famous Buddhist work called *Milindapañha* we find the view that there is no self that is over and above the changing states.[3] Vatsyayana's comments are probably directed against such a theory.

> The self having seen the kind of object the experience of which has been pleasant wants to acquire that. This desire to acquire, since it involves the synthesis of cognitions, becomes a sign for a self which is one and has many experiences. If there were only different cognitions each restricted to its object, this would not be possible as in the case of a different body. In the same way from the synthesis of cognitions of the same one having many experiences there is aversion towards the source of suffering. When a kind of thing is familiar as a source of pleasure and one sees that, one strives to get that. This kind of volition would not be possible without a synthesizer of cognitions who is one and has many experiences. If there were only cognitions each restricted to its object, this would not be possible as in the case of a different body. This also explains the volition [of

avoiding] the source of suffering. From the remembrance of pleasure and pain it [the self] procures the causes of those, experiences pleasure and pain and becomes aware of pleasure and pain; the sign is as said before. Out of inquisitiveness it enquires "what is it?" After enquiring it comes to know "it is this." This kind of cognition prompted by inquisitiveness and enquiry is known to be that of an identical agent: thus it becomes a sign for the self in the way already said. "As in the case of a different body" may be analyzed as follows. Just as even for those who reject the self different cognitions each restricted to its object belonging to a different body cannot be synthesized, so also those belonging to the same body cannot be synthesized—for there is no difference. Thus is gathered the existence of an identical self: one may remember only what one has seen and not what has been seen by some one else nor what has not been seen. For different beings the fact is that what is seen by one is not remembered by another. Thus one who rejects the self cannot account for this [remembrance]. Hence it follows that the self exists. (NSB 1.1.10)

The Buddhist has rejected the standard Hindu commitment to a permanent and unitary self and held that the self is an aggregate (*saṃghāta*) of internal states. These states are each fleeting and transitory and are in a continual flux. There is nothing different from these states which endures through time and retains its identity and continuity. In this Hindu view when I say that I am happy, I distinguish myself from my happiness, which is something that belongs to me but is not the same as me. For I would also say that I am sad, which implies that I am different from my sadness which too is something that belongs to me but is not the same as me. Neither my happiness nor my sadness can be the same as me; for happiness and sadness are two incompatible states and the same thing could not be identical with both. The Buddhist counters that this would be a problem if the self were an entity different from these states and the same entity were identified with two or more incompatible states. But the Buddhist thesis is that there is no such entity over and above the internal states. So the question does not arise. Since the existence of the self as the self same owner of the internal states is rejected, the Buddhist position is described as the no-self theory (*anātmavada*). From the Buddhist standpoint knowledge of the no-self theory is taken to be a means to the attainment of liberation.[4] The no-self theory is also found in the *Upaniṣads*.[5]

Some Buddhists speak in particular of an aggregate of five *skandhas* or seats of suffering:

1. *Rūpa* or nature, which comprises the sense organs and their objects
2. *Vijñāna* or cognition, which comprises both self-consciousness (*alayavijñāna*) and consciousness of objects (*pravṛtti-vijñāna*).
3. *Vedanā* or feeling, which comprises pleasure and pain arising out of the interface of the first two called nature and cognition
4. *Saṃjñā* or name, which comprises cognitions featuring names
5. *Saṃskāra* or disposition, which comprises attachment, aversion, pride, high spiritedness, merit, and demerit prompted mainly by feeling (*vedanā*). (SD 39–40)

All the five *skandhas* are in a state of flux, with the previous states being causally connected with the succeeding states. As long as the causal connection is not interrupted, we have a flowing stream (*santāna*) of internal states. The flowing stream is the ground of personal identity. There is no need for the Hindu posit of a permanent self to account for personal identity. The permanent self is a false construction (*vikalpa*) that should be exposed and got rid of.

To refute this theory the six signs are offered to show that a permanent owner of the internal states should be admitted. All the six signs utilize the fact of memory and seek to show that memory is inexplicable without a permanent self. Vatsyayana lays down three undisputed facts about remembering something:

1. One cannot remember what has not been seen.
2. One cannot remember what has been seen by someone else.
3. One can only remember what one has seen before.

It follows that the one who has seen before and the one who remembers now should be the same entity. This proves that this same entity is something over and above the internal states. For the state of seeing has ceased to exist; what we now have is the state of remembering.

So the self-same entity that has seen before and is now remembering is different from both. Since the self, as the unitary agent of both seeing and remembering, must endure through time, it is proved that the self is permanent.

Suppose that the self is not permanent. Vatsyayana offers the reductio that then a person would be nothing more than a bundle of different fleeting states. Each such state is restricted to its own object and has no information about the object of some other state. So the state of remembering has no inkling about the state of seeing and cannot do the job of remembering. Since the two states are different and each has no information about the other, the situation is no different from having two different persons neither of whom can remember what the other has seen.

Vatsyayana has explained how each of the six signs involves memory. Desire involves memory in that when one has found something to be pleasant one may later have the desire for it from remembering that it is pleasant. Aversion involves memory in that when one has found something to be harmful one may later have aversion toward it from remembering that it is harmful. Volition involves memory in that when one has found something to be pleasant one may later have the volition to acquire it from remembering that it is pleasant. Similarly, volition involves memory also in that when one has found something to be unpleasant one may later have the volition to avoid it from remembering that it is unpleasant. Pleasure and pain may involve memory in that from the remembrance of pleasure and pain one may direct one's efforts toward the sources of those and experience pleasure and pain accordingly. Finally, cognition may involve memory in that curiosity may lead one on to an enquiry that may yield knowledge of what one is enquiring about. It is not claimed that pleasure, pain, and cognition always involve memory. Since Gotama has offered them as grounds for the permanence of the self, Vatsyayana has explained how these may involve memory and thereby serve as the ground. The first three signs—desire, aversion, and volition—however, always involve memory. The point of Gotama and Vatsyayana is that whenever an internal state involves memory, it becomes a legitimate ground for inferring the permanence of the self. It is the self that organizes experience, originates actions for acquiring something beneficial and avoiding something harmful, and accounts for our identity as persons. All of this requires memory, from which the self is inferred.[6]

The Buddhists have countered by saying that the reason one cannot remember what has been experienced by someone else is that the prior experience is a causal condition of the impression (*saṃskāra*) without which no remembrance can take place. If one lacks the prior experience and the impression left by it, one obviously cannot remember it. So what is needed for an account of remembrance is not necessarily an identical, enduring self. Remembrance can be accounted for also by the continuity of the causal chain of succeeding internal states making up the life of an individual. When an experience leaves behind an impression, the latter generates a succeeding stream of impressions the present member of which gets revived by some stimulus when a remembrance takes place. So remembrance is possible because it is linked by an unbroken causal chain with the previous experience. Another person cannot remember that experience because there is no such causal link. The position has been succinctly stated as below:

> Because of the relation of cause and effect from previous cognitions later cognitions are generated in accordance with the power of the previous cognitions. . . . Hence, although the cognitions are many, there is synthesis through the cause-effect relation as in the case of a seed, etc. Just as rice saplings . . . produce rice seeds in accordance with their power and not barley seeds, so also from the cognitions belonging to the same stream there is synthesis based on the relation of cause and effect and not from cognitions belonging to a different stream, the latter not being preceded by that (the original experience). (NV 64–65)

The sameness of the stream does not imply the continuity of any identical thing. All that is implied by sameness is that the later cognitions in the stream are related to the earlier cognitions as effect and cause.

But failing back on the continuity of a causal connection does not wholly solve the problem posed by the Nyāya philosophers. A part of their argument is that the self same cognizer who had the prior experience recognizes himself as the agent of remembrance when the latter takes place. In other words, the recognitive perception (*pratyavijñā*) is of the form "I who saw X before now remember it." It is such recognitive perception of the identity and continuity of the same self that Vatsyayana has in mind when he speaks of the recognitive synthesis (*pratisandhāna*) of cognitions. So the self was a content (but not an object) of the previous experience; it is also a content of the present remembrance. Since the self is the content of two cognitive states between which there is considerable lapse of time, it must be an enduring entity. If the previous experience of a cat merely left behind an impression of that cat and that impression is revived, that alone cannot account for the recognitive perception of the identity and continuity of the self same cognizer. So the Buddhist must dismiss such recognitive perception as false. However, since such recognitive perception is a common experience, it cannot merely be assumed to be false, but must be proved to be so. But the Buddhist has not produced any compelling reasons to show why such a common and almost universal belief should be false. Until that is done it is reasonable, a Nyāya philosopher claims, to use it as a ground for the permanence of the self.

Uddyotakara has argued that in spite of the causal connection the earlier and the later cognitions are still different: "it is being said that recognitive synthesis is based on the relation of cause and effect; but that does not wipe out difference" (NV 65). As long as the two cognitions are different and there is no self-identical cognizer of both, the recognition of the same person having both cognitions cannot be true. "It is agreed to by both sides that there is no recognitive synthesis if there is difference" (NV 65). That is to say, both agree that one does not recognize the experience of another person as his own. Here also the two internal states, in spite of the causal link, are completely different. So the later state cannot recognize the experience of the earlier state as its own. "It is recognized through the remembrance that the earlier and the later cognitions have the same kind of object. Such remembrance is not accountable from your [= the Buddhist] viewpoint" (NV 66). Although the later state may be caused by the earlier state, still it is a different state and cannot know, Uddyotakara claims, that it has the same object. The difficulty does not arise if there is a permanent self other than the changing states. But the problem remains if the self is denied, "for the cognitions are impermanent" (NV 66). Only something permanent is known to have desire and so on. But the cognitions are impermanent and so cannot fill that role.

The Buddhist could, of course, reiterate that impermanent cognitions could fill the role of the desirer by virtue of the causal connection. But that does not work, for causal connection alone does not account for desire. Desire involves much more than the mere revival of the impression of a past experience. One may not have desire for something being remembered. For desire what is needed is that one recognizes the remembered object to be of the same kind as what has been pleasant or useful before. So one must, it is claimed, endure through time to be able to do that. Moreover, all activities,

Uddyotakara points out, have a substratum. Remembering is an activity. So remembering too must have a substratum (NV 66). This points to the existence of a self different from the act of remembering: the self serves as the substratum or support of the activity. Without the self the needed support is lacking. The object of memory cannot be that support, for it may be something nonexistent and something nonexistent cannot support anything. So the support has to come from the subject or the agent of remembering (NV 67).

Further, all effects, Uddyotakara adds, need a support. Since remembering is an effect, it needs a support. It could be said that the momentary state that becomes the cause supports the momentary state that becomes the effect. But this is not acceptable. The two states are not contemporaneous; so one could not support the other (NV 67).

It may be noted that these two arguments from remembering being an activity and being an effect presuppose the ontological distinction between a substance and what is supported by a substance and a certain theory of causation that all effects (which are positive entities) have a support. Nyāya philosophers have offered arguments for both these views. If these views are found to be reasonable, the two arguments here will deserve attention too.

Since the Buddhist cannot account for memory and since recognitive synthesis presupposes memory, Uddyotakara concludes that the Buddhist cannot account for recognitive synthesis (*pratisandhāna*). Thus the admission of the self as an additional, unitary owner of experiences is justified (NV 67–68). As he says:

> There can be no recognitive synthesis when the agents are different, the objects are different and the causes are different. . . . Since the different cognitions are each restricted to its object and are different from each other, the no-self theorist cannot account for recognitive synthesis. Therefore, that which does the recognitive synthesis is the self. (NV 64)

Vacaspati Misra has observed that since each cognition is restricted to its object, that they belong to the same stream (*santāna*) is of no help. The stream is not an additional entity different from the cognitions and so fares no better. On the other hand, if it is supposed to be an additional entity, it would amount to conceding the existence of the self (TP 211).

The Buddhist could argue that that one cannot remember what has been experienced by another person is not due to the fact they are different persons but due to the fact that there is no causal connection (TP 212). Although the stream is not an additional entity, the cognitions belonging to it are causally connected. This is why a later member of the stream can remember what has been experienced by a previous member. But it cannot remember what has been experienced by a member belonging to a different stream because there is no causal connection between the two.

But causal connection alone does not suffice for explaining recognitive synthesis. For example, a mango may be replaced by another mango and one may recognize both to be of the same kind. But the two mangoes are not causally connected (TP 213).

Again, there is a causal connection between a piece of cloth and its threads or between a pot and its two halves. But that does not provide the ground for recognition (TP 213).

Further, not all Buddhist philosophers accept causation as a real relation. For those who do not the appeal to causation would be of no use (TP 213).

Finally, causal connection does not provide the kind of connection needed for recognition. Even if a later member of a stream is causally connected with a previous member, the later cognition cannot know that its object is also the object of that former cognition. To recognize that something present is the same as or of the same kind as something past. one must be present at both periods of time. This presupposes permanence and cannot be accommodated by a Buddhist advocating that everything is momentary (TP 213).

The Buddhist could say that when two momentary cognitions belonging to the same stream are causally connected and the difference between the two is not known, recognition would be possible. But this does not go far enough. What is needed for recognition is not merely lack of knowledge of difference, but knowledge of sameness of the owner of both cognitions (TP 214).

The bottom line is that memory is not explicable if all cognitions are momentary and there is no permanent self. As Vacaspati Misra says: "Memory is such that the earlier and the later cognitions have the same agent, for both are recognized as having the same object. Those which do not have the same agent are not so recognized, e.g., the memory of Devadatta is not recognized by Yajnadatta. This is not so. Therefore, it is so" (TP 216). The argument may be reformulated as follows.

1. Those cognitions that do not have the same agent as that of an earlier cognition are not recognized as having the same

object as that of an earlier cognition, like the cognitions of X and Y.

2. All remembrances are recognized as having the same object as that of an earlier cognition.
3. Therefore, all remembrances have the same agent as that of an earlier cognition.

The argument is formally valid. So if the premises are reasonable and acceptable, so must be the conclusion. Is the first premise adequately supported by empirical evidence? It should be noted that Vacaspati Misra has put the argument in the *vyatirekin* form. This means that the first premise should not be replaced by its contrapositive, namely, all cognitions that are recognized as having the same object as that of an earlier cognition have the same agent as that of an earlier cognition. The reason for this is that the Buddhist would dispute any instances of memory, desire, and so on, as being cognitions that have the same agent as that of an earlier cognition. So a Nyāya philosopher cannot produce any corroborative examples that are above controversy and claim that the premise is reasonable and acceptable. However, in the *vyatirekin* form undisputable corroborative examples are available. Neither the Naiyāyika nor the Buddhist would dispute that there are cognitions of X which are not recognized by Y. The Buddhist would offer earlier and later cognitions as counterexamples claiming that the later cognition can recognize its object as being the same as that of the earlier cognition although the two cognitions do not have the same agent. But the Nyāya would undoubtedly dispute them and claim that they do have the same agent. It is thus clear that the Buddhist cannot cite any counterexample that is undisputable while there are corroborative examples that are undisputable.

Under the circumstances, the Buddhist has tried to weaken the above argument by claiming that the first premise is still questionable, because it is possible that the cognitions of X cannot be recognized by Y, not because they do not have the same agent, but because they are not causally linked. This is a plausible suggestion and accepted by the Nyāya in part. The Nyāya too accepts that the earlier cognition has left behind an impression the revival of which has made recognition possible. Although such a causal link is a necessary condition for recognition, it is not, in the Nyāya view, a sufficient condition. Another necessary condition is the unity of the agents of both the earlier and later cognitions. To drive home this point Vacaspati Misra has shown that causal connection alone does not provide the explanation of recognition, for there are clear cases of causal connection that have nothing to do with recognition. In other words, it is plainly false to say that all cognitions that are causally connected are recognized to have the same object. To show this Uddyotakara and Vacaspati Misra have cited examples such as: "it is not that I recognize that the color I have seen is this touch" (NV 64; TP 212). The point is that touching a thing may follow seeing the color of something else or touching a thing may follow seeing its color. Since the touch and the color are different objects, one would not recognize the cognitions as having the same object (so far as the touch and the color are concerned) although the two, by virtue of the temporal succession, are causally connected from the Buddhist perspective.

Since causal connection alone cannot account for recognition, (to weaken the first premise) the Buddhist has suggested that momentary cognitions that are causally connected and belong to the same stream are the bases of recognition. But, Vacaspati Misra claims, since the stream is not an additional entity and since the only basis for sameness of the stream is nothing other than causal connection, this explanation fares no better than that in terms of causal connection alone.

To salvage their position and to weaken the first premise the Buddhist has next suggested that momentary cognitions that are causally connected, belong to the same stream and have the appropriate potency (*śakti*) or similarity (*sādṛśya*) provide the bases for recognition (NV 66). But, Uddyotakara argues, this still does not explain how the two momentary cognitions which are not contemporaneous get connected for recognition (NV 66). The mere appeal to potency (or similarity) does not suffice for the purpose. Neither potency nor similarity are unique to internal phenomena but are found in nonconscious external things. If these latter do not qualify as carriers of memory in spite of having potency or similarity, why should potency or similarity be the explanans when the phenomena are internal? For the Nyāya since both the cognitions have the same agent, the later cognition, through the revival of the impression of the earlier cognition, is recognized to have the same or the same kind of object as that experienced by that agent earlier. In the end, then, since the first premise is supported by undisputable corroborative instances and there are no undisputable counterexamples, it, given GAIE, is justified. The remaining premise—that all remembrances are recognized to have the same object as that of an earlier cognition—is not disputed by either the Nyāya or the Buddhist. Thus the conclusion, the Nyāya claims, is justified.

Uddyotakara has presented another version of the argument from recognition: "Devadatta's perceptions of color, taste, smell and touch have many [objects as] causes but also have a unitary [agent as a] cause, for they are recognized as mine with the help of memory" (NV 68). Perceptions of color, taste, and so on, are caused by different external stimuli. If they were not all apprehended by the same agent, they would not have been apprehended as all belonging to the same person. Such a common agent of many perceptions taking place at different times should be permanent.

The Buddhist view is similar in some respects to that of Hume that the self is nothing more than a bundle of particular perceptions, feelings, and the like. Hume writes: "When I enter most intimately into what I call myself, I always stumble on some particular perception or other. I never catch myself without a perception" (*Treatise* 1.4.6). Significantly, some Nyāya philosophers come close to agreeing with at least the wording of Home that we can never catch ourselves without a perception and so on. Visvanatha writes clearly: "the self is perceived as related to cognition, pleasure, etc., and not otherwise—through such awareness as 'I know,' 'I do,' etc." (BP 410). Thus Visvanatha rules out that the self can be perceived without some particular perception.

Still the disagreement with Hume remains fundamental. The real point of Hume is that he fails to find the self or the common subject. This is not accepted by the Nyāya. The latter view rather is that the self is perceived through I-consciousness (*aham-pratyaya-gamyatvāt ātmā pratyakṣa*) (NM 2:4). Again, "the awareness that I am happy directly reveals the self also" (*aham sukhīti tu jñaptirātmanah api prakāśikā*) (ibid., 4). Moreover, the awareness that I know cannot be maligned even by a small grain of fault: of this the self is the chief content (*na khalu aham jānāmi iti pratyayah kenacit alpīyasā doṣareṇunā dhūsarīkartum pāryate tadasya ātmā eva mukhyo viṣayah*) (ibid., 4). The last point about the incorrigibility of I-consciousness is in tune with the Cartesian and the Samkarite views of the indubitability of the self.

However, the appeal to incorrigibility is not the only platform of the Nyāya case for the self. As we have seen, it is the view of some Nyāya philosophers that the self is not perceived. So arguments from desire and so on, pointing to the permanence of the self as the common and abiding owner of internal state, are offered. This is where the Buddhist gets into difficulty as we have seen. This is also where a Humean gets into difficulty. We shall not discuss Hume's own account in detail, for it is too brief and leaves much to be desired.

In stead we shall look at some recent Hume-like and Buddhist-like views.

Before we do that we first quote the following passage, which contains a crushing objection to the Buddhist (and by implication also the Humean) view that accepts only fleeting internal states but not an enduring self:

> If momentary, what has been experienced long ago cannot be remembered, for the cognizers are different. If it is said that what was experienced by an earlier momentary state may be remembered by a later state because of their being related as cause and effect, this is inappropriate. If there were no self, the relation between cause and effect could not be ascertained. The cognitive state which would be the effect is yet to come into being when the cognitive state which is the cause is there, and by the time the former comes into being the latter ceases to be. Since there is no knower other than these two, how could it be known that these two successive entities are related as cause and effect? It may be suggested that the earlier state which is self-revealing also becomes aware of its nature as the cause which is non-different from itself; similarly, the self-cognizing later state also becomes aware of the fact of its being the effect which is non-different from itself. . . . But this is an undue fabrication. Each of the two earlier and later cognitions is confined to itself. How then could the awareness that I am the effect of this or the awareness that I am the cause of that take place? The fact is that each is ignorant about the other. (PDS 170–17)

Although the objection is targeted to the view that replaces the enduring self with momentary states, the point of the objection has force against any position that grounds personal identity on anything changing (if certain things are granted). Suppose permanent bodily states that are nevertheless subject to change, are the bases of personal identity. Suppose also that one such state is a causal condition of another such succeeding state. The point is: How can either be aware of being causally related to each other? The earlier state cannot know (though it may know what kind of a thing may succeed it) that the later state is its effect, for the latter is yet to be and, for all we know, it may never materialize and by the time it may materialize the earlier state must be gone. The later state cannot know (though it may know what kind of a thing may precede it) that the earlier state is its cause, for the earlier state is gone and the later state does not have the means to individuate the earlier state. Something enduring other than these two states that is aware of both and also of their succession may, of course, know of their causal connection. One may suppose that the body or perhaps the brain is such an enduring thing. But that would only push the difficulty one or more steps backwards. The difficulty would still crop up when the body or the brain would change and be a causal condition of something succeeding it. How could these two themselves know that they are causally connected? Hence the knowledge of causal connection can be entrusted only to the self, which is simple and does not change.

Now we turn to some recent Hume-like and Buddhist-like views, one of which is that of Sydney Shoemaker. Shoemaker has challenged the thesis that memory presupposes personal identity. To this end he has introduced the notion of quasi-memory.[7] The latter does not require that the same person who had the original experience must also be the rememberer. What the latter requires is that there should be some kind of causal connection between the previous experience and the present remembrance. To quote Shoemaker:

> Let us take 'remember-W' to be synonymous with 'quasi-remember'. Clearly to establish that S remembers-W an event E it is not necessary to establish that S himself witnessed E, for it will be enough if S is the offshoot of someone who witnessed E. [1970:281]

This kind of causal connection would obtain if the impression of the previous experience is transferred to another individual through some procedure, say a brain transplant. Then the latter would be able to remember the previous experience although it is not the same person who originally had that experience. Thus quasi-memory does not presuppose personal identity. Accordingly, personal identity may be explained through quasi-memory without inviting the charge of circularity. One may object that if quasi-memory requires only some kind of causal connection between the previous experience and present remembrance, there would be some cases where remembrance would have to be admitted in spite of that being counterintuitive. Shoemaker anticipated this objection and argued that all such cases can be avoided by adding the condition that in every case the rememberer should be the best available candidate.

But even this does not avoid all the undesirable results. For example, suppose that a newborn's mother dies at the time of the former's birth without leaving behind any other child. There is a causal connection between the mother and the child and that connection does not hold between any one else. So the child should be able to remember the mother's experience there being no better candidate left to remember it. It seems that to avoid all such possible counterexamples, what we have to require is that the person who had the original experience and the one who remembers it must be the same person. Then the introduction of quasi-memory would serve no real purpose. The difference between Shoemaker's view and that of the Buddhist is that while, according to the latter, the rememberer should belong to the same stream as the original experiencer in a continuing and uninterrupted flow, according to the former, the rememberer should be the best available candidate who is causally connected with the original experiencer. Both agree that mere causal connection is not enough and have provided additional conditions to avoid possible counterexamples. But the additional conditions fall short in both cases.

Another view that is of the same genera as the above two views is that of Parfit.[8] The latter has argued that what matters is not the survival of the same person but rather that of someone suitably related to the original person. Thus in a fictional case of split-brain transplant it would be irrational, Parfit claims, to try to ensure some personal gain by getting rid of one of the brain hemispheres, so that there is only one survivor who could be identified with the original person. David Lewis has objected to this argument by saying that Parfit has unwarrantedly assumed that the original person ceases to exist after the fission.[9] We do not find this objection very persuasive for it involves the thesis of two spatially coincident people becoming spatially distinct after the fission. Unless there are independent reasons for accepting that two (or more in case there is more than a two-way split) people are normally coincident in the same body, Parfit may simply disown the thesis and save his argument. But to us an objectionable assumption in this argument is that A the survivor with only half the brain is a better candidate for identity with the original person than B the two survivors each with one half of the original brain. At least from the Nyāya point of view of strict identity neither A or B are suitable candidates for identity with the original person and it is not of any merit to give A a higher rating than B. So one may accept Parfit's claim that it would be irrational to try to get rid of one of the brain hemispheres in this case. But one may still disagree with the conclusion that what matters is not the survival of the same person. A plausible explanation is that since in this case the survival of the original person is impossible, the person has nothing more to gain by trying to ensure the survival of only one person with half the brain. Instead, the person accepts the inevitable and prefers the survival of two different persons each carrying on with something of importance belonging to the original person. This has no bearing on a case where the survival of the original person is possible and fails to show that in latter kind of case such survival is immaterial. In fact, the above case has some analogy with parents having children (in spite of the obvious disanalogy of two individuals rather than one being required for having a child). Having a child does not mean the survival of the parent. Whether the parent has one child or two children has no bearing on the survival of the parent himself or herself. So a parent cannot rationally prefer to have only one child rather than two children to promote the cause of personal survival. Accordingly, a parent may very well prefer to have two (or more) children rather than one child for various reasons (provided economic or social or health factors, etc., do not stand in the way). However, if having one child rather than having two (or more) children meant ensuring one's personal survival, the situation would have been dramatically different with very different results.

Parfit's own view is that what matters in survival is a sufficient degree of psychological continuity that is causally grounded in any way whatsoever and is nonbranching. But this is not tight enough, for it allows for causal dependence of any kind. Suppose that a person's brain is preserved after his death (and the destruction of his body) and transplanted into a new body ensuring nonbranching psychological continuity. Then we have a Parfitian survivor A. But we would also have a Parfitian survivor B if the said brain is somehow totally damaged and still miraculously happens to be causally linked with the production of a new brain exactly like the original brain and then fitted to a new body. Parfit's account provides no ground for A being a better candidate than B and this does not fit with our usual preference for self-preservation measures that are normal and dependable over those that are abnormal and undependable. As far as we can see, no quick fix is available and any significant revision may very well bring in personal identity through the backdoor in a question-begging way.

It should be noted that while memory is a crucial sign for personal identity, memory cannot provide a criterion of personal identity as some neo-Humeans have held. This modern approach, as explained, claims that personal identity is constituted by a manifold of mental states connected by co-consciousness and psychological continuity. However, from the Nyāya point of view, as we have seen, there can be personal identity even when the mental states are not connected by co-consciousness and even when there is no psychological continuity. In the Nyāya view, consciousness arises in the self only when certain other conditions are fulfilled. So gaps in our conscious lives are inevitable and psychological continuity is unavailable as well as unnecessary. This will be clearer from the following discussion of the Hume-like view of the theory of stream of consciousness developed by William James.[10] James' view has recently been defended by Owen Flanagan.[11] Just as the Buddhist replaces the permanent (*sthira*) self (*ātman*) with a flowing stream of cognitions (*cit-pravāha*), (*cit-santati*), so also James and Flanagan replace the identical and permanent self with a stream of consciousness. We focus on the account of Flanagan.

According to Flanagan, "individual consciousnesses are streamlike" (CR 155). The Nyāya would agree in part, for it accepts the seemingly obvious truth that internal states occur successively. But the Nyāya does not agree to the dismissal of the substantival self and the special tasks the stream is required to take over for the self.

First, there is the question: What happens to the flowing stream when we are apparently unconscious, as in a deep sleep? The Nyāya view on this is that the self abides with the latent impressions of previous experiences, for the person is later able to reconnect with himself. But since there is no evidence of any conscious activities going on, the Nyāya holds that there are no conscious states happening then. The Nyāya does not hold like Descartes or the Sāṃkhya that consciousness is the essence of the self. Consciousness is an adventitious (*āgantuka*) characteristic of the self and arises when the conditions are suitable.

But this solution is not easy for a stream theorist. If no conscious states are taking place, what happens to the stream? Is the stream then dry? But if so, how can we speak of a single stream? And without a single stream how can we account for personal identity? As Flanagan says: "James's likening consciousness to a stream is jeopardized by his own honest admission that we might indeed sometimes be wholly unconscious" (CR 157).

Can the single stream survive in the face of this crushing objection? We first look at what is suggested by the Buddhist. The Buddhist claimed that although there is no consciousness of objects (*pravṛttti-vijñāna*) in deep sleep, the I-consciousness (*ālaya-vijñāna*) persists as an uninterrupted series, so that we can still speak of a single stream (ATV 260).

But this claim, according to the Nyāya, is no more than a gratuitous assumption to save the stream theory. It also shows why the latter is less economical. To account for memory the Nyāya introduces the abiding self as the owner of impressions. Nothing additional is needed to account for deep sleep then. On the other hand, the Buddhist introduces a flowing stream to account for memory. But when confronted with gaps in conscious life, the Buddhist has been forced to assume additionally that I-consciousness persists through such gaps.

The Buddhist view appears to be less economical in another respect. To explain deep sleep, all that the Nyāya admits is the self and the impressions that have already been admitted to exist to account for memory. But to maintain the streamlike nature of consciousness the Buddhist must not only assume that I-consciousness persists in deep sleep, but also that I-consciousness is constantly being regenerated then. This amounts to admitting an indefinite number of gratuitous I-consciousnesses (in deep sleep and so on) together with their prior absences (*prāgabhāva*) and their posterior absences (*dhvaṃsābhāva*). The prior absences should be admitted because each transitory I-consciousness is nonexistent before its origin. Similarly, the posterior absences should be admitted because each transitory I-consciousness is nonexistent after it is gone. Such absences may not carry as much ontic weight as things such as bricks and stones. But in the Nyāya view they still have some weight and add to the ontic burden of the Buddhist theory. To shed the additional ontic burden, the Buddhist could suppose that I-consciousness does not constantly regenerate but persists unchanged in deep sleep. But then, with an abiding I-consciousness added, the Buddhist position will soon become too close to the Nyāya position (ATV 269).

Now we look at Flanagan's own observations on a stream. He points out that a single thought lacks the streamlike feature (CR 158). Still the whole process has some important characteristics. First, "*every state is part of a personal consciousness*." "Each thought is owned." "It is just that you cannot have my thoughts" (CR 158, 159).

All these are accepted by the Nyāya, for the self is *ex hypothesi* the owner of each internal state. But how does this help James or Flanagan to resolve the gaps in consciousness? All that we know is that if there are conscious states, they are owned. If there are no conscious states in deep sleep, surely they are not owned either. Could the talk about ownership suggest anything like a flowing I-consciousness as it does for the Buddhist? Presumably not. But even if it does, that is not a very comfortable position as we have seen. Further, each state in the so-called stream is different, as the Nyāya philosophers point out. Why should then each be felt as mine and as having the same subject, namely, me, particularly when there probably are gaps in conscious life? A stream theorist owes an explanation of why each state is felt as being personally owned. The explanation does not come simply from acknowledging that it is so.

Second, the physical, neurological and phenomenological evidence suggests, Flanagan reports following James, that consciousness is in constant change. This is also the Nyāya and the Buddhist view (with the Nyāya holding that internal states usually endure for two moments but the Buddhist insisting on some metaphysical grounds that all internal states endure for only one moment). The latter too hold that no new state is ever identical with an earlier state. However, it should be kept in mind that this throws no light on how the stream can be single in spite of gaps in conscious life or on how personal identity is possible in case the streams are many.

Third, although we in fact are not always subjectively conscious, Flanagan notes, each consciousness reconnects to its past and feels continuous (CR 162). Here some Buddhists would disagree on the first part and claim that I-consciousness invariably accompanies every cognitive state. However, the Nyāya would agree on the first part and both the Nyāya and the Buddhist would agree on the second part. But for the Nyāya a stream theorist should nevertheless explain why consciousness is subjectively felt to be continuous although there are probably periods in our lives when we are nonconscious. To a self-theorist, consciousness reconnects to its past in spite of periods of nonconsciousness because both the new and the old consciousnesses belong to the same self. This explanation is not available to a stream theorist.

Fourth, consciousness has the fringe, the penumbra, the halo of relations. "The fringe suffuses the present thought with the resonating feel of past thoughts, and it is the carrier of the network of memories already acquired and of expectations about the future" (CR 164). Again, "A stream has length and breadth. It appropriates its past as it moves forward" (CR 165).

The Nyāya does not dispute that consciousness has a focus and a fringe but would dispute that the fringe is the carrier of the network of memories. Flanagan's suggestion is somewhat similar to the Buddhist suggestion that momentary states become carriers of memory by virtue of causal connection, or potency or similarity. The Nyāya countered that these are also found in nonconscious things. If nonconscious things do not become carriers of memory by virtue of these, why should we believe that conscious states would be so by virtue of these? The same applies to the fringe, the penumbra, or the halo. These are also features of nonconscious things that are not carriers of memory. So why should conscious states become carriers of memory by virtue of these?

Fifth, according to Flanagan, identity, direction, and agency are grounded in the memorable connections of the stream. If the conscious stream is eliminated (because of severe brain damage as in final-stage Alzheimer patients), the sense of identity and personhood are jeopardized (CR 166–67).

The Nyāya explanation of severe loss of memory and sense of personal identity would presumably be that much of the network of impressions, interests, and anticipations are lost in such cases. Hence the self can no longer perform its normal functions, for the requisite auxiliaries are missing. But identity cannot be grounded in the stream and if the stream is the whole story, the past cannot be appropriated by present consciousness. The latter can be causally connected with the past and contain its impressions. But still the present consciousness is different from the past and so cannot recognize its object as the same or as of the same kind as that of the past.

Sixth, according to Flanagan, Dennett is wrong to think that consciousness flows in multiple channels rather than as a single stream (CR 172–74). On this the Nyāya philosophers are not unanimous. Most following Gotama (NS 1.1.19) favor a gappy but linear succession of internal states with the self as the abiding owner. This is why they hold that the inner sense (*manas*), the principal auxiliary of the self for the generation of internal states, is unifunctional. Although the inner sense is unifunctional, it can move in a blazing speed and appear to be multifunctional. Others such as Raghunatha Siromani favor the idea of multiple channels and hold that the inner sense is multifunctional (GD 799).

Flanagan rejects the traditional view that all consciousness is self-conscious and that every conscious state not only reveals its object but also its subject, the self (CR 177). On this he is in disagreement with some Buddhists, for, according to the latter, I-consciousness or "I think" accompanies all experience. However, he is for once in agreement with the Nyāya. As we have seen, according to the Nyāya, a cognitive state requires another cognitive state to reveal itself and does not always have the self as a content.

James and Flanagan are opposed to the Cartesian self, which is removed from space, and the Kantian noumenal self, which is removed from time (CR 184). But so far as the Nyāya is concerned, the self is considered to have dimension (*parimāṇa*) and also to be in time. The Nyāya does not find it impossible for the self to be both dimensional and immaterial (discussed in chapter 2). The Nyāya self is not anti-naturalistic, for it is inferred as the best available explanation for the natural phenomenon of memory.

But, according to James and Flanagan, thoughts themselves are the thinkers (CR 182). The Buddhist accepts this and brings in the I-consciousness (*ālaya-vijñāna*) and the causal network to account for it. The Buddhist also rejects the metaphysical distinction between a substance and its qualia and a substance and its action. The Nyāya rejects that I-consciousness accompanies all consciousness. The Nyāya is also committed to the thesis that an action requires a substratum which belongs to a different ontic category and also that a quale requires a substance that also is ontically different. Since thoughts are both qualia (*guṇa*) and acts (*kriyā*), they require the self as their supportive substance and the thinker. We note it as a ground of disagreement, then, that if the substance ontology is accepted, thoughts cannot be thinkers.

Apart from the metaphysical disagreement the explanation offered by James and Flanagan for thoughts as thinkers is not acceptable to the Nyāya. "[T]houghts . . . carry rich information about the past course of the stream and the direction in which it is headed" (CR 182). Again, "'I' names this judging thought only insofar as this thought is appropriative, only insofar as it appropriates my life and brings to bear some appropriate model of who I am" (CR 186). The trouble is that appropriation without a permanent self is not explanatory of the sense of identity. In the world of nonconscious events, too, previous events get appropriated into the later ones through the causal network, as when one drop of water flows and blends into another drop of water. If that does not endow drops of water with a sense of identity, why should it work for thoughts?

Of course it is possible that by appropriation or by fringe, penumbra, or halo as mentioned earlier Flanagan means something that is unique to conscious states. Then the choice of the terminology is unfortunate, to say the least. What is needed then is a set of features that are unique to consciousness and explains the sense of identity in a noncircular way that is significantly different from the introduction of a permanent self. This implies that the stream cannot be ontically different from the states in the stream. But then all we seem to have left are different states related by way of a highly complex causal network. Since such causal networks are also found in nonconscious processes that lack a sense of identity, it is difficult to see how that can provide something unique about consciousness and be explanatory of the sense of identity.

The difficulty is compounded by the admission made by James and Flanagan that though, viewed subjectively, consciousness is streamlike, viewed objectively, it is less streamlike (CR 169). For a Nyāya philosopher this amounts to admitting that we do not have a single stream. If there is no evidence of any conscious states happening in deep sleep, we should not admit, as the Nyāya insists, that any conscious states are happening in deep sleep. Then we still have left the impressions and dispositions. But there is no evidence that the impressions and dispositions continue to regenerate in a flowlike manner and moreover in a single flowlike manner. Of course, the impressions are there and the Nyāya accepts it. But where is the evidence to show that they are in a streamlike state? The issue is not whether neural and other bodily changes are taking place in deep sleep and so on. The Nyāya would accept that they are. But this does not prove that mental functioning is going on and that such neural and bodily changes are generating mental functioning in a flowlike manner. Thus the single stream seems to be lost irrecoverably and with it the hope of grounding the sense of identity in the single stream.

But the continuation of the self and of the impressions in the gappy periods of our conscious lives is not difficult to understand from the Nyāya viewpoint. The impressions are not constantly changing like the occurrent states. The impressions do become firmer (*dṛḍatara*) or fainter (*līnatara*). But they are not known to be fleeting like the occurrent states. So the Nyāya regards them as being relatively stable; these may persist in deep sleep and so on. The self too persists when no conscious activity is going on. The self is inferred as a substance that supports such activities. The lack of such activities does not imply the nonexistence of the self. If the substance ontology and the inference of the self as a substance are defensible, so is the continuation of the self during periods of nonconsciousness.

Finally, Flanagan, following James, disputes that "the mind *must* have a control center and that the conscious self must be *the* control center in the mind" (CR 189). An alternative possibility is that there is no center of control. To explain how this is possible Flanagan cites the example of certain bird flocks that maintain cohesion without a single leader or even a small group of leaders (CR 191). (Another similar example would be that of a sports team that may retain its name after changing the captain or other players.)

From the Nyāya point of view this is not acceptable. What is true of certain bird flocks is not true of individual birds in the flock. No one bird within the flock may be indispensable for the survival of the flock. But there are parts of the bird's body that are indispensable for the survival of the individual bird. So the flock analogy is not very illuminating. (Similarly, what is true of a sports team is not true of individual players in the team.) The high level of coordination needed for the survival of an individual animal is hard to explain without a single supervisor (*adhiṣṭhātā*). Without a chain of commands headed by an overall controller, the life of an individual would be like the exploits of an army without a commander-in-chief. The commander-in-chief does not get to learn about every detail, nor does he get to make every decision. In fact, the actual body of information used by the commander and the actual number of decisions made by him may be relatively small. Still the efficiency of the army depends in a significant way on the commander-in-chief. In the same way the efficiency of the individual depends in a significant way on the hierarchy of commands with something heading it. Flanagan himself notes: "It is normative for us that each person has one and only one self" (CR 199). The Nyāya theory requires this to be the way each person is.

CHAPTER 6

The Self as a Substance

According to Gotama, as seen in the previous chapter, internal states such as desire serve as the definiens of the self and provide the grounds for its permanence. We now discuss how and why they also provide the grounds for regarding the self as a substance (*dravya*).

We begin with the following comments of Vatsyayana:

> [The kind of inference] called 'known through the universal' (*sāmānyatodṛṣṭa*) is when the relationship between the sign (*liṅga*) and the sign-possessor (*liṅgin*) is imperceptible and the imperceptible sign-possessor is inferred on the basis of the sign's universal connection with a certain something. For example, desire, etc., are qualia; and qualia are supported by a substance; that which is their support is the self. (NSB 1.1.5)

Here the inference of the self as the substance that supports desire, and so on is given as an example of a kind of inference called 'known through the universal'. This is the third kind of inference mentioned by Gotama (NS 1.1.5). Vatsyayana offered two different explanations for this kind of inference that, for the lack of a better term, may perhaps be called genus-mediated inference. The comments quoted above give the second explanation.

According to the second explanation, in a genus-mediated inference the sign-possessor (*liṅgin*) is imperceptible and therefore the relationship of the sign (*liṅga*) and the sign-possessor is also imperceptible.[1] This is not usually so in other kinds of inference from a cause to its effect or from an effect to its cause. For example, in inferring fire from smoke, both fire, the sign-possessor, and its togetherness with smoke, the sign, are perceptible. So it is possible to infer fire directly from smoke as the sign. But sometimes the sign-possessor is not perceptible and so a different logical strategy is called for. Since the sign-possessor is imperceptible, no matter what is chosen as the sign, the relationship between the sign and the sign-possessor will be imperceptible too. At the same time the foundational requirement for inferring laid down by Gotama, namely, that inferring must eventually be grounded in perception, has to be met. (Without this restriction inferring would open the door for idle speculation bereft of empirical basis.) So the genus of the sign as well as the genus of the sign-possessor are brought into play. Although the sign-possessor is imperceptible, its genus may be perceptible. So the relationship between the genus of the sign-possessor and the genus of the sign may also be perceptible. Thus a roundabout ticket for inferring an imperceptible sign-possessor in a way that is eventually grounded in perception is secured. The example of inferring the self shows how this is possible. Since the self is imperceptible, its relationship with whatever is chosen as the sign is imperceptible too. Still, the inference must eventually be perception based. So the genus of the self, substance (*dravya*), is brought in as also the genus of desire, the sign, that is, quale (*guṇa*). The togetherness of qualia and substances is perceptible. (This is explained below.) Thus the perceptual basis for inference of the self is secured. The inference is still rigorous, for it is a logical truth that what is true of the genus (*sāmānya*) is true of the species (*viśeṣa*).

In inferring the self, Vatsyayana claims first that desire, and so on are qualia. The Nyāya-Vaiśeṣika school accepts qualia such as color or smell that belong to physical (*bhautika*) substances. The substances are ontologically different from the qualia and also support the latter.[2] That qualia are supported by a substance is, according to the Nyāya-Vaiśeṣika, an empirical generalization. Qualia such as color or smell are observed to be supported by a substance. Like the qualia, the substance too may be perceived. For example, we not only perceive the color or smell of a mango; we also perceive the mango. This view then is different from that of modern Western philosophers such as Locke who recognize the substance but regard it as an imperceptible know-not-what. For the Nyāya-Vaiśeṣika the substance is not a mysterious entity hiding behind the phenomena. It is perceived and perceived to be different from its qualia. It is also perceived as the principal (*pradhāna*) and the qualia as secondary (*gauṇa*). On the basis of such observations, then, of qualia being supported by substances (when both the qualia and the substance are perceptible), it is generalized that all qualia are supported by substances. The ontological distinction between a substance and its qualia or actions is then grounded, according to the Nyāya, in common perceptions.

To elucidate: We have such common perceptions as that the mango is red, the mango is sweet smelling, and so forth. Such common experiences reveal color, smell, and so on, as qualia of the mango. We also have such common experiences as that the mango is falling and so on. These reveal falling and so on as actions of the mango. On the strength of such common experiences (*anubhava*), it is reasonable to claim that these different qualia and actions belong to the same substratum. The substratum is called a substance. The substance is accordingly described (but not strictly speaking defined) as the substratum of qualia and actions. The substance is conceived as the causal substratum (*samavāyi-kāraṇa*) of its qualia and actions. The qualia and actions originate as inhering (*samaveta*) in the substance to which they belong. This implies that the qualia and actions are dependent on the substance but the latter is not dependent on the former. Accordingly, change in qualia and actions does not imply that we have a different substance.

It may be useful to elaborate on the above point. We have such common perceptions as that the mango was green before and is yellow now. Since this is a common experience, on this basis it is reasonable to claim that the mango is the same though its color has changed. That the mango remains the same although the qualia and actions have changed is explicable if the mango is a unitary entity different from the qualia and actions. Otherwise all that we have left are the changing qualia and actions. Then the perception of the mango as one thing that is undergoing changes of qualia and actions must be judged to be false. But that the mango is one thing is a common perception and a common perception is not to be thrown out without sufficient reason. Rather than rejecting the common perception as false, the Nyāya offers the theory of substance as the best available explanation that preserves the truth of the common perception. If the mango is a unitary substantial whole which is different from its qualia and actions, the perception of the mango as one thing in spite of changing qualia and actions may be accepted as true.

The Buddhists regard the common perception of the mango as one thing with many qualia and actions as false (NV 217–39). In the Buddhist view, the mango is nothing but an aggregate of qualia and actions (*guṇa-karma-samudāya*). Each quale is a separate entity and so is each action. But their collection is not a separate entity just as a forest is not a separate entity apart from the trees making it (SV 444). Thus the mango does not exist as a unitary substance. When we analyze the experience of a mango we find nothing but the qualia and actions themselves. In other words, when we analyze the perception of a mango, we find the perception of a color, perception of a smell, and so on but not the perception of anything that is different from these. The ordinary language does contain words like mango with a singular reference. But language is no sure guide to the nature of things. What is really referred to by words like mango is a collection of qualia and actions.

Thus the Nyāya and the Buddhist disagree on the phenomenology of the perception of a mango. While for the Buddhist such perception reveals only a plurality of qualia and actions, for the Nyāya it reveals, besides the plurality of qualia and actions, also a unitary whole.

The Buddhists have also raised some dialectical objections against the theory of substance to show that the linguistic usage of the mango as a single thing is false. Suppose that the mango is a unitary substance different from its qualia and actions. Then the question is: Does the mango reside in its entirety in each quale and action or partially? If it resides in its entirety in a quale or an action, it cannot reside in any other quale or action. But if it resides only partially in a quale or an action, it follows that it has many parts and then the same question is repeated for the parts. Does it reside in its entirety in a part or only partially? If it resides in its entirety in a part, it cannot reside in other parts. But if it resides only partially in a part, it has still other parts and this opens the door of an infinite regress (NSB 2.1.32).

Vatsyayana dismisses the above question as being illformed and misleading. The words 'entire' (*kṛtsna*) and 'partial' (*ekadeśa*), he points out, have no application to a thing that is *one*. The word 'entire' means "all of many things" and the word 'partial' means "some among the many" (NSB 2.1.32). Hence both apply only to a plurality but not to a substantial whole that is a unity.

This illustrates the way in which the Nyāya philosophers tried to resolve or dissolve various Buddhist attempts to prove that the common usage about a substance being one thing is false. The outcome of the discussion, from the Nyāya point of view, is that there is no sufficient reason to label such common usage as false.

Besides such defensive action the Nyāya has also argued that the Buddhist view is less economical. For the Nyāya the word 'mango' refers to the substance mango and mangoness is the specifier (*avacchedaka*) of what the word refers to. By the specifier is meant that which delimits the reference within the intended boundary. But for the Buddhist there is no such unitary whole; rather what the word 'mango' refers to is an aggregate of qualia and actions. So 'being an aggregate of qualia and actions' will have to be the specifier of what 'mango' refers to. As between the two specifiers, namely, mangoness and being an aggregate of qualia and actions, the latter is more complex. Other things being equal, a more complex specifier should be discarded for a simpler one (AN 7). Thus considerations of economy (*lāghava*) favor the admission of a substance. We have seen above that the Nyāya prefers to base the case for the category of substance on common perceptions such as the mango is red, the mango is sweet, and so on, which reveal the mango to be one thing having many qualia and actions. But the Buddhist challenges that. Hence the argument from economy is offered from the common platform of logical theory to show that the theory of substance is more reasonable than the theory of aggregate.

Further, if there are no substantial wholes (*avayavin*), it is difficult, granted the atomic theory (the arguments for which will be presented in the tenth chapter), to explain how measurable and perceptible (*mahat*) things arise out of a mere collection of atoms (NSB 2.1.35). The atoms are indivisible and therefore immeasurable and imperceptible. If they were measurable or perceptible, they would have been divisible. Here immeasurability and imperceptibility means immeasurability and imperceptibility (excluding the limiting case of divine knowledge) in principle and not just in practice. So it is not permissible to say that although atoms are not measurable or perceptible by any available means, they could in some distant future be measured or perceived by some new sophisticated device. So atoms are not just small things that are hard to measure or perceive. When small things that are hard to measure or perceive are collected, they may become bigger and easier to measure and perceive. But that does not apply to atoms. So how can a mere conjunction of atoms produce things that are bigger, measurable, and perceptible? There is simply no basis for claiming that two or more immeasurables when merely conjoined together will make something measurable. So the Nyāya argues that the admission of substantial wholes obviates this difficulty. Then it is possible to say that the substantial whole is a different unitary entity and has features like measurability missing in the ultimate parts. Not every Buddhist accepts the atomic theory but some do. This argument is addressed to those who do and others who may eventually be inclined to accept the atomic theory.

Can the argument from perceptibility be separated from the context of the atomic theory and offered independently? Gotama and

Vatsyayana have shown that it can be, though with a new twist. Even if one does not admit atoms, one would not deny that things like trees are made of parts. Now the problem is that it is not possible to have sensory contact with all the parts of the tree at a given time. One can perhaps at best have sensory contact with the front but not with the back. So only some parts of the tree can at best be perceived but never the tree. The tree then can only be inferred (NS 2.1.30). So if one holds that the tree is perceived, one may be well advised to regard the tree as a substantial whole over and above a mere collection of its parts. Then it makes sense to say that sensory contact with each or even a majority of the parts of a whole is not necessary for the perception of the whole. So the whole may be perceived in spite of there being sensory contact with only some of its parts. Needless to say, some philosophers including some Buddhists hold that things like trees are inferred and not perceived. The above argument is addressed only to those who hold or may be persuaded to hold that such things are perceived. The Nyāya philosophers have indeed shown that perceptibility of wholes yields rich dividends in epistemology.[3]

Again, things like pots and houses function as unitary wholes rather than as aggregates (NS 2.1.35). Clearly a pot can be used in ways (such as holding water) for which a mere lump of clay will not be suitable. As Vatsyayana says, making such a thing involves more than gluing or cementing the parts together (NSB 2.1.35). For the parts cemented in an unplanned way do not a house make. The argument from economy may be brought in at this point to reinforce this argument. If a pot is accepted as a substantial whole, potness as a simple property may be regarded as the specifier (*avacchedaka*) of the causal functions of a pot. It is important to recognize such a specifier, for a pot has distinctive uses and it should be explained why such uses are restricted to pots. however, if a pot is not a unitary whole, but a collection of parts in a specific way, potness can no longer be regarded as a simple property. Instead potness will then have to be explained as having a narrow necklike structure and so on. It is often very difficult, if not impossible, to come up with a complete list of what falls under 'and so on' in such cases. Since we can know what a pot is without having to completely spell out (in many cases without ever completely spelling out) such a list, potness as a simple property turns out to be attractive as the said specifier (and certainly more economical than a highly complex and perhaps unfinished conjunction of features). This favors the admission of substances as unitary wholes.

Moreover, a thing such as a pot is perceived to be one thing. If it is not a substantial whole but a mere aggregate, the perception of it as one thing must be dismissed as false, for it amounts to cognizing something as one that is not really so. The Buddhist may maintain that there is no harm in labeling it as false. But then the question remains: What is the true source of the perception of unity? A false perception of something presupposes a true perception of it. For example, one cannot misperceive a rope as a snake unless one has seen a snake before. But if we disallow substantial wholes, as Vatsyayana argues, we are hard put to find something that is truely perceived to be one (NSB 2.1.36). Things like pots cannot be such things, for they are by supposition a plurality of parts, qualia, and actions. One could say that a quale or an action could still be truly perceived as one. But this is far from clear. The question remains: How can a quale or an action be one if it belongs to a collection and not to some one thing? Should we not say that each part in the collection has its own quale and that each such quale is as particular as the part itself? At least the Buddhist should say so, for he rejects all nonparticular reals. Clearly, if a quale belongs to many parts, that is, if one and the same quale is truly in many things, it is no longer a particular but a universal. So it seems that we must eventually get down to the ultimate parts and their qualia that are as particular as the parts themselves. But can such qualia be perceived and perceived as one when these ultimate parts themselves are not perceptible? Thus there does not seem to be anything that may truly be perceived as one thing from the Buddhist perspective. The Buddhist then appears to be unable to account for a true perception of unity. The difficulty does not arise if substantial wholes are admitted, for these (and some of their qualia and actions) may truly be perceived as one.

It appears then that the ontological distinction between a substance and its qualia and actions, in spite of serious challenges, is defensible and acceptable. Vatsyayana applies this ontological thesis to the internal states like desire. These are directly perceived, according to the Nyāya, and are perceived as dependent (*paratantra*) and secondary. We have such common experiences as that I desire this, I cognize this, and so on. Common experiences are true, according to the Nyāya, unless there is compelling evidence to the contrary. On the strength of such common experiences it is reasonable to claim that desire, cognition, and so on, are dependent on something else. It is also part of the common experience that desire and so on are characteristics of the 'I', for it is commonly felt that I am desirous of this, I am cognizant of this, and so on. Desire, cognition, and so on, are internally perceived to be characteristics of the 'I' just as color and smell are externally perceived as characteristics of a mango. Hence these are qualia and these too must have a substance as their support. The self is inferred as their support (NV 64–68). So all substances are not perceived. Sometimes a substance is inferred as the needed support for some observed or unobserved (but inferred) qualia. The self has some observed qualia like desire or cognition. It also has some unobserved qualia, that is, dispositions (inferred to account for memory) and merit and demerit accruing from voluntary actions (inferred to account for discrepancies in personal reward and punishment so that God is not blamed for favoritism or cruelty).

The self has nine qualia that it does not share with any other substance. These are desire, aversion, volition, pleasure, pain, cognition, disposition, merit, and demerit. These are the specific qualia (*viśeṣa-guṇa*) of the self (SM 488). With the help of these the self is inferred as an imperceptible substance. The self also has five qualia which it shares with other substances, namely, number, distinctness, dimension, conjunction, and disjunction (SM 488). Thus there is a plurality of selves. This implies that number is a real quale of the self. The plurality also implies that each self is distinct from every other, so that distinctness is also an actual quale of it. Like other substances the self is supposed to be the substratum of dimension (*parimāṇa*). It is also supposed to be conjoined or united with the body (at the time of birth) and to be disjoined or separated from the body (at the time of death).[4]

We have seen that the self is inferred as the substance to which desire and so on belong. This is a two-stage inference. First, it is inferred that since desire and so on are qualia they must belong to a substance. Second, it is inferred that the self is that substance. Even if desire and the rest belong to some substance, it does not follow immediately that the self is that substance. There are eight other kinds of substances in the Nyāya-Vaiśeṣika ontology. In principle desire and so on could belong to any one of them. Before it may be concluded that the self is that substance to which desire and the rest belong, the other substances must be eliminated. Such elimination is done through elaborate reasoning that we discuss in the next three chapters. For the time being we assume that the elimination is sound and simply concern ourselves with the results of the elimination. The two-stage inference may then be reformulated as follows.

> All qualia belong to a substance, for instance, color and so forth.
>
> Desire and the other marks of the self are qualia.
>
> Therefore, desire and so on belong to a substance.

> Either desire and so forth belong to one of the eight recognized kinds of substances, or they belong to an additional ninth kind of substance.
>
> Desire and so forth do not belong to one of the eight recognized kinds of substances.
>
> Therefore, desire and so on belong to an additional ninth kind of substance.

This additional ninth kind of substance is called the self.

Thus the inference of the self is a chain argument with the first argument being in the form of a categorical syllogism and the second argument being in the form of a disjunctive syllogism. The deductive part of the argument may be put in the symbolic notation as below: [Dx = x is a desire; Qx = x is a quale; Sx = x belongs to a substance; Ex = x belongs to one of the eight substances; Nx = x belongs to an additional ninth substance]

$(x)\ (Dx \supset Qx)$
$(x)\ (Qx \supset Sx)$
Therefore, $(x)\ (Dx \supset Sx)$

$(x)\ (Dx \supset Ex) \vee (x)\ (Dx \supset Nx)$
$(x)\ (Dx \supset -Ex)$
Therefore, $(x)\ (Dx \supset Nx)$

In the passage quoted earlier Vatsyayana does not say explicitly that the second half of the inference of the self is an eliminative reasoning. However, he had explained the form of an eliminative reasoning (*pariśeṣa*) in the passage immediately above the passage quoted earlier and had also explained the nature of such reasoning with an example. It is more than likely, given the compactness of his style of writing, that he expects the reader to see for himself that the second half of the argument for the self is an eliminative reasoning.[5] He has argued elsewhere (to which we shall turn in the next three chapters) that desire and so on cannot be the qualia of other recognized substances. He naturally expects the reader to connect that discussion with the passage cited earlier. However, Uddyotakara says explicitly that the second half of the inference of the self is an eliminative reasoning (NV 52).

This shows that ancient Indian logicians produced argument chains by combining arguments in the categorical syllogistic form with arguments the formal validity of which depends on truth-functional connectives. It is worth noting that no such specimen is found in the ancient Greek Aristotelian or Stoic writings. Many Aristotelians and Stoics seem to have wrongly believed that the syllogistic logic and the truth-functional logic are somehow opposed to each other and that one should make way for the other. Clearly some ancient Indian logicians did not think so and saw the merit of combining the fruits of both in a logical theory.

Vacaspati Misra has given another interpretation of the above argument: "Together with proof of desire, etc., not belonging to the eight substances being a quale itself becomes an exclusion based probans (*vyatireki hetu*) for (desire, etc.) belonging to the self" (TP 184). Thus he takes all internal states such as desire and the like as the subject (*pakṣa*: similar to the minor term) of the inference, "being a quale that belongs to the additional ninth substance called the self" as the probandum (*sādhya*: similar to the major term) and "being a quale that does not belong to the other eight substances" as the probans (*hetu*: similar to the minor term).[6] We reformulate the argument as follows:

> Whatever is a quale that does not belong to the additional ninth substance called the self is not a quale that does not belong to the other eight substances, for example, color and so on.
>
> All internal states are qualia that do not belong to the other eight substances.
>
> Therefore, all internal states are qualia that belong to the additional ninth substance called the self.

The deductive part of the argument may be put in the symbolic notation as follows [Ix = x is an internal state; Sx = x is a quale that belongs to the additional ninth substance called the self; Ex = x is a quale that belongs to the other eight substances]:

$(x)(\sim Sx \supset \sim\sim Ex)$
$(x)(Ix \supset \sim Ex)$
Therefore, $(X)(Ix \supset Sx)$

That internal states such as desire do not belong to the other eight substances including the body is of course a huge claim that must be justified. Leaving that aside for the present, it should be noted that here the first premise should not be replaced by its contrapositive, namely, whatever is a quale that does not belong to the other eight substances is a quale that belongs to the additional ninth substance called the self. If the skeptic or the materialist challenges this proposition, the Nyāya should come up with undisputable corroborative examples on the basis of which the general claim is made. But no such examples are there. An opponent who disowns the immaterial self may refuse to accept any quale as something that does not belong to the other eight substances, for such an opponent is likely to hold that desire and so on are qualia of the body. Moreover, since all internal states such as desire are the subject of the inference, none of them are usable as confirming instances. The subject of the inference is part of the bone of contention; so to avoid the charge of circularity the subject must be excluded from the evidence supporting the said generalization.

That is why the premise has been put in the *vyatirekin* or exclusion mood.[7] If the premise is challenged now, undisputable supporting instances can be found. Color, smell, and so on, are accepted by both the Nyāya and the critic as qualia that do not belong to any additional substance but belong to one or more of the other eight substances. Further, there are no undisputable counterexamples. The only available counterexamples are the internal states and the critic may very well claim them to be qualia of the body. But that does not make them acceptable as undisputed counterexamples, for they are included in the inferential subject. Since the inferential subject is part of the bone of contention, just as the Nyāya is not allowed to use it as evidence for supporting the generalization, so also the critic is not allowed to use it as the evidence for refuting it. So the generalization, being supported by undisputable confirming instances and not being challenged by any undisputable counterexamples, can now, given GAIE, be accepted. If the other premise that the internal states are qualia that do not belong to the other eight substances is justified, the conclusion that the internal states are qualia that belong to the additional substance called the self becomes justified. The question then remains as to whether the other premise is justified, to which we shall turn in the next three chapters.

For further reflection on the value of arguing in the exclusion (*vyatirekin*) mood, we look at another such argument given by Uddyotakara to prove the existence of the immaterial self: "Exclusion based (*vyatirekin*) . . . the living body is not without the (immaterial) self because it does not lack breathing, etc." (NV 46). Here the living body is the inferential subject (*pakṣa*), 'being with the immaterial self' is the probandum and breathing is the probans. By saying 'breathing, etc.' it is implied that other distinctive features of a living body, such as blood circulation, may be brought in as supplementary probantia if necessary. We reformulate the argument below:

> Whatever is without the immaterial self does not breathe, for instance, a stone.
>
> The living body does not lack breathing.
>
> Therefore, the living body is not without the immaterial self.

In the symbolic notation the deductive part of the argument looks like [Lx = x is a living body; Sx = x is with the immaterial self; and Bx = x is breathing]:

$$(x)\,(\sim Sx \supset \sim Bx)$$
$$(x)\,(Lx \supset \sim\sim Bx)$$
$$\text{Therefore, } (X)\,(Lx \supset \sim\sim Sx)$$

Here again the first premise should not be replaced by its contrapositive—all that breathes is with the immaterial self. If the critic demands justification for it, the Nyāya cannot produce any undisputable supporting instance. Such an instance must be something that is acceptable to both the Nyāya and the critic as being breathing and as being associated with an immaterial self. But the critic may oppose the existence of an immaterial self altogether, so that no such instance can ever be found. Further, the only things that both breathe and are with the self in the Nyāya view are the living bodies. (In the Nyāya view all living bodies including those of animals are associated with immaterial selves.) But the living bodies are the inferential subject and hence cannot, except on the pain of circularity, be offered as evidence for the generalization.

To resolve the difficulty Uddyotakara switches from the inclusion (*anvaya*) mood to the exclusion mood. That is, instead of using the pervasion (*vyāpti*) between breathing (the probans) and being with the immaterial self (the probandum) as the premise, he uses the pervasion between being without the immaterial self (the negation of the probandum) and not breathing (the negation of the probans) as the premise. This switch does not make any difference from the point of view of formal validity. The argument is formally valid both in the inclusion mood and in the exclusion mood. But the switch does make a difference from the point of view of soundness. Now the premise is that whatever is without the immaterial self does not breathe. This generalization can be supported by undisputable examples such as bricks and stones. Both the Nyāya and the critic accept that bricks and stones do not breathe and are also without immaterial selves. At the same time this generalization cannot be refuted by any undisputable counterexamples. The only counterexamples that may be offered are living bodies that the critic may claim, do breathe but are without the immaterial self. But this is disputed, for the Nyāya claims that the living bodies are with immaterial selves. The living bodies are the inferential subject and part of the bone of contention and hence cannot be accepted as impartial evidence that refutes the generalization. Being supported by undisputable examples and not being challenged by undisputable counter examples the premise now, given GAIE, turns out to be reasonable and acceptable. The other premise, namely, that the living body breathes, is accepted by both the Nyāya and the critic. So the conclusion—that the living body is not without the immaterial self—becomes reasonable and acceptable too. The great Greek philosopher Plato too has utilized the phenomenon of life to argue for the immaterial self. But his arguments have often been rejected by the critics as circular. The merit of Uddyotakara is that he has shown how one can utilize the phenomenon of life to argue for the immaterial self in a way that is not question begging and also is formally valid. The burden is now on the shoulder of the critic who should either find some convincing way of neutralizing the power of the argument or accept the existence of an immaterial self. We continue the discussion in the next three chapters as we move deeper into the Nyāya defence of psychophysical dualism.

CHAPTER 7

The Self and the External Sense Organs

The Nyāya holds, as we have noted, that there are material as well as immaterial substances and neither is reducible to the other. There are many kinds of material substances, such as earth, water, and so on. But there is only one kind of substance that serves as the substratum of consciousness and is called the self (*ātman*). We have already discussed the Nyāya arguments for the existence of the self as a permanent entity and then for its existence as a substance. We now discuss why the self is an additional kind of substance and why it differs from the rest of the permanent substances.

We begin with the remarks of Vatsyayana introducing the section on the examination of the nature of the self:

> The self is to be examined. Is the self merely an aggregate of the body, the external senses, the inner sense, cognition and feeling or is it an additional [substance]? There are such usages as 'sees with the eye', 'knows with the inner sense', 'examines with the intellect', 'experiences pleasure and pain through the body', etc. There it is not settled as to whether these speak of . . . something additional. (NSB 3.1.1)

The self or the I is the understood subject in the above examples of ordinary usage. Vatsyayana finds such usage to be indecisive. We commonly say such things as that I am fat, I am fair, and so on. Here bodily charaters of being fat, being fair, and so on, are being attributed to the self. This would support the identification of the self with the body. But we also commonly speak of "my body," "my eye," and so on. This would support the idea that the self is different from the body, the eye, and so on. Since the common usage goes both ways, it does not by itself show whether the self that sees with the eye and so on is an aggregate of the eye and so on or is an additional entity.

There are, however, other grounds that may show that what is referred to as the self or I is an additional entity and different from other permanent substances such as the body. First it may be shown that the self is different from the external sense organs. Some Indian materialists have identified the self with the external senses because of their prominence in the acquisition of knowledge.[1] Clearly, the self is the knower. According to these materialists, perception is the only source of knowing and there are five kinds of perception corresponding to the five external sense organs: the eye, the ear, the skin, the nose, and the palate.[2] Since the primary function of the self is to know and there are basically five kinds of knowing, the self is held to be none other than the five external sense organs themselves each of which is indispensable for each basic kind of knowing.

The Nyāya does not agree that perception is the only source of knowing and argues at great length to show that inferring and the like must also be accepted as separate sources of knowing.[3] It also regards internal perception as a separate kind of perception and acknowledges (as discussed in the next chapter) the existence of the inner sense organ as something different from the external senses. So the Nyāya must reject the above materialistic argument for holding that the self is the aggregate of the five external senses. But we do not enter into these issues here, for the above view may also be attacked on some other grounds. First, in the words of Gotama: "[The self is different from the external senses] because the same thing may be cognized through seeing and touching, (NS 3.1.1) Vatsyayana explains:

> That which is apprehended by the sight may also be apprehended by the touch: 'that which I saw through the eye I cognize through touching also', 'I see through the eye that which I touched with the skin'. These two cognitions are recognized to have the same object and the same subject; they are not recognized as being due to the agency of an aggregate nor as having one sense organ as the agent. That which grasps the same thing by both the eye and the skin and recognizes two cognitions having different causes but the same object and the same subject is the additional entity called the self. Why [is this] not due to the agency of the same sense organ? A sense organ can grasp its own object . . . but not the object of another sense organ. Why [is this] not due to the agency of

> an aggregate? The two cognitions having different causes are recognized as being of the nature of having one and the same agent. . . . In the case of an aggregate the lack of recognition by each of other apprehended things is not prevented as in the case of another sense organ. (NSB 3.1.1)

Here the aim is to show that the self cannot be identified with one or more of the external sense organs. The experiential datum cited by Gotama to this end is that the same thing, say a mango, may be both seen and touched. This shows that there is a common agent of both these perceptions and that the agent is different from both of the organs involved. Each organ is clearly indispensable for each perception. Still, each organ is restricted to its own object. The eye can grasp the color of the mango but not its smoothness. The skin can grasp the smoothness but not the color. So neither organ by itself nor both together can grasp that both the color and the smoothness are features of the same thing. This judgment is possible only on the part of something that has been the witness to both perceptions and can synthesize the two. Such a synthesizer must be different from each of the external senses and is called the self.

It could be suggested that the synthesis is achieved by the aggregate of the sense organs. This too is not acceptable. Each organ of the aggregate is restricted to its object and has no information about what is grasped by another organ. So the aggregate (*saṃghāta*), being nothing other than these organs themselves, cannot perform the role of the common witness needed for the synthesis. On the other hand, if, to avoid this difficulty, the aggregate is held to be an additional entity over and above the external sense organs and the self is identified with such an aggregate, the self can no longer be identified with the external sense organs.

Gotama anticipates an objection: "No [the self is not different from the external senses], because there is restriction (*vyavasthā*) of objects." (NS 3.1.2). Vatsyayana elaborates on the point as follows:

> The sense organs are restricted to their objects. Color is not perceived without the eye and is perceived only if it is there. . . . Therefore, perception of color belongs to the eye. the eye perceives the color. The same applies to smell and so on. These senses are conscious because each grasps its own object. . . . If this makes sense, why another conscious entity? But this is not a good reason because of being subject to doubt. That the senses are so, is this due to their being conscious or due to

> their being instruments of something conscious?—such is the doubt, for even if the senses were instruments, such would be the case. (NSB 3.1.2)

By way of an objection, a materialist proposes that the senses themselves are the conscious perceivers, for they are indispensable for perception. Then admission of the self as an additional substance is jeopardized. Vatsyayana counters by saying that although the senses are indeed indispensable for perception, it does not follow necessarily that they are the perceivers. Even if the senses were not the perceivers but were the necessary means without which perception could not take place, the above fact would have been explained. Since both the agent and the instrument are indispensable for perception, it does not follow from indispensability alone that the senses are the perceivers.

Gotama replies to the objection: "It is verily because of that restriction that there is ground for the existence of the self, so that there is no denial [of the self]" (NS 3.1.3). Vatsyayana comments:

> If there were a sense organ which was not restricted in its scope and could grasp everything consciously, who could infer a different conscious entity? But since the sense organs are restricted in their objects, a different conscious entity which can grasp everything and is not restricted in what it can grasp is inferred. In that connection this recognitive synthesis which cannot be disowned and is [effected] by something conscious is illustrated: by seeing color it infers taste or smell [say, of a mango] previously perceived; having perceived smell [it] infers color and taste; similarly about the remaining objects. . . . It synthesizes perceptual, inferential, authoritative, and doubtful cognitions of various things as of its own agency and knows from the synthesis. It understands a systematic treatise (*śāstra*) dealing with all kinds of subjects. Having heard letters in succession, recognizing how they are related as words and sentences and understanding the boundaries of linguistic expressions and their meanings it knows what is meant comprising many things which cannot be grasped by any one sense organ. (NSB 3.1.3)

Since the organ of touch has never been involved in perceiving color, it cannot synthesize the perception of touch with that of color and infer color from touch. Similarly, since the organ of sight has never been involved in perceiving smell, it cannot synthesize the perception of smell with that of color and infer smell from color. Such inferences can be made only by a synthesizer that has been privy to both perceptions in the past and is therefore different from both the organs. Further, the synthesizer must be conscious and there is no clear evidence that the sense organs themselves are conscious. If there is no proof that the senses are conscious and if synthesis requires consciousness, it becomes harder to claim that the senses are the conscious knowers. Finally, the synthesizer must be capable of assimilating data from various sources of knowing, namely, perception, inference, authority, and so forth, and also grasp the connection between language and meaning including abstract and theoretical matters. It is far from clear how the organ of sight or that of touch can do all these things. This lends further support to the thesis that the self as a conscious synthesizer that is not restricted to specific kinds of perceptual data, is different from the external senses or their aggregate.

Gotama cites another observed fact and directs it against the materialist view that the sense organs themselves are the conscious perceivers: "[The self is different from the external senses] for there is change in another sense organ" (NS 3.1.12). Vatsyayana observes:

> When some sour fruit is tasted together with its color and smell and the color or smell is [later] perceived by some organ, there is change in another organ, namely, the organ of taste, in the form of salivation . . . caused by the remembrance of the taste. This is not explicable if the senses themselves are conscious. What is perceived by one cannot be remembered by another. (NSB 3.1.12)

Neither the organ of sight nor the organ of smell has been involved in the perception of the sour taste. So neither can be responsible for the salivation triggered by the remembrance of the sour taste. One cannot remember what one has not perceived before. Thus the salivation is explicable only if there is a conscious agent that has been the witness to each of the perceptions of color, smell, and taste of the sour fruit and, therefore, is different from each of these organs.

Gotama takes note of a possible objection from the materialist: "No [the self is not different from the external senses], for remembrance is due to the thing remembered" (NS 3.1.13). Vatsyayana glosses: "The phenomenon called memory is due to a cause; it has a remembered content; the change in the other sense organ is caused by that and not by the self" (NSB 3.1.13). Thus the objector is saying that memory is caused by two factors, namely, the impression (*saṃskāra*) and the remembered thing. No other cause is called for to explain memory. The self is neither the cause of memory nor an object of memory. So the self can be inferred neither as the cause of memory nor as the object of memory. The change in the organ of taste from the remembrance of the sour taste is due to the previous experience of sour taste and not due to the self. So what may be inferred from the change is the sour taste and not the self.

Gotama replies: "Since it [memory] can exist only as a quale of the self, there is no denial [of the self]" (NS 3.1.14). Vatsyayana observes:

> Since it can exist only as a quale of the self, there is no denial of the self. If memory is a quale of the self? Only then can memory be explained, for what is seen by one is not remembered by another. If external senses were themselves the conscious [knowers], there would have been no recognitive synthesis of experiences of things by different knowers; alternatively, if there were recognitive synthesis, there would be no explanation for the restriction of objects. The one and the same conscious [knower] which witnesses many things [as contents] of previous experiences caused by various factors, remembers. Since perceptions can be synthesized only by one thing which has been the witness to many perceptions, there can be memory only if it is a quale of the self; it cannot be explained if there is no [self]. The activities of all living beings are based on memory. The change in another organ is cited as a sign of the self only by way of an illustration. [Numerous other signs from activities which require memory could also added.] (NSB 3.1.14)

Since the external senses are found to be restricted in their scopes (the eyes can grasp color but not smell, the nose can grasp smell but not color), the synthesis of different perceptions through different sense organs cannot be done by the organs themselves. The synthesis requires memory of the experiences and there is memory of only what one has experienced. Since one external sense organ cannot grasp what can only be grasped by another organ, it cannot remember and synthesize that experience with what it can grasp. So there is another conscious knower that serves as the common witness of different perceptions by different senses and remembers and synthesizes them. Vatsyayana remarks that the reference to the change in a sense organ that is different from the one that has been used in a given occasion to perceive something is only illustrative. Any other behavior, such as building nests, hunting, and so on, that requires the memory and synthesis of perceptions derived from more than one sense organ would also be useful for the purpose. The inference of the self as the common witness of many perceptions from more than one sense is thus backed by virtually an endless supply of empirical data. The objection that memory cannot be a proper sign, for the self as the common witness is then groundless.

Vatsyayana adds the following remarks:

> This is said [by the objector] without a proper understanding of the object of memory. In the remembrance of something which is currently unperceived [but previously perceived] as (1) that which I cognized before the cognizer and the previously cognized thing become the contents and not merely the thing. (2) I cognized that thing, (3) that thing was cognized by me and (4) the thing became the object of my cognition—these four sentences spelling out the content of remembrance are equivalent in meaning. In every case [of such remembrance] the cognizer, the cognition and the cognized are grasped. In the remembrance of something perceived three cognitions referring to the same thing are synthesized by the same knower and not by many knowers nor without any knower. . . . "I saw this thing which I see now." In "I saw" (1) the seeing and (2) the awareness of seeing (become the contents). I would not know that I saw if my seeing remains unknown. These are then the two cognitions. [That is, in the remembrance "I saw" the past perception and the internal awareness of that perception become the contents.] "I am seeing that now" is the third cognition. Thus the three cognitions connected with the same thing [that is, the memory or the recognitive perception] are neither without any knower nor by many knowers but [are known] by one and the same knower. . . . This is not merely a remembrance, nor does it have only the remembered thing as the content: it is the recognition of remembrance like the recognition of an awareness and the same [knower] cognizes all. The one and the same knower which can know everything recognizes and synthesizes the cognitions belonging to itself, such as "I shall know that thing," "I know that thing," "I knew that thing"; it ascertains that it knows the thing after not having known it for a long time: "I enquired

> about that thing and I know it." In this way it recognizes and synthesizes memory which is marked by the desire to remember and which pertains to the three orders of time. . . . Without the experience the recognition of cognition and memory as mine does not arise as in a different body. Therefore, it is inferred that there is a unitary entity in each body which is capable of cognizing everything and which recognizes and synthesizes its own stream of cognitions and its own stream of memories. Since it does not exist in a different body, there is recognition or synthesis [pertaining to a different body]. (NSB 3.1.14)

The objector had said that memory is not a sign of the self, for memory is confined to only what is remembered. Vatsyayana disputes that by showing that the self or the I can be the content of a memory.[4] He cites the example "I knew this thing before" (with other versions of it) to show that not only the thing previously seen but all the three—the cognizer, the cognition, and the cognized—are the contents of the remembrance. Also when I know "I saw this before and see it now," the previous perception, the internal perception of that perception, and the present perception—all these three cognitions become the contents. Unless the previous perception is also revealed through an internal awareness of it, I could not know that I saw. The three cognitions are also known as having the same knower, for it is clearly felt that whoever had the previous perception and the internal perception of that perception is having also the present perception. All three perceptions, having the same knower, leave behind their impressions with the help of which they are recognized and remembered as having the same knower. Thus the same knower is found to recognize and synthesize cognitions and memories pertaining to the past and the present as being its own cognitions and memories. So it is wrong to say that remembrance is only about the thing remembered as the thing previously seen. The remembrance also includes the self or the I as the common knower.

This is even clearer when someone enquires about something over a period of time, finds the subject hard to decifer, and eventually is able to find the answer one has been searching for. Here the person clearly remembers himself as the one who has been searching for an answer that has been eluding him for a long time and as being the same person who has the answer now. This kind of remembrance is explained if we admit a knower that can grasp all the things involved and retain its identity over the whole period of time. If the knower were restricted in its scope, as each sense organ is, or were something that is no longer the same, each such remembrance must be dismissed as false. But there is not enough evidence for doing so. It also goes against the verdict of experience that what is experienced by one person cannot be remembered by another person. If the person enquiring about the answer for a long time were not the same as the one who found the answer, he could not remember that he was searching for the answer over a long period of time. So this one person must be different from the aggregate of sense organs, in which case we would have only a plurality of knowers and not one and the same knower.

We look at one final reason given by Gotama to show that the self is not identical with the external senses: "[Consciousness] does not belong to the [external] sense organs nor to the [external] things, for consciousness persists even after their demise" (NS 3.2. 18). Since the self is the conscious entity, it cannot be identified with either the external senses or the external things. The consciousness of a color may persist after the color is gone and also after the eye involved in the perception of the color has been irreparably damaged. Neither the color seen nor the eye needed for seeing the color can then be the support (*ādhāra*) of consciousness. What is supported cannot exist when the support is gone. Since consciousness can exist without these, these cannot be the true support of consciousness. Vatsyayana clarifies:

> Consciousness is not a quale of either the [external] senses or the [external] things, for conscousness persists even after their destruction. It does get known after the sense and the thing are destroyed that I saw this. Cognition could not be there if the cognizer were destroyed. . . . There is the remembrance that I saw this regarding something previously seen. There cannot be remembrance of what was previously seen if the knower is gone, for what is seen by one is not remembered by another. (NSB 3.2.18)

Since the self can remember something seen before even when that thing and the organ needed for seeing are gone, it must be different from both. If either the organ or the external thing were the bearer of the impression needed for the remembrance, the impression would have been destroyed along with the destruction of the organ or the thing and the remembrance could not have taken place. Uddyotakara says: "'I saw' does not arise from sense-object connection, for it is a remembrance. . . . But it remains the same regarding a remembrance as well. Just as there can be no cognition without the cognizer so also there can be no remembrance without the experiencer had the experiencer been destroyed" (NV 4211).

This argument not only works against identifying the self with the external senses but also against identifying the self with external things. If some materialist wishes to deny the basic dichotomy between the external (*vāhya*) and the internal (*āntara*) and seeks to lay the foundation of our internal lives in the external things themselves, this argument shows that such a position would not be tenable.

To sum up, there are two main reasons for rejecting the view that the self is the aggregate of the five external senses. First, it is then impossible to explain who or what supervises the activities that require the coordination of more than one sense organ. Since each sense organ is restricted to its object and cannot grasp the object of a different sense organ, none of them individually or collectively can assimilate and synthesize the data received from two or more senses. Second, it is then impossible to explain how one can remember something perceived through a sense organ even after that organ has been destroyed. The fact that the remembrance takes place after the organ is destroyed proves that the rememberer is different from that destroyed organ. It also proves that the perceiver of the original experience (when that organ was still intact) that is being remembered now is different from that organ, for the perceiver and the rememberer are the same.

CHAPTER 8

The Self and the Inner Sense

After arguing that the self cannot be identified with any one of the external sense organs or their aggregate, Gotama proceeds to show that the self cannot be identified with the inner sense organ (*manas*) either. We shall not explore the Nyāya doctrine of inner sense in detail but confine the discussion to what is immediately relevant for our present purpose.[1] The inner sense is not perceived. Like the self it too is inferred. There are two main reasons for admitting an inner sense. First, consciousness is unifunctional, Gotama claims, in the sense that two or more cognitive acts do not take place at the same time. In spite of our having ample opportunities for performing several cognitive acts at a time we do not. Thus one may be sitting on a chair at the same time as reading a book, hearing a clock ticking away, and so on. But it is not that, Gotama claims, all these perceptions of touching, seeing, and hearing take place at the same time. Rather they take place in very quick succession. We do not often notice the succession and, sometimes, as when tasting a sour and smelly fruit, several perceptions may seem to take place simultaneously. But in Gotama's view these also are rapidly succeeding perceptions.

One may object that the sensation of touching seems to go with the sensation of tasting, and the like, and that this shows that such sensations are simultaneous. The Nyāya disagrees. It accepts that the organ of touch is involved in other external perceptions as well (SM 272). So the sensation of touch may seem to accompany other perceptions. But even here, the Nyāya claims, there is a temporal gap, however small, between different sensations.

At any rate, the important thing is that we do not often notice more than one thing at a time in spite of having the opportunity to do so, that is, in spite of more than one external sense being activated at the same time. So Gotama infers that there is an inner, unperceived sense organ that is unifunctional and that also needs to be activated for any cognition (NS 1.1.19). The Nyāya philosophers admit that in some cases consciousness appears to be multifunctional with several things being attended to at the same time. Some Naiyāyikas such as Raghunatha also think that consciousness is multifunctional and that the inner sense acts through multiple channels rather than a single channel (GD 858–59; PTN 9). But many of them side with Gotama and hold that consciousness is always unifunctional. In their view, when we seem to attend to several things at the same time, the inner sense still remains unifunctional but moves at a blazing speed between successive states with infinitesimally small temporal gaps that escape our closest notice. This is analogous to the situation when many pages of a book appear to be pierced at the same time by a needle although the latter can only go through one page at a time.

The inner sense is also required to account for detachment or distraction (*vyāsaṅga*). Thus one may be oblivious of pain in the foot (*pādavyathana*) because of being preoccupied with something else. If one fails to be aware of the pain in spite of having all the opportunity for being so, it is reasonable to infer that the said failure is due to the failure of an internal attention organ that may be called the inner sense. The existence of an attention organ further draws support from the fact that our attention can be under voluntary control and our ability to concentrate (*ekāgratā*), with the twin results of paying closer heed to selected stimuli and disregarding other stimuli, can be heightened through training and practice (*abhyāsa*). Indeed, the word *vyāsaṅga* (distraction, detachment) also means intent attachment or close attention. This is a reflection of the fact that close attention to one thing involves nonattention to other things. So the attention organ should be such that its capacity as well as attention span is limited. In the Nyāya view, the inner sense is involved in the origin of any conscious states whatsoever: it is an indispensable instrument that the self needs to be aware of anything.

The other main reason for admitting the inner sense is that we have internal perceptions of our cognitions, and so on. Since these are internal perceptions without the involvement of the external senses and since perception requires an instrument (*karaṇa*), the inner sense is inferred as the instrument of internal perception (NSB 3.1.16). It may be noted that each of the external sense organs has its proper object, for example, the nose senses smell and so on. In the same way the inner sense too has its proper objects, namely, the internal states. The reasoning may be more formally set up as below.

All perceptions require an instrument, for example, seeing color and so on.

The direct awareness of cognition is a perception.

Therefore, it requires an instrument.

This instrument is either one of the external senses or an additional inner sense.

But it is not one of the external senses (for internal perceptions may take place independently of the external senses).

Therefore, it is an additional inner sense.

The doctrine of an inner sense that is different from the self is not influential in Western philosophy. Aristotle does speak of a 'common sense' (*sensus communis*), a term that was also adopted by many medieval philosophers. But the common sense is not an organ as the Nyāya inner sense is. Shoemaker seems to be accurate in reporting: "No one supposes . . . that there is an *organ* of introspection."[2] In the standard Western view the self (whether it is identified with the body or some part of the body such as the brain or not) is supposed to absorb the functions of the inner sense. A common Sanskrit word for the inner sense—*manas*—is also part of the Indo-European word root from which the word 'mind' is derived.[3] But the above argument as a whole is formally valid. Each premise also appears to be reasonable and acceptable. For one thing, that all perceptions require an instrument is supported by undisputable positive examples such as the perception of color (where the eye is needed as an instrument) and is not countermanded by any undisputable counterexamples. The direct awareness of cognition (and of other internal states) may be offered as a counterexample. But, given GAIE, it does not qualify as a counterexample, for it is included in the inferential subject and is a part of the bone of contention. Further, there is broad support for the view (defended by numerous Nyāya arguments that we do not discuss due to lack of space) that perception alone provides cases of direct awareness while inferring and the like are cases of indirect awareness. So the inference of the inner sense turns out to be of philosophical interest.

The admission of an inner sense that may fail to perform would not go well with a Cartesian incorrigibilist. But the Nyāya would disagree with a Cartesian here too and extend the usual fallibilism to our awareness of internal states as well. In this regard Gangesa, the reputed founder of Navya Nyāya, has made an exception for the internal state "I cognize," which is taken to be incorrigible in so far as it is restricted to the claim of merely having some cognition.[4] But even this, in spite of the high stature of Gangesa, is not accepted by many in the Nyāya tradition. So far as our cognitions of pain and so on are concerned, these are fallible and such states may sometimes go unnoticed. Needless to say, the doctrine of inner sense is bitterly challenged by other Indian schools such as the Advaitins. The controversy turns partly on the analysis of perceptual awareness and related epistemological issues. But any meaningful discussion of this long-drawn-out controversy would demand a lot of space and we have to skip it.

We do note, however, that some contemporary philosophers, for example, William Lycan, accept something like an inner sense (understood in the functionalist sense as a capacity), as the following quote shows: "The inner-sense theory as I have formulated it makes at least one brutally empirical commitment: to the actual existence of internal attention mechanisms."[5] Lycan also stoutly defends the doctrine of inner sense against a variety of objections in a way that reminds one of the Nyāya view. It seems that an old Indian controversy may finally heat up in the contemporary philosophy of mind.

Lycan is a physicalist and would have no truck with an immaterial self. Indeed, the admission of an inner sense may provide further ammunition to disowning an immaterial self, for the self may be identified with the inner sense (which may be physical). It is no wonder then that Gotama anticipates the objection that the self is the inner sense: "No [the self is not different from the aggregate of the external senses, the inner sense, etc.], for the grounds for the admission of the self are applicable to the inner sense" (NS 3.1.15). Vatsyayana says: "the probantia for the self are applicable to the inner sense, for the inner sense can grasp everything." The self has been inferred to be different from the external senses on the ground that each external sense is restricted in its scope. But this ground surely does not exclude the inner sense, for the very reasoning that supports the admission of the inner sense shows it as something that is not restricted in its scope but capable of grasping anything. To account for the unifunctional nature of consciousness, Gotama has supposed that not only the eye but also the inner sense needs to be activated for the perception of color. Similarly, not only the ear but also the inner sense needs to be activated for the perception of sound and so on. He has also supposed that since the inner sense is unifunctional, only one perception arises at a time even when several external senses are activated at the same time. It follows that the inner sense can grasp information about both color and sound, unlike the eye, which can grasp color but not sound, and the ear, which can grasp sound but not color. If the inner sense can grasp everything, why infer the self?

Gotama replies: "Since an instrument of knowing presupposes a knower, there would only be difference in name" (NS 3.1.16). Vatsyayana comments:

> There can be an instrument of knowing only if there is a knower. Sees with the eye. Smells with the nose. Touches with the organ of touch. Similarly. there is an inner sense which is the cognizer's instrument of cognizing everything with the help of which it [the self or the cognizer] cognizes. . . . If this is denied, the consequence will be the rejection of all senses. If this is denied and it is held that there is no instrument of the cognizer for cognizing everything, the consequence would be that there are also no instruments for cognizing color, etc. (NSB 3.1.16)

Gotama says that if one likes to call the self by the name of the inner sense, the difference would only be in the name and not in substance. The inner sense has been inferred as the instrument of knowing. Hence it would still be necessary to admit a knower different from the instrument, for all instruments presuppose a user of the instrument. Gotama has no objection if the change is merely linguistic. He would not mind if the self is called the inner sense and the inner sense is called by some other name. But the difference between the self as the cognizer and the inner sense as the cognitive instrument should not be wiped out.

Vatsyayana points out that if this is denied, the external senses should be rejected too. They are admitted as the instruments of perceiving. Since perceiving is a kind of knowing, it may be generalized, with perceptions of color and so on as the confirming instances, that all cognitions require an instrument. An objector may cite thinking as a counterexample and claim that thinking is a kind of knowing that does not require an instrument. But this is not acceptable, for the counterexample should be undisputed by both the Nyāya and the objector. In the Nyāya view thinking does require an instrument, that is, the inner sense.[6] Since the Nyāya supposes that all cognitions require an instrument, the objector cannot come up with undisputable counterevidence. So that all cognitions require an instrument is supported by undisputable confirming examples but is not challenged by any undisputable counterexamples and, given GAIE, is justified. Accordingly, the inner sense (which has inner states as the proper objects) may be admitted as the universal cognitive instrument. One who denies this would not be justified, Vatsyayana argues, in admitting the external senses either. To be consistent one should accept both the external senses and the inner sense or deny both.

Why should the inner sense not be the cognizer that uses the external senses as the instruments of external perception? Because the inner sense, the Nyāya argues, can only be inferred as an instrument. Since there is no known case of an instrument that is not used by a cognizer different from it, it is reasonable to suppose that the inner sense, too, serves as a tool for a different cognizer that is called the self. We return to this issue later in this chapter.

Gotama adds: "The restriction [that although the knower possesses instruments for the perception of color, etc., there is no instrument for the internal perception of cognition, etc.] is without any inferential basis" (NS 3.1.17). Vatsyayana explains:

> The intended restriction that it [the knower] has instruments [namely, the external sense organs] for the perception of color, etc., but there is no instrument for the cognition of all things—this restriction lacks inferential support, i.e., there is no inference here to justify the restriction. Since pleasure, etc., are different from knowable objects like color. etc., there is an instrument for the perception of them [pleasure, etc.]. Just as since smell is not perceived by the eye, the nose is a different sense organ and similarly, since the taste is not perceived by either the eye or the nose, the gustatory organ is a different sense organ and so also with the rest, in the same way since pleasure, etc., are not perceived by the eye, etc., there should be another sense organ. It is also inferred from non-simultaneity of cognitions. . . . That is, because of its connection with a given sense organ and lack of connection with other sense organs, cognitions do not arise simultaneously. (NSB 3.1.17)

The objector claims that the self perceives pleasure and so on without the aid of an inner sense organ as the instrument. Gotama argues that this amounts to theorizing that although the self has instruments for the perception of external things, it has no instrument for the perception of internal states. Such a theory, Gotama claims, has no evidentiary support. He implies that the objector's claim is no less a claim and should be vindicated with reasons. Vatsyayana rehearses the two reasons for which the inner sense should be inferred. The first is that since pleasure and other states are directly perceived but not through the external senses, the inner sense should be admitted to account for that. The second, already familiar reason is that since cognitions do not arise simultaneously, although several sense organs may be activated at the same time, it should be inferred that there is another inner organ that is connected with only one organ at a time so that several cognitions do not arise together.

Uddyotakara observes: "There is no known case of intentional (*savisaya*) awareness which arises without an instrument" (NV 364). His point is that intentional states such as perception of color require an instrument for their origin. So other intentional states like the internal awareness of a perception should also require an inner sense as the instrument for their origin. Apart from containing an argument for the inner sense this passage is of historic importance for another reason. Here Uddyotakara (6th century CE) explicitly and unambiguously describes internal states as intentional. While the notion of intentionality may be found to be implied in works of similar or greater antiquity, we are not aware of any other earlier philosophical work in the East or in the West in which intentionality of internal states has been explicitly put to use to further the cause of a philosophical theory. If earlier instances of similar use of the concept of intentionality are not unearthed by more research, this may be the earliest explicit record of the emergence of this important idea. Because of the likely historic importance of this passage, we reformulate and set out the argument explicitly:

> All intentional cognitions require an instrument, for example, the perception of color and the like.
>
> The internal perception of a cognition is an intentional cognition.
>
> Therefore, it requires an instrument.

> This instrument is either one of the external senses or an additional inner sense.
>
> It is not one of the external senses, for such internal perception takes place independently of the external senses.
>
> Therefore, it is an additional inner sense.

Once again, each part of the argument as well as the whole argument is formally valid and each premise is reasonable and defensible. Hence the conclusion drawn about the existence of an inner sense is also reasonable and defensible.

Vacaspati Misra says: "This [an internal awareness like memory or inference] must arise through a sense organ, for it is an awareness like the awareness of color, etc. Since this arises without the eye, etc., this sense organ is an additional one and is called the inner sense" (TP 514). We have already explained a similar reasoning above and studied a modified and explicitly reformulated version.

Again Gotama argues: "Not of the inner sense [i.e., cognition is not a quale of the inner sense], for [the latter is inferred] on the ground of non-simultaneity of cognitions" (NS 3.2.19). Vatsyayaya comments:

> Non-simultaneity of cognitions is the sign of the inner sense. . . . [C]ognition is not a quale of that. Whose then? Of the knower, by virtue of being the controller (*vaśī*). The knower is the controller, the instrument is the controlled (*vaśya*). (NSB 3.1.19)

Here the objector is again of the view that the inner sense is the conscious knower and that cognition is a quale of that. So the difference between the self and the inner sense is emphasized by calling the former the controller and the latter the controlled. When, for example, we speak of concentrating our (mind or the) inner sense on something, we think of the self as the controller and the inner sense as the controlled. Vatsyayana argues that only a conscious entity can be the controller. The inner sense has been inferred as an instrument. No instrument is conscious. That no instrument is conscious is a generalization supported by undisputable confirming instances provided by such bodily instruments as the external sense organs and other instruments such as a pen. There are no undisputable counterexamples. So, given GAIE, the said generalization is acceptable. Accordingly, the inner sense, being an instrument, is not conscious and not the controller either. Uddyotakara says:

> There is no rule that the knower is only a controller, for it may also be controlled. But there is a rule regarding the non-conscious: all that is non-conscious is subject to control. The inner sense is subject to control [and not the controller], for it is unconscious like the nose, etc. (NV 422)

The argument is: All that is unconscious is subject to control, such as the nose and so on. The inner sense is unconscious. Therefore, it is subject to control. The inner sense thus cannot be the self, for the latter is the controller. Why is the inner sense unconscious? Because, as said above, it has been inferred as an instrument and all instruments are unconscious. When it is said that the self is the controller, it is not denied that the self can also be subject to control. That is why Uddyotakara brings out the true implication of Vatsyayana's description of the self as the controller by adding that the controller too may be under another's control. Rather the point is that the self alone can be self-controlled. Vacaspati Misra makes that clear:

> By the knower being the controller is meant that the knower is the agent for being capable of self-control. It is known that from among the agent, the instrument, etc., consciousness belongs to the agent alone and not to the instrument, etc. For example, from among clay, the rod, the wheel, water, the thread and the potter [consciousness] belongs only to the agent potter and not to clay, etc. (TP 564)

Being capable of self-control (*svātantrya*), then, is a decisive difference between the conscious and the unconscious. Self-control requires a sense of personal identity, purposiveness, forethought, planning, and so forth, and none of these is possible without consciousness.

In the light of the above an argument to prove that the self alone is conscious (and not the external senses or the inner sense) may be developed: The self is conscious because of being capable of self-control and being unrestricted in scope (*avyavasthita*) (NV 341; TP 504). The argument may be reformulated as follows:

> Whatever is unconscious is not both capable of self-control and unrestricted in scope, for example, the eye and so on.
> The self is capable of self-control and unrestricted in scope.
> Therefore, the self is conscious.

As Uddyotakara and Vacaspati Misra point out, this argument is based on universal exclusion (*vyatireka*) alone. So the first premise should not be replaced by its contrapositive, namely, whatever is capable of self-control and unrestricted in scope is conscious. Then no undisputable confirming instances for the generalization would have been available. But in the exclusion mood as stated, the external senses are available as undisputable positive examples. There are also no undisputable counterexamples. The inner sense is the only counterexample that may be cited. But it would be disputed by the Nyāya, for, as already said, it has been inferred as an instrument which therefore in the Nyāya view is incapable of self-control. Accordingly, Vacaspati Misra observes that being capable of self-control suffices as a probans for proving that the self is conscious (TP 504). The argument, then, could be simplified as follows:

> Whatever is unconscious is incapable of self-control, for example, the eye and so on.
>
> The self is capable of self-control.
>
> Therefore, the self is conscious.

Some of the functions attributed by the Nyāya to the inner sense are in modern parlance attributed to the physical brain. For example, the brain is supposed to provide the activity needed for the direct awareness of the internal states. The materialistic thesis of the identity between the mind (or the self) and the brain is a well-known and popular view in twentieth-century philosophy. Thus, as may be expected, in marshalling arguments against the identification of the self with the inner sense, the Nyāya is in a sense anticipating such modern developments and in effect arguing against some versions of materialism. There is no known undisputable instance of anything material, including the most sophisticated computers designed to date, that is truly capable of self-control. Clearly, the most advanced computer could not function without the built-in design provided by the conscious inventor. So, as long as the brain is understood as something physical, the Nyāya would object to assuming that the brain is self-controlled. With some modifications and revisions the brain could be accepted from the Nyāya point of view as a necessary tool for internal perception, thinking, and so on. Still, capability of self-control must, for the Nyāya, be reserved for the immaterial self. Since innumerable material things such as stones and bricks are known not to be capable of self-control, the advocate of the identity between the self (or the mind) and the brain must prove and not assume that the brain is capable of self-control. For this it is not enough to prove that the brain appears to be capable of self-control. If the brain appears to be capable of self-control, that may be because it is actually capable of self-control or because it is guided by something else that is truly self-controlled. The identity theorist then should produce evidence to discount the second possibility. Otherwise Gotama and Vatsyayana would get the opportunity to use one of their favorite critiques that "the reason is not good because of being open to doubt" (*saṁdigdhatvāt ahetuh*). Until the identity theorist proves his case the Nyāya can defend its position by simply offering the following formally valid arguments the premises of which are reasonable and acceptable:

> No material object is self-controlled, for example, a brick and so on.
>
> The brain is a material object.
>
> Therefore, the brain is not self-controlled.

> No material object is conscious, for example, a brick and so on.
>
> The brain is a material object.
>
> Therefore, the brain is not conscious.

No doubt, an objector may dispute the truth of the first premise in each of the above arguments by offering the living brain or the living body as a counterexample. Nevertheless the premises remain reasonable and acceptable. These counterexamples are disputed by the Nyāya and, given GAIE, do not qualify as proper grounds of refutation. The premises are also supported by innumerable supporting instances acceptable to both the objector and the Nyāya. The objector presumably does not challenge the truth of the second premise in each of the above arguments and does hold that the brain is a material object. It then follows that the brain is not the self, for the latter stands for something conscious and self-controlled. Since this conclusion is reasonable and acceptable, the ball is now in the court of the identity theorist to come up with a convincing refutation.

The Nyāya does not make such claims as that the self (or the mind) is essentially conscious or that matter is essentially extended. From the Nyāya viewpoint what the dualist needs to prove is the weaker claim that the self (or the mind as long as we do not confuse it with the inner sense) alone is conscious. A major part of this has been sought to be accomplished in trying to prove that the self is not identifiable with the external senses or the inner sense. To complete the case, it needs to be shown further that consciousness is not a quale of the body and that the self cannot be identified with the body. We turn to these questions in the next chapter.

CHAPTER 9

The Self and the Body

While the immaterial self is the substratum of consciousness, the body, in the Nyāya view, is the receptacle (*āyatana*) of worldly enjoyment (*bhoga*). The body is not the enjoyer (*bhoktā*), for it is unconscious (*acetana, jaḍa*). The self, being conscious, is the enjoyer. But the self must be associated with a body to have enjoyment. The self must also be associated with a body for it to be alive. The body can exist without the self; but then it is dead. The self too can exist without the body; but then it is unconscious and devoid of all enjoyment. The self and the body must be together in order to have a living being in the ordinary sense. The association between the self and the body is described as a conjunction (*saṃyoga*). The conjunction between a particular self and a particular body is a particular relationship that holds between only that self and that body. This hypothesis of the particularity of the conjunction is necessary to account for the privacy of our mental lives. If the self were conjoined with more than one body at the same time or if the body were conjoined with more than one self at the same time, it becomes difficult, without bringing in other more complex assumptions, to explain why our experiences are private. So far as the Nyāya is concerned, the privacy of our mental lives is a datum of common experience that, unless overridden by more reliable evidence, is reliable and acceptable. Accordingly, the Nyāya offers the said hypothesis as the most reasonable explanation to account for it. It should be noted that not only the conjunction between the self and the body, but also all conjunctions are regarded as nonrepeated particulars. A conjunction is a relationship that holds only between particular substances and is always a particular. But the reasonableness of the above hypothesis turns to a large extent on the demonstration that consciousness is not a quale of the body. If consciousness were a quale of the body, the hypothesis of the conjunction between the immaterial self and the body would be significantly weakened and then some other explanation for the privacy of our mental lives might be in order. So we discuss the reasons why consciousness is not a quale of the body.

Vatsyayana begins the discussion by raising the materialistic objection: "Consciousness is a quale of the body, for it exists if there is the body and does not exist if there is not the body" (NSB 3.2.46). What exists or originates only if something else is there is a quale of that. For example, qualia like color exist or come into being only if things such as pots are there. So color and so on are qualia of pots and the like. In the same way, consciousness exists and comes into being only if there is the body. It follows that consciousness is a quale of the body. According to the Cārvāka school, consciousness is an emergent quale of the body. There is no consciousness in bodily elements such as earth or water. But when they are combined in a certain way, consciousness emerges (CD 29). This is similar to new qualia emerging from chemical (*pākaja*) change, for example, although rice, water, and so on, are not inebriating substances by themselves, they become so when brewed in a certain way. The Cārvāka adds that in common usage the self is often identified with the body. For example, when one says "I am fat," "I am fair," and so on, one identifies oneself with one's body.

Gotama begins the critique of materialism thus: "There is room for doubt, for in a substance both its own qualia and qualia of another thing are found" (NS 3.2.46). Vatsyayana elaborates:

> That something exists only if something else exists is [as an argument for materialism] subject to doubt. In water its own quale of liquidity is perceived, but so also is heat, which is a quale of another thing. Hence this doubt: Is consciousness found in the body a quale of the body or is it a quale of some other substance? (NSB 3.2.46)

In the Nyāya view heat is a quale of fire. So the heat found in hot water is not its own quale but a quale of something else. This could also be true of consciousness. Although it is found in the body, it may not be a quale of the body. Uddyotakara observes that conjunction, disjunction, and velocity are produced by motion and exist only if there is motion.[1] But still it does not follow that these are qualia of motion. Similarly, sound is produced by conjunction and disjunction.[2] But this does not show that sound is a quale of conjunction and disjunction (NV 433). So the materialistic argument is inconclusive.

Gotama now offers an argument aimed at refuting materialism: "[Consciousness is not a quale of the body], for color, etc., endure as long as the substance ["body" instead of "substance" in some manuscripts] does" (NS 3.2.47). Vatsyayana explains: "The body is not known to be without color, etc., but is known to be without consciousness, like water which is no longer hot. Therefore, consciousness is not a quale of the body" (NSB 3.2.47). Though water is sometimes found to be hot, heat is not regarded as a quale of water because water is also found to be cold. Since water is hot some of the time but not all of the time, it is surmised that heat is not a quale of water but of another substance that happens to be associated with water some of the time and makes it hot. In the same way the body is found to be conscious some of the time but not all of the time. (The body is certainly devoid of consciousness when it is dead and may arguably be without consciousness in deep sleep, coma, etc.) So (assuming the ontology of substance and qualia and assuming that consciousness is a quale as explained earlier) it is surmised that consciousness is not a quale of the body but of another substance that happens to be associated with the body some of the time and that makes it possible for the latter to appear to be conscious. This other substance should be such that some of its qualia may not belong to it all the time. The argument may be interpreted as saying that since most or nearly all qualia of the body and other physical substances are found to belong to them as long as they exist, it is unlikely that consciousness, which is always missing in a dead body, is a quale of the body. Unless the materialist is able to find a clear and non-question-begging explanation of why consciousness should always be missing in a dead body in spite of being a quale of it, it follows that probably consciousness is not a quale of the body. The argument may also be presented in a stronger version:

> All qualia of the body endure as long as the body does, for example, color and the like.
>
> No conscious states endure as long as the body does.
>
> Therefore, no conscious states are qualia of the body.

In the stronger version the argument is formally valid. But its weak point is that it gives the materialist an easy escape route by claiming that the first premise is false or at least doubtful. As the subsequent discussion shows, Gotama and Vatsyayana have anticipated and tried to answer various objections to close such an easy escape route.

Gotama is well aware that all physical substances are not colored and also that a physical substance may change its color (and other qualia). The point of his aphorism quoted above is that if a physical substance is colored, it retains some color as long as it exists. He implies that if consciousness were a true quale of the body, it would have retained some consciousness all the time. Vatsyayana anticipates and answers a likely materialistic objection to this:

> If like velocity? [That is, the lack of consciousness in a body some of the time may be explained analogously to that of lack of velocity in a body some of the time.] No, for there is no cessation of the cause. Velocity does not cease to exist in a body when it is in the same condition as when it has velocity. Velocity ceases to exist there absolutely because of the cessation of the cause [of velocity]. But consciousness is not perceived in the body which is in the same condition as when it is perceived in the body. Therefore, "like velocity" is an uneven solution. (NSB 3.2.47)

Velocity is a quale of the body although it is found there only some of the time. The same is true of consciousness, the materialist objects. Vatsyayana counters by saying that there is a cause for the origin of velocity in a body, namely, motion. The presence and absence of velocity can be explained by the presence and absence of that cause. But there is no such explanation available for the presence and absence of consciousness in a body. According to Carvaka, the materialist, consciousness emerges when the material elements are combined in a certain way. If such combination is the cause of consciousness, there should be consciousness in a dead body, for the elements are still combined in a dead body. Vatsyayana is demanding that the materialist should produce some kind of a physical cause of consciousness, which is always available in a living body and never available in a dead body. Otherwise, the analogy to velocity is not appropriate. In the light of this the stronger version of the argument above may be recast as below:

> All bodily qualia the causes of which continue to be available, endure as long as the body exists, for example, color and so on.
>
> No conscious states endure as long as the body exists.
>
> Therefore, no conscious states are bodily qualia the causes of which continue to be available.

The first premise is no longer open to the objection from qualia such as velocity that belong to the body for a limited time. These qualia are excluded, for their causes do not continue to be available as long as the body exists.

The materialist may still object by claiming that some of the causes that produce conscious states do not continue to be available when the body is dead. For example, the lack of consciousness may be sought to be explained by the lack of vital processes such as blood circulation, respiration, and so on. But this would not be satisfactory. From the Nyāya point of view, to explain the loss of consciousness in a dead body as being due to the loss of such vital processes as exhalation or inhalation or some other biological phenomenon would be circular. The very presence of these biological processes in a living body, according to the Nyāya, serves as a pointer to the existence of an immaterial self as we have already seen in the sixth chapter. As long as the argument there stands, the objection has no force. The Nyāya would not be deterred by the fact that if the presence of life is to serve as a sign for the self, not only the bodies of humans but also the bodies of animals (and also plants if they are alive) would have to be regarded as being inhabited by immaterial selves. It is a part of the Hindu-Buddhist-Jain worldview that animals (and plants) also have immaterial selves (which is also the view of Plato). The Nyāya accepts that, though due to the limitation of space we avoid a discussion of the issue.[3]

Vatsyayana adds:

> Also, should the cause of consciousness be in the body or in another substance, or in both? Not so, for there is no ground for the rule [that consciousness is produced only in the body and only some of the time]. If in the body, there is no basis for the rule that consciousness is produced some of the time and not produced some of the time. If in another substance, there is no basis for the rule that consciousness should be produced only in the body and not in other things like a stone, etc. If in both, there is no basis for the rule that consciousness is not produced in the substance similar [in the respect of sharing the cause of consciousness] to the body but is produced only in the body. (NSB 3.2.47)

Once again Vatsyayana is pressing the materialist to find the cause of consciousness. Should such a cause be located in the body itself? But then why is not consciousness ever produced in a dead body in spite of the cause being there? To avoid this difficulty, the materialist may say that the cause is located in another substance and that the dead body is not able to take advantage of that. But then why is consciousness never produced in that other substance? To get out of this problem, the materialist may suggest that the cause is located in both the body and another substance and the cooperation of both are needed. But then too it should be explained why, in spite of the cause being located in both, consciousness is produced only in one of the two and not in the other.

Uddyotakara observes that if the cause of consciousness is located in the body, it should be explored whether the cause remains available as long as the body exists or not. If it remains available as long as the body exists, consciousness should be found in the body always, including the dead body. If the cause is in the body only some of the time and is itself dependent on the availability of another cause, it should be explained why that other cause is not available always and why never in a dead body (NV 434).

Gotama addresses another possible objection: "No [i.e., in a substance that is black or of some other color there is never total lack of color], for another quale is generated by chemical change" (NS 3.2.48). Vatsyayana explains:

> It may be thought that in a substance which is of black color, etc., the cessation of the black color, etc., is observed. Similar should be the cessation of consciousness. But the substance does not become absolutely devoid of color; when the black color [say, of a pot] is gone, another quale, viz., red color, is generated by chemical change. However, in a [dead] body there is absolute cessation of consciousness. (NSB 3.2.48)

In the Nyāya view consciousness is a specific quale (*viśeṣa guṇa*) of the self. By a specific quale is meant a quale that belongs to only one kind of substance. With the help of a specific quale, a substance may be distinguished from every other species of substance. Previously the materialist objector had pointed to the quale of velocity as something that belongs to a physical substance only some of the time and suggested that the same could be the case with consciousness, which belongs to the body only some of the time. But velocity is not a specific quale, for it belongs to more than one kind of substance. A Nyāya philosopher could take cover by urging that the counterexample may only apply to nonspecific qualia and may not apply to specific qualia. To avoid this the materialist has now cited black color, which, in the Nyāya view, is a specific quale of the earth but which too may not last as long as the earthen substance may last. His point is that just as specific qualia such as black color may not belong to the substance all the time so also consciousness, in spite of being a specific quale, may not belong to the body all the time.

Gotama replies by saying that the analogy does not hold. Although its color may change, an earthen substance will never be devoid of color. But the body can be completely devoid of consciousness. Further, there is a clear explanation of why the color changes. For example, in a pot the change may be due to the process of baking. Where is the explanation for the complete loss of consciousness in a dead body? What physical element or what physical combination is always missing in a dead body? It is squarely the responsibility, the Nyāya argues, of the materialist to come up with the answer, but he has not, according to some, even after more than two thousand years of research.

Gotama continues: "There is no refutation, for there is the origin of competing qualia due to chemical change" (NS 3.2.49). Vatsyayana explains:

> In all substances in which there is chemical change there is the origin of qualia which rival the previous qualia, for it is observed that the qualia resulting from chemical change do not coexist with the previous qualia. But in a [dead] body it is not observed that there is the origin of another quale which competes with and does not coexist with consciousness, so that it may be inferred that it is opposed to consciousness. Hence there is no denial of that consciousness should belong to the body as long as it exists; but it does not; therefore, it is not a quale of the body. (NSB 3.2.49)

Here Gotama argues that the change of color and the like in cases of chemical change is also marked by the origin of new qualia that are incompatible with the previous qualia. For example, red is incompatible with black, for it is observed that nothing is both black and red at the same time in the same part. So the loss of the previous quale can be understood as also being due to the emergence of a new, opposed quale. But when consciousness is lost in a dead body, there is no evidence that a new quale has emerged there that is opposed to consciousness. On the contrary, what the materialist has supposed to be the cause of the origin of consciousness—the combination of the bodily elements—is still there. So once again, the analogy fails. In the light of this further exchange a second reformulation of the stronger version of the above argument may be offered as follows:

> All bodily qualia that are not replaced by their opposite qualia endure as long as the body does, for example, color and so on.
>
> No conscious states endure as long as the body does.
>
> Therefore, no conscious states are bodily qualia that are replaced by their opposite qualia.

Both the first and the second reformulations of the stronger version are formally valid and the premises of each are supported by ample empirical evidence. So the conclusion of each is reasonable and acceptable. Of course, in either case the conclusion is not that consciousness is not a quale of the body, but rather that it is not a bodily quale that is replaced by its opposite and the cause of which continues to be available as long as the body exists. A materialist can accept this and say that consciousness can still be a bodily quale that is replaced by an opposite quale in a dead body and that the cause of consciousness is absent in a dead body; nevertheless, this puts considerable pressure on the materialist. Now the latter should show that an opposite and incompatible quale is originated in a dead body, so that consciousness should not be there and also that the causes of consciousness in a living body are not available in a dead body. Otherwise the latter will be hard put to explain why consciousness, in spite of being a bodily quale, is not found in a dead body. If the latter fails in this task, the dualist would have the opportunity to push for the view that consciousness is found in the body only when it is associated with another substance to which consciousness really belongs. This other substance could also be held to be associated with the body only when it is alive and not when it dead.

To throw more light on the above reasoning, we now look at a recent argument for the mental-physical contrast developed by Saul Kripke.[4] Kripke has pointed out that some expressions, for example, the teacher of Aristotle, refer to things contingently while some others, for instance, Aristotle, refer to things necessarily. (The latter are called rigid designators.) The reason for the distinction is that in the latter case the possibility of referring to something other than the reference is ruled out while in the former case there are possible situations in which the expression could refer to something else, for example, someone other than Plato could also be the teacher of

Aristotle. Now, according to Kripke, expressions like 'pain' or 'bodily state A' determine their references necessarily. So, if physicalism is true and pain is identical with some bodily state A, the statement 'pain is the bodily state A (say, the firing of C fibers)' must be necessarily true and its denial must be necessarily false. But 'pain is not the firing of C fibers' is certainly not necessarily false. This goes against identifying mental states with bodily states.

The plausibility of this argument turns (partly) on whether there are unfelt pains. Kripke claims that pain is necessarily felt as pain. So if a bodily state A were identical with pain, it could not be that there is A but no feeling of pain. But it is possible that there is A but no feeling of pain. This shows that the connection between the two is contingent.

A physicalist may respond by denying that pain is necessarily felt as pain.[5] On this the Nyāya is in agreement with Kripke and would reject such a physicalist response. That is, in the Nyāya view, too, while some cognition may be uncognized or unintrospected, pain (or pleasure) is always felt without exception. But it is difficult to show that we need to be aware of pain at every moment (in spite of distraction, etc.). So the physicalist may have the opportunity to score a point here. Accordingly, it is useful to explore if the main point of the argument can be sustained without being committed to the claim that there can be no unfelt pain. (This would not harm any major Nyāya view. In fact, the Nyāya doctrine of inner sense can with minor changes be pressed into the cause of arguing for the existence of unfelt pain or pleasure.)

It seems that it can be by considering the case of dead bodies that are admittedly devoid of pain. Kripke does mention the case of dead bodies in a footnote but does not develop fully the argument as the Nyāya does.[6] The case of dead bodies shows without any doubt that there are bodily states that cannot be identified with any mental states. It is conceivable that with the help of some (existing or future) medical technology the brain or the heart or any other part of the body can be activated even when it is dead. Then the bodily state A could be found in a dead body; but this cannot be identical with pain. As Visvanatha has put it eloquently: that consciousness cannot be attributed to the body follows from the deviation in a dead body. (*śarīrasya na caitanyam mṛteṣu vyabhicāratah*: BPP 210) While nondeviation (*avyabhicāra*) does not suffice to prove identity, deviation (*vyabhicāra*) does suffice to prove nonidentity. This deals a major blow to the mind-body identity theory (and does not, it may be noted, critically turn on the acceptance of rigid designators).

The argument from lack of consciousness in a dead body should also be distinguished from a well-known Cartesian argument: I am different from my body because while I cannot doubt my own existence, I can doubt the existence of my body.[7] From the Nyāya point of view such an argument begs the question, for it presupposes that thinking or doubting can take place without the body—something that neither a materialist nor the Nyāya is prepared to grant. The Cartesian argument is sometimes reinterpreted in recent times as follows: I am not my body, for there is something that is true of me but not of my body.[8] This presupposes the law of indiscernibility of identicals that things not sharing all their properties are not the same. The Nyāya does accept the law.[9] But this does not help the dualist, for, according to the Nyāya, the law does not apply to psychological predicates such as thinking or believing.[10] Another recent version of the Cartesian argument is that I am different from my body, because I can conceivably exist without my body.[11] But this is open to the objection that it can be counterbalanced by arguing from the possibility and conceivability that I am identical with my body.[12] The Nyāya argument is not vulnerable to this objection: it is not an argument from possibility or conceivability of disembodied existence but from an actual lack of consciousness in the body under some conditions.

We now move on to consider a second argument offered by Gotama: "[Consciousness is not a quale of the body], for it pervades the body" (NS 3.2.50). This may suggest that if something pervades something else, the former cannot be a quale of the latter. But there is little support for such a view in Nyāya ontology. Uddyotakara, accordingly, does not regard this as being directly a ground for consciousness not being a quale of the body but rather as being a ground under the materialistic assumption for the presence of many cognizers in the same body (NV 435–36). Vatsyayana interprets it in a similar vein:

> The body and all the parts of the body are pervaded by the origin of consciousness. There is no part where consciousness does not originate. Since like the body the bodily parts are also conscious, the plurality of cognizers follows as a necessary consequence. In that connection just as the restriction of the awareness of pleasure and pain is a sign for there being different cognizers in each different body, it should have been so in the same body as well. But it is not so; hence consciousness is not a quale of the body. (NSB 3.2.50)

What follows from consciousness pervading the body and its parts is that there are many cognizers in the same body if one were to suppose that consciousness were a quale of the body. Since every part is conscious and is also different from other parts, these cognizers have to be different. But that there are many cognizers in the same body is not supported by evidence. We infer that there is a different self or cognizer in each different body because each is aware of its own pleasure or pain and not of the others. This is not true of the so-called many cognizers in the same body, for one and same person is aware of what is happening in different parts of the body. So the acceptance of many cognizers in the same body is unwarranted. But this would be a consequence of the materialist view that consciousness is a quale of the body. If consciousness were to be a quale of the body, since it would have to be a quale of all the different parts of the body, there would have to be a plurality of cognizers in the same body. The latter is not acceptable. So the assumption that leads to this unacceptable result is also not acceptable. The reasoning applies the law that if *a* implies *b* and *b* is not acceptable, *a* too is not acceptable.

One could dispute the claim that consciousness is found in each and every part of the body. What about hair and nail? Gotama and Vatsyayana admit that there is no consciousness in these (NS 3.2.51). But they propose that since no sensation is felt in these, these are not parts of the body in the strict sense (NS 3.2.52). Needless to say, the issue here is that consciousness is found in many parts of the same body, so that it follows that there are many cognizers in the same body. Vatsyayana has expressed his objection to this in another place as well:

> The plurality of cognizers in the same body is without logical support. For a materialist there would be in the same body many materials which are possessed of the qualia of cognition, desire, aversion and volition, so that the plurality of cognizers follows necessarily. (NSB 3.2.37)

So the charge is that a materialist cannot account for the unity of consciousness. This becomes clear if one ponders over common bodily qualia such as weight, color, and so on. What the body weighs is a function of what each part of it weighs. The body does not have a separate weight of its own. Similarly, the color of the body is a function of the colors of each part of the bodily surface. If three different parts of the body are colored red, blue, and green, the color of the body is also red, blue, and green. The body does not have a separate unitary color of its own.[13] In the same way, if many different parts of the body are conscious, the bodily consciousness will be the sum total of each of these consciousnesses. The body as a whole would not have a separate unitary consciousness of its own.

The point then is that if consciousness were a quale of the body, since the parts of the body are numerous, there should have been numerous cognizers and selves in the same body (*prāptam cetana-bahutvam*). The materialist could reply that the body as a substantial whole (*avayavin*) is different from its parts and numerically one. Consciousness could be regarded as a quale of only the body as a substantial whole and not of the numerous parts; then the difficulty of there being many selves in the same body would be avoided. But this reply would be futile, for there is no satisfactory way to explain why, from the materialist viewpoint, consciousness should be a quale of only the whole body and not of the parts. Familiar holistic or organizational properties do not belong to different parts of varying magnitude in the same proportion. But every part of the living body is conscious in the same way. It would not help to suppose that consciousness is a quale of only one particular part of the body. For then it cannot be explained satisfactorily why consciousness is found in every part of the body. The materialist cannot escape by boldly supposing that there are many selves in the same body. Then the experiences of one part would be accessible only to that part (*pratyaya-vyavasthā-prasaṅga*) just as the experiences of one person are accessible only to that person.

A materialist could suggest that since different bodily activities are controlled by one and the same brain, the coordinating consciousness belonging to the brain is the unitary consciousness the dualist is searching for. But the brain is a highly complex substance with many specialized functions performed by many of its different parts. How the innumerable brain activities get coordinated and whether that can provide the foundation for a unitary consciousness is, according to some, a mystery that is yet to be fathomed. So the materialist is not entitled to assume that the brain is the seat of the unitary consciousness. He has to prove it. Needless to say, the problem of the unity of consciousness requiring that all conscious states of a person are witnessed, if witnessed at all, by the same cognizer would be solved if the immaterial self is instead accepted as the seat of consciousness. Since the self is one and has no parts, there is no occasion for allowing many cognizers in the same body (in usual circumstances).

Gotama offers yet another argument for psychophysical dualism: "[Consciousness is not a quale of the body], for it is utterly dissimilar to bodily qualia)" (NS 3.2.53). Vatsyayana explains:

> For this, too, consciousness is not a quale of the body, viz., because of utter dissimilarity from bodily qualia. Bodily qualia are of two types: (1) imperceptible, such as weight, and (2) [externally] perceptible, such as color, etc. But consciousness is of a different type. It is not imperceptible, for it is internally perceptible; nor is it [externally] perceptible, for it is grasped by the inner sense. Therefore, [it] is the quale of a different substance. (NSB 3.2.53)

The weight of a body is inferred by measuring it on a scale. Thus it is an example of a bodily quale that is imperceptible. Other bodily qualia such as color are perceived by an external sense organ. Consciousness is not of either type. It is directly grasped by the inner sense; hence it is not imperceptible. At the same time it is not graspable by the external senses. Since it is so completely unlike bodily qualia, it should be inferred that it is the quale of a substance different from the body. Once the body is eliminated, the other recognized substances in the Nyāya ontology may be eliminated in a few more steps. Thus it is proved that consciousness is the quale of an additional substance called the self.

Gotama takes note of a possible objection from the materialist: "No [that consciousness is not a quale of the body is not proved], for color, etc., are mutually different" (NS 3.2.54). Vatsyayana comments: "Just as color, etc., which are different from each other, do not cease to be qualia of the body, so also consciousness, in spite of its difference from color, etc., does not cease to be a quale of the body" (NSB 3.2.54). Bodily qualia such as color and smell are quite different from each other. Color is perceived by the eye, smell is not; smell is perceived by the nose, color is not. Still, these are qualia of the body because they are all found in the body. In the same way, consciousness is not perceived by the eye, the nose, and so on, and is clearly different from color and so forth. Still, it can be a bodily quale, for the basic reason has not changed. Like color and the rest, consciousness is found in the body. Hence, in spite of being quite different from color and so on, it should be regarded as a bodily quale.

Gotama replies: "Since color, etc., are externally perceived, there is no refutation" (NS 3.2.55). Vatsyayana elaborates:

> Because of imperceptibility as well. Just as color, etc., which are mutually different, do not go beyond the two types, so also consciousness which too is different from color, etc., should not go beyond the two types if it were a bodily quale; but [it] does

> go beyond [the two types]. Therefore, it is not a bodily quale. (NSB 3.2.55)

Although color, smell, taste, and so on, are quite different from each other and each is grasped by only one sense organ to the exclusion of the others, still they are all objects of external perception and this is an important feature that they all share. If a quale is not perceptible by one external sense organ but is perceptible by another, there is no difficulty in accepting it as a bodily quale. It is a general feature of material things that they are (usually) perceptible by the external senses. But consciousness is not an object of external perception. That makes it absolutely dissimilar to color and so on. If it is a bodily quale, why is it not externally perceived like so many other bodily qualia? It is true that some bodily qualia, such as weight, are not externally perceived. But they are not perceptible at all. On the other hand, although consciousness is not externally perceived, it is internally perceived. That makes it radically different from bodily qualia. This is why Vatsyayana says that while the bodily qualia do not go beyond the two types of being either externally perceptible or being imperceptible, consciousness does go beyond these two types and, therefore, is not attributable to the body. This argument may be reformulated as below:

> All bodily qualia are either externally perceptible or imperceptible, for example, color and so forth.
>
> No conscious states are either externally perceptible or imperceptible.
>
> Therefore, no conscious states are bodily qualia.

This argument is formally valid. So the conclusion is acceptable if the two premises are acceptable. The first premise is clearly an acceptable generalization, for there are undisputable confirming instances such as color and weight and there are no undisputable counterexamples. The only counterexamples that the materialist could offer are internal states such as cognition, desire, and so on. But they are included in the inferential subject (*pakṣa*) and, being part of the bone of contention, not acceptable as counterexamples. The second premise too is acceptable, for it is widely agreed (in spite of some hard-core behaviorists who may think otherwise) that internal states like cognition, desire, and so on, are not externally perceptible. It is also widely agreed (in spite of the likely objection from some Wittgensteinians and Ryleans) that one is directly aware of one's desire, pleasure, and so on, so that these are not imperceptible either. Again, that internal states are objects of introspection and not of extrospection is one of the few nontrivial and nontautological philosophical claims that (notwithstanding significant challenge from some quarters both in Indian and Western philosophy) have retained a large measure of respectability. It appears then that Gotama and his followers have succeeded in proving (in the sense of arguing validly down to a conclusion from reasonable and acceptable premises) that consciousness is not a bodily quale. Nyāya philosophers are fallibilists. They are all too aware that both the premises are empirical generalizations that are not, and will never be, above challenge. But they are, to put it bluntly, as good as they get. So the conclusion is justified (although not beyond controversy).

The point of the above argument may be further explained with reference to some recent arguments for the indispensability of the first-person perspective. Thomas Nagel has persuasively argued that even if one knows everything about a bat's brain, neurophysiology, sensory activities, and so on, one still cannot know what it is like to have the sensory experiences of a bat from the unique perspective of that creature.[14] As he pointedly observes: "If the subjective character of experience is fully comprehensible only from one point of view, then any shift to greater objectivity—that is, less attachment to a specific viewpoint— . . . takes us farther away from it."[15] Frank Jackson has argued along these lines that a neuroscientist who knows everything about the human visual system but is color-blind cannot know what it is like to have a normal visual sensation of red—this shows that there are subjective facts that are inaccessible to the 'objective' or the third-person perspective.[16] What is the point of such arguments? Is the point merely that the color-blind neuroscientist cannot know what it is like to see red because that person lacks a part of the visual system that people with normal vision have, or that humans cannot know what it is like to be a bat because humans lack a bat's sensory system? This is true enough, but this need not be the point; for the point could be that I can know the quality of such and such sensation and what it is like to have the sensation only if I have that sensation myself; that is, when a person experiences subjective phenomenality, there is something it is like to be that person.

At least, this is the point of the Nyāya argument from privacy (irrespective of whether this is the point of the arguments of Nagel and Jackson). The point of the Nyāya is not that my experiences are private to me merely because my neural network is off limits to anyone else. On this ground indeed Paul Churchland has criticized the arguments of Nagel and Jackson: "[E]ach person has a self-connected . . . way of knowing that will function successfully and independently of what that person can see or hear, . . . and independently of whatever book-learned scientific knowledge he might . . . possess. . . . But nothing in these facts entails . . . that something . . . transcends understanding by the physical sciences."17 A similar objection has also been voiced by William Lycan. "I have monitors that scan my brain, you have monitors that scan yours, . . . this is part of what it is to be an organism. . . . But this fact too poses no threat to materialism.[18]

But such objections miss the target so far as the Nyāya argument from privacy is concerned. The mere fact that my neural network is different from yours does not explain why my (and also your) experiences are private. If living organisms were nothing but unconscious automata, they too would come up with the same outputs to the same inputs as computers do. But they do not. There is nothing in the physicalist or functionalist accounts that explains why they do not. This cannot be explained by pointing to the difference in the material. Two different computers are made of different material and have different circuits. Still, if they are so designed, they come up with the same answers to the same questions. This is where a living organism parts company with a machine like a computer. For we can, per impossible, suppose that two different living organisms have the same internal or functional design. That is, they have exactly the same kind (and maybe number) of neurons, synapses, and so on, organized in exactly the same way. It does not follow therefrom that they would respond to the same stimuli in the same way. Indeed, it makes perfect sense to suppose that they would respond to the same stimuli in different ways. For example, it is conceivable that two identical twins or somebody and its clone or just any two people who, per impossible, have exactly the same physical constitution and are raised in exactly the same environment still grow up to be quite different in some of their preferences. This is where the analogy with a computer breaks down: we do not suppose that, except for malfunctioning, different computers that are so designed would respond to the same stimuli in different ways. Why the difference? That is, why do we not suppose that two different living organisms with the same functional design would respond in exactly the same way, while we do suppose that two different computers with the same functional design would respond in the same way? Until a physicalist or a functionalist comes up with a satisfactory explanation for this difference, no progress can be made in accounting for privacy by appealing to the uniqueness of the neural network in each person. There is nothing unique in the neural network, qua a neural network. The same material could conceivably be reused in exactly the same way with the same structure to make another neural network. (Cf. Theseus' ship.) Hence there is nothing in the physicalist or functionalist accounts that can disallow such reduplication and preserve personal uniqueness. Accordingly, such claims as that of Lycan that privileged access is simply a fact but not a problem is a gross understatement. Privileged access is no doubt a fact. But it is a fact that goes a long way in vindicating dualism and poses one of the worst problems for a physicalist or functionalist. As Lycan himself says, privileged access must be accounted for by any viable theory of mind. The problem for a physicalist or a functionalist who chooses to be a nondualist is that they have not accounted for it and if the argument above is sound, cannot account for it even in principle. Needless to add, the appeal to the distinctness of an organism to account for privacy is circular in the first place, for in the Nyāya view all organisms have an immaterial self.[19]

Further, Lycan (and others) think that the arguments of Nagel and Jackson rest mistakenly on the intensionality of knowledge. That is, the latter are said to wrongly assume that if a person knows that *p* and if *p* and *q* are the same, then a person knows that *q*.[20] But this has no force against the Nyāya argument from privacy. It is true enough that one may know about water and yet not about H_2O although water is H_2O. Such lack of knowledge can usually be explained by one's lack of knowledge of other relevant facts, lack of following through the logical connections, and so on. But no such explanations (which all bear on "third person" facts) are available for the third person's lack of knowledge of the so-called subjective or "first person" facts. That is, in every other case the lack of knowledge can be remedied in principle. But the point of the Nyāya argument from privacy is that such a lack cannot be remedied even in principle. A mere appeal to the natural difference between two organisms cannot explain why this is so, for it is conceivable that the neural network of one organism could directly access the neural network of another organism. A full-blooded dualistic metaphysics of the self is needed to explain why this cannot be remedied even in principle.

To reiterate: my neural network, my sensory system—they may be inaccessible to others and necessary conditions for having my experiences; but they are all physical systems that are subject to change and accordingly, as argued earlier, cannot provide the basis of my personal identity. Further, what if another self happens to inhabit my body and have my neural network? Could that other self still be me and have my experiences? Or what if through some medical technology I am fitted with the exact sensory system of a given bat? Could I be that bat and have its perceptions? If the answer is no, merely having my neural network or my body is not a sufficient condition for having my experiences. Clearly the answer is no from the Nyāya dualist point of view. This is partly because my seeing and the like belong to a beginningless network of experiences that could never be reduplicated merely by cloning my nervous system or my body. In the same way that bat's perceptions belong to a beginningless network of experiences that also cannot be reduplicated merely by cloning its sensory system or its body. But this is also because the simplicity of the self guarantees that it could not be reduplicated, period. Physicalists and functionalists sometime complain that dualism is essentially a negative thesis and has nothing positive to offer. This is wrong. The thesis of a beginningless, simple, immaterial self is directly useful to account for privacy, unity and uniqueness of an individual ego, and personal identity.

To continue the thought further: In a case of multiple personality it is conceivable that two or more selves may inhabit the same body and make use of the same nervous system. Still, none of these personalities may be aware of the others. For the Nyāya this is not puzzling, for the experiences of each such person inhabiting the same body still remain private and inaccessible to the others. Since it is logically possible that two or more selves could inhabit the same body, personal identity cannot be grounded on anything in the body.

This applies with equal force to brain cells that are atypical and can last a full lifetime as also to each person's unique and persisting genetic program in the DNA. If two or more selves happen to cohabit the same body, the experiences of each would still remain incommunicable to each other although all these selves would interact with the same brain cells and the same genetic program contained in the cells. Moreover, it is conceivable that the existing stock of brain cells may be divided and transplanted into two different bodies (perhaps preserving the localization of functions as found in an ordinary brain). The resulting persons may or may not look similar and may or may not behave similarly. Should we then say that the same person has now been reduplicated into two persons? Or should we say that only one of the two is the same person?

The same question arises with the genetic program. The cells with the same genetic program could be reproduced, divided, transplanted, and so on. Another animal or human being could be produced with the same genetic program in the DNA through cloning. What would happen to personal identity then? How can personal identity be preserved if the same person is reduplicated into two or more persons?[21] Further, according to the Nyāya, a substantial whole made of parts is totally dependent on its parts and ceases to exist if even one of its parts is lost. From this viewpoint, since the initial stock of brain cells continues to get depleted throughout the lifetime of an individual, substantial identity cannot be preserved with only the remaining stock of brain cells whenever even one brain cell is lost. A similar problem crops up with new cells with the same genetic program, for there too the replacement of parts is unavoidable.

Besides the arguments of Nagel and Jackson, another influential argument in recent philosophy of mind called the Chinese Room Argument was developed by John Searle. This argument refutes the thesis that minds are computer programs by pointing out that such programs are defined syntactically by way of the manipulation of formal symbols while mental states have semantic contents that are more than a syntax.[22] Searle's argument is welcome from the Nyāya viewpoint though not many of his related views.[23] Traditional Nyāya texts do not try to refute the view that minds are computer programs. However, an anticipation of an argument from semantic contents is found in the following passage:

> Hearing the letters in succession, understanding the word meanings (*padārthagraha*) by way of remembering the semantic connections (*samayasmṛtyā*), . . . understanding the meaning of the sentence as a whole (*vākyārthsampiṇḍanam*) by means of the expectancy and other relationships (*ākāṃkṣādinibandhanānvayakṛtam*)—these will be extremely difficult to explain without the self. (NM 2.15)

Other arguments similar to the Nyāya argument from privacy may be constructed by developing the idea of the fundamental difference between consciousness and recognized physical qualia. Uddyotakara argues that since physical qualia are perceptible by both oneself and others (ātma-parātma-pratyakṣa) and since consciousness is not so, it is not a physical quale (NV 52). The argument may be set out explicitly as follows:

> All perceptible physical qualia are perceptible by both oneself and others, for example, color and so on.
>
> No conscious states are perceptible by both oneself and others.
>
> Therefore, no conscious states are perceptible physical qualia.

Once again we have a formally valid argument with two reasonable and acceptable generalizations as premises; accordingly, the conclusion is reasonable and acceptable. It is true that the argument does not prove that conscious states are not bodily qualia, for they could still be imperceptible bodily qualia. But if it were to be claimed in order to hold on to materialism that conscious states are imperceptible, that would only expose the difficulty of materialism. It is very widely held that conscious states are directly knowable and, in one version of this view, are introspectible and perceptible. If conscious states are perceptible, the above argument is a serious obstacle to materialism. For it follows that conscious states, by virtue of their perceptibility by only oneself and nobody else, that is, privacy, are not bodily qualia. No wonder then that in the recent philosophy of mind arguments for and against the privacy of our mental states are considered to be crucial for the choice between materialism and dualism.

Another familiar argument may be built out of the feature of intentionality (*saviṣayatva, saviṣayakatva*) to drive home how fundamentally different cognition is from known bodily qualia, so that cognition should be the quale of an immaterial substance. Although not explicitly offered by Gotama or Vatsyayana, the argument may be set out thus:

> No bodily qualia are intentional, for example, color and so on.
>
> All cognitive states are intentional.
>
> Therefore, no cognitive states are bodily qualia.

Characteristically, in the current philosophy of mind the debate over intentionality and its implications for dualism is in the center stage. Some Indian philosophers, the Advaitins in particular, allow for cognition that is nonintentional (*nirviṣayaka*). But the Nyāya rejects that and holds emphatically that all cognitive states are intentional (BP 397). We have seen that Uddyotakara has utilized intentionality to argue for the admission of the inner sense. Others have used it to refute the view that the self is the same as cognition (and not different from and the owner of cognition), a view supported in some sense by philosophers of such diverse persuasion as the Humeans, the Buddhists, the Sāṃkhyāns, and the Advaitins. The supporters and critics of the nonownership theory should find the following argument to be of interest: It makes sense to speak of cognition of a pot; but it does not make sense to speak of the self of a pot (by substituting 'self' for 'cognition' in accordance with the thesis that self = cognition). So the self and cognition are not the same (BP 398). The self, in the Nyāya view, is the cognizer and cognition, its quale.

We now look at some other antimaterialistic arguments. The first is simply that consciousness cannot be a quale of the body because the latter is a material product. Far from being circular, this argument is based on the premise that whatever is a material product is not conscious (*yat bhūtakāryam na tat cetanam*) (NKD 173). This generalization is supported by countless positive examples such as pots and stones that, according to both the dualist and the materialist, are material products and unconscious. There are no undisputable counterexamples. Although the materialist claims that the living body is a material product and is conscious and would offer that as a counterexample, it is rejected by the Nyāya dualist. Since the counterexample should be acceptable to both parties in the dispute, the living body is not a proper counterexample, given GAIE, that can refute the generalization. It is then reliable like an ordinary empirical law, such as that arsenic is poisonous. One can be a skeptic and say: there could still possibly be a material product that is conscious. The Nyāya would agree that it is logically possible. In the same vein a skeptic could also say: there may be some arsenic that is not poisonous. The Nyāya would agree to this as well. But such a skeptical doubt merely based on some logical possibility does not, in the Nyāya view, diminish the reliability of an otherwise healthy, empirical generalization.[24] If this is acceptable, we have the following formally valid argument the premises of which are reliable and, accordingly, also the conclusion:

> Whatever is a material product is unconscious, for example, a stone.
>
> All living bodies are material products.
>
> Therefore, all living bodies are unconscious.

Once it is shown that the living body is unconscious the inference of the self as the substratum of consciousness gains ground. The philosophical burden is then shifted to the materialist to come up with an effective rejoinder or accept dualism or withhold judgment.

Another similar argument is that consciousness is not a quale of the body because the latter is colored. The argument is based on the generalization that whatever is colored is unconscious (*yat rūpavat na tat cetanam*). Again, the premise is supported by innumerable positive examples such as bricks and stones. The living body is the only colored thing that a materialist can offer as a counterexample.

The effort will fail, given GAIE, for the dualist disputes that. The argument may be reformulated as:

> Whatever is colored is unconscious, for example, a stone.
>
> All living bodies are colored.
>
> Therefore, all living bodies are unconscious.

The deductive part of the argument may be put in the symbolic notation as (C = colored, U = unconscious, L = living body):

$(x)\,(Cx \supset Ux)$
$(x)\,(Lx \supset Cx)$
Therefore, $(x)\,(Lx \supset Ux)$

Other similar arguments to show that consciousness is not a quale of the body may be coined from the fact that the body is changeable (*pariṇāmitvāt*) and from the fact that the body has a composite structure (*sanniveśa-viśiṣṭatvāt*) (NM 2.12). These two arguments rely respectively on the generalizations that (1) whatever is changeable is unconscious and that (2) whatever has a composite structure is unconscious. For these premises, too, there are virtually endless undisputable supportive examples such as bricks and stones but no undisputable counterexamples.

Some twentieth-century materialists have advanced the view that mental states, including conscious states, are brain states. This view, as already mentioned in an earlier chapter, will be criticized by the Nyāya on the ground that while the brain, being somewhat functionally similar to the inner sense (*manas*), may be indispensable as an instrument (*karaṇa*), it by no means follows that the brain is itself the conscious knower. Moreover, the above arguments drawn from being colored, being a material product, being composite, and being changeable apply with the same force to the brain and vindicate that consciousness is not a state (or quale in accordance with the ontology preferred by the Nyāya) of the brain. Additionally, the earlier arguments based on the lack of cotemporality, pervasiveness, and utter dissimilarity also go to show that consciousness is not a state (or quale) of the brain. The cumulative weight of these arguments shows that the inference of the self as an immaterial conscious entity is reasonable and acceptable and poses a serious challenge to all forms of materialism, including the mind-brain identity theory. While the Nyāya arguments are designed for substance dualism, with suitable changes they can be brought in defense of some other forms of dualism as well. Nyāya philosophers do not claim to provide universal and necessary truths as Descartes or Spinoza do. The goal of the Nyāya is to show that the inference of the immaterial self meets the standards of reliability. Without any doubt, they have achieved that goal.

While the Nyāya has made good its claim, that may not be so with the physicalists. Recent physicalists argue that although no other physical states are subject to privileged access, the brain states are so because of their greater complexity.[25] In other words, the brain is the unique physical thing that can do something that no other physical thing can. While this is logically possible, the very structure of this argument is suspicious from the Nyāya point of view. It seeks to show that internal states that are subject to privileged access, are brain states and, therefore, are physical states. And it claims that brain states are subject to privileged access in spite of being physical states, because the brain states have something that no other physical states have, namely, a certain kind of complexity. What is suspicious is not the claim about the brain states having a certain complexity that no other physical states have. This is a factual question and may be settled by science one way or the other. Suppose, however, that this is true. That is, brain states do have some complexity that no other physical states have. How does that show that this makes them suitable candidates for privileged access? From the very nature of the case, the claim cannot be independently verified. Nothing else has this complexity and no other physical state has privileged access. So we cannot verify, by examining anything else, whether this complexity has anything to do with being eligible for privileged access. Surely the physicalist may make that claim. But is it justified and not merely an assumption? What if such complexity has nothing to do with privileged access and merely helps the brain states to be among the necessary conditions for some internal states that are nonphysical and that are subject to privileged access? At least, this is the claim that may be made by a dualist. The physicalist has not produced any evidence to rule this out. So the physicalist is guilty of assuming what is clearly part of the bone of contention.

The following example may help to see what is wrong in trying to settle a philosophical dispute by merely falling back on some unique feature. Suppose there is disagreement over whether sound is eternal or noneternal. Suppose again that sound has some unique feature, say, some complexity that does not belong to anything else. Clearly, nothing else that is either eternal or noneternal, then, has that complexity. For example, a brick is noneternal but does not have that complexity.

Similarly, space, assuming that space is eternal, is eternal but does not have that complexity. So we have no other case where something has that complexity and is also either eternal or noneternal. Now suppose one argues that sound is eternal because it has that complexity. Clearly, one has made no progress, for, if this is permitted, one may also argue with equal plausibility that sound is noneternal because it has that complexity. We may call this the flaw of uniqueness (*asādhāraṇya*), which is recognized as such in the Nyāya logical tradition.

There may be disagreement over whether this is a flaw, and we do not wish to settle that here. But if it is, the above physicalist argument is flawed. The issue is whether brain states are subject to privileged access or not. Let us suppose for the sake of argument that brain states have some complexity that nothing else has. There are numerous states that are subject to privileged access. For example, a state of anger is subject to privileged access. But it does not have the said complexity. Similarly, there are numerous states that are not subject to privileged access. For example, the changing color of a mango is not subject to privileged access. But it, too, does not have the said complexity. Now suppose one argues that brain states have privileged access because they have the said complexity. Clearly, one has made no progress, for, if this is permitted, one may also argue with equal plausibility that brain states do not have privileged access because they have the said complexity. A physicalist could object that a state of anger, being the same as some brain state, does have the said complexity. But this would be nothing more than an assumption made by a physicalist (a state of anger is not known to have the complexity of a brain state) and, unless shown to be justified, would have no merit as an objection.

We now develop in more detail one of the Nyāya arguments for dualism mentioned earlier, namely, the argument from changeability. If consciousness were a quale of the body, it becomes difficult to explain how a person is able to remember in his old age his experiences from childhood (*śarīrasya caitanye vālye vilokitasya sthavire smaraṇānupapatteh*). If consciousness belonged to the body and the body itself were the cognizer, the old body would have to be the agent of remembering and the infant body would have to be the agent of the original experience. But the old body and the infant body are different. It is also beyond doubt that what is experienced by one cannot be remembered by another. So the old body, being different from the infant body, cannot remember what was experienced by the latter (NM 2.10).

The materialist could claim by adopting the Aristotelian view that in spite of the phenomenal difference in shape, size, and so forth, the old body, in so far as it is a substance, is the same as the infant body. From the Aristotelian standpoint what makes a substance the same as an earlier substance is that its matter is the same, or derived from the matter of the former substance by gradual replacement, without losing the essential properties that represent its form. For living things, moreover, even total replacement of matter—provided it is gradual, and provided the structural change too is gradual—will not destroy identity. Since in this way the old body may be claimed to be the same substance as the infant body (in spite of the total replacement of matter), the former may be credited with the job of remembering the experiences of the latter.

But this solution, it must be said, is not acceptable to the Nyāya-Vaiśeṣika. According to the latter, even the replacement of a single part (*avayava*) would destroy a substantial whole (*avayavin*) and give rise to a new substance which though utterly similar, is different from the former substance. This view has been developed by the Nyāya-Vaiśeṣika, not as an ad hoc assumption to suit the present case, but as a solution for the wider issues of substantial change and sameness. Thus the Aristotelian view, if applicable to artifacts, faces a formidable challenge in something like Theseus's ship where a second ship is built gradually out of the same wooden pieces (by replacing each, one at a time) used to build the first ship so that the second one becomes an exact replica of the first and we end up with two ships each of which seems to have an equal claim to be the same as the first ship. Some neo-Aristotelians have offered solutions to this and other problems and have tried to keep the ship of materialism afloat. [26] But it would take too much space to enter into a meaningful discussion of the merits/demerits of the Nyāya-Vaiśeṣika and the Aristotelian/neo-Aristotelian doctrines of substantial sameness here. Suffice it to note that, given the Nyāya-Vaiśeṣika view, the old body would have to be a different substance from the infant body and then accounting for childhood memory would be a difficult problem for the materialist.

The materialist may offer the following rejoinder. Even if it is conceded that the old body is different from the infant body, the former is still related to the latter by an unbroken causal chain. So the impression of the childhood experience could be passed on through the causal chain and be revived on the appropriate occasion for memory to be possible (VU 242). But we have already seen in connection with the discussion of the Buddhist stream theory of consciousness that an account of remembrance based on merely the thesis of impressions being passed down through the causal connection is open to various difficulties.

An additional problem here is that the materialist should now find an explanation of why the experiences of the mother are not passed on to the child (BP 393). Clearly, the mother's body is causally related to the infant's body. So the mother's experiences should have been transferred to the baby up to the time of birth and the child should be able to remember them if the occasion so arises. A materialist could say that the mother's impressions are stored in her brain and that there is no suitable causal connection between the mother's brain states and the baby's developing brain during pregnancy. But the question is: Why is there no suitable causal connection between the mother's brain and the baby's brain during pregnancy? Since the mother's brain has channels of communication with various parts of the body, with some changes such channels of communication could also conceivably be set up between the mother's brain and the baby's brain and the mother's impressions transferred to the baby. Since that never happens, something other than causal connection is involved in memory. Not that it is impossible for a materialist to solve this problem. But he should come up with an answer and the dualist should get an opportunity to examine it and respond to it. Needless to say, the dualist has a ready answer to this problem. To a dualist even during pregnancy and before the birth the baby is a different person with a self of its own. No amount of causal or other connections can transfer, according to the dualist, the experiences of one person to another person. The experiences are private and one must have them in order to be able to remember them. So there is no question of the mother being able to pass on her impressions to her child.

Further, if impressions are to be passed on through the bodily causal chain, it would have to be supposed also that each time a new body is added to the causal chain, the impression residing in the previous body is destroyed and a new impression is produced. Then the materialist would have to be committed to the origin and destruction of an indefinitely large number of impressions (BP 383). From the dualist point of view, however, the self is different from the body and remains the same in spite of the bodily changes. There is, then, no need to suppose that the impression is replaced by a new impression each time a new body is added to the causal chain. In this respect, the dualist position turns out to be more economical than that of the materialist.

Moreover, the causal connection between earlier and later impressions is problematic. The cause and the effect are co-located (*samānādhikaraṇa*). For example, the potter making the pot, the clay and the pot are all in the same location. But the earlier impression is in the earlier body and the later impression is in the later body and the two bodies are different. So the two impressions are not going to be co-located; the materialist then should explain how the causal connection can still hold. Again, the materialist may have an answer; but it should be put on the table and the dualist should get a look at it. The dualist, of course, can account for the co-location of the earlier and the later impressions. Both are located in the same self and the earlier impression could thereby be the causal condition of the later impression. The materialist can avoid some of these problems by adopting, as already said, an Aristotelian view of matter, form, and substantial identity. But these views are by no means above controversy; if the success of materialism has to hinge on that, so much the worse for materialism. On the other hand, the dualist here is on safer grounds, for he is making the commonsense claim that the body of old age is different from that of childhood and, accordingly, is demanding an economical and reasonable explanation of how remembrance of childhood experiences in old age is still possible from the materialist standpoint.

Now we move to another point. Gotama says: "Since moving toward and moving away are due to the cognizers's desire and aversion, (desire, aversion, etc., are qualia of the cognizer)" (NS 3.2.34). (*Ārambha* and *nivṛtti*, which we have translated as "moving toward" and "moving away," may also be translated as moving and cessation of moving.) Vatsyayana explains:

> This comes to know that this causes me pleasure and that this causes me pain. Having known this it desires to acquire the cause of pleasure and to avoid the cause of pain. Moving toward is the special effort to acquire the cause of pleasure being motivated by the desire to acquire; moving away is the avoidance of the cause of pain being motivated by the desire to avoid. Thus it follows that cognition, desire, volition, aversion, pleasure and pain are connected with the same entity, have the same agent and also that cognition, desire and volition have the same support. Therefore, desire, aversion, volition, pleasure and pain are qualia of the cognizer and not of something unconscious. (NSB 3.2.34)

One could hold that while cognition is a quale of the self, desire, aversion, volition, pleasure, and pain are not qualia of the self but of the inner sense (*manas*). Gotama is arguing against such a view and showing that not only cognition but also desire and the rest also are qualia of the self. His reason for repudiating such a position is that the inner sense, being an instrument, is unconscious, but desire and the others require consciousness and cannot belong to something unconscious. We desire something and move to acquire it when we are aware of it as something likeable and pleasant; we turn away from something when we are aware of it as unpleasant or painful. So desire, aversion, volition, pleasure, and pain are all linked to consciousness and must all belong to the same substance to which consciousness belongs.

At this point Gotama anticipates an objection from the materialist. In the words of Vatsyayana:

> In this connection the materialist asserts: "Since those are the signs of desire and aversion, that [consciousness] belongs to the [body] made of earth, etc., cannot be denied." Moving toward and moving away are the signs of desire and aversion. Hence that which moves toward and moves away is that to which desire and aversion belong. It follows that consciousness belongs to that. Since bodies made of earth, water, fire and air are observed to move toward and move away, they are connected with desire, aversion and cognition. So [it should be admitted that] consciousness [belongs to the body]. (NSB 3.2.35)

In this passage the quoted sentence is Gotama's aphorism 3.2.35. The materialist is arguing that since moving toward and moving away require desire and aversion and since the latter require consciousness, it is clear that all these belong to the same thing. But that thing is the body, for it is the body that moves toward something or moves away from it. So it is proved that consciousness is a bodily quale. In particular, cognition of being pleasant is the cause of desire and desire is the cause of moving toward. Similarly, cognition of being unpleasant is the cause of aversion and the latter is the cause of moving away. The cause and the effect should be co-located. Since cognition, desire, aversion, moving toward, and moving away are causally connected, they must all be co-located. Since moving toward and moving away are bodily activities, cognition, being the cause of the cause of that, must also be a bodily activity.

Gotama replies: "Since moving toward and moving away are observed in an axe, etc. [the inference that consciousness belongs to the body is not sound]" (NS 3.2.36). Vatsyayana comments:

> That consciousness is of the body is to be denied. If connection with desire, aversion and cognition were to be gathered

> from the observation of moving toward and moving away, it follows that instruments like an axe, etc., too, being observed to move toward and move away, were conscious. It may be said that the connection between the body and desire, etc., [is proved] and that moving toward and moving away are deviant with respect to instruments like an axe, etc. But then that desire, aversion and cognition belong to the body made of earth, water, fire and air because the body moves toward and moves away is not a sound reason. (NSB 3.2.36)

Thus Gotama shows that the inference of cognition, desire, and so on, from moving toward or moving away from something is not sound. Instruments like an axe, too, are found to move toward and away from things, but an axe is unconscious. So it is not justified to generalize that all that move toward and move away are possessed of cognition; without such a general premise it cannot be validly inferred that the body is possessed of cognition because it moves toward and away from things.

Vatsyayana adds the argument that if the materialist were to claim that consciousness emerges from a special combination (*vyūha*) of material elements found in a body, it should be specified what that special combination is. Otherwise it cannot be explained why the body gets to acquire this feature but not other things such as pots that also are made of the combination of elements. Further, the materialist should explain, as already said, what prevents the emergence of many cognizers in the same body (NSB 3.2.36). In other words, since the hands and the legs are different parts of the body and are, *ex hypothesi*, both conscious, why is it that these two are not two different cognizers? The same consideration applies to other parts of the body and it should be explained why the other parts are not different cognizers as well. Needless to say, it cannot be admitted, as said earlier, that there are many cognizers in the same body, for then the experiences of one part would have been inaccessible to the other parts.

We finally consider a moral argument to prove that the self is not the body. This argument is not addressed to a materialist but to someone who accepts the authority of the Veda and believes in transmigration. Gotama says: "Since there would be no sin from [or after] the destruction of the body, [the self is not the body]" (NS 3.1.4). Gotama's point is that if the self were the same as the perishable body, the self would cease to exist when the body dies. Then there can be no certainty that the self would continue to exist until it has suffered the consequences of the sins committed by it. So an eternal self that is different from the body and survives the death of the body should be admitted. Vatsyayana explains:

> By the body is meant the living aggregate of the body, the sense organs, cognition and feeling. By sin is meant the sin arising from the destruction of life of one who destroys a living body. The absence of that is due to the lack of relationship of the result of that with the sinner and of relationship with the non-sinner [that is, the sinner may not suffer the consequences and someone else who is not the sinner may suffer the consequences]. If there were a succession of the body, the sense organs, cognition and feeling, another aggregate would come into being different from the one which ceases to exist. The succession within a stream of origin and cessation does not conflict with difference. . . . Accordingly, the aggregate of the body, etc., which causes the destruction of life does not get related with the consequence of the destruction and the one who gets related is not the one who caused destruction. Thus if there were different beings, it follows that there is loss of [the merit or demerit] of what is done and the accrual of [the merit or demerit of] what is not done. Further, if the being originates and ceases to exist, the birth of being would not be due to karma. Then there would be no justification for celibacy for the sake of liberation. Therefore, if the being were merely the aggregate of the body, etc., there would be no sin from [or after] the destruction of the body. This is undesirable. Therefore, the self is different from the aggregate of the body, etc., and is eternal. (NSB 3.1.4)

Gotama is here arguing that the self is not the body with a fellow Hindu in mind who believes that bad karma results from bad action (and good karma results from good action). The body is burnt (according to the Hindu custom) upon death and is destroyed. If the self and the body were the same, the merits and demerits accruing from one's voluntary actions would belong to the body. All these merits and demerits would then be destroyed when the body is destroyed, for a characteristic that is supported by a substance is destroyed when that substance is destroyed. One should not then have any fear of suffering from the consequences of one's sins committed before one's death. Why should one then refrain from committing sins? (Equally, one would not have any hope of being rewarded for the virtuous deeds performed before one's death. Why should one then bother? Without the hope of reward in afterlife it is difficult to be motivated to undertake laborious, time-consuming [and sometimes even costly] enterprises the mundane rewards of which are often unclear.

Vatsyayana interprets the aphorism with a different twist and turns it into a critique of the Buddhist theory of the self as an aggregate of internal states. The Buddhist accepts the karma theory and especially condemns the destruction of life as sinful. But the self is nothing more than a flowing stream of everchanging bodily and internal states. So there is no room, Vatsyayana charges, for personal identity and accountability. There is always a new aggregate that is different from the previous aggregate that committed the sin. If the new aggregate suffers for the sins of the former, it is suffering for the sins committed by someone else, which is not right. If the new aggregate is rewarded for the virtuous deeds of the former, it gets a reward that it has not earned, which also is not right. Again, the former aggregate that committed the sin does not face the consequences of its bad deed, which is not right. Similarly, the former aggregate that performed the virtuous deed did not get its reward, which also is not right. Where then is the rationale for celibacy and other kinds of abstinence so important to the Buddhist as well?

The Buddhist could say that in a flowing stream the earlier state is the cause of the later state, so there is room for accountability. Since both the earlier and the later states belong to the same stream, the latter can be said to be rewarded or punished in accordance with what it has done. But that would miss Vatsyayana's point. As Vatsyayana so eloquently insists, the new state and aggregate is a different entity. So it should not get punished or rewarded for what the previous state or aggregate has done. The previous state or aggregate should not also be denied the fruits of its own actions. True, the new state the former has caused bears the fruits of the former's actions. Still, the new state is a different state and the former is irrevocably debarred from reaping the consequences of its own actions. Since the stream is not an additional entity and is as transitory as any state in the stream, there is still no room for the same person's being rewarded or punished. By contrast, the Nyāya theory of an abiding self that endures and remains the same throughout the lifetime of an individual and the cycle of life and death fits in nicely with the karma theory and provides the ground for moral accountability. Uddyotakara, too, makes these points in agreement with Vatsyayana while discussing the above aphorism of Gotama.

Gotama anticipates an objection: "There is absence of that [sin] from [or after] the destruction of also the ensouled [body], for that [the self] is eternal" (NS 3.1.5). Even if the self is admitted to be different from the body, there can be no explanation for sin, the objector says. The self is eternal and cannot be destroyed. So why should it be a sin to destroy the body? Vatsyayana comments:

> Even for whom the body associated with the eternal self is destroyed there can be no sin of the destroyer from [or after] the destruction of the body. Why? For the self is eternal. No one can destroy something eternal. On the other hand, if it is destroyed, it cannot be eternal. Thus while from one point of view injury is without consequence, from the other [point of view] it is not possible. (NSB 3.1.5)

So the theory of an eternal self is in worse shape for an explanation of sin. If the self were the psychophysical aggregate, it could at least be destroyed. The problem then is that the destroyer is irrevocably gone as the aggregate undergoes change and cannot reap the consequences of its action. But if the self were eternal, it could not be destroyed at all and so the possibility of sin would be ruled out.

Gotama replies: "Not so, for there is destruction of the locus of effect and of the agent" (NS 3.1.6). Although the self is eternal, the body with which the self is associated can be harmed and sin would result from that. Vatsyayana clarifies:

> The experience of pleasure and pain is the effect; the receptacle or locus or support of that is the body. By injury is meant the destruction of the body which is the support of the effect and of the sense organs which are the agents of the perception of their objects and not [destruction] of the eternal self. (NSB 3.1.6)

Injury could be taken in the primary sense of causing harm directly to the self or in the secondary sense of harming the body and the sense organs that are indispensable to the self for having experience. Since the self is eternal, the first is ruled out and the second is to be accepted. The Buddhist may argue that the self should be identified with the aggregate of the body, and so forth, which can be harmed. Then injury can be understood literally as injury directly to the self. But the difficulty of this, as explained above, is the loss of the merits and demerits of what is done (*kṛtahāna*) and accrual of the merits and demerits of what is not done (*akṛtābhyāgama*). So the secondary meaning of injury is called for.

CHAPTER 10

Miscellaneous Arguments

We have discussed the major Nyāya arguments for the existence of the self as a permanent, immaterial substance. In this chapter we first look at some arguments developed by opponents to undermine this Nyāya view and then at some arguments supportive of the Nyāya position on the existence and eternality of the self. Some of these arguments are discussed by Uddyotakara in a preamble to the detailed examination of the nature of the self. It is not certain which philosopher or philosophical school is the source of the polemical, anti-Nyāya arguments. But from the context it is likely that these philosophers are Buddhists. In the discussion of the proofs we find the notions of *skandha*, *rūpa*, *vedanā*, and so on, which are familiar Buddhist ideas. The use of the hare's horn as a corroborative example is also suggestive of Buddhist lineage as also the fact that the Buddhists are among the chief critics targeted by Uddyotakara for refutation. However, a materialist Carvaka philosopher may also be the author of some of these anti-Nyāya arguments.

1. We start with this argument: "The self does not exist, because it is unoriginated, like the hare's horn" (NV 336). The argument may be reformulated as below:

> Whatever is unoriginated is nonexistent, for example, the hare's horn.
>
> The self is unoriginated.
>
> Therefore, the self is nonexistent.

The argument is formally valid. A Nyāya philosopher cannot challenge the truth of the second premise, for in the Nyāya view the self is unoriginated. The first premise is a generalization supported by such confirming examples as the hare's horn, which the Nyāya accepts. The hare's horn, being unreal, does not exist and is unoriginated. The Nyāya does reject the first premise as false, for it accepts the self, the atoms, and so on, as eternal entities that do exist and are unoriginated. But the Nyāya cannot offer the self or the atom or any other unoriginated entity as a counterexample, for an opponent like the Buddhist is entitled to dispute that and prevent it from being accepted as a counterexample by both parties in the debate. So how can the Nyāya counter such an argument?

Uddyotakara responds by saying that unless the opponent can show how the concept of the self has been built out of other concepts that are referential, the conclusion—namely, that the self is nonexistent—would be meaningless. When it is said that the pot does not exist, it is a meaningful denial of existence. What is meant is that the pot does not exist at some place at some time. The judgment makes sense, because what is denied is already familiar and the subject term is nonempty. The opponent cannot offer a similar explanation for the nonexistence of the self. It would not make good sense to say that the self does not exist at some particular place, for the self is conceived as an immaterial entity that does not fill space at all. In fact, the opponent does not intend to say that the self does not exist at this particular place at this particular time. Rather he intends to say that the self does not exist at all and is unreal. That makes the concept of self empty and uninstantiated like the concept of the hare's horn. But the concept of the hare's horn has been built out of the concepts of hare and horn, each of which is nonempty.[1] In other words, a complex concept like that of hare's horn is meaningful in spite of being empty, because it is made only out of nonempty concepts. So the opponent should show which nonempty components are contained in the concept of the self, so that the conclusion can be meaningful. Otherwise, the conclusion cannot be accepted to be meaningful and to follow validly from the premises.

The opponent could suggest that his thesis really amounts to saying that there is no immaterial self in a living body. If this boils down to refuting the proofs of the existence of the immaterial self, that is welcome. The opponent is entitled to offer arguments against such proofs. But a distinction must be drawn between refuting proofs of existence and proving nonexistence. While the former is a legitimate exercise, the latter runs the risk of arguing about an empty, useless subject. For example, arguing about whether a rabbit's horn is sharp or not or whether the round square is big or not is philosophically barren for the simple reason that there are no rabbit's horns and that there are no round squares.[2]

The opponent could suggest that what is meant by his thesis is that what is intended by you (the Nyāya philosopher) as the self does not exist. However, to the Nyāya philosopher the "self" and "I" are synonymous. So "the self does not exist" is equivalent to "I do not exist." But the latter is self-defeating, for the very denial of my existence by me is possible only if I exist. This argument is analogous to the famous Augustinian and Cartesian argument that the very doubt about the self's existence proves its existence. It is also similar to the Sāṃkhya argument (SS 6.1) that any proof of the nonexistence of the self implies its existence and is self-refuting.[3]

Moreover, the opponent has offered 'being unoriginated' as the sign to prove the nonexistence of the self. It should be explored what is precisely meant by being unoriginated. Does it mean "not being born"? Then the premise that the self is not born would appear to go against common opinion. Although the self is eternal and goes through transmigration (in the Nyāya view), its conjunction with the new body at the time of birth is commonly understood as "the birth" of the self. On the other hand, if the sign of being unoriginated is addressed to the Nyāya philosopher, it amounts to begging the question. What is unoriginated may also be eternal and existent forever. So the opponent's sign is subject to doubt. When it is said that something is unoriginated, what is meant is that it is not brought into existence by any causes. This does not preclude its existence.

Finally, the opponent claims that the sentence 'the self is unoriginated' is true. Does this imply that the property of not being originated actually belongs to the self in the same way in which in the true sentence 'the pot is red' the red color actually belongs to the pot? But then it should be explained why this does not conflict with the thesis that the self does not exist. How can a property actually belong to something that does not exist? On the other hand, if the property does actually belong to the self, how can it be nonexistent? A similar problem arises about the thesis that the self does not exist. Does this imply that nonexistence actually belongs to the self, that is, is a real property of the self? But then it should be explained how something nonexistent can have any real properties? On the other hand, if something does have any real properties, how can it be nonexistent? A property, after all, is not self-existent and needs a support (if it belongs to the category of quale or *guṇa*). If nonexistence were a real property and if the self were a real support of that, how can it fail to exist? In other words, how can something nonexistent be the real support of a real property? (NV 335–41)

2. The opponent may argue for the nonexistence of the self on the ground that it is not cognized: "The self does not exist because it is not cognized (NV 341). Since the thesis is still the same, that is, the self does not exist, the relevant difficulties pointed out above still apply. Additionally, the sign, namely, not being cognized, is questionable, for the self may be claimed to be cognized by way of perception, and so on. How is the self perceived? It is perceived as the object of I-consciousness (*aham iti vijñānam*). If there is any perception that is indubitable (*mukta-saṃśaya*), the I-consciousness is so and it reveals the self (*svātma-saṃvedya*). If I can doubt my own existence, I cannot avoid being skeptical about everything else either. If universal skepticism is to avoided, I cannot doubt my own existence.[4]

Could it be that I-consciousness is accepted but not that the self is the object of that? But then what is the object of I-consciousness? Are things such as color the objects of I-consciousness? But this is not acceptable, for it is not cognized that I am color. Are internal states such as pain the objects of I-consciousness? This too is not acceptable, for it is not cognized that I am pain. It is true that we do say that I am fair, I am dark, and so on. But this does not unequivocally support identifying the self with the bodily complexion. It may very well be that in such cases the concept of I has been extended to what is mine (*mama*) or possessed by me. Needless to say, any cognition of the self's identity with bodily attributes must eventually be dismissed as false if the antimaterialistic arguments are sound.

Besides being perceived as the object of I-consciousness the self is inferred from desire and so on. This too shows that the above sign of not being cognized is questionable. The opponent cannot simply assume that the self is not cognized. If he wishes to stick to his point, he must refute the various grounds for inferring the self.

Again, when one argues that the self does not exist because it is not cognized, one may be guilty of circularity. One may be asked: Why is the self not cognized? One may reply: Because what is to be cognized (*upalabhya*) does not exist. But that would make the thesis and the reason mutually dependent.

The opponent may say that not being cognized is the feature of what has been imagined to be the self, that is, the thesis is that what has been imagined to be the self is nonexistent. Then the question is: Is the self imagined as existent or as nonexistent? If the self is imagined as existent, not being cognized is no longer its feature, that is, it is no longer true that it is not cognized. On the other hand, if it is imagined as nonexistent, it is futile to offer the sign to prove its nonexistence.

3. Another argument is: the living body is without the self because it exists" (NV 344). It may be reformulated as:

Whatever exists is without the self, for example, a pot.

The living body exists.

Therefore, the living body is without the self.

This argument is formally valid. The second premise is obviously true and cannot be challenged by the Nyāya. The first premise is supported by confirming instances such as a pot that the Nyāya cannot dispute, that is, the Nyāya too accepts that material things such as pots exist and are without any self. There are also no undisputable counterexamples, for the living bodies are the only things that are not without the self, according to the Nyāya. But the living body is the subject and part of the bone of contention. Hence it is not acceptable as a counterexample.

Although the argument may look impressive, it may be counterbalanced by an argument such as the following:

Whatever exists is useful to the self, for example, a pot.

The living body exists.

Therefore, the living body is useful to the self.

This counterargument is formally valid. The second premise is obviously true and accepted by the opponent. The first premise is supported by confirming examples such as pots accepted by the opponent. The opponent cannot produce any undisputed counterexamples, for the Nyāya claims that everything is useful to the self. (This claim is to be taken seriously. In the Nyāya view while eternal entities like selves, atoms, and space exist forever, God creates all noneternal things in accordance with the merits and demerits of individual selves.) Since being useful to the self implies that the self exists, the opponent's conclusion that the living body is without the self can no longer be claimed to be proved without first showing that the counterargument is weaker in some respect.

Another problem is: How should being without the self be understood? One understands how a house can be without mosquitoes (*nirmaśaka*), for both the house and mosquitoes are familiar. As pointed out above, when one negates something, one is already familiar with what is negated and the negation refers to nonexistence in some place or some time. Thus in the above example the mosquitoes are said to be nonexistent in the house at some given time. But the self, according to the opponent, does not exist anywhere anytime. So how can there be the negation of something that is totally unfamiliar?

The opponent could say that the negation of the self that does not exist anywhere and anytime should be understood in the same way in which we understand the negation of hare's horn and the like, which are unreal. But the analogy with nonentities such as a hare's horn cannot be taken for granted. Although there are no hare's horns, we can understand the concept, for it is built out of concepts of (1) hare, (2) horn, and (3) having or possessing—each of which is familiar. The notion of hare's horn is exactly like the notion of cow's horn, which is familiar. We know that horns belong to a cow as its body parts and that the horns are related to the cow as cause and effect. (Since the cow's body as a substantial whole is dependent on its parts, each body part may be regarded as a causal condition of the cow's body. If the horns are accepted as parts of the cow's body, they are among the causal conditions of the cow's body. Alternatively, the horns may be treated as outgrowths of the body like hair and nail. Then the horns are related to the cow's body as effects to the cause [TP 501].) When we say that there are no hare's horns, we may simply mean that hares do not have horns or that horns are not among the body parts of a hare and are not related to a hare's body as cause and effect. What we do not ordinarily mean is that "not having" (as part of hares not having horns) may be understood in any vague and general sense; rather we ordinarily imply that some specific kind of relation (which is familiar and holds between, say a cow and its horns) does not hold between hares and horns (NV 340). So the opponent needs to show by analysis that the concept of self is as a matter of fact a complex concept like that of hare's horn constructed out of a number of other nonempty concepts. But these are debatable claims and must be demonstrated and not merely taken for granted. It may very well be that the concept of self or I is not a complex notion and rather is a basic notion with a unitary reference.

4. The opponent may again argue that the word *self* refers to something noneternal, for it is made of letters (NV 344). The implied premise is: whatever is made of letters refers to noneternal things. For example, the word *pot* is made of letters and refers to noneternal pots. In the same way, since the word *self* is made of letters, it too should refer to something noneternal, such as a cognitive state. (In the

Buddhist view the self is nothing but an aggregate of particular, fleeting internal states.) But if something noneternal, such as cognition, is taken to be the self, the Nyāya position that the word *self* refers to something eternal is jeopardized.[5]

Uddyotakara responds by saying that all words made of letters do not refer to noneternal things. For example, the word *eternal* does not refer to something noneternal. While all letter sounds may be noneternal, some of them may still refer to something eternal.

The opponent may as a way out suggest that what is claimed to be different from the body and so on and to be an additional kind of substance is noneternal. Uddyotakara points out that even then the opponent's position will be undermined, for he does not actually admit the existence of any such thing. Further, if it is granted that the self is different from the body, and is an additional kind of substance, it can no longer be said to be necessarily originated or destroyed with the body. Then the eternality of the self may be proved with the help of some further arguments as the Nyāya tries to show.

5. Now comes an argument in favor of the Nyāya position that the self is an additional entity over and the above the body, the sense organs, and so on. Thus one may argue that the eye and so on are for the use of someone else, for they are aggregates, like a bed (NV 344). The argument[6] may be formally set out as:

> Whatever is an aggregate is for the use of someone else, for example, a bed.
>
> The eye and so on are aggregates.
>
> Therefore, the eye and so forth are for the use of someone else.

This formally valid argument is part of an effort to prove that the external senses are for the use of (by way of additional arguments eliminating the body and the inner sense) the immaterial and conscious self, which utilizes them as instruments just as a bed is there for the use of one who makes or owns or occupies it. The argument is addressed to the Buddhists, who as antisubstance philosophers support the aggregate theory. The Buddhists accept the second premise that the eye and the rest are aggregates. The first premise is a generalization supported by confirming instances such as a bed or a seat, which the Buddhists also accept. There are also no counterexamples that are undisputed by both the Nyāya and the Buddhists. So how can the Buddhists respond?

To stop the inference of the unitary, substantial self the Buddhist may counterargue that although an aggregate is always for someone else, the latter too is an aggregate. (In the Buddhist view, it may be remembered, the self is an aggregate of the internal states.) The counterargument may be set out as:

> Whatever is an aggregate is for the use of another aggregate, for instance, a bed.
>
> The eye and so forth are aggregates.
>
> Therefore, the eye and so forth are for the use of another aggregate.

If the counterargument is an equal match to the Nyāya argument given above, the Nyāya fails to prove its case. The Nyāya cannot easily dispute the second premise, for in the Buddhist view all phenomenal things, including the eyes and so on, are aggregates. Further, in the Nyāya view also the eye and so forth are parts of the body, which is a substantial whole (*avayavin*). Although the parts of a substantial whole may be made of other parts, none of these can be treated as independent substantial wholes as long as they remain parts of a substantial whole. The Nyāya may wish to offer the self as a counterexample to the first premise. But this would be disputed by the Buddhist, who denies the existence of the self. So how can the Nyāya show that the counterargument is weaker?

Uddyotakara responds thus. If the first premise of the counterargument were to be accepted, a vicious infinite regress would result. Since the other aggregate that makes use of the former aggregate is itself an aggregate, the other aggregate must itself be for the use of still another aggregate and so on to infinity. So everything cannot be an aggregate. There must be at least one thing that is not an aggregate (*asaṃhata*) to stop the regress and make the very existence of aggregates possible.

Another difficulty is that the aggregate is not anything over and above the particular things in the aggregate. So the Buddhist position boils down to that some particular things are for the use of some other particular things. This by itself is not illuminating and does not shed any light on why the former is for the use of the latter. So the Buddhist owes an additional explanation for that.

6. A final argument in favor of the Nyāya position (in this section of Uddyotakara's NV) is this: The word self (or the word *I*) has a reference that is different from that of words such as color, for it is

different from words such as color, and has a singular reference, like the word *pot* (NV 343). So different words, except when there is counterevidence, have different references. Further, words that appear to have singular references, except when countermanded by evidence, refer to single things. Accordingly, the word *self* (or the word *I*) should not refer to the aggregate of color, pain, and so on, as the Buddhist suggests.

Clearly, the word *self* and the word *I* have the same reference and these words appear to refer to something different from color, pain, and so on. Ordinarily, we do not say that I am color or I am pain. This exposes the difficulty of identifying the self with the aggregate of color, pain, and so on. We have already seen that the aggregate is not an additional entity apart from the color, pain, and so forth. Identifying the self with the aggregate amounts to identifying the self with color, pain, and so on. But, as just said, it is not part of common knowledge or usage that I am color, I am pain, and so on. It could be said for the sake of argument that the aggregate is ontically different from the particulars in the aggregate. But then the difference between the Buddhist and the Nyāya positions will be in the danger of being merely terminological. If the aggregate is ontically different from the changing qualia and motions, there is no reason not to regard it as an abiding and unitary support for these. Then the aggregate will in substance be the same as what the Nyāya is arguing for under the label of the self. Nor do we ordinarily say that each of us is a collection of a sort without a unity. The word *self* (or *I*) appears to refer to a single entity. For example, when we say that I am happy, I am sad, I want to eat, and so on, what we ordinarily mean is that the reference of the word *I* is one and the same in each of these cases and that is how this should be construed (unless there is counterevidence). Thus the argument is a typical expression of the Nyāya confidence in and committment to common sense and ordinary usage (except when there is sufficient ground for revision).

Uddyotakara takes note of the Buddhist objection that a word such as *pot* does not refer to a single thing but to a plurality of qualia and motions. But he points out that the matter has been settled and the Buddhist view refuted by the arguments for the category of substance (already discussed by us in an earlier chapter). He also notes that there are words such as *darkness* (*tamas*) that, according to some, do not to have a reference (and the same could be the case with the word *self* or the word *I*). He disagrees and argues that even the word darkness has a reference: it refers to substances, qualia, and motions devoid of light.[7] He rests his case with the optimism that the burden of proof lies squarely on the Buddhist to show that the word self (or the word I) should be treated differently from the way common sense does and that a revision of ordinary usage is here necessary but that the Buddhist will not succeed in doing this.

We have noted that in the Nyāya view the self is eternal. This implies that the self is both beginningless and endless. If the self is different from the body, the former need not begin to exist or cease to exist when the latter does. So the self may very well exist both before and after the body. Further, as the agent of remembrance, the self must remain the same throughout the lifetime of an individual. It is also a substance, as the Nyāya argues, different from the internal states. If it were a substance made of parts, it would not remain the same, according to the Nyāya, if any parts were lost or added. Then it could not remain the same throughout the lifetime of an individual and be the agent of remembrance. So the self should be a partless substance (unlike the body which is a substance made of parts). A partless substance can be neither produced nor destroyed, for a substance is produced by conjoining the parts and destroyed by disjoining the parts and neither is possible if there are no parts. If thus the self is a partless substance, it must be beginningless and endless and eternal.

An eternal self need not be associated with only one body in one lifetime. It may very well be associated with many different bodies in many different lifetimes. Thus the self may have gone through many lives before the present one and may go through many more after the present one. For an eternal self changing bodies in different lifetimes and moving from an old body to a new body is like a person discarding worn out clothes and wearing a new one (BG 2.22).

There are also reasons for thinking that the self was actually associated with different bodies in previous lives. The evidence is drawn from the phenomenon of biologically inherited instinctive activities, such as suckling by a newborn mammal (NS 3.1.21). Suckling is a purposive act the result of which is getting nourishment and satisfying hunger. In an adult the act of getting nourishment is prompted by the awareness that nourishment is beneficial (*iṣṭa-sādhana*). If causal connections are objective and uniform, as the Nyāya holds, a new born's act of getting nourishment should also be prompted by the awareness of the act being beneficial. Such causal connection is established through a process of trial and error that requires previous experience. Since the possibility of previous experience is ruled out in the present life, the inference of a previous life becomes in order.

The critic could object that the movement of a new born baby toward the mother's breasts is like that of an iron toward a magnet (NS 3.1.22). That is, the iron moves toward the magnet although it has no awareness that such movement is beneficial. In the same way the baby moves toward the breasts although it has no awareness that the movement is beneficial. Thus the need for a previous life is avoided.

But the objection is not sound. The iron moves not toward other things but toward the magnet (NS 3.1.23). This is so by virtue of the causal connection that there is between the movement of the iron and the magnet. Thus the movement of the iron is in accordance with the causal laws. Similarly, the movement of the baby should also be in accordance with the causal laws. In this case the causal connection is that between the movement for acquiring food and awareness of the resulting benefit. Since the effect cannot take place without the cause and since the effect, that is, the said movement, is there, the cause, namely, the said awareness, should also be there. But the awareness cannot arise in this life. So a previous life should be admitted. There is no reasonable basis for drawing an upper limit once a previous life is admitted. Accordingly, the self is beginningless and, since a (positive) thing that is beginningless is also endless, it is endless as well.

From the modern point of view the instincts are carried on through the genes contributed by the parents. Such a genetic link between the parent and the offspring does not weaken the above argument. The admission of genes is in accordance with causal laws. Unless unconscious teleology is acceptable and unless a justifiable exception can be made to an otherwise established causal law, instincts (as unlearnt goal-oriented activities done right without instruction) provide a reasonable ground for preexistence (granted that the self is an immaterial substance different from the body).

Finally, no one is born without preferences (NS 3.1.24). Everybody displays from very early in the childhood certain preferences. Some like music, some like to paint, some like sports, etc. These preferences are not always explained by family traits or environmental influences. Further, there are prodigies who show exceptional skills, such as playing some musical instrument, doing difficult mathematical calculations, with very little or no significant training. These are skills that an average person needs a lot of practice and training to master. But prodigies master them with little training or practice. Since skills require practice and since a prodigy has the skill without the benefit of practice in the present life, a previous life when the prodigy had the practice should be inferred. Otherwise, we have to make an exception to the established causal connection between a skill and practice. The burden of justifying the exception must be borne by the critic. Until it is provided, the inference of preexistence is in order.

What is true of prodigies is true in a less dramatic sense of everyone. That is, everyone has certain skills or preferences rather than some other skills or preferences. And these cannot always be explained by family traits or environmental influences. Whenever we find evidence for some skill or preference that is not explicable by hereditory or environmental connections, it may be considered to be innate. Such innate skills or preferences, if any, point to previous lives, for no skill or preference is acquired without prior experience and there is no opportunity for such experience in the present life.

CHAPTER 11

A Nyāya Causal Proof of the Existence of God

We have discussed how the Nyāya argues for the existence of the self as an immaterial substance. The Nyāya also offers various arguments for the existence of a supreme self or God. To throw further light on the subject we now look at one such well-known proof that runs as follows: the first product (*kṣityaṅkura*) has a causal agent (*sakaṛtrka*) because it is an effect (*kārya*) such as a pot.[1] In this argument the first product is the subject (*pakṣa*), having a causal agent is the probandum (*sādhya*) and being an effect is the probans (*hetu*). The subject, the probans, and the probandum are represented by respectively the minor term, the middle term, and the major term of a categorical syllogism.[2] The argument may be explicitly reformulated as:

Every effect has a causal agent, for instance, a pot.

The first product is an effect.

Therefore, the first product has a causal agent.[3]

This argument is deductively valid, that is, the conclusion necessarily follows from the premises. Hence if both the premises are justified, the conclusion must be justified too. The question then is: Are both the premises justified?

Let us first consider the second premise. It is a truism that the first product, if there is one, is an effect. But then what is the first product? The answer, in the Nyāya view, is: the dyad (*dvyaṇuka*). A dyad is the conjunction of two atoms. This is how the origin of things must begin, given the atomic theory. In other words, if it is true that the atoms (*aṇu*) are the ultimate, indivisible parts out of the combination of which all noneternal substances (*dravya*) are produced, the process of the origin of noneternal substances must begin with the dyad. The dyad thus turns out to be the ontologically first product. What is ontologically first should not be confused with what is chronologically first. The Nyāya philosophers hold that the universe is beginningless (*anādi*) and also that there was no absolutely first moment of time when the origin of noneternal things began. So they do not accept that there is a chronologically first effect in time. But they do accept the atomic theory and therefore also the dyad as the ontologically first product.

Why does the Nyāya hold that the universe is beginningless? First of all because nothing comes out of nothing. Particular noneternal things do begin to exist at particular times. So we can point to the absolutely first moment when something begins to exist. But it does not make sense to say that there was a time when nothing whatsoever existed and that there was a moment when some one thing or many things began to exist for absolutely the first time. For then the inevitable question is: What made that possible? Whenever something begins to exist, there is some cause that makes that happen. But from the very nature of the supposition there could not be anything that made the first thing happen. This is contrary to what we know to be the case in any given case of origin. Since something must always come into existence depending on something that is already there, the supposition that the whole universe was nonexistent before some time is unacceptable.

Moreover, if the universe as a whole has a beginning, time also must have a beginning. This would invite the difficulty that there was a time before which there was no time that is questionable, for then we seem to have to speak of a time when there was no time. Some medieval Western philosophers as well as the Sāṃkhya philosophers in India do not find this puzzling. In their view, time is not an absolute entity in itself but a function of change in the universe. Such a view may be defensible but is consciously rejected by the Nyāya, which regards time as an absolute entity and also regards change as beginningless. The Nyāya does offer arguments for defending these claims, but the underlying issues here are complex and cannot be discussed in a short space. Suffice it to say that if time and change are beginningless, the universe must be beginningless as well. Further, granted the atomic theory, matter can have no beginning (and no end). So the supposition that the universe as a whole has a beginning must, according to the Nyāya, be rejected.

Even if the universe is beginningless, why should not there be an absolutely first moment of time when noneternal things begin to exist? By way of an answer, the Nyāya points to the difficulty of determining which came first—the tree or the seed (*vījāṅkura-nyāya*). Since there can be no tree without the seed and there can be no seed without the tree, the best course is to accept an infinite regress of trees and seeds. Otherwise, one would have to stop the regress at some point and say that either the tree was the first or that the seed was the first—which would be dogmatic and arbitrary. The acceptance of an infinite regress (*anavasthā*) in such a case is not only harmless but also reasonable (*prāmāṇika*).

Why should one accept the atomic theory? Because otherwise we cannot account for the great diversity of sizes of different material things such as a mountain and a mustard seed (*meru-sarṣapa*).[4] To explain: It is a fact of observation that things such as pebbles and shells are divisible into parts. This process of division can be supposed to either go on indefinitely and end in nothing, or to go on infinitely and endlessly, or to end at some point when we reach the indivisibles. These three alternatives are mutually exclusive and collectively exhaustive. Of these the first, according to the Nyāya, is not acceptable, for then we are committed to saying that material things come out of nothing. Some Western and Indian theists would object to this and claim that God creates matter out of nothing. In this particular theistic view, matter is produced out of nothing in the sense of out of no preexisting material but nevertheless by a preexisting cause, namely, God, that produces the total being of the thing. Although the Nyāya defends theism, it rejects such a view of the origin of matter. In each and every known case of the origin of a material thing it is found to come out of some preexisting material. There is also no counterexample that is undisputed and above board. So one is entitled to generalize that in all cases a material thing comes out of some preexisting material, which conflicts with the view that God creates matter out of nothing and renders that view questionable, to say the least.[5]

The second alternative is that the process of dividing a material object such as a pebble could go on infinitely. This too is not free from difficulty, for then we have to say that each and every material thing is infinitely divisible and then we cannot explain how there can be the virtually endless diversity of sizes found in the universe.

One may object that some infinities are bigger than others. For example, the power set of natural numbers is bigger than the set of natural numbers although each set is infinite. So even if things are infinitely divisible, there can be diversity of sizes.

But the objection overlooks the crucial point that these larger infinities are generated in an orderly way to suit the needs of a mathematical theory. Since these theoretical infinities are generated in an orderly way, they cannot provide the basis for the random and specific variety in sizes found in nature. For example, while one table may measure five feet, another may measure twelve feet, and so on. The transfinite numbers do not show why this is specifically so in each such case. This difficulty does not arise if we accept that the process of division ends in the indivisible atoms. Then we can suppose that the second thing, which is twelve feet long, just has that many more of the atoms than the first thing, which is five feet long, and so on. If this makes sense, by elimination (*pariśeṣa*) we are left with only the third alternative, which the Nyāya accepts. There are an infinity of indivisible particles called the atoms that are the building blocks of the material universe. These can be combined in smaller or larger numbers and thus can generate the seemingly endless diversity of sizes.

The atomic theory then may be accepted and also that the universe is beginningless. Thus the second premise amounts to this: the dyad, which is the ontologically (but not chronologically) first noneternal thing, is an effect.

From the standpoint of the three great world religions of Judaism, Christianity, and Islam, God is the creator of the universe, which did not exist before creation. If this means that nothing noneternal existed before creation, the Nyāya accepts that. But if creationism means that nothing but God existed before creation, the Nyāya rejects that for the reasons explained above. These reasons show that from a philosophical perspective creationism faces serious challenges.

We may now turn to the first premise, namely, that every effect has a causal agent, such as a pot and so on. Here it may be useful to explain the notion of a causal agent (*kartā*). The latter is a causal condition (*kāraṇa*) with some special features, that is, perceptual awareness (*aparokṣa-jñāna*) of the material (*upādāna*) needed for the effect and the desire (*icchā*) as well as the will (*kṛti*) to make the effect.[6] For example, the agent of a pot is the potter who is able to perceive the lump of clay out of which a pot is made and also has the desire and the will to make a pot. If someone has merely an inferential knowledge or knowledge derived from some authoritative source of the lump of clay, one would not be an agent of a pot. For the lump of clay must be actually handled to produce a pot, and for that, perception of the lump of clay is needed. Similarly, if someone perceives the lump of clay but does not have the desire and the will to make a pot or if such a person has the desire but not the will to make a pot, the pot would not be made and hence such a person would not be an agent of a pot. Thus all the three features of perception of the material and the desire and the will to produce are implied in the concept of agency (*kartṛtva*).[7]

This does not rule out devising an automaton (which being a material thing lacks perception of the material) for making pots. Even then the desire and the will to make a pot is implied on the part of the designer of the automaton. Further, although the designer need not perceive the particular clay used to make a given pot, he must possess direct knowledge of some lump of clay and of the properties that make clay suitable as a material to be able to design an efficient automaton. Thus the designer of such an automaton may be regarded as an agent through an indirect (*paramparā*) relationship.

To say that an agent is a causal condition implies that it is a necessary condition for the effect. The first premise then asserts that nothing would come into being unless someone has direct knowledge of the material (that in which the effect inheres: *samavāyin*) cause of the effect and also has the desire and the will to make the thing.

Is this justified? In other words, since this is a generalization, does this satisfy the requisite conditions of a generalization? Now in the Nyāya view a generalization (*vyāpti*) is not reliable (*prāmāṇika*) unless it is supported by acceptable positive instances or acceptable negative instances and is not contradicted by any unquestionable counterexample. For example, the generalization that all swans are white is supported by observing white swans. These white swans are called positive instances (*anvayi-dṛṣṭānta*) because both the (assumed) pervader (*vyāpaka*) property—being white, and the (assumed) pervaded (*vyāpya*) property—being a swan—are present (*vṛtti*) in them. The said generalization is also supported by observing things such as black cats that are neither white nor swans. These are called negative instances (*vyatireki-dṛṣṭānta*) because both the (assumed) pervader property and the (assumed) pervaded property are absent (*avṛtti*) in them. However, although this general claim is amply supported by hundreds of positive instances and negative instances, it turns out to be false when one observes a swan that is black. A black swan is a counterexample (*vyabhicāri-dṛṣṭānta*) because the (assumed) pervaded property of being a swan is present but the (assumed) pervader property of being white is absent. This conclusively proves that some swans are not white and that therefore 'all swans are white' is false. Thus a general statement may be refuted by a single counterexample even when it is found to hold in innumerable instances. It may be noted that in the Nyāya view both the supportive instances and the counterexamples should be acceptable to parties on both sides of the issue. For example, a white swan produced as a confirming instance should be acceptable as being both white and being a swan by both those who may claim that all swans are white and those who may reject it. Similarly, a black swan produced as a counterexample should be acceptable as being both nonwhite and being a swan by the same two parties.

Does the above premise then satisfy the said conditions? The Nyāya claims that it does and this is indicated, through a well-established convention within the Indian logical tradition, by adding the words 'such as a pot and so on' as an appendage to the general statement that every effect has a causal agent. The words 'such as a pot and so on' are intended to be a summary of the inductive evidence in support of the general claim. The words 'and so on' are usually added to the particular specimen cited to make it clearer that it is a summary. Some modern scholars have speculated that the inclusion of examples in an argument shows that such an argument is not deductively valid and is as a matter of fact an analogical argument from particulars to a particular.[8] But this is a mistake. The purpose of citing examples is to show that the general proposition being used as a premise has adequate inductive support and so is acceptable. Otherwise, if the premise were false or doubtful, the conclusion validly following from the premise could be false or doubtful too. The reason for interest in the acceptability of the premise is obvious. The acceptability of the premise guarantees that the conclusion following validly is also acceptable.

Now the general premise that every effect has a causal agent is supported by acceptable positive instances. For things such as pots and other artifacts are without any doubt both effects and made by agents. It is also clear that if there are any eternal entities in one's ontology, they will provide suitable negative instances. In the Nyāya view, of course, atoms and so on are eternal, are neither made by agents nor effects and therefore serve as negative instances in support of the premise. Needless to say, if in one's ontology there are no entities that are beginningless, no negative instances can be found. But that there are acceptable positive instances cannot still be questioned.

Are there any unquestionable counterexamples to this general premise? An atheist may offer nonartifacts such as stones as counterexamples to refute the premise. But while these are accepted by the atheist to be effects that are not made by any agent, they are regarded by the theist to be effects whose sum total of causal conditions includes at least God as an agent. In fact, in the theistic view, God is a causal condition of anything and everything that comes into being. Under these circumstances, the atheist cannot produce any counterexamples that are not rejected by the theist. It appears then that while the general premise is supported by acceptable positive instances (and also by acceptable negative instances if there are any eternal entities at all in one's ontology), it is not contradicted by any undisputable counterexample. It is, the Nyāya claims, justified (given the principle that both confirming and disconfirming examples should be acceptable to both parties).

It appears that the theist here has formulated the premise in such a way that the possibility of a counterexample is ruled out *ab initio*. This may appear to be questionable to some. But what the theist has done is not unusual in philosophical circles. Philosophers sometimes make similar general claims. For example, a materialist claims that all real things are physical. He may support the claim by producing positive instances such as stones that are both real and physical and accepted as such by both a materialist and a psychophysical dualist. The dualist may submit an act of consciousness that the dualist claims is a mental state and is nonphysical, as a counterexample to the materialist thesis. But the materialist may then dispute it and claim that while an act of consciousness is real, it is not a mental state but a physical state. In this way, the materialist may justifiably object to anything that the dualist may offer as a counter example. Thus it seems that the theistic move is within the norms of known philosophical exercise.

Both the premises then seem to be justified and acceptable. Thus the conclusion—that the dyad has a causal agent—which follows validly from the premises, seems to be justified and acceptable.

With this conclusion the monotheistic position can be reached in a few more steps. It is obvious that the agent of the dyad must be a superhuman spirit (*ātman*). First, a human agent cannot function without a body. Since no human body (which is a complex product) can exist before the dyad, human agency for the dyad is ruled out. Second, the agent of the dyad must be able to perceive the atoms out of which the dyad is made. But atoms are imperceptible to humans and therefore, too, no human can be the agent of the dyad. Thus the agent of the dyad must be a superhuman, disembodied spirit. It must also be beginningless, for it exists before the ontologically first product. Its knowledge, desire, and will, too, must be beginningless, for these also exist before the ontologically first product. But in order for it to be beginningless it must be simple (*niravayava*), for something complex and made of parts can exist only after the parts have been combined. Since it is simple, it is also endless, for destruction implies separation of parts and something simple cannot be destroyed. Thus, the agent of the dyad must be an everlasting (*nitya*) spirit. This spirit is needed not only for some given dyad but also for any dyads, past, present, or future. Hence it remains involved with the changing world, which forever becomes dependent on it, for no future dyads could come into being without its agency. There is no compelling reason to admit more than one such spirit. Hence based on considerations of economy (*lāghava*) only one such spirit is admitted and monotheism is established.[9]

This proof is set in the context of the atomistic ontology favored by the Nyāya. But the essential steps of the proof are autonomous and can be set in the context of some nonatomistic ontologies as well so long as they accommodate the fact that there are effects and that some things are ontologically prior to some others. Then it can still be argued that the ontologically first product (be it the dyad or not) has a causal agent that is a disembodied, everlasting, and unitary spirit for the sort of reasons outlined above.

Further light may be thrown by comparing this proof with some of the celebrated theistic proofs given by the great Christian philosopher St. Thomas Aquinas. The latter argues as follows:

> That some things change is certain and evident to the senses. But whatever is changed is changed by something else, for nothing can be altered unless it has a capacity or potentiality for the end result of the change. Now only some actual being can alter a thing. For to change is merely to bring something from a potential state to one of actuality. But only some being that is actual can bring something potential to actuality. . . . Anything in the process of change, therefore, must be altered by an agent other than itself, and this agent by still another. Infinite regress here is out of the question, for otherwise there would be nothing to initiate the change and hence nothing else would be altered. For secondary agents of change only function when moved by some primary mover, even as a stick moves nothing unless stirred by some hand. One is bound to arrive, then, at some first mover which is not changed or moved by any other, and this is what all understand by God. (*Summa Theologiae*, I, q. 2, art. 3)

The argument may be reformulated as:

1. Some things change.
2. Whatever changes has the potentiality for becoming what it is changed into.
3. Whatever is changed is altered by an actual agent other than itself.
4. The latter if itself undergoing change must be altered by still another agent and so on.
5. This regress of one thing being altered by another is either infinite or finite.
6. But the regress cannot be infinite because then there would be nothing to begin the change and then there could be no change.
7. Hence the regress must be finite.
8. From this it follows that there must be a first mover called God that begins the change but is not changed by anything else.

Aquinas begins from the observed fact of change and argues to the existence of a first unmoved mover that begins the change in something else but is not itself changed by anything. The proof is set in the framework of the Aristotelian ontology of potency and act. In this light Aquinas argues that there must exist one thing that is pure actuality devoid of all potentiality while other things possess actuality with reference to what they change and also potentiality with reference to what changes them. However, the proof may also be understood without any particular reference to that framework, and it is often explained without any special ties to the Aristotelian ontology in the modern parlance.[10] We (partly) follow this modern practice.

A crucial stage in the proof is step 6 designed to rule out the possibility of an infinite regress of one thing being altered by another thing. If there is an infinite regress, there would be nothing to initiate the change—Aquinas argues. But this presupposes that change must be linear and not circular. If the latter were the case, there would be no absolute initiator of change. For it may very well be that A changes B, B changes C, and so on, and that Y changes Z but Z in its turn changes A so that the whole thing is a circular process without any first point (or last point). But Aquinas does not show why change cannot be circular.

However, if one assumes the Aristotelian distinction between potency and act, the process of one thing being altered by another thing cannot be circular. In the Aristotelian scheme the actual (the mover) is ontologically prior to the potential (the moved) and this relationship can never be reversed. This may be why Aquinas assumes here that change is linear and not circular.

Is an infinite regress ruled out if change is linear? The reason given by Aquinas to rule it out is that then there would be nothing to bring about the first change, from which it is taken to follow that there could be no change, which is absurd.

That there is no change may be absurd. But does this follow? Clearly, that there is nothing to bring about the first change does not by itself logically imply that there can be no change. So once again some additional reason is necessary but Aquinas does not give one.

One could try to fill this gap in the reasoning by arguing that in the case of an infinite regress, an infinite number of causes must precede any change. But that makes any change impossible, for an infinite series cannot be completed.

This added reasoning, however, is open to challenge. First, while there may be some difficulty in holding that an infinite series is completed in a finite time, the difficulty would disappear if it is supposed that the time preceding any change is not finite but infinite. So to defend Aquinas one would have to show that the time preceding some change cannot be infinite. But Aquinas has not shown that and we do not see how that can be satisfactorily done. Second, whether time is finite or infinite, to speak of an infinite regress of causes before some change does not imply that an infinite series has been completed. It simply means that there is no finite number that is the upper limit for the series of preceding causes. This should be understood in the same sense in which it is true that any distance, however big or small, is divisible infinitely, or that the series of even numbers starting from 2 is infinite. In all these cases infinity means being open ended in one direction although the starting point of the series is fixed and finite. Since the starting point in each such series is already given and the very possibility of the infinite series depends on its acceptance, the regress cannot jeopardize the status of the starting point. Hence the infinite regression of causes before some change does not jeopardize the reality of that change, for the regression presupposes the reality of such change. This shows that an infinite regress is not always the downfall of a theory.[11] Thus the dismissal of the infinite regress of causes is on shaky ground and this renders the proof vulnerable.

The situation is different if the Aristotelian doctrine of potency and act is assumed. Since potency presupposes act, an infinite regression in this case is ruled out, for potentiality could not exist without actuality. Here the starting point of the regress could not exist unless the end point of the regress were granted first. Hence although an infinite regress is not harmful in the above case, it is unacceptable in this case. Thus the proof remains viable with the support from Aristotelian ontology, but not without it.

Another major flaw in the proof is that even if the proof were sound, it fails to show that the unmoved mover is a spirit. As Hume objected, there is nothing to rule out the possibility that the unmoved mover is a chunk of matter.[12]

Once again, this objection would lose force if the Aristotelian theory of potency and act were invoked. Since pure actuality must be devoid of all matter, the former can only be a spirit. This conclusion, however, would then depend on a particular metaphysical theory of spirit, form, and matter.

Aquinas has offered two other causal proofs of the existence of God. One of them is based on efficient causality and seeks to prove that there is a first uncaused efficient cause. The other is from necessity and contingency and seeks to prove that there is a necessary being. Even if these were sound, these too would not show that the uncaused cause or the necessary being is a spirit.

Aquinas has also presented an argument from design and tried to prove the existence of God as the designer of the universe. If this proof were sound, God as the designer would have to be a conscious being and a spirit. But the major weakness of this proof is that whether the universe has a design is very much open to doubt and would have to be proven first—but Aquinas merely takes that for granted.

Compared to the proofs of Aquinas, the Nyāya proof discussed earlier unambiguously shows God to be a spirit without assuming that the universe has a purpose. It infers God as the designer of the dyad, which indirectly makes God the designer of the universe as well. For the dyad is the ontologically first product and by setting the order of what is ontologically prior, God also sets indirectly the order of what is ontologically posterior. The Nyāya presents a well-argued case for the existence of atoms and thereby secures God as the designer of the dyad and indirectly of the whole world of change. Thus the universal purpose follows as a corollary of the proof and is not assumed as in the proof of Aquinas.

Further, as remarked earlier, the Nyāya proof is not critically dependent on the atomic theory. What it critically needs is something as the ontologically first product. The ontologically first product is identified with the dyad on the basis of the argument for the existence of atoms. The proof will work with some other theories of the ontologically first product as well. The viability of this proof also does not depend on the dismissal of an infinite regress of causes and the acceptance of an absolutely first temporal beginning of the world of change as it is with the proofs of Aquinas. The Nyāya proof, however, will still work if one dismisses the infinite regress of causes and accepts an absolutely first temporal beginning of the world of change. For then the dyad (or something else that will be the chosen candidate in some nonatomistic ontology) will be not only the ontologically first product but also the temporally first product and God will be inferred as the agent of that. Thus the ontological burden of the Nyāya proof is lighter than that of the causal proofs or of the teleological proof of Aquinas. The Nyāya proof combines a causal argument with a teleological argument and achieves that with a significantly thinner ontological base.

Another famous causal proof of the existence of God has been advanced by Descartes, the father of modern philosophy.[13] The essential steps of this proof are the following:

1. Nothing comes out of nothing.
2. Since nothing comes out of nothing, the cause may contain more than what is contained in the effect but cannot contain any less. (For example, the lump of clay out of which a pot is made may have more clay than what is found in that pot but cannot have any less.)
3. We have the idea of God as an infinite and perfect substance.
4. This idea, like every other idea, must have a cause.
5. We, human beings, cannot be the cause of this idea, for we are finite and imperfect while what is contained in this idea is infinity and perfection.
6. Since nothing finite or imperfect can be the cause of this idea, it follows that the cause is an infinite and perfect substance and thus that God exists.

In this way Descartes seeks to prove the existence of God as the cause of the idea of God. God, so to speak, has left his imprint or trademark in us, his favorite creatures.

One could object that since infinite means not finite, one could form the idea of the infinite merely by negating the finite. Thus a finite self could be the author of the idea an infinite substance. For such a self can be the cause of the idea of a finite substance and then derive the idea of God by adding the negative prefix.

Descartes anticipates this objection and responds by denying that infinity is a negative idea. He argues that since finite means being limited, it presupposes the idea of what is beyond the limit, that is, the infinite. Thus the infinite is logically prior to the finite and the former cannot be derived from the latter.[14] This reminds one of a key step in the well-known argument from recollection offered by Plato to prove the preexistence of the soul.[15] Plato too argued that knowledge of Forms such as that of equality cannot be derived from knowledge of particulars, for the former knowledge is presupposed in judging the particulars to be falling short of the ideal standards. In a similar vein Hegel argued, while criticizing Kant's view that our knowledge is limited to the phenomena and does not extend to the noumena, that to know the limit is to know what is beyond the limit.

However, the above argument is open to a number of objections, two of which may be indicated here. First, in many causal situations, particularly in those that involve chemical rather than physical change, the effect comes to acquire new properties missing in the cause. For example, water is H_2O, but water has properties such as that of liquidity that are not found in either hydrogen or oxygen. So the causal adequacy principle, namely, that the cause must contain all the features of the effect in at least as great a proportion, on which the proof is based, is questionable.[16]

Second, the causal adequacy principle is not applicable to causing ideas. What is contained in an idea should be distinguished from what is contained in something as a real feature of that thing. This is why the author of a fairy tale may cause the idea of a fairy in our minds without having the distinctive features of a fairy. The proof then seems to be based on a confusion between ideation and causation and between being the content of an idea and being the content of something as a characteristic of that thing.[17]

Needless to say, neither of these objections have any relevance for the Nyāya causal argument. In fact, the Nyāya philosophers have actively opposed anything like the causal adequacy principle, for they have argued for the view that an effect is a new (*asat*) entity that possesses features that are not potentially (*śakta*) contained in the cause. They have also sharply distinguished between the content (*viṣaya*) of an idea and the feature (*dharma*) of a thing. Last but not the least, they are opposed to the view that the immortal souls are created. One main argument for the immortality of the soul is based on that it is simple (*niravayava*). A simple substance cannot be created for the same reason for which it cannot be destroyed, namely, that it has no parts that can either be put together or taken apart.

The Nyāya causal proof, however, may be counterbalanced (*satpratipakṣita*) by the following argument:

> Whatever is not produced by anything with a body is not produced by a causal agent, for example, an atom.
>
> The first product is not produced by something with a body.
>
> Therefore, the first product is not produced by a causal agent.[18]

Clearly this counterargument is formally valid. A Nyāya philosopher should not question the truth of the second premise, for God, according to the Nyāya, is the causal agent of the first product and God does not have a body.[19] The first premise is supported by acceptable positive instances, for eternal entities such as atoms are not produced by anything. It is supported by acceptable negative instances too, for artifacts such as jars are produced by causal agents and are also produced by something with a body, such as a potter. No undisputable counterexamples are available. Thus the Nyāya proof and the counterargument appear to be equally matched. The opponent wins in such a situation, for the conclusion can no longer be claimed to be any more reasonable than its denial.

The way out for the Nyāya is to show that the counterargument is not an equal match but is actually weaker in some respect. One way to achieve this is by way of showing that while the first premise of the counterargument is not supported by a cogent subjunctive argument (*tarka*), the first premise of the Nyāya proof is so supported.[20]

This may be elaborated as follows. Although the general claim in the first premise is confirmed by both positive and negative examples and is not nullified by any counterexample, one could still harbor the doubt (*śaṃkā*) that the pervaded—that is, not being produced by anything with a body—could deviate from the so-called pervader, that is, not being produced by a causal agent. That is to say, one could still suppose it to be possible that something that is not produced by anything with a body is produced by a causal agent. Such a doubt entertaining the possibility of deviation (*vyabhicāra*) must be countered by a suitable subjunctive argument showing that if such were the case some undesirable consequence (*aniṣṭa-prasaṅga*) would result.[21] But the critic is unable to do this.

On the other hand, the general claim that every effect is produced by a causal agent can be backed up a cogent subjunctive argument if one were to entertain the doubt that there might be effects that were not produced by any causal agents. One such subjunctive argument is the following. If there were effects that were not produced by any causal agents, effecthood (*kāryatva*) could not be the limitor (*avacchedaka*) of the characteristic of being volitionally produced (*kṛtijanya*). A limitor, it may be noted, must be coextensive (*samaniyata*) with the limited (*avacchedya*).[22] But clearly, if there were effects that were not produced by any causal agents, there would be effects that were not volitionally produced; hence effecthood or the property of being an effect could not then be coextensive with being volitionally produced.

When it transpires that effecthood cannot be the limitor of the said property, the critic could suppose that each particular thing produced by a causal agent is in a particular effect-cause relationship (*viśeṣa-kārya-kāraṇa-bhāva*) with each particular volition and that there is no general causal connection (*sāmānya-kārya-kāraṇa-bhāva*) in such a situation. But this goes against the accepted rule (*niyama*) that those that are in particular effect-cause relationships embody, unless proven otherwise (*asati bādhake*), a general causal connection.[23] The critic could try to accommodate a general causal connection in such a case by offering the conjunction (*kūta*) of each particular volition as the limitor. But such a conjunction is a highly complex (*guru*) property and cannot be preferred over effecthood unless there are overriding considerations to the contrary.[24]

Yet another way in which the counterargument could be weakened is by challenging the second premise. It is true that in the standard Nyāya view God is a disembodied spirit. But this could be revised. It could be supposed that the eternal atoms constitute God's eternal body.[25] Unless the critic is able to show why such a supposition must be rejected, the truth of the second premise would become questionable and the counterargument weakened.

To conclude: There may not be any proof of the existence of God that is free from objections or controversies. But it should be apparent that the Nyāya causal proof is not open to the various objections to which some other famous causal proofs are open may, accordingly, be more defensible. It, therefore, given its place as a classical proof, deserves careful scrutiny.

CHAPTER 12

The Sāṃkhya View and the Nyāya Critique

In this chapter we look at the theory of the self developed by the Sāṃkhya school and some Nyāya critique of it. The Sāṃkhya, one of the oldest schools of Hindu philosophy, advocates a dualism of two ultimate principles (*tattva*) called *puruṣa* (person, soul) and *prakṛti* (nature, cause). The former is pure consciousness that never becomes the object of cognition (*aviṣaya*) and never undergoes any change (*apariṇāmin*). It is the witnessing subject (*sākṣin*) and the knower (*draṣṭā*) and free (*mukta*) and aloof (*udāsīna*) forever (SK 19).

By contrast *prakṛti*, though eternal like *puruṣa*, is constantly changing (*pariṇāmin*). It is devoid of consciousness (*jaḍa*, *acetana*) and the ultimate source of all objects of cognition including both physical objects such as pots and stones and internal states such as pleasure and pain (SK 11).

Prakṛti contains three kinds of substance called *sattva* (literally, being; essence, vitality, inherent power, courage, etc.), *rajas* (literally, dust; any small particle, menstrual discharge, passion, etc.), and *tamas* (literally, darkness; error, grief, etc.) (SK 11). These are called *guṇas*. A *guṇa* for the Nyāya signifies a quale and something dependent on a substance. But it would be a mistake to take the word *guṇa* in this sense here. *Guṇa* also means a connecting thread and *sattva rajas*, and *tamas* are called so because they are the common constituents or natures of all noneternal things. Moreover, *guṇa* means being subordinate and *sattva* and so on are so called because they are also for the use of something else (*parārtha*). However, they do have features such as whiteness and heaviness, and hence are better represented as substances (though the Sāṃkhya does not draw the distinction between a substance and a quale in the way the Nyāya does).

Sattva is of the nature of pleasure, *rajas* of pain, and *tamas* of perplexity and confusion (*moha*). *Sattva* is bright, light, and white and needed for revelation; *rajas* is red and needed for mobility, change, and effort; while *tamas* is dark and heavy and is responsible for inertia and ignorance (SK 13). These are each engaged in a battle for supremacy over the other two and remain intertwined. Each of the three substances is found in each noneternal thing though in varying proportions and dominance. Thus *sattva* is dominant in a rocket propelling upwards and *tamas*, in a stationary piece of stone. Still *tamas* is present in the rocket going upwards and helps to regulate and set a limit to its motion without which it would have gone on indefinitely. Similarly, *sattva* is present in a subdued form in a stationary stone, for otherwise it could not ever move upwards. Thus some measure of each *guṇa* is present in each thing. Here is another example: a poisonous snake may be a source of pleasure for its mate, but a source of pain for the one bitten by it and a source of confusion for one who is not yet bitten but near enough to be in the danger of being bitten by it—thus indicating the presence of all the three constituents in the snake. Again. all the three forces are at work in the processes of water vaporizing, forming clouds, and coming down as rain. The upward motion requires the lightness provided by *sattva* and the downward motion requires the weight provided by *tamas*; further, neither the upward nor the downward motion would be possible without the mobility of *rajas*. Both *sattva* and *tamas* are incapable of producing anything noneternal by themselves: it is only through the intervention of *rajas* that anything in particular takes place. In other words, nothing particular (*vyakti*) can happen unless all the three substances work together, although each seeks its own ascendancy over the other two.

Prakṛti is the primordial state when the three substances are in a perfect equilibrium (*sāmyāvasthā*). In this state no substance can dominate the other two though each continues to change independently into its own kind by itself and in complete isolation from the other two. That is, in this condition *sattva* transforms only into *sattva*, *rajas*, only into *rajas*, and *tamas*, only into *tamas*. So nothing particular evolves in this condition. Common predicates for particular things are not, accordingly, attributable to *prakṛti*. For example, a particular mango may be green and sour but *prakṛti* cannot be described as being of any particular color or particular taste. All noneternal entities evolve out of *prakṛti* and it contains them potentially within itself. Hence it is called their ultimate ground (*pradhāna*). But no specific features such as some particular shape or smell can be truly predicated of *prakṛti* and it is, therefore, described as the unmanifest (*avyakta*).

Creation or the origin of particular things begins when *puruṣa*, in accordance with the law of karma, comes into contact with *prakṛti*. *Sattva* being bright and transparent gains most from the proximity with *puruṣa* or consciousness (which also is transparent) and attains initial dominance over the other two. This inevitably brings the three *guṇa* substances together and sets off the process of each trying to dominate the others and the world of noneternal things evolves as a result (SK 21).

The first thing to evolve with the preponderance of *sattva* is called *mahat* or great because it is prior to and greater than all other noneternal things (SK 22). It represents the general determination (*adhyavasāya*) of something as something—the foundation of any act of judging and may, for the lack of anything better, be called reflectivity.[1]

The next thing to evolve is the sense of egoness (*ahaṃkāra*) which is represented in the awareness of I and mine to the exclusion of others (SK 22).

From egoness evolve the eleven sense organs (*indriya*) (SK 24). There are five cognitive organs (*jñānendriya*): the organs of seeing, hearing, smelling, tasting, and touching. There are also five action organs (*karmendriya*): the organs of speaking, handling, walking, excreting, and procreating. There is finally the inner sense (*manas*), which directly grasps internal states and coordinates the activities of all the ten other organs—thereby functioning as both a cognitive and an action organ (SK 26–27).

It may be noted that *Buddhi* (reflectivity), *ahaṃkāra* (egoness), and *manas* (the inner sense) are also together referred to as the internal organ (*antaḥkaraṇa*). Their usefulness may from one point of view be explained as follows:

1. Without the inner sense we cannot account for absent-mindedness (*vyāsaṅga*) when a cognitive organ receives an impression from an external object but no notice is taken of that thing.

2. Without egoness we cannot account for such dream states as "I am a tiger," for the inner sense is incapable of making a judgment about an external object unless it is activated by an external organ.

3. Without *buddhi* we cannot explain how vital processes go on even in a deep sleep when no activity of either the inner sense or egoness can be noticed.

The internal organ comprising the inner sense, egoness, and *buddhi* has priority over the external organs like the eye. Without the internal organ, the external organ cannot function as a cognitive organ at all. The external organ can only come into contact with an external object, but cognition is possible only when the internal organ is activated. Another indication of the priority of the internal organ over the external organ is that each external organ is restricted to a particular kind of object. For example, the eye can grasp color but not smell. The nose can grasp smell but not color and so on. But the internal organ is not restricted in this way.

From egoness also evolve the subtle matter essences (*tanmātra*) (SK 25). From the latter evolve five kinds of gross matter: earth, water, fire, air, and *ākāśa*, from the last of which space and time emerged. Then are evolved particular physical objects and internal states.

It should be pointed out that the order of creation or evolution is not chronological. Both space and time are products of the process of evolution. In the Sāṃkhya view neither space nor time is indispensable for the basic act of judging something as something. They are also not indispensable for egoness nor for the mere possibility of sense organs and matter. But they are useful for the explanation of particular material objects as well as internal states. However, neither space nor time should be thought to be additional entities (as held by the Nyāya-Vaiśeṣika). Spatial divisions (such as the space of this room) and temporal divisions (such as a moment) can only be made with reference to the things and events in space and time. This suggests that spatial and temporal divisions and, in the next step, space and time themselves are onotologically reducible to the things and events in space and time. So the order of creation is transcendental and represents what should be the case, given the Sāṃkhya understanding of the basic scheme of things.

It is also clear that *prakṛti*, the ultimate source of all noneternal things, cannot be described as physical or mental. Both material objects and internal states come out of the same basic stuff, which is beyond the physical/mental division.[2] The crucial difference between the so-called noneternal physical objects and internal states is that while in the former the opaque and heavy *tamas* becomes relatively predominant, in the latter the relative domination belongs to the transparent *sattva*—all three constituents being nevertheless present in both physical objects and internal states. It may be remembered that both subtle matter and the sense organs are held to evolve from egoness. Subtle matter evolves from egoness out of its *tamas* constituent called *bhūtādi*. On the other hand, the sense organs evolve from egoness out of its *sattva* constituent called *vaikārika*. *Sattva* is light (*laghu*) and revealing (*prakāśaka*). So the sense organs, which act swiftly in grasping an object or getting something done, are linked to *sattva*. By contrast most ordinary material things are heavy and serve as barriers to revelation. So their source is linked to *tamas*, which too is heavy (*guru*) and serves as a concealer (*āvaraka*) rather than a revealer. The important point of course is that both the sense organs (i.e., cognitive and action capacities) and subtle matter essences are held to evolve from the same principle called egoness and not from radically different sources.

So for ordinary physical objects and internal states the Cartesian type or the Nyāya-Vaiśeṣika type of dualism is unacceptable from the Sāṃkhya point of view, for the ultimate constituents for both are one and the same—the three *guṇas*. But the Sāṃkhya does advocate the dualism of the subject and the object. The subject or *puruṣa* is pure consciousness and unchanging. All objects including both particular physical objects and internal states are unconscious and changing.

The Sāṃkhya thus advocates the thesis of unconscious cognitive states. A cognitive state is a transformation (*vṛtti*) of *mahat*, which is also called *citta* or *buddhi*. This is to be taken literally. The cognition of a pot is literally the transformation of the *buddhi* as a pot. The *buddhi* is unconscious and so also is its transformation. It makes no difference whether what is cognized is a physical object such as a pot or an internal state such as pleasure. In either case the cognitive state is an unconscious transformation of the unconscious *buddhi* or reflectivity.

Let us look at the Sāṃkhya account of perception (*pratyakṣa*). When a sense organ becomes related to an external object such as a pot, the reflection (*pratibimba*) of that object is cast on that organ. Then the organ carries that reflection over to the *buddhi*. The *buddhi*, being dominated by *sattva*, is transparent and luminous. When the reflection of the object is carried on to it, the *buddhi* assumes the form (*ākāra*) of that object. This transformation of the *buddhi* in the form of an object is an unconscious state. But since it is transparent, it is capable of receiving the reflection of *puruṣa* or consciousness. When the reflection of *puruṣa* falls on the transformation of the *buddhi* as some object, there is cognition of that object (SKN 264). The cognition is not a quale (*guṇa*) of the self as held by the Nyāya. The cognition is a modification of the *buddhi* and belongs to the latter. Thus cognition is a real modification of the *buddhi* but not of *puruṣa*. The latter remains unaffected by the process just as the sun is not affected by its reflection in the water. If there is current in the water containing the reflection of the sun, the sun may appear to be moving. But the movement is of that water alone and not of the sun. Similarly, the transformation taking place in the event of cognition or any other internal state is that of the *buddhi* alone and not of *puruṣa*. However, the reflection of *puruṣa* enables the unconscious *buddhi* to reveal the object in the way the moon is able to reveal things by borrowing the light of the sun although the moon has no light of its own.

Can more than one cognitions take place simultaneously? Vacaspati Misra, following Isvarakrsna, says that it happens sometimes. He gives the following as an example. Suppose that lightning strikes when it is totally dark and one suddenly sees in that light that there is a ferocious animal in front. Then on the spur of the moment one decides instantly to flee or take some other action. Since there is no time for deliberation here, the modifications of the external sense organ, the inner sense, egoness, and *buddhi* or reflectivity must be said to take place at the same time (STK 364).

However, in the Sāṃkhya view there is a causal sequence in such a case. First the external sense organ must be activated. Only after that can the inner sense make a judgment that this is (for example) a tiger. The eye, in the Sāṃkhya view, cannot make this judgment, for it can only receive the impression. The inner sense cannot make the judgment on its own, for it is totally dependent on the eye to first pass on the information. The egoness (producing the awareness that this concerns me) can be operative only after the inner sense makes the judgment that this is, say, a tiger. Only after that modification of egoness takes place can *buddhi* or reflectivity make the decision that I should flee (or take some other action). Because of this causal sequence, which involves a chronological order, it is far from clear how all these cognitions can take place at the same time. Should the causal sequence be understood in a nontemporal sense? If so, neither Isvarakrsna nor Vacaspati Misra have given any indication of how that should be construed.

It may be noted here that Gotama and many other Nyāya philosophers deny that cognitions are ever simultaneous. They hold that in cases where more than one cognition appear to take place at the same time, the temporal gap between the cognitions is too small to be noticed. Perhaps this is a better option for the Sāṃkhya as well. In other words, if the causal sequence in the modifications of the external organ, the inner sense, egoness, and *buddhi* is to be accepted, it appears to be more sensible to deny that cognitions are ever simultaneous. On the other hand, no major Nyāya doctrine (except the one involving the atomicity of the inner sense) is compromised if cognitions are allowed to be (sometimes) simultaneous. That is why Nyāya thinkers such as Raghunatha Siromani have disagreed with Gotama, accepted that more than one cognition may take place simultaneously, and made the needed revision in their theory that the inner sense is a nonatomic, physical substance. No such easy solution appears to be open to the Sāṃkhya in order to admit the possibility of simultaneous cognitions, unless the causal sequence can be shown to be nontemporal. The latter seems to be a difficult option. We are not here dealing with the evolutionary process of basic principles such as *buddhi*, a process that is admittedly nontemporal. What we have here are cognitions of a living person that, in the Sāṃkhya view as well, are temporal events. So it is unclear how can this be reconciled with the possibility of simultaneous cognitions, given the Sāṃkhya analysis of the process.[3]

Why should one accept the existence of *prakṛti*? The Sāṃkhya offers a variety of arguments, one of which is the following. All ordinary things serve as sources of pleasure, pain, and confusion (or indifference) in varying degrees under different circumstances (SK 15). There is nothing particular that is absolutely pleasurable or absolutely painful or absolutely confusing (or indifferent). From this it may be inferred that each such thing has in varying degrees the sources of pleasure, pain, and confusion in itself. Similarly, all ordinary things are found to possess in varying degrees the characteristics of being light, being heavy, and being mobile. There is nothing particular that is absolutely light or absolutely heavy or absolutely mobile. From this it may be inferred that each such thing has in varying degrees the sources of lightness, heaviness, and mobility within itself. These three sources are called *sattva*, *rajas*, and *tamas*, which, therefore, are the three basic substances within the constitution of all ordinary things. We also find that all ordinary things change and the degree of lightness or pleasantness, and so on, of the same thing undergoes change. From this it may be inferred that the three substances are together within the nature of each such thing but are engaged in a process of trying to dominate each other.

It is important to note that all effects are potentially contained in the cause. For example, a clay pot is potentially in the lump of clay out of which it is fashioned, a statue is potentially in the rock out of which it is carved, oil is potentially in the oil seed, and so on. It should also be noticed that the cause is greater than the effect. From these two theses, if accepted, it may be inferred that all ordinary things are potentially contained in an ultimate causal ground (*upādāna*) that is greater than any such things and from which they are evolved (SK 15). Such an ultimate ground of all evolved things can only be the equilibrium of the three substances found in each evolved thing. If one of the substances were dominant in the ultimate ground, the latter would have acquired some degree of specificity and could not have the potentiality for every evolved thing. The equilibrium of the three substances is called *prakṛti*, which literally means nature, cause, and so forth.

Why should one accept the existence of *puruṣa*? The Sāṃkhya offers various arguments, one of which is based on the premise that the subject and the object of cognition must be different. This is strictly interpreted to imply that the subject cannot be the object and the object cannot be the subject. If this is granted, since all evolved things, including the internal states, are objects of cognition, it must be inferred that there is a subject that is different from all of them. Such a subject is called *puruṣa* (SK 19). It can only be pure consciousness. There can be no object without consciousness, that is, nothing can be cognized without consciousness. At the same time, there can be no object without the subject, that is, nothing can be cognized without the subject. Thus the pure subject presupposed by each and every object is pure consciousness.

A living person is an evolute of *prakṛti*, which is devoid of consciousness. In other words, a living person is a product of the three unconscious substances called *sattva*, *rajas*, and *tamas*. The body is dominated by tamas and the internal states are dominated by *sattva*. Cognition and other internal states appear to be conscious, as we have seen, because of the reflection of *puruṣa* or consciousness in them. But in reality they are devoid of consciousness. Thus in a way the Sāṃkhya agrees with the materialist who claims that consciousness is nowhere to be found either in the body or in the internal states. The bodily states and the internal states are not radically different (as a Cartesian dualist claims, in the former being unconscious and extended and the latter being conscious and unextended). Insofar as this goes, the Sāṃkhya promotes a kind of reductionism, for it traces both the bodily states and the internal states back to the same kind of source. But it would be a mistake to label this common source as matter and describe the Sāṃkhya as "clearly tending in the direction of a reductive materialism."[4] We have seen that both material and mental phenomena in the customary senses evolve from the same basic stuff, which, therefore, cannot be categorized as either material or mental. This basic stuff is better represented as something neutral.

Accordingly, insofar as the Sāṃkhya traces both bodily states and internal states back to the same neutral source, it may with some reservation be said to be tending in the direction of a reductive neutralism. Further, the Sāṃkhya is far from espousing materialism, for it advocates the existence of pure consciousness (*puruṣa*) and denies the very possibility of there being a living person or a body or other material objects or internal states unless there is reflection of consciousness on (or at least the compresence of consciousness with) the transformations of *prakṛti*, the neutral source of everything non-eternal, objective (*viṣaya*), and manifested (*vyakti*).

It is worth noting that neither gross matter (*mahābhūta*) nor subtle matter (*tanmātra*) can evolve unless there are the sense organs, egoness (*ahaṃkāra*), and reflectivity (*buddhi*). There is a priority of the sense organs since otherwise everything could become the object of consciousness all at once. Clearly, not everything is revealed to *puruṣa* all at once and this is because revelation is channeled through the sense organs, the capacities of which are limited. Further, revelation is always tied to a particular ego or I who alone gets to cognize in distinction from the others. So egoness should precede the sense capacities for revealing objects. This applies equally to internal states and physical objects. Both internal states and physical objects are revealed to some egos in distinction from the others. Revelation is also not possible without reflectivity or the determination of something as something. So egoness and reflectivity precede physical objects and internal objects alike.

Thus reflectivity and egoness are sources, though not immediate, of ordinary material states as well. These sources do not fit the ordinary notion of matter as something filling space. These sources in turn have evolved from *prakṛti* and its light, mobile, and heavy constituents with the help of the compresence of *puruṣa* or consciousness (which is not a source). The actual sources are, like *prakṛti*, devoid of consciousness. Still, they point to an evolutionary process that unmistakably links the emergence of both material and mental phenomena to manifestation (*vyakti*). The process cannot be described as exclusively material or exclusively mental. The process points to the deeper, common foundations of both materiality and mentality as ordinarily conceived—foundations that potentially have features of both but not specifically and actually. The internal states are subtle (*sūkṣma*) and private (*āntara*) and ordinary material objects are gross (*sthūla*) and public (*sāmānya*). The same neutral process accounts for both kinds of evolutes with their relatively distinctive features. Reflectivity and egoness contain the kind of transparency that can account for the privacy of internal states. At the same time, they also contain heavy and dark *tamas*, which can account for the grossness of physical objects.

We now move on to consider how Gotama and Vatsyayana have, from their Nyāya perspective, criticized an important Sāṃkhya view. Vatsyayana begins the discussion with a prefatory remark on Gotama's aphorism 3.2.1: "now is the time to examine cognition as to whether it is eternal or noneternal. Why the doubt?" As an answer to the question why the doubt is there, Vatsyayana cites NS 3.2.1: "There is doubt because of similarity with [both] action [which is noneternal] and *ākāśa* [which is eternal]." Vatsyayana explains the point of the aphorism: "The lack of touch, which is the common feature of those two, is found in cognition, but no distinctive feature . . . is found; hence the doubt" (NSB 3.2.1). So what is to be examined is whether cognition is eternal or noneternal. Cognition lacks touch. Some noneternal entities like action lack touch. Some eternal entities like *ākāśa* (the substratum of sound) also lack touch. Since cognition is found to be similar to both eternal and noneternal entities in the respect of lacking touch and since no feature of cognition which belongs only to something eternal or only to something noneternal is known, there is doubt over whether cognition is eternal or noneternal.

The present point of disagreement between the Nyāya and the Sāṃkhya over cognition may be explained thus. In the Nyāya view, *buddhi* or cognition is a fleeting quale (*guṇa*) of the self and does not usually endure for more than two moments. But in the Sāṃkhya view *buddhi* or reflectivity is the first evolute of *prakṛti*. Each *puruṣa* has its own distinctive *buddhi* that endures from the beginning of evolution to the time of liberation (*mokṣa*)—a time span that may last for billions of years. So *buddhi* is not strictly eternal in the Sāṃkhya view but is still something that endures for a very long time. It should also be kept in mind that in the Sāṃkhya view *buddhi* as an effect preexists in *prakṛti* in a potential form before evolving and again returns to *prakṛti* in a latent form after ceasing to exist. So Vatsyayana may have described *buddhi* as eternal with this Sāṃkhya view in mind. However, in spite of Vatsyayana's terminology, the real issue is whether cognition is something fleeting or something that lasts for a very long time.

Vatsyayana continues:

> This doubt is inappropriate. Every person knows directly himself that cognition is noneternal like pleasure, etc. There is also the cognition 'I shall cognize', 'I cognize', and 'I

> cognized'. . . . [I]t is thus known that cognition is non-eternal. . . . Still the section is for refuting a received viewpoint. . . . [T]he Sāṃkhya holds that *buddhi*, which is the internal organ of *puruṣa*, is eternal. An argument is also offered. (NSB 3.2.1)

So Vatsyayana observes that there is no real room for doubt as to whether cognition is eternal or noneternal. Every person already knows directly from his or her own experience that his or her cognitions are noneternal. We commonly have such experiences as that I cognized something (which cognition is now gone) or that I cognize something (which cognition did not exist before) or that I shall cognize something (which cognition is yet to take place). This clearly shows that some cognitions are past, some are present but did not exist in the past, and some are future and do not exist now. Such cognitions must be noneternal. There is no evidence from our personal experience of any kind of cognition that endures in all the three orders of time. Still the discussion is called for to examine and refute the Sāṃkhya view that *buddhi* as the internal organ of *puruṣa* is eternal, that is; strictly speaking, enduring for a very long time.

Gotama cites a reason that may be offered for holding that *buddhi* endures for a very long time: "Because there is recognition of objects" (NS 3.2.2). Vatsyayana elaborates:

> What is such recognition? 'I cognize this thing which I cognized before'—thus recognition involves the awareness of two cognitions sharing the same object; this can be accounted for if *buddhi* is enduring. If there were many incoming and outgoing *buddhis*, recognition cannot be explained, for one cannot recognize something cognized by another. (NSB 3.2.2)

According to the Sāṃkhya, *buddhi*, and not *puruṣa* or consciousness, is the active agent (*kartā*) and cognition, pleasure, and so on, are transformations of unconscious *buddhi* and not of *puruṣa*, which never undergoes any change. That is to say, since *puruṣa* or consciousness never undergoes any change, cognitions and so on, which are transformations, can only be transformations of something else that is unconscious and that is called *buddhi*. The latter must be enduring and not something fleeting. Otherwise there could be no recognition of the same thing at a later time. If cognitions were as fleeting as the Nyāya holds, the former cognition could not endure till the time the later cognition takes place and recognize that both cognitions have the same object.

Gotama replies: "Not a reason because of being in need of proof" (NS 3.2.3). Vatsyayana comments:

> Just as it needs to be proved that *buddhi* is eternal [i.e., enduring] so also it needs to proved that recognition belongs to *buddhi*. Why? Because that which belongs to something conscious cannot be ascribed to an instrument. Cognition or awareness or apprehension or knowledge or determination is clearly the property of a person. Indeed, it is what is conscious that recognizes a thing previously cognized; it stands to reason that that [= the conscious self or cognizer but not an unconscious instrument] should be eternal [i.e., enduring] on this ground. If an instrument is admitted to be conscious, the nature of what is conscious should be spelt out. It cannot be claimed to be known that a self which is different exists unless its nature can be specified. If it is admitted that cognition belongs to the internal organ [= *buddhi*], then what is the nature of what is conscious? What is its character? What is its essence? What does this conscious entity do with the cognition belonging to *buddhi*? Suppose it is said to be conscious? No, this does not speak of anything different from cognition. 'The person becomes conscious', '*buddhi* cognizes'—this does not amount to speaking of anything different from cognition. Becomes conscious, cognizes, sees, apprehends—these are synonymous. Suppose it is said that *buddhi* makes known? That is, *buddhi* makes known and the person cognizes. This is true. But if this is admitted, cognition is shown to belong to the person, not to *buddhi*, the internal organ. Again, if different notions are exclusively predicated of different persons, the ground for rejection should be stated. It may be proposed that one person is conscious, another cognizes, yet another apprehends, still another sees: that is, the conscious, the cognizer, the apprehender, the seer—these are different persons and these properties do not belong to the same being. What is the ground for rejecting this? Suppose it is said that the thing is the same? But then there is parity. That is to say, it may be claimed that these notions are synonymous and hence the differentiation is unjustified. Then there is parity. The person is conscious, *buddhi* cognizes—here also the thing does not become different. Since in this way both turn out to be conscious, either has to go. Suppose it is said that by *buddhi* is meant that which serves as the instrument of cognition

> and that it is the same as the inner sense (*manas*), which is (in the Nyāya view as well) eternal? Let it be so. But still the inner sense cannot be said to be eternal on the ground that there is recognition of things. Even when the instruments are different, recognition becomes possible if the cognizer is the same. For example, what is seen by the left eye may be recognized by the other . . . again, what is seen with one lamp may be recognized with another lamp. So this [= recognition] is a ground for the eternality [i.e., endurance] of the cognizer. (NSB 3.2.3)

Vatsyayana raises several objections against the Sāṃkhya position. First, it cannot be automatically assumed that *buddhi* is the agent of recognition, so that *buddhi* can be shown to be an enduring entity on that ground. *Buddhi* after all is unconscious; but only something conscious can cognize and recognize something. So how can *buddhi* be the recognizer? The point is: while the conclusion may be open to contention, the premise should not be so. The Sāṃkhya claims that *buddhi*, the unconscious internal organ, is enduring because it is the recognizer. But whether something unconscious can be the recognizer is open to contention, for, at least in the Nyāya view, only something conscious can be the recognizer. So what should be debated first is whether something unconscious can be the cognizer or recognizer—a debate that the Nyāya fully expects the Sāṃkhya to lose or at least to be open enough to render the present argument fallacious. That is why Gotama labels the ground offered as a nonreason (*ahetu*), that is, as a pseudo-probans (*hetvābhāsa*). 'What is equally or similarly in need of being proved' (*sādhyasama*), it may be noted, is the fourth kind of pseudo-probans listed by Gotama.[5]

Second, in the Nyāya view, the arguments for which have been presented in the earlier chapters, consciousness (*cetanā*), cognition (*jñāna*), seeing (*darśana*), apprehension (*upalabdhi*), understanding (*bodha*). determination (*adhyavasāya*), and so on, are all internal activities or states that belong to the self or person (*ātman*, *puruṣa*). So the fact of recognition supports the idea that the self or person, but not the unconscious internal organ called *buddhi*, is an enduring entity.

Third, one may claim, though this is not the Sāṃkhya view, that although the internal organ is an instrument (*karaṇa*), it is still conscious. The Nyāya would dispute this, for that all instruments are unconscious is a generalization well supported by undisputed positive instances such as an axe, a hammer, and so on, there being no undisputed counterexamples. If, in spite of this, one insists that both the person and the internal organ are conscious, the problem will be: On what ground, then, can the person be properly distinguished from the internal organ? We cannot merely say that while the person is conscious, the internal organ is the cognizer. For consciousness and cognition are synonymous. The point is better appreciated if we consider the following scenario. One may hold for the sake of argument that the person who is conscious, the person who cognizes, the person who apprehends, the person who sees—these are different persons. That is, a living being is a conglomeration of many persons. This is not the Sāṃkhya view; but on what ground will this view be rejected? One obvious ground is that consciousness, cognition, and so on, stand for the same activity, state, or process, so that the admission of all these different persons is not justified. If this is accepted, that goes equally against holding that the person and the internal organ are both different, conscious entities making up the life of the same individual. It appears then that the nature of such a conscious person that is different from the conscious internal organ may not even be clearly specified or spelt out. Under the circumstances, the admission of both would be superfluous and the existence of either the conscious person or the conscious organ would have to be denied.

Fourth, the Nyāya has no objection to accepting the internal organ as an instrument of the self and as an enduring thing but does object to accepting recognition as a ground for that. For there are cases where the instruments are different and recognition still takes place because the cognizer is the same. For example, one can recognize that something seen with the help of a lamp is the same as what was previously seen with the help of another lamp. Since the two lamps are different (apart from the obvious fact that the lamps are unconscious), the second lamp cannot recognize what was seen with the first. Since in this case recognition cannot be a ground for the endurance of the lamps, in the given case of *buddhi* as an instrument as well recognition becomes a wrong ground. What recognition points to is the endurance and unity of the conscious cognizer that uses *buddhi* as an instrument, just as in the given example recognition points to the endurance and unity of the conscious cognizer that uses both the lamps.

Gotama raises another issue: "No, because there is lack of simultaneous cognitions" (NS 3.2.4). "And if there is lack of recognition, the cessation [of *buddhi*] follows as a consequence" (NS 3.2.5). Vatsyayana amplifies:

> It is held (by the Sāṃkhya) that from the existing *buddhi* there come out transformations which are cognitions in accordance with what the objects are and that the transformation and the transformed are not different. That "is not acceptable, because there is lack of simultaneous cognitions." If the transformation and the transformed were nondifferent, since the transformed is existent, the transformations would be existent too. Then, all these cognitions of objects being existent, there would have been simultaneous cognitions [of all objects]. (NSB 3.2.4)

> And if there is cessation of recognition, there is cessation of the transformed as well. This involves as a consequence the destruction of the internal organ. If this is denied, difference [of cognitions from *buddhi*] follows. (NSB 3.2.5)

Gotama is attacking the Sāṃkhya view that cognitions are transformations of *buddhi* and that, as transformations, are nondifferent from *buddhi*. This position is a consequence of the over all Sāṃkhya stand that an effect is already existent potentially in the cause and that nothing new ever comes into being nor is anything existent ever lost. The viewpoint is attacked by the Nyāya in various ways. Here Gotama is simply spelling out one special difficulty of this view when applied to the case of cognition. The difficulty seems to be based on an application of the [implied] law of indiscernibility of identicals: that if two things are nondifferent, what is possessed by or true of one is also possessed by or true of the other and vice versa. If cognitions and the internal organ called *buddhi* are nondifferent, since the internal organ is existent, cognitions are existent too. Then there should be cognition of virtually everything at the same time, for all past, present, and future cognitions of whatever is cognized are existent. But of course there is no recognition of all these different objects at the same time. From this would follow that those cognitions are nonexistent. For if those cognitions were existent, there would have been recognition of all the objects of the cognitions. However, if the cognitions are nonexistent, the internal organ, being nondifferent from them, is nonexistent too. This would go against the Sāṃkhya view that the same internal organ endures until there is liberation. One can surely deny all this and hold that although the internal organ endures, cognitions do not. But then one would also embrace the Nyāya view and hold that the internal organ and the cognitions are different.

CHAPTER 13

The Advaita View And The Nyāya Critique

We now consider another highly influential view of the self in the Indian philosophical tradition, that of the Advaita Vedānta school. The Advaita shares with the Sāṃkhya the view that the self is pure consciousness. But while the Sāṃkhya admits two ultimate principles called *puruṣa*, which is pure consciousness, and *prakṛti*, which is the source of all objects of consciousness, in the Advaita view consciousness alone is real (*sat*). Everything other than consciousness is unreal (*asat*) and, from the ultimate (*pāramārthika*) standpoint, does not exist now, has not existed in the past, and will not exist in the future. Since the self and consciousness are the same, it follows that the self alone is real and everything other than the self is unreal. The individual self (*jīva*), according to the Advaita, is nothing other than the supreme self (*paramātman*, *brahman*). Accordingly, the Advaita disowns the Sāṃkhya view that there is a plurality of selves and holds that *ātman* or the self and *brahman* or the absolute are one and the same, both being nothing but pure consciousness, the only reality.

In such Vedic statements as that *brahman* is infinite existence and consciousness (*satyam jñānam anantam brahma*) *brahman* and consciousness are declared to be the same. Again, in other Vedic statements as "Thou art that" (*tattvamasi*), "I am he" (*soham*), and so on, the individual self is identified with the universal self. According to the Vedas, then, *brahman*, *ātman*, and consciousness are one and the same and this rules out treating consciousness as a quale (*guṇa*) of the self. In the Nyāya-Vaiśeṣika view, consciousness is a quale of the self and different from the latter. This, according to the Advaita, conflicts with the Vedic statements cited above. Further, the self is that which makes possible the cognizing of anything cognized, of the hearing of any sound, of the tasting of any food, or the use of any sentence. In the same way consciousness is that which makes possible the cognizing of anything cognized, of the hearing of any sound, and so on. This goes to support that the self and consciousness are not different.

According to the Advaita, the main evidence for the view that the self is consciousness comes from Vedic statements. All Vedic statements are true and like all other true statements the truth of Vedic statements is intrinsic (*svataḥ*). In other words, the truth of the cognition communicated through such a statement is apprehended through that cognition itself.[1] In the Nyāya view the truth of a cognition is extrinsic (*parataḥ*). That is, truth is gathered from a subsequent confirmatory process, such as success of some action (*pravṛtti-sāmarthya*) resulting from such cognition or coherence (*saṃvāda*) with other accepted views. But if truth were extrinsic, the Advaitins object, how can the truth of subsequent cognition be itself confirmed? Granting that truth is extrinsic, the truth of the subsequent cognition can only be confirmed by yet another cognition. But this surely opens the door of an infinite regress. If the regress is stopped at some point and some cognition is accepted as self-certifying, why not accept other true cognitions as self-certifying too? In the words of Vacaspati Misra:

> How can all these, the truth of which has not been determined, come to the rescue of the initiating cogition? On the other hand, if the truth of it [confirmatory cognition] is regarded as *svataḥ*, what is wrong with the initiating cognition, so that it too should not be so? (*Tīkā* 24)

Although truth is intrinsic, the falsity of a cognition, according to the Advaita, is extrinsic. That is, the falsity of a cognition can be gathered from a subsequent disconfirmatory process, such as unsuccessful activity resulting from the cognition. So arguing for the truth of a Vedic statement declaring that the self and consciousness is the same is not useless. Such arguing can show that an alleged disconfirmation of a Vedic statement is itself liable to be disconfirmed.

Accordingly, the Advaitins offer dialectical support for Vedic statements saying that the self is consciousness. If the self were different from consciousness, it would have to be *jaḍa* or matter, for the division between consciousness (*cetanā*) and matter (*jaḍa*), like that between the subject (*viṣayain*) and the object (*viṣaya*), is not only mutually exclusive but also collectively exhaustive.

In the Advaita view cognition or *jñāna* (which is the same as the self) primarily means pure consciousness, which is the only reality and timeless as well as changeless (AD 252). But from the empirical (*vyavahārika*) perspective a modification (*vṛtti-jñāna*) is regarded as cognition in a secondary sense. This is similar to the Sāṃkhya view to some extent, for the Sāṃkhya too distinguishes between *puruṣa* or pure consciousness, which is timeless as well as changeless, and cognition as *vṛtti*, which is a modification of *buddhi* (reflectivity) or *mahat* (the great), the first evolute of *prakṛti*, the latter being the primordial source of all objects of cognition.[2] However, in the Sāṃkhya view both cognition in the primary sense of pure consciousness and cognition in the secondary sense of modification of *buddhi* or reflectivity are real. But in the Advaita view cognition in the secondary sense exists only from the empirical standpoint (*vyavahārika-sattā*) and has no reality from the ultimate standpoint (*pāramārthika-asattā*).

Further, the Advaita, unlike the Sāṃkhya, distinguishes between two kinds of modification: modification of the inner organ (*antaḥ-karaṇa*) and modification of nescience (*avidyā*). The former is our awareness of public objects such as a pot or a cloth that are common to many cognizers. It is considered to be veridical (*pramā*) from the empirical point of view, for its object is not sublated (*bādhita*) until there is the liberating knowledge of *brahman*. In the Advaita view the inner organ is a composite substance that is capable of contraction and expansion. It is predominantly made of the transparent *guṇa* called *sattva* (again, similarity with the Sāṃkhya is noticeable) and receives the reflection of consciousness. When something is perceived, the inner organ exits through an external sense organ and assumes the form (*ākāra*) of the perceived object. Thus it removes the cover of ignorance and allows the perceived thing to be revealed like light dispelling darkness.

The second kind of modification is that of nescience. This is illustrated by such a misperception as that of mistaking a shell for silver. It is nonveridical (*apramā*), for the silver is sublated by the corrective cognition of the shell as shell. In the Advaita view nescience is the underlying stuff (*upādāna*) of all nonveridical cognition. Such cognition fails to remove the cover of ignorance and fails to reveal the nature of the object (GB 545).

The Advaitins argue that when the victim of an illusion gets to know his mistake, he also knows that the illusory object does not exist in the locus (*adhiṣṭhāna*) of illusion. For example, when a person realizes that the thing before him that he misperceived as silver is actually a shell, he also realizes that nothing silvery existed in the thing before him—that the thing in front (which was misperceived and which, therefore, is the locus of illusion) was not a piece of silver. So the illusory object cannot be real (*sat*). If it were real, the perception could not be false. But, at the same time, it cannot be unreal, for nothing unreal, given that the perceived object activates our sense organ, can be perceived. So the illusory object is neither real nor unreal and is, therefore, indescribable (*anirvacanīya*). For example, in the Advaita view, an indescribable silver is produced when the shell is misperceived as silver (VP 93). It does not exist in the empirical (*vyavahārika*) sense but it does exist as an appearance (*pratibhāsa*) as long as the illusion lasts.

The locus of illusion, the shell in our example, of course exists in the empirical sense, for it is not sublated by the corrective awareness. If an illusion is described as 'this is that', the ontological statuses of the 'this' part and the 'that' part are different. The 'this' part is empirically (*vyavahārika*) existent. But the 'that' part is only apparently (*prātibhāsika*) existent. Since the perception of the 'this' part is empirically true, it is said to be a modification of the inner sense. But since the perception of the 'that' part is false, it is said to be a modification of nescience or ignorance. Put differently, illusion results from ignorance about the emprical nature of the locus of illusion, so that the cover of ignorance is not removed.

It may be gathered from the above that in the Advaita view a cognition is veridical if its object is not sublated (VP 9). In the misperception of a shell as silver the latter is sublated by the later corrective awareness of the shell as shell. The shell is not sublated by another empirical awareness; hence the awareness of the shell as shell is veridical from the empirical standpoint. As already said, all empirical objects are sublated, according to the Advaita, by the transcendent knowledge of *brahman*. The latter alone is veridical in the ultimate sense.

According to some Advaitins, a cognition is not excellent unless it has novelty and its object is not previously cognized (VP 7). This rules out memory as ever being accepted as excellent cognition. However, the continuing perception of the same thing (*dhārāvāhika pratyakṣa*) may still be accepted as excellent cognition. The continuing perception is a unitary cognition and endures till its place is taken by another internal state (VP 11). So it does not lack novelty.

From the transcendent (*pāramārthika*) standpoint cognition (as well as the self) is nondual (*advaita*). If many cognitions were admitted, we end up admitting many other entities, such as the common property of cognitionness (*jñānatva*) shared by all cognitions, the relation of inherence (*samavāya*) between the universal cognitionness and particular cognitions, the prior absence (*prāgabhāva*) and posterior absence (*dhvaṃsābhāva*) of cognitions and so on. This, according to the Advaita, goes against considerations of economy (*lāghava*).

At the same time, even a nondualist cannot deny that there is a difference between the cognition of a pot and that of a cloth, for such difference is a matter of experience (*anubhava*). However, the Advaitin offers to explain such difference by bringing in the specifiers (*avacchedaka*) of cognitions. That is, the cognition of a pot is ontologically the same as the cognition of a cloth. Still the former may be distinguished from the latter on the ground that the former has a pot as its object and is, therefore, specified by a pot while the latter has a cloth as its object and is, therefore, specified by a cloth (GMS 2.17). It is a matter of common experience that what is true of one entity when specified by some character may not be true of the same entity when specified by a different character. For example, the president of a country may have the authority to pardon a convicted criminal on death row but would not have that authority when he is no longer the president. Here we have the same individual. But what is true of him insofar as he is the president is not always true of him otherwise. This shows that an entity may remain the same even when its specifiers are different.

This is not denied by the Nyāya philosophers who are staunch pluralists. In their view also space is one and infinite; but it is demarcated into different spaces, such as the space of the building (which is space as specified by the building), the space of the room (which is space as specified by the room), and so on, with the help of specifiers. Clearly, what is true of the space of the building (which may be bigger than the room) may not be true of the space of the room. Just as space remains the same in spite of being demarcated into different spaces with the help of specifiers, so also cognition remains the same although it is specified as cognition of a pot, cognition of a cloth, and so on.

It may be objected that the cognition of one person is private and directly accessible only by that person; similarly, the cognition of another person is also private and directly accessible only by that other person: this proves that cognitions belonging to different persons are different. But this does not follow. We know that the building space does not belong to the room space; still space is one and the same. In the same way, cognition as specified as belonging to one person and being directly accessible by that person is distinct from cognition as specified by belonging to another person and being directly accessible by that other person; still cognition is one and the same.

In the Advaita view *brahman* or the self is the same as cognition. Hence from the transcendent perspective cognition is not only non-dual but also eternal. If this were denied and cognition were held to be noneternal, it follows that there could be a time when cognition would not exist. But then everything would have also been covered by the darkness of ignorance (*jagadāndhya*) that would not have ever come to an end.

According to the Advaita, the self is the same as cognition; but on the mundane, empirical level there remains ignorance about the true nature of the self. When the true nature of the self is known and the ignorance is dispelled, the self is known to be self-revealing, that is, revealed without dependence on any other manifestor (*vyañjaka*). This is also the Vedic view as the following quotation shows: "This person [*puruṣa*] is self-luminous [*svayam jyotiḥ*]" (BU 4.3.14). This conflicts with the Nyāya view that an inferential process (or anything else) is needed for revelation of the self.

Metaphorically, this point of view is explained as follows. In the daytime we carry on our activities with the help of the light of the sun. In the nighttime we use the light of the moon. When there is no light of the moon, we may use the light of fire. When there is no fire, we may use the light of speech, that is, communicate through language in darkness. But when there is no speech, there is still the light of the self (*ātma-jyoti*). In other words, the self does not require the light of the sun or of the moon or of fire or speech or anything else to reveal itself. The self as pure consciousness is self-revealing.

Philosophically, the significance of this may be gathered as described below. Since this topic has generated a lot of controversy in the Sanskrit philosophical tradition, we expound it through a number of succeeding steps and add the Nyāya rejoinder on the way. First, it is accepted by everyone that nothing is revealed or known without cognition or consciousness. A lamp is an aid to seeing and reveals things; but it is useless for seeing unless there is consciousness. Although a lamp is only an aid to seeing, it does not need another lamp to reveal itself. Why should then consciousness, which is clearly that without which no revelation can take place, need something else to reveal itself? (AD 770)

From the Nyāya point of view, however, this argument is inconclusive. Although nothing is revealed without cognition, a cognitive state, if there are many such states, may still be revealed by another cognitive state. The analogy between a lamp and cognition is also unilluminating. A lamp serves as an aid to eye contact with the flame and things illuminated by the flame. Since the eye comes into contact with the flame when the eye comes into contact with the things illuminated by the flame, another flame is not needed. However, the job of cognition is to reveal its object. This does not rule out needing another cognition to reveal itself just as it does not ruled out that another lamp may be needed to reveal what is under the lamp.

Second, it is generally accepted that cognition removes ignorance and that these two are opposed like light and darkness. Just as light does not need another thing to remove darkness, to which it is opposed, so also cognition does not need anything else to remove ignorance, to which it is opposed. If two things are opposed, the presence of one implies the absence of the other. Since cognition and ignorance are opposed, there can be no ignorance or lack of cognition of cognition. Cognition, therefore, must be self-revealing. Put in another way, cognition is the negatum (*pratiyogin*) of lack of cognition. That is, when we speak of the lack of cognition, cognition is that which is negated. The negatum and its absence (*abhāva*) are opposed. For example, the pot and absence of the pot are opposed. If there is the pot, there is no absence of the pot; if there is absence of the pot, there is no pot. Accordingly, if there is cognition, there is no absence of cognition; also if there is absence of cognition, there is no cognition. Cognition then is self-revealing (GB 770).

But from the Nyāya point of view this argument is faulty. If there is cognition, there is no absence of cognition. This is true. Still if there is cognition, there may be absence of cognition of cognition. Absence of cognition and absence of cognition of cognition are not the same.

Third, nothing can be revealed by something that is itself unrevealed (BH 190). So if the self or cognition were unrevealed, the object of cognition could not be revealed as well.

From the Nyāya viewpoint, of course, this is not true. In order to have cognition of a pot, it is not necessary to have cognition of cognition of a pot, the Nyāya claims. So one should prove and not merely assume that nothing can be revealed by something that is itself unrevealed.

Fourth, if cognition were not self-revealing and were to be revealed by another cognition as the Nyāya holds, a vicious infinite regress would be inevitable (GB 770). We then need a second cognition to reveal the first cognition, a third cognition to reveal the second cognition, and so on to infinity. On the other hand, if we stop the regress at some point and regard some cognition as self-revealing, why not get rid of the regress altogether and regard the first cognition itself as self-revealing?

In the Nyāya view a vicious infinite regress is uncalled for. Since cognition of cognition of a pot is not needed for cognition of a pot, there is no need for the second (and then the third, etc.,) cognition if a pot is all that one cares to cognize. Similarly, in order to have cognition of cognition of a pot, it is not necessary to have cognition of cognition of cognition of a pot. So if one is interested in cognition of cognition of a pot, one can have that without being compelled to have cognition of cognition of cognition of a pot.

Fifth, in the Nyāya view no cognition can take place unless there is first contact between the self and the inner sense. So when, for example, a pot is cognized, there is no bar to the self also being cognized at the same time.

However, although the contact between the self and the inner sense is a necessary condition (in the Nyāya view) for any cognition, it is not a sufficient condition. So it does not follow from that something, say a pot, is cognized that the self (or the inner sense) is also cognized.

Sixth, according to the Nyāya, cognition reveals its object but not itself. Hence a second cognition is needed for revealing the first cognition which becomes the object of the second cognition. But this amounts to treating cognition on a par with ordinary unconscious (*jaḍa*) objects such as a pot or a cloth. These latter do need something else to reveal themselves. But since cognition is nothing but consciousness, the very task of which is to reveal, it does not need another cognition to reveal itself.

The Nyāya disagrees. Although the task of cognition is to reveal, it too becomes the object of cognition like ordinary unconscious objects. So the same theory—that cognition is always different from its object—should apply to cognition of cognition. That is, cognition of cognition should be different from cognition. If an exception must be made here, the burden of proof lies on those who make that claim. But various efforts in that direction, such as that invoking the threat of a vicious infinite regress, have been found to be open to rebuttal.

Seventh, the Nyāya argues that an object like a lamp helps to reveal things. So cognition could still reveal its object although it becomes the object of a second cognition. But this misses the entire point. Cognitive aids such as a lamp are useful because there is consciousness that makes revelation possible. That without which revelation is impossible cannot be merely an object (*viṣaya*) (BH 20). If this is overlooked, a vicious infinite regress of one cognition requiring to be revealed by another cognition will result.

But the Nyāya is not persuaded by the threat of an infinite regress, as we have already seen. Accordingly, it refuses to endorse the thesis that the same cognitive state should be both the subject (*viṣayin*) and the object (*viṣaya*), that is, should both reveal itself and its object. Since there is nothing else that is both the subject and the object, the burden of proof lies once again squarely on the Advaitin who makes such a claim for cognition.

Eighth, there is a difference between the revealing function of an unconscious thing such as a lamp and that of cognition. Cognition removes ignorance and is opposed to that. But a lamp removes darkness and is opposed to that. A lamp is not opposed to ignorance and that is why the latter is not removed by the former. Since the very task of cognition is to remove ignorance, it does not need another cognition to remove ignorance about it (GMS 2.18).

The Nyāya agrees that there is a difference between the revealing function of a lamp and that of cognition. But the agreement extends upto the point that cognition removes ignorance about its object. However, from the agreed point that cognition removes ignorance about its object, it does not follow that it also removes ignorance about itself. This is an additional claim that must be argued for and not taken for granted.

Ninth, a lamp cannot reveal things hidden by a barrier (*vyavahita*). Similarly, cognition could not reveal its object if it remained hidden and unrevealed (*aprakāśita*) (VPS 67).

This is a wrong analogy from the Nyāya point of view. A lamp cannot reveal the hidden thing because it fails to reach it. Cognition does not fail to reach its object and, therefore, does not fail to reveal it.

Tenth, even the Nyāya admits that there is a heterogeneity between cognition and its object. While in the cognition of a pot, the pot is characterized by objectivity (*viṣayatā*), cognition is characterized by subjectivity (*viṣayitā*). Why must then cognition need another cognition to reveal itself? (GMS 2.18)

But the Nyāya admits the subjectivity of cognition only with reference to its object and not with reference to itself. If the latter claim is to be made, it must still be argued for and not merely assumed.

Eleventh, in the Nyāya view the divine cognition is self-revealing and not dependent on introspection for revelation. Why should not this be true of ordinary cognition as well? (GMS 2.18)

The divine cognition is eternal. So there can be no introspection of it, for introspection takes place only after the cognitive state ceases to exist. Ordinary cognitions do cease to exist; so introspection is possible for them. If it is accepted that the subject cannot be the object and the object cannot be the subject, cognition of cognition must be different from cognition and should be an after-cognition or introspection. The analogy of divine cognition is misleading. Divine cognition encompasses everything, including itself. Ordinary cognitions do not encompass everything and need not encompass themselves.

Twelfth, according to the Nyāya, introspecion or cognition of cognition of X is the causal condition of any usage about cognition of X. But in the Advaita view, cognition of X is the causal condition of the usage of X as well as that of cognition of X. This shows that the latter view is more economical (GMS 2.18).

However, the crucial question is whether cognition is self-revealing and whether the subject and the object of a given cognition can be the same. If not and if introspection is settled as the means of knowing about cognition on various grounds, the lack of economy would not be a decisive factor against the Nyāya view.[3] If there are good reasons for accepting two cognitions instead of one cognition, although the latter is more economical, the former is still to be preferred.

As a final point in our account of the Advaita position, we briefly look at why in the highest-level knowing and being become one. In the Advaita view cognition at the highest level is the direct knowledge of *brahman* of the form "I am brahman." This takes place through a final modification of the inner sense after the knower has completed all the necessary preparation (BH 55). Three levels of knowing may here be specially taken note of. First, there is knowledge of *brahman* from the study of Vedic statements such as "That art thou." This is called the level of hearing (*śravaṇa*) the truth. Then the doubt about the truth of what is heard or read is removed through a process of ratiocination. This is the second level, called reasoned knowledge (*manana*). Finally, there is continuous succession (*jñānadhārā*) of the knowledge that the self is *brahman*. This is the third level called meditation (*nididhyāsana*) of the truth. This final knowledge carries complete conviction, removes all kinds of duality and the ignorance that the self is different from *brahman* and accomplishes the unity of the self and *brahman* that is always there. This removes all desires for everything else and bondage is overcome. Accordingly, knowledge is the proper means of liberation (which is knowing and being *brahman*) in the Advaita view.

We now move on to consider the Nyāya critique of some major Advaita views (bearing on issues other than that cognition is self-revealing). First we take some passages from Jayanta Bhatta's *Nyāyamañjarī* (10th century CE).

> Is non-difference accepted on the ground that difference is refuted by a source of knowing or on the ground that non-difference is established by a source of knowing? Neither is the case. All the sources of knowing like perception, etc., are grounded on difference. Difference from whatever presupposes the other. When things . . . made out of a lump of clay are known to be of the same nature as clay, the identical nature of clay is gathered but not otherwise. The Buddhists say that what is perceived is difference from the other and not identity, which presupposes the other. The awareness 'this is other than that' presupposes the other just as the awareness 'this is common to these' presupposes the other. Thus both you and the Buddhist are in difficulty. . . . Both differentiation and inclusion presuppose the other. . . . Determination of the nature of something is not possible without the negation of other natures. Only when things are known to be different from the yellow, etc., that many things are known to be blue and not otherwise. As it is said: determination as that involves differentiation from what is different. (NM 96)

Jayanta Bhatta here attacks the Advaita position on nonduality. Neither nondifference of everything nor eradication of all kinds of difference can be proved through sources of knowing, for the latter presuppose difference. Could nonduality be proved by showing that all things share the same nature? No, says Jayanta Bhatta. Things such as pots made out of clay can be found to share the same nature. But this presupposes that pots and other clay vessels are different from each other and also from the common nature they share. The Buddhists here disagree and argue that pots and so on are not found to have a common nature but to be different from everything not of the nature of clay. But this presupposes the common nature of clay the determination of which in its turn presupposes the different things made of clay. Jayanta Bhatta finally reminds us of the basic dictum that every determination involves negation which presupposes difference. So nonduality cannot be proven and is contradicted by the very foundations of the sources of knowing.

> What is nescience which is said not to be describable as real or not? Nescience is beginninlessly and continuously operative, capable of covering up and subject to removal—but why is it said to be unreal? Objection: Who could remove it if it

> were real? Reply: But only real things like trees are found to be removed, not something unreal like rabbit's horns. Since nescience is subject to removal, it should not be eternal but must be real. . . . But if nescience is real, since it is the second thing, non-duality cannot be accepted. It may be said that since *brahman* is eternal knowledge, it cannot be the locus of nescience. The individual selves are the loci of nescience. When nescience is gone, they merge in the supreme *brahman* like pot-space. But this is not smart. The specifiers of space are real; the supreme self, however, is said to be specified by nescience which is unreal—thus the example is improper. . . . It may be said that nescience is the means to knowledge. . . . But this also serves no purpose, for every means is found to exist in its own nature and unreal things like sky-flowers, etc., cannot serve as the means. . . . It may be said that a false statement like . . . a lion is coming in this direction is also found to produce real effects like the fleeing of the cowards and enthusiastic preparation with weapons of the brave. But there the awareness of a lion is the effect of that [false statement] and since that is real, this is not a case of something unreal serving as the means. (NM 98)

Here Jayanta Bhatta joins issue with the Advaita view that plurality is the product of ignorance or nescience and that there is no plurality but only nonduality when ignorance is removed. Such nescience is beginningless but is said to be neither real nor unreal. But since nescience is removed, it can only be real, argues Jayanta Bhatta. The Advaitin asks: How could nescience be removed if it were real (since only that which can never be sublated is real)? The reply is that something unreal like a rabbit's horn cannot be removed and only something real such as a tree can be removed. But if nescience is real, nonduality must go, for nescience is different from *brahman*, which is pure, eternal, and changeless knowledge.

The Advaitin may suggest that since *brahman* is eternal knowledge, nescience cannot belong to *brahman*. On the other hand, nescience may plausibly belong to the individual selves, which merge without a trace in the supreme self once ignorance is removed by knowledge. This is comparable to the divisions within space (which is one and infinite) like the pot-space, and so on, which are gone when pots and the like are gone. But the analogy is improper, says Jayanta Bhatta. The divisions within space are made with reference to real things such as pots. But the divisions within the supreme self are made with reference to nescience, which is unreal. Divisions made with reference to something unreal are not intelligible.

The Advaitin may again suggest that nescience is the means or method to knowledge. Jayanta Bhatta replies that even then nescience must be real, for only something real can be the means and something unreal cannot be the means.

The Advaitin may point out that even a false statement that is about a state of affairs that does not exist may produce real changes. For example, the false statement that a lion is approaching may induce the coward to flee and the brave to get ready with arms. Jayanta Bhatta agrees. But he adds that a false statement produces an awareness that is real and that the real changes are brought about by such real awareness. So this is no exception to the rule that something unreal cannot serve as the means.

> If there is proof of non-duality, that itself is the second thing and hence there is no non-duality. But if there is no proof, non-duality is not . . . established. (NM 98)

The point is that the proof must be different from what is to be proved. So if nonduality is to be proved, the proof must be different from it, which shows that there is duality and not nonduality. On the other hand, if there is no proof of nonduality, it is nothing more than an unproven claim. This critique is similar in spirit to the critique of skepticism that if the latter is true, nothing is certain. But if nothing is certain, at least it is certain that nothing is certain which refutes skepticism. On the other hand, if it is not certain that nothing is certain, something may be certain, in which case skepticism is not established.

> Vedic statements like "Only one without a second—there is no plurality here" . . . should not be taken literally. . . . When there is conflict between what is meant and sources of knowing like perception, the primary meaning is given up and an interpretation based on the secondary significance is resorted to. Since this statement says something which is contradicted by another source of knowledge, . . . it should be construed as something like that the self . . . does not become different in spite of the different states like pleasure, pain, etc., or that the plurality of this [the self] does not follow from the plurality of the body, the sense organs, etc. (NM 97)

An Indian philosopher of the Cārvāka or the Buddhist or the Jaina school may simply dismiss a Vedic statement as false if it does not suit his purposes. But Jayanta Bhatta belongs to the Nyāya school and, like the Advaita, accepts that Vedic statements are authoritative sources of knowledge. So he opts for the way out that Vedic statements that seem to go against the pluralistic ontology should not taken at their face value and should be given a suitable interpretation based on the secondary meaning (*lakṣaṇā*), which is consistent with pluralism.[4] The hermeneutic principle invoked is widely used. It says that if a scriptural statement is found to contradict what is accepted from some reliable, nonscriptural source, the primary meaning (*śakti*) of the former should be given up in favor of a secondary meaning that is consistent with the nonscriptural source. This is consistent with the epistemological stance implied by Gotama, the founder of the Nyāya, that of the four recognized sources of knowledge—perception, inference, *upamāna* (which has an analogical component), and authority—the one listed before in the given order gets precedence over the one listed afterwards. Since authority is the last in this list, Jayanta Bhatta says, following the Nyāya tradition, that when authority is in conflict with another source of knowledege, it should be so interpreted as to be consistent with that other source of knowledge.

Another Nyāya critic of the Advaita named Visvanatha, the author of the *Nyāyasiddhāntamuktāvalī* (18th century CE) raises the following question:

> Not so. If it had everything as the object, there would be the objection of being omniscient. But if it had some one thing as the object, there is lack of decision. There is also the consequence that there should be awareness of some object in a dreamless sleep, for cognition is intentional. . . . There is no evidence to show that cognition is nonintentional. (SM 222–23, 232)

The question is: Does the nondual, all-inclusive cognition (admitted by the Advaita to be the only reality) have everything as its object or some one thing? If it has everything as the object, since the individual self is identical with *brahman* and the cognition, the individual self would turn out to be omniscient (which it is not). On the other hand, if the cognition has some one thing as the object, there would be no good reason why the self should be identified with the cognition having that one thing as the object rather than with the cognition having some other thing as the object. Further, one should then be aware of something even in dreamless sleep (though this does not happen), for the nondual cognition, according to the Advaita, persists all the time including the state of dreamless sleep. What if the nondual cognition is held to be nonintentional so that neither everything nor some one thing would be its object? Visvanatha replies that such a suggestion lacks merit, for there is no evidence to show that cognition is ever nonintentional, cognition being always specified as cognition of some object.

CHAPTER 14

Conclusion

As we survey Nyāya-Vaiśeṣika philosophy of mind certain features of its dualism emerge very clearly. Nyāya-Vaiśeṣika dualism is not disrespectful toward matter. It wholeheartedly accepts the reality of the latter and gives it pride of place where it is due. In this way it differs from such extreme positions as those of Yogācāra idealism or Advaita monism or Berkeleyan immaterialism according to which matter does not ultimately exist. To a Yogācāra idealist only particular conscious states are real and physical states are unreal (like hare's horns or dream objects that are cognized but are nothing more than constructions or *vikalpa*). But to the Nyāya both conscious and physical states are real, different from each other, and objects of veridical awareness. To an Advaita monist, matter has more than apparent (*prātibhāsika*) reality, for it is granted empirical (*vyavahārika*) reality. But it is still held to lack ultimate (*pāramārthika*) reality, which is granted only to consciousness. This the Nyāya rejects and holds that both matter and consciousness are ultimately real. To a Berkeleyan immaterialist sensible things such as color or size are in the mind: the admission of a material substance is unnecessary and also fraught with difficulties. The Nyāya is wholly opposed to such a view. Color, size, and so on, are not in the mind, according to the Nyāya, but belong to material substances, the admission of which is fully justified.

Nyāya dualism also differs sharply from Sāṃkhya dualism. The latter traces all our internal states back to the same source from which all material states evolve and holds that even internal states are devoid of consciousness. That is, in the Sāṃkhya view even the internal state of cognition only appears to be conscious but is not really conscious. The Sāṃkhya does recognize consciousness as an irreducibly different ontological principle but removes it as far as possible from our mundane lives. For consciousness or *puruṣa* is unchanging, totally aloof, and a mere witness and never an object of any awareness or an agent of any action. On the other hand, for the Nyāya-Vaíseṣika, consciousness is an integral part of our everyday lives. Our internal states (except for merit, demerit, and disposition) are conscious and causally interact with our bodily states, which are unconscious.

The interaction of bodily states and internal states is not a mystery as it is in Cartesian dualism. For the Nyāya subscribes to a Hume-like view (but not exactly the Humean view: see DI, chapter 11) that a causal condition is an invariable and contiguous antecedent of the effect. From this understanding of causation, there is no difficulty in accepting that a physical state may be the cause of an internal state and vice versa in the sense that either may be the invariable and contiguous antecedent of the other. Further, both internal states and bodily states belong to two different substances each of which has extension (*parimāṇa*) and both of which are in contact (*saṃyoga*) with each other. Just as the states of one physical substance can causally interact with those of another physical substance with which it is in contact, so also can the states of the body causally interact with the internal states belonging to the self with which the body is in contact and vice versa. The Nyāya does not endorse the Cartesian assumption that the immaterial self is unextended. Although the immaterial self is not solid (as bricks or stones are), it is still in contact with the physical body. Only something having extension (*parimāṇa*) can come into contact with a body. The immaterial self is the substance in which the internal states such as cognition and desire inhere. Still, since the self is in contact with the body and internal states cannot arise without such contact, the latter can be said to be located in the body in the sense that they arise only within the confines (*avaccheda*) of the body.

This kind of dualism has a life of its own and a philosophical appeal that goes beyond any particular religion. This is clear from the way the Nyāya argues for an immaterial self. One argument is based on the difference of internal states from bodily states. Just as earth is a different kind of substance from air because their distinctive states or qualia are different, so also is the self a different kind of substance from the body because the internal states are different from the states of the body. One main reason (the main reasons are summarized later) for the difference between internal states and bodily states comes from perception, which is accepted as a reliable source of information. We learn from perception that bodily states are public and can be observed by more than one subject. We also learn from perception that internal states such as pleasure are private and can be directly experienced only by one subject. If such perception is credible, we can justifiably claim that internal states are different from bodily states and, therefore, given the ontology of substance, that they belong to a different kind of substance. There is nothing antinaturalistic or unscientific in admitting an immaterial self unless it is assumed in a question-begging way that 'natural' or 'scientific' means physical.

It is worth emphasizing that the charges of antinaturalism or mysterianism aimed at psychophysical dualism are hollow: the reasoning for the immaterial self is subject to the same standards that apply to familiar philosophical or scientific reasonings. If a physicist claims that electrons are different from protons, he tries to show how they are different, relying largely on perceptions, deductions from them, hypotheses, and the best available explanations of any phenomena that appear to be problematic. The Nyāya uses the same method to try to show that the body and the self are different. One can always disagree by either pointing out an alleged mistake in the deduction or by questioning one or more of the premises or by promoting alternative hypotheses and explanations. But this is the fate of any philosophical or scientific theory. Needless to say, like any other well developed system, the Nyāya does offer an elaborate ontology and epistemology to back up its claims if and when challenged.

Some dualists stop short at what might be called 'property dualism' and disown substance dualism. This is not acceptable to the Nyāya. If one merely holds that internal states are ontologically different from bodily states and denies the existence of an enduring, immaterial self that remains the same in spite of its changing qualia, one is hard put to account for personal identity. The Nyāya subscribes to what may be called the simple view of personal identity: personal identity is grounded on the simplicity (*niravayavatva*) of the self. Personal identity cannot be grounded, the Nyāya argues, on the body or any part of the body or the bodily states or the internal states, for these all undergo change. And without an identical self, memory is difficult to explain, for it is generally agreed that one cannot remember what some one else has experienced. A critic may invoke a stream of causally connected internal states to account for memory (as a Buddhist or a follower of Hume-James may do). But, as the argument goes, causal connection fails to provide either a necessary or a sufficient condition for (1) memory as well as (2) the awareness of causal connection. The critic's position cannot also be salvaged by diluting the notion of memory to something weaker, such as that of quasi-memory (as suggested by Shoemaker, etc.).

Further, the thrust of the Nyāya arguments is that memory presupposes an identical self. This implies that memory cannot provide the criterion for personal identity. In the same way, the psychological continuity criterion of personal identity (popularized in recent times by Parfit, etc.) must be rejected, for once again, psychological continuity is neither necessary nor sufficient for personal identity. In this respect the Nyāya view is closer to those of Butler and Reid, who were highly critical of Locke and opted for 'strict and philosophical' identity (in the case of Butler) and 'perfect' identity (in the case of Reid).[1]

A distinctive feature of Nyāya dualism is that it admits an inner sense that is different from both the external senses and the self. The inner sense accounts for inattention in such cases as when one fails to hear a clock ticking away nearby while one is absorbed in reading a book although the sound has reached the ear. The inner sense also accounts for one's direct awareness of internal states such as pleasure. A direct awareness, the Nyāya claims, is always sensory and, since the external senses are ruled out and since no sensory awareness can take place without a sense organ, an inner sense should be admitted. The inner sense coordinates the external senses and in this respect has some of the functions generally attributed nowadays to the brain. But the former is not the brain. In the older Nyāya view the inner sense is atomic as well as nonphysical and so cannot be the brain. In the later Nyāya view developed by Raghunatha Siromani, the inner sense is nonatomic and physical. Still, it is not the brain as it is ordinarily understood. In Raghunatha's view, the inner sense is constituted by the noninherent (*asamaveta*) material particles.[2] So it cannot be the gross brain but can only comprise the subtle particles located in the brain as well as other parts of the body. The self must be distinguished from the inner sense. In spite of its ascendancy over the external senses, the inner sense is still an instrument (*karaṇa*) and cannot be the self-controlled (*svatantra*, *vaśin*) agent (*kartā*). This is useful for countering the recent view that the self is the brain, which is, in turn, a sophisticated computer.[3] Even the most sophisticated computer is not self-controlled, for it has been designed by someone else. The difference between the tool and the toolmaker, the Nyāya holds, cannot be wiped out.

Consciousness, in the Nyāya view, is an adventitious (*āgantuka*) quale of the self. This distinguishes it from Cartesian dualism, according to which consciousness is an essential attribute of the self.

Unlike Descartes, the Nyāya does not disallow the possibility that (ordinary) consciousness may have arisen through the evolution of animal life forms. The latter view gains ground from the fact that only organisms with developed nervous systems are found to exhibit higher forms of conscious activities.[4] But this in no way should be thought to harm the Nyāya kind of dualism. Something adventitious may very well be contingent on the presence of some other phenomenon. But it does not follow therefrom that it is reducible to that phenomenon. So the Nyāya does not object to holding that (ordinary) consciousness is contingent on the availability of biological phenomena, but does object to any attempt to reduce it to biological phenomena.

Further, the contingency applies to only particular coginitive states of particular mortals. In the Nyāya view the conscious states belong to the immaterial self, which is eternal. So the existence of the self does not depend on anything else. However, the origin of conscious states is dependent on other causal conditions, such as biological phenomena; the self may very well exist devoid of conscious states if other necessary conditions are not available. Again, the evolution of higher animals from lower animals and that of the latter from inanimate matter is evident and raises no problems for the Nyāya. In fact, standard Hindu scriptures routinely speak of vast expanses of time when only the selves and indestructible material substances exist. Life forms are typically supposed to emerge later and evolve from the lower to the higher. But that does not imply that the Darwinian type of evolution can be the whole story. For that leaves the evolution of conscious states to a process of natural selection without the guidance of intelligence—and this is not acceptable to the Nyāya. In other words, the Nyāya has no objection to holding that the selves existed devoid of conscious states for millions or billions of years when biological phenomena were not present and the earth was too inhospitable for that. Still, for the Nyāya, the evolution of ordinary conscious states out of matter must be subject to the merits and demerits of the individual selves as well as divine intelligence and must be beginningless.[5] The arguments for these views are well articulated and defensible.

Although life forms and ordinary conscious states emerge later, internal states such as volitions have, in the Nyāya view, genuine causal powers. So it would not support a supervenience theory of internal states according to which the internal character of a thing is wholly determined by its physical nature and if two things are indiscernible physically, they must be indiscernible mentally as well.[6] The Nyāya has no objection to the indispensability of the neural network that makes my limb movements possible when I wish to get up and do get up.[7] Still, there is no individually identifiable neural event that can be singled out as the relevant cause of my limb movements and nothing, from the Nyāya point of view, on the physical side that can be identified with my volition. The Nyāya wholeheartedly accepts the commonsense view that individual internal states like particular volitions really exist and are causally active. This is incompatible with the thesis that notions of folk psychology have no place in a scientific study of the causes of living behavior.[8] For the Nyāya the neural events that culminate in my limb movements would not exist unless my volition preceded them. So the latter is indispensable for a scientific account of my behavior. There should be no genuine apprehension that this conflicts with a naturalistic view of living beings. If our perceptions are credible, we are entitled to hold that internal states and bodily states are mutually interactive. This is not non-naturalistic unless it is assumed in a question-begging way that only a physicalist account of internality can be naturalistic or scientific.

The admission of nonphysical conscious (and other internal) states is defensible for a variety of reasons.

1. If conscious states are physical, why does not the best available study of neural (or any other physical states with which cognitive states may be sought to be identified) states throw any light on such integral features of cognitive states as the distinction between the qualifier and the qualificand or their layeredness? When there is an explanatory gap between two physical phenomena one of which supposedly provides the explanation for the other, there is usually evidence about what other physical phenomenon would fill the gap. But in this case there is no evidence that the explanatory gap can be remedied by anything physical any time soon (or even in principle).

2. If conscious states are physical, why are not they either imperceptible or externally perceptible as all other physical states are? In other words, if conscious states are physical, why are they open to immediate or at least privileged access while no other physical states are? As we have argued, a physicalist or a functionalist who courts nondualism cannot get out of this morass by merely appealing to the fact that each organism is distinct. There is nothing in a physicalist or functionalist account of neural networks, and so on, that can rule out the possibility of reduplication

and guarantee personal uniqueness. Thus the mere possession of a neural network or any other bodily feature is not a sufficient condition for privileged access. Further, such appeal by a physicalist to distinct organisms to account for privileged access is circular, for the Nyāya holds on the basis of well-articulated arguments that each organism is associated with an immaterial self.

3. If conscious states are physical, why are not there many selves in the same body belonging to the many different bodily parts?

4. If conscious states are physical, why are not there any in a dead body, which retains all other (relevant) physical attributes? The loss of consciousness in a dead body cannot be explained by a physicalist or functionalist, except in a question-begging way, by merely appealing to lack of life, for everything alive, in the Nyāya view, has an immaterial self.

Of the several arguments above we restate one as follows:

All physical states are either externally perceptible or imperceptible.

No internal or mental states are externally perceptible or imperceptible.

Therefore, no internal or mental states are physical states.

This argument is in a valid form which may be displayed by replacing 'physical states' with P, 'externally perceptible or imperceptible' with S and 'internal or mental states' with M as below.

All P is S.

No M is S.

Therefore, no M is P

The form satisfies the rules of validity. The middle term S is distributed in the second premise as the predicate of a universal negative proposition. Both the subject and the predicate of the conclusion are distributed; they are also distributed in the premises. One of the premises is negative while the conclusion is also negative. Thus the conclusion follows necessarily from the premises. The remaining crucial question then is whether the premises are acceptable. Of the two premises the second premise—that no internal states are either externally perceptible or imperceptible—enjoys broad support not only among the dualists but also the physicalists (though it is challenged by some behaviorists, neo-Humeans, etc.). The first premise—that all physical states are either externally perceptible or imperceptible—is confirmed by innumerable examples such as bricks and so on. The only possible counterexamples are internal states, which are treated differently by dualists. Accordingly, given GAIE, internal states do not count as counterexamples. Further, since internal states are the subject of the conclusion, they cannot, except on pain of circularity, be adduced as counterexamples or positive examples or negative examples. Both the premises thus are acceptable. So, therefore, also is the conclusion that internal states such as desire are nonphysical.

A physicalist may argue that although no other physical states are subject to privileged access, the brain states are so because of their greater complexity. In other words, the brain is the unique physical thing that can do something that no other physical thing can. While this is logically possible, the very structure of this argument, as we have seen, is suspicious from the Nyāya point of view. What is suspicious is not the claim about the brain states having a certain complexity that no other physical states have. This is a factual issue and may be settled by science one way or the other. Suppose, however, that this is true. That is, brain states have some complexity that no other physical states have. How does that show that this makes them suitable candidates for privileged access? Nothing else has this complexity. So we cannot verify by examining anything else whether this complexity has anything to do with being eligible for privileged access.

The following example may help to see what is wrong in trying to settle a philosophical dispute by merely falling back on some unique feature. Suppose there is disagreement over whether sound is eternal or noneternal. Suppose again that sound has some unique feature, say, some complexity that does not belong to anything else. Now suppose one argues that sound is eternal because it has that complexity. Clearly, one has made no progress, for, if this is permitted, one may also argue with equal plausibility that sound is noneternal because it has that complexity. We may call this the flaw of uniqueness (*asādhāraṇya*) which is recognized as such in the Nyāya logical tradition.

There may be disagreement over whether this is a flaw and we cannot settle that here. But if it is, the above physicalist argument is flawed. The issue is whether brain states are subject to privileged access or not. Let us suppose for the sake of argument that brain states have some complexity that nothing else has. Now suppose one argues that brain states have privileged access because they have the said complexity. Clearly, one has made no progress, for, if this is permitted, one may also argue with equal plausibility that brain states do not have privileged access because they have the said complexity.

It is sometimes charged that psychophysical interactive dualism violates the fundamental scientific principle of conservation of energy, which holds that the total amount of energy in the universe remains constant in spite of constant and endless transformations. If my non-physical state of volition causes my limb movement, physical energy in my body should increase in such a way that it is not attributable to a physical source. Further, an amount equal to the new energy should depart from the existing physical stock so that the total amount of energy remains constant. But of course there is no evidence that shows that any such new energy is introduced by my volition nor any evidence that shows that any of the existing energy has departed as a result of that. So interactive dualism can be saved only by making one ad hoc assumption after another, which is utterly question-begging.[9]

This objection, however, springs from assuming that my non-physical volition can cause my limb movement only if it introduces some new physical energy in and around my body. A Cartesian dualist who holds that *ex nihilo nihil fit* may (or may not, as we understand it) be persuaded to make this assumption. But a Nyāya dualist does not (and cannot be persuaded to) subscribe to this. My nonphysical volitional state has no physical energy and so the question of its introducing any new physical energy to my body or to anything else does not arise. Such a question may (in a limited way) be pertinent from the Sāṃkhya viewpoint, which accepts that *ex nihilo nihil fit*. Characteristically enough, since the Sāṃkhya accepts this and also accepts the interaction between internal states and bodily states, it holds further, quite consistently, that both internal states such as volitions and bodily states such as limb movements are totally unconscious and are both derived from the same ultimate stuff.

But the Nyāya does not hold that *ex nihilo nihil fit*. It also rejects the doctrine of causal power in all its forms. Accordingly, the principle of conservation of energy, for the Nyāya, can only have a limited application and (when suitably reformulated to fit Nyāya ontology) must be restricted to cases of causation where the part-whole relation (*avayava-avayavi-bhāva*, to which the physical conception of an isolated or closed system is applicable) holds. Since my volition is not a part (*avayava*) of my limb movement in spite of being a cause of it, the said principle does not apply in such a case. What is implied in the Nyāya claim that my volition is a cause of my limb movement is that my volition is invariably present in my body immediately before my limb movement. And this is not incompatible with the principle of conservation of energy as understood in either the classical Newtonian physics or the recent relativistic physics. In the Nyāya view life and consciousness emerge from the causal conglomeration of the self and the body and have causal roles that are missing in either the self alone or the body alone. This is not ruled out by the conservation principle, which allows for the possibility of an effect having new features and causal functions not found in its causal conditions. For example, the principle is not violated by such facts as that water is compounded out of hydrogen and oxygen and has causal functions that are missing in hydrogen or oxygen.

Further, the view that life and consciousness emerge from the aggregate of the self and the body does not contradict physics. Physics, consistently with its point of view, is confined to the study of physical phenomena alone. We have made great strides in exploring and understanding the physical foundations of life and consciousness. But while the physical foundations should be accepted as necessary conditions for life and consciousness, the evidence falls short of showing that they are also the sufficient conditions. No one has ever produced life exclusively out of matter without the assistance of some form of life. (Frozen sperms and eggs still have to be collected from bodies that are alive or have very recently been alive.)[10] Since there is no known aggregate of (nonliving) physical conditions that suffices to produce life, there is warrant for the inference that the association of something nonphysical is necessary for the emergence of life, which under suitable conditions helps the emergence of consciousness.

It thus appears that a conflict between dualism and physical naturalism can be avoided and that Nyāya dualism has the resources to do that. It also has the resources to make it attractive to religion as well as morality. Without any doubt Nyāya dualism draws its inspiration from the Hindu doctrine of reincarnation, which holds that the self becomes associated with different bodies in different lives in accordance with the law of karma. Such a view becomes impossible if the self is identified with a body which patently disintegrates and disperses after the death. In the same way the Judeo-Christian-Islamic doctrine of personal immortality and of the virtuous being rewarded with a life in the heaven after physical death cannot be maintained if the self is identified with the body.

Of course, Nyāya dualism provides for the continued existence of the self not only after the physical death but also before the physical birth. The continued existence of the self before the phyical birth is rejected in the Judeo-Christian-Islamic traditions. One main reason why the Nyāya disagrees with these religious traditions is that the self is conceived to be simple. A simple self cannot be destroyed, for only a substance made of parts can be destroyed by taking the parts apart. This is accepted in the above traditions as well and sometimes used as a ground for the immortality of the self. But a simple substance cannot also be created, for only a substance made of parts can be created by putting the parts together. If philosophical consistency were to be the main consideration, the Nyāya view is clearly to be preferred here.

Further, a preexistent self allows room for the law of karma, which can be invoked to explain the many incongruities in life. Some prosper with little effort without any rhyme or reason, while others fail in spite of all their efforts. If the world is created by an all-powerful, all-knowing, and all-good God, such disparity becomes hard to explain. According to the Nyāya, such a creator will have to be charged with partiality (*vaiṣamya*) and cruelty (*nairghrṇya*). These charges cannot be brought against the God of Nyāya, for the inexplicable success or failure (and other such incongruities) can be attributed to the good or bad karma accrued in previous lives.

Again, the phenomenon of biologically inherited instinctive activities, such as that of suckling by a newborn mammal, provides evidence for preexistence. If (1) unconscious teleology is not acceptable, (2) causal connections are uniform and objective, and (3) the act of suckling is aimed at getting nourishment (which in other known cases in adults is prompted by the awareness that nourishment is beneficial), the inference of a previous life becomes warranted, for there is no opportunity for acquiring the said awareness in the present life.

Although preexistence and transmigration are not acceptable from the Judeo-Christian-Islamic points of view, the elegant philosophical base that Nyāya dualism provides for the fundamental distinction between the self and the body is attractive to the Hindu (and the Buddhist and the Jain) as well as the Judeo-Christian-Islamic schemes of things. The base can be utilized to build a rational defense of the doctrine of personal immortality and of eternal life in heaven. As we have seen, Nyāya dualism also seeks to provide a rational basis for monotheism and offers proofs of the existence of God. The classical Nyāya causal proof does not seem to be vulnerable to the objections raised against the traditional Western causal proofs of the existence of God offered by Aquinas and Descartes. There are significant differences between the Nyāya viewpoint and the traditional

Judaic, Christian, and Islamic viewpoints. Still the differences are less important than the agreements. What is more important is that they all agree in rejecting physicalism and materialism as adequate bases for the fundamental values and goals of life. They all agree further that the immaterial self is essential for the ultimate dispensation of reward and punishment.

Again, morality assumes that people are more than machines and are capable of controlling their actions, setting goals, and giving conscious direction to their lives. Physicalists and materialists, in spite of many valient efforts, have been hard put to accommodate free will and moral responsibility within the framework of physically closed systems. A dualism that makes room for the self to be different from the body and to rise above the necessities of mechanical causation (to which the reflex actions of the body are subject), is accordingly welcome for the moral discourse.

The great modern European philosopher Descartes, also a great mathematician and scientist in his own right, developed a sophisticated dualism that accommodates the interests of religion and morality. Nyāya dualism too is attractive to religion as well as morality. However, unlike Descartes, the Nyāya does not base its dualism on such claims as that 'I think' is indubitable. For many Nyāya philosophers our internal perceptions and self-awareness, though private, are still fallible.[11] (The Nyāya also does not hold that consciousness is the essence of the immaterial self.) The Cartesian view of an unextended, essentially conscious self has been held to be antinaturalistic (and to make the mind-body interaction a mystery). These charges are not effective against the Nyāya view, as we have tried to show. Because of such views as that the self (though immaterial) is extended, that consciousness is an adventitious phenomenon and also because of using a method of reasoning that is based on empirical observations and generalizations, valid deductions from them and inferences to the best available explanations, Nyāya dualism is not only attractive to religion and morality but also well equipped to resolve the perception of conflict with scientific naturalism. This has significance for the overall philosophical point of view.

Appendix:
An Annotated Translation of Ātmatattvaviveka

The *Ātmatattvaviveka* (ATV) or *Discerning the Nature of the Self* is a famous work of Udayana (11th century CE). It is mainly a defense of the Nyāya view of the self by way of a critical examination and refutation of a number of Buddhist, Advaita, and Cārvāka philosophical views. The major views that Udayana seeks to refute are (1) that everything is momentary, (2) that consciousness alone is real and that the object of consciousness is not ontically different from consciousness, (3) that the substance is reducible to the aggregate of qualia, and (4) that the nonexistence of the self is known by way of nonapprehension (*anupalabdhi*). The first view is held by the Buddhists. The second view is held by the Buddhists of the Vijñānavāda (idealistic) school. The third view is held by the Buddhists and the Advaita Vedāntins. Even for those Buddhists who hold that the object of consciousness is real and is different from it, the substance (*guṇin*) is reducible to the collection of qualia (*guṇa*). For example, color, smell, and so on, are, from this point of view, different from the cognitions of color, smell, and so on, and are external (*vāhya*) objects. But a mango is not a separate substance over and above these qualia; it is a mere aggregate (*samudāya, saṃghāta*) of them. In the Advaita (and the Bhātta Mīmāṃsā) view, on the other hand, the relation between a substance and its qualia is that of identity in and through difference (*bheda-sahiṣṇu-abheda*). That is, a substance and its qualia are neither utterly identical nor utterly different. However, the self and consciousness, in the Advaita view, are utterly identical and it is a mistake to label consciousness as a quale of the self. In other words, the self is ontologically identical with consciousness and not a separate substance which is its support. The fourth view is held by the Buddhists and the Cārvāka. The first four parts of ATV are devoted respectively to the refutation of these four theses in the above order. The fifth and the final part is devoted to the discussion of and arguments for Udayana's own position. Thus the last part is an elaboration of the accepted view (*siddhānta*) and the first four parts are refutation of philosophical opponents' views (*purvapakṣa*).

Udayana's own position is that the self (*ātman*) is an abiding (*sthira*) substance (*dravya*) that is the substratum of (and utterly different from) consciousness and other internal states, which are all adventitious (*āgantuka*) qualia of the former. This view cannot be maintained if any of the above four views are accepted. First, if everything were momentary, nothing, including the self, could be permanent. Hence in the first part Udayana has sought to refute the major Buddhist arguments for the doctrine of momentariness.

Second, if consciousness alone were real, the self could not be a different entity of which consciousness is a quale. Hence the second part is devoted to a critical examination of the Buddhist arguments for the view that nothing external (*vāhya*) to and other than particular conscious states is real.

Third, if the substance were not ontologically different from its qualia, the self could not be a substance that is the substratum and support of consciousness as a quale. Hence the third part argues for the ontological difference between a substance and its qualia.

Fourth, if nonapprehension of the self as something different from the body and so on, were a legitimate ground for inferring the nonexistence of such a self, the Nyāya view of the self as an immaterial substance could not be maintained. Accordingly, in the fourth part, Udayana argues against nonapprehension as truly providing such a ground.

All through the work Udayana maintains a high level of rigor, technical precision, philosophical depth, and originality. At the same time his prose is terse and compact. Without any doubt he is relying on the continuing Nyāya tradition of teacher-student dialogue and expert counseling by the teacher to the student to make clear what he means. It has, therefore, been necessary to add copious notes to clarify (a part of) what is implied or left understood. It has also been necessary to use technical expressions like negatum (*pratiyogin*), prior absence (*prāgabhāva*), substratum (*anuyogin*), and so on, as and when necessary. It would take too much space to properly explain these neologisms. So in our exposition, because of the very nature of Udayana's work, familiarity with elementary works is presupposed. For the best available exposition of these notions in English one may consult

Tarkasaṃgraha-Dīpikā of Annambhatta, translation and exposition by Gopinath Bhattacharya (Calcutta: Progressive Publishers, 1976).

In the Nyāya tradition Udayana is sometimes considered to be the last stalwart of the old (*prācīna*) Nyāya. (We have heard Pt. Madhusudana Nyayacarya and others say this.) The so-called new (*navya*) Nyāya that emerged soon afterwards was decisively influenced by his many works. It is a testimony to his high stature that in later Nyāya writings he is often referred to simply as "the teacher" (*ācārya*), an epithet reserved for no one else. Besides the *Ātmatattvaviveka* Udayana authored the *Kiranāvalī*, a free commentary on Prasastapada's *Padārthadharmasaṃgraha*, which is mainly a metaphysical treatise on the substance, qualia, and so on. Another work of his is the *Pariśuddhi*, a free commentary on the *Tātparyatīkā* of Vacaspati Misra dealing with the major Nyāya epistemological and metaphysical issues and themes. Another famous work is the *Nyāyakusumāñjali*, in which Udayana offers proofs of the existence of God after a sustained defense of causality, induction, and so on, against skeptical criticism. Two other works called the *Lakṣaṇāvalī* and the *Lakṣaṇamālā* are devoted to definitions (*lakṣaṇa*) of principal Nyāya concepts. He also authored the *Nyāyapariśiṣṭa*, which deals with informal fallacies, pseudorefutations (*jāti*), and grounds of defeat (*nigrahasthāna*).

In our translation and exposition we have consulted the three classical Sanskrit commentaries of Sankara Misra (SM), Bhagiratha Thakkura (BT), and Raghunatha Siromani (RS). These are included in the *Ātmatattvaviveka* of Udayana (edited by MM Vindhyesvariprasada Dvivedin and Pt. Laksmana Sastri Dravida [Calcutta: Asiatic Society, 1984], abbreviated as ATV). We have also utilized the recent Bengali commentary on the *Ātmatattvaviveka* by Pt. Dinanatha Tripathi (Calcutta: Sanskrit College, part 1, 1984, abbreviated as DT). We would like to emphasize that more often than not the text is interpretable and translatable in several different ways. Although we have tried to choose the one that makes most philosophical sense, in many places the choice is not as clear cut as one would like it to be.

> *Svāmyam yasya nijam jagatsu janiteṣvādau tatah pālanam vyutpatteh kāraṇam hitāhitavidhivyāsedhasambhāvanam bhūtoktih sahajā kṛpā nirupadhiryatnastadarthātmakastasmai purvagurūttamāya jagatamīśāya pitre namaḥ.* (ATV 1)

He who has in the beginning his own [natural] authority over the world, he who preserves thereafter, coins the

> names and advises on what should be done as being beneficial and what should be prohibited as being harmful, he whose utterances are true and whose compassion and consequent volition are natural and unconditional—homage to him, the parent, the lord of the world, and the most elevated among the preceding preceptors.

Note: Udayana begins with a prayer to God upholding the custom in the Nyāya tradition.

SM (p. 2) explains the lord (*īśa*) of the world (*jagat*) as one who possesses the power and the volition to create all noneternal things. However, RS (p. 6) explains it as one who has omniscience and so on. Thus, according to RS, the homage is to one whose direct knowledge is eternal and encompasses everything, who is contented (*tṛptaḥ*) and absolutely lacks any desire for his own pleasure, who is independent (*svatantra*) and not subject to the law of karma and whose volition is eternal and a necessary causal condition of the origin of anything noneternal.

Since God is the creator, his authority (*svāmitva*) over all created things is natural (*nija*: literally, own) in the sense of being independent of contractual transaction (*krayādyanapekṣa*), BT and RS say (pp. 4 and 7). Accordingly, God is also described as a parent (*pitṛ*: also means father), for a parent's authority over the child is also not dependent on any contractual dealing. Just as a parent is a causal condition of the child, God is a causal condition of all creatures. As a parent protects the child, God also helps the preservation (*pālana*) of his creation. As a parent teaches the child what thing is called by which name, so also God determines which word refers to which thing (*vyutpatti*) as part of the core vocabulary. (God procreates himself both as the teacher and the student so that humans and other animals can learn how to use language.) As a parent tells the child what is good and should be done and what is bad and should not be done, so also God lays down the basic injunctions and prohibitions. These are contained in the Veda, of which God himself, and not any human, is the author.

All the divine sayings are true (*bhūtoktiḥ*), for God is not tainted with attachment, aversion, error, or intent to deceive. This is gathered from the very proofs from which the existence of God is known (*dharmigrāhakamāna*).

God has already achieved whatever is desireable (*āptakama*) and has no desire for anything (*tṛpta*). Still God gets the process of creation going out of his compassion (*kṛpā*) for the creatures. His compassion and the attendant volition (*yatna*) are natural (*sahaja*) and eternal. The compassion is also unconditional (*nirupadhi*) and not motivated by any gain for himself.

God is the greatest among the earlier preceptors. Other venerable preceptors like Kapila were dependent on their bodies which could not come into being without the wiil of God, BT points out (p. 4).

It should be kept in mind that in the Nyāya view the universe and the cycle of creation and dissolution are beginningless. So God gets the process of creation going in the sense that the first conjunction of two atoms (which are the ultimate, indivisible parts of noneternal substances) in each creative cycle takes place as the result of the divine will.

> *Iha khalu nisargapratikūlasvabhāvam sarvajanasamvedanasiddham duḥkham jihāsavaḥ sarva eva taddhānopayamavidvāṃsaḥ anusarantaśca sarvādhyatmavidekavākyatayā tattvajñānameva tadupāyamakārṇayanti na tataḥ anyam. Pratiyogyānuyogitayā cātmaiva tattvato jñeyaḥ. Tathāhi yadi nairātmyam yadi vātmaivāsti vastubhūtaḥ ubhayathāpi naisargikam ātmajñānam atattvajñāmeva ityatrāpi ekavākyataiva vādināmata ātmatattvam vivicyate.* (ATV 10)

> Here everyone seeks to avoid suffering, which is inimical by nature and experienced by everyone; but not knowing what is the means to that one keeps on exploring. In this regard all spiritualists say [*ākarṇayanti*: literally, cause to hear] in one voice that the knowledge of the truth itself and nothing else is the means to that. It is the self itself the nature of which should be known either in its capacity as the superstratum (*pratiyogin*) or as the substratum (*anuyogin*). Thus irrespective of whether the self exists or not on both counts as a matter of fact the ordinary [*naisargikam*: literally, natural] awareness of the self is certainly not knowledge of the true nature. Since the theorists agree on this also, the nature of the self is investigated.

Note: Udayana explains why it is important to investigate the nature of the self, the theme of his work.

Here (i.e., in the world in which one lives) there is one thing that everyone knows about but no one likes and that is suffering. Although some sufferings can be temporarily eliminated by various other means, there is broad agreement among the spiritualists that knowledge of the reality alone is the only sure means to eradicate all suffering for all the time. Thus knowledge of the reality turns out to be one of the ultimate goals of life.

But knowledge of what reality? Udayana argues that it can only be knowledge of the self. Philosophers disagree on theories about the self. However, even when the self is held not to exist, the self becomes the negatum and the superstratum of the absence of the self. On the other hand, if the self is held to exist and to be different from the body and so on, the self becomes the substratum of the diference from the body and so on. Thus either as the superstratum or as the substratum of some negation, the self becomes the proper object of exploration. Further, irrespective of what one holds to be the correct theory of the self, the ordinary perceptions about the self, such as that I am fair, are false from many points of view. (If the self does not exist, the opinion that I am fair is false, for there is nothing real corresponding to the expression 'I'. On the other hand, if the self exists and is held to be different from the body and so on, the opinion that I am fair still turns out to be false, for the self, being different from the body and being nonphysical, cannot be fair or of some other complexion. This would, of course, be disputed by some materialists who hold that the self is the body.) This too makes the investigation necessary.

Some Hindus believe that if one meets one's death in the holy city of Benares, one is assured of freedom from all suffering. SM and RS point out that by implication Udayana is joining issue with such a belief (pp. 11 and 15). Dying in a holy place without knowledge of the truth cannot bring an end to all suffering, Udayana implies. On the other hand, if one acquires knowledge of the reality, one does not have to die in a holy place in order to gain freedom from all suffering.

> *Tatra bādhakam bhavat kṣaṇabhaṅgo vā vāhyārtha-bhaṅgo vā guṇaguṇibhedabhaṅgo vā anupalambho veti*. (AṬV 20)

> There the opposite views are that everything is momentary or that external things do not exist or that the substance is not different from the qualia or that nonapprehension (provides the ground for the nonexistence of the self).

Note: Here Udayana lists the four major views he seeks to examine and refute. As SM, BT, and RS point out (pp. 20, 21, 22), it is not enough to merely argue for one's own position. Even if one's arguments for one's own position are cogent and powerful, they cannot achieve the purpose unless the opposite views are properly examined and set aside. As DT (p. 17) remarks, the refutation of the opposite views may also provide indirect support for one's own view.

We describe a typical debate scenario that Udayana may have had in mind. The proponent (*vādin*) asserts that the self is permanent and non-momentary (*sthira*, *akṣaṇika*). The opponent (*prativādin*) then asserts that the self is impermanent and momentary (*asthira*, *kṣaṇika*). The mediator (*madhyastha*) then presents both viewpoints to the congregation, which is left with the doubt as to whether the self is permanent and non-momentary or impermanent and momentary. The aim of the debate is to resolve the doubt by eliminating one of the opposite views.

What precisely is meant by being momentary? One of several explanations given by SM and BT (p. 21) is that this is being something that is the negatum of the destruction (i.e., which is destroyed) in the moment immediately after its origin. Since the thing ceases to exist in the very moment following the moment of its origin, the thing exists for only one moment and is thus momentary in the strictly literal sense. The idea may also be expressed by saying that something existing at a given moment does not exist at any other moment (BT, p. 21).

RS (p. 25) explains a momentary entity as something that exists only for some time (*kādācitka*) and is not originated at a moment that is the locus of the prior absence (*prāgabhāva*) of (i.e., not originated in a moment that precedes) the moment of its existence. This rules out that the thing may endure for two or more moments. If the thing were to exist for a second moment, it would have to be originated in a moment that precedes the moment when it exists.

In this account of momentariness it is necessary to add that the thing exists only for some time. If this were left out, what we have left is that a momentary thing is that which is not originated at a moment that precedes the moment when it exists. This applies to something eternal as well and hence is too wide. Something eternal is not originated at all and so not originated at a moment that precedes the moment when the said thing exists.

Still, even after adding that the thing exists only for some time, this account overextends to prior absence. Prior absence, in the Nyāya view, is not originated but still does not exist for ever and is not eternal. Hence RS offers a second account (p. 25). Instead of saying that the thing exists for only some time, we may say that the thing has an origin and leave the rest as it is. This would rule out prior absence, for the latter has no origin (DT 19). The second account comes to this: a momentary thing is that which has an origin and is not originated at a moment that precedes a moment when it is existent.

This account of momentariness contains the notion of origin (*utpatti*). What is origin? It may (roughly) be explained as something's being related to the time that is not the locus of the destruction of a time when that thing is existent (DT 20). This description applies to the thing's existence only in the very first moment (*ādyakṣaṇa*) even if it were assumed that the thing is non-momentary and endures for some time. For in any subsequent moment there will be the destruction of some earlier moment of time when the thing is existent.

What is a moment (*kṣaṇa*)? It may be explained as not being the locus of the negatum of any prior absence belonging to itself (DT 26). At any given moment there is the prior absence of the noneternal things yet to exist. These noneternal things are the negata of these prior absences. Since none of these negata are existent at that moment, the latter does not become the locus of any of them. Thus the description may apply to any given moment of time.

However, it is conceivable that all noneternal things may be destroyed without any new beginning. Such a state is called a "great dissolution" (*mahāpralaya*). The above description would fail to apply to the first moment of such a great dissolution. Since no new entities are going to come into existence, it is false to say that at that moment there is the prior absence of any such entity.

Hence RS explains a moment as that which is not the locus of the prior absence of any entity belonging to itself (p. 25). Since a noneternal entity existing at any given moment of time is already there, its prior absence must cease to exist then. Hence no given moment can be the locus of any such prior absence. This account does apply to the first moment of the great dissolution. Since no new entities are to be originated, this moment is not the locus of any prior absence whatsoever.

However, this account works only if all things are accepted to be momentary. If some things are instead accepted to be non-momentary, even the second and later moments of time would not be the locus of the prior absence of any entity belonging to itself. Thus the description will hold not only of exactly one moment of time but also of a collection of moments of time. This difficulty does not arise if all things are momentary. Then the thing would cease to exist in the following moment and the latter cannot be the time to which the thing could still belong.

If things are accepted to be non-momentary, the definition of a moment should include the further qualification of not possibly being the locus of the negatum of any destruction belonging to itself. Since in the second and later moments some other noneternal things may be destroyed, these moments will possibly be the locus of the negata of these destructions. Hence the definition would be retricted to exactly any one given moment. Thus a moment may be defined as that which is not the locus of the prior absence of any entity belonging to itself and which cannot be the locus of the negatum of any destruction belonging to itself.

> *Tatra na prathamah pramāṇābhāvāt. Yat sat tat kṣaṇikam yathā ghatah saṃśca vivādādhyāsitah śabdādiriti cet na pratibandhāsiddheḥ*. (ATV 22)

> There the first [alternative that everything is momentary], is untenable, for there is no proof. Suppose it is argued that whatever has being is momentary, like a pot, and that sound and so on, which are the subject of contention, have being? No, for the pervasion is not justified.

Note: The argument for momentariness is based on the generalization that whatver has being is momentary. If this is granted and also that sound and so on have being, it follows that sound and so on are momentary. The force of saying that sound and so on are momentary is, of course, that everything is momentary. The Nyāya is entitled to object to citing a pot as a confirming example, for although a pot is momentary in the Buddhist view, it is not so in the Nyāya view. That is why Udayana says that the generalization is not justified.

However, the Buddhist can supply an undisputed confirming example. In the Nyāya view, too, the final sound in a series of sounds is momentary. So the final sound is something that, according to both the Buddhist and the Nyāya, has being and is momentary. This is hinted at by stating the second premise as "sound and so on, which are the subject of contention, have being." The final sound is not the subject of contention: both the Nyāya and the Buddhist accept it as momentary. But other sounds are the subject of contention. In the Buddhist view these are momentary but not in the Nyāya view. So the argument is over other sounds and anything else that has being. We find then that the final sound is not included in the inferential subject (*pakṣa*) and is an undisputed corroborative example. There are also no undisputed counterexamples. Although the Nyāya claims that stones, pots, and so on, have being and are non-momentary, the Buddhist disputes them. Thus the said generalization is prima facie acceptable.

Nevertheless, one can raise the doubt that there may be something that has being and is non-momentary, that is, one may have the apprehension (*śaṃkā*) that the sign, namely, having being, deviates from the probandum, namely, being momentary. In other words, the Buddhist argument is: Whatever is existent or has being is momentary. Thus having being or existence is the probans or ground of an object's momentariness. But some may doubt this relation of universal concomitance between being and momentariness: What is the harm if the object possesses being but is non-momentary? Such a doubt would hinder us to draw the inferential conclusion that everything is momentary. In order to counteract such a doubt the Buddhist has to present an argument in the form of a reductio ad absurdam (*tarka*) to show that if such were the case, that is, if there were something that had being and were non-momentary, something unacceptable would result. By saying that the generalization is unjustified, Udayana seems to imply that the Buddhist is not in a position to produce any such reductio argument that is above reproach.

Udayana next takes note of and responds to an objection:

> *Sāmarthyāsāmarthyalakṣaṇaviruddhadharmasaṃsargeṇa bhedasiddhau tatsiddhirit cet. Na viruddhadharmasaṁsargāsiddheḥ*. (ATV 34)
>
> Suppose it is said that that [momentariness] is proved from proof of difference based on the ascription of the opposed characters of ability (*sāmarthya*) and inability (*asāmarthya*)? Not so, for the ascription of opposed characters is not justified.

Note: The implied premise of this Buddhist argument is that causal efficacy or the ability to bring about change (*kāritva*) is the ticket to reality or having being. If something lacks the ability to bring about change, it is unreal, such as the hare's horn. Now consider the moment when a thing brings about some change. Since it has done the job, it clearly has the ability to do it. But then consider the moment after the job is done. The Nyāya, being the upholder of permanence, claims that the same thing continues to exist then. But it cannot be so. Since the thing has already brought about the effect, it can no longer bring about the effect and have the ability to do so. However, ability to bring about the effect and inability to bring about the effect are opposed characters. Both cannot belong to the same thing.

So we must suppose that the thing at the moment when it is productive is different from the moment when it is not productive. Momentariness now follows as a consequence. Something must be productive in order to be real. But when it produces something, it ceases to be the thing that has the ability to produce that thing. So we now have a new thing and the previous thing is gone. The same consideration applies to any subsequent or previous moment. So nothing can remain the same for any two moments.

Udayana replies that the ascription of opposed characters is not an admissible ground. He implies that if two characters are opposed, both cannot truly belong to the same thing at the same time; so the ascription must be false. Then the premise stating that the sign truly belongs to the inferential subject must be false, irrespective of whatever may be chosen as the inferential subject. Then the conclusion (about momentariness of everything) can no longer be claimed to be necessarily true. On the other hand, if the ascription of those characters to the same subject is true, those characters cannot be opposed. The argument fails on either count.

In particular, the Buddhist is suggesting an argument like the following: the thing in the previous moment is different from the thing in the succeeding moment, for otherwise the two opposed characters of causal efficacy and lack of causal efficacy must be ascribed to the same thing. Udayana's refutation is that if causal efficacy and lack of causal efficacy are truly opposed, both cannot belong to the same thing. On the other hand, if it is true that the same thing is both causally efficacious and not, then causal efficacy and lack of causal efficacy (in spite of their appearance) are not opposed characters.

The Buddhist raises another objection and Udayana replies:

> *Prasaṅgaviparyayābhyām tatsiddhiriti cet. Na sāmarthyam hi karaṇatvam vā yogyatā vā. Nādyah sādhyāviśiṣṭatvaprasaṅgāt.* (ATV 34)
>
> That [the ascription of opposed characters] is proved with the help of a reductio proving as a consequence [presence and] absence. No. Is efficacy being instrumental or being capable by nature? Not the first, for then it becomes indistinguishable from the probandum.

Note: The reductio offered by the Buddhist is of this type:

1. If the thing (at the given time) were incapable of producing the effect, it could not have done that; but it does; therefore it is not incapable of producing the effect.
2. If the thing were capable of producing the effect (at the following moment), it should have done that; but it does not; therefore, it is not capable of producing the effect.

These two subjunctive arguments together prove both the presence and absence of capability of producing the effect. It follows that the thing at the time it is capable of producing the effect is different from the thing at the following moment when it is incapable of producing the effect and, therefore, that it is momentary.

Udayana begins the reply by distinguishing between two different senses of being a causal condition. The first sense is that of being a causal condition which is immediately followed by the origin of the effect. Such a causal condition is called an instrument (*karaṇa*). (In another sense an instrument is that causal condition that has an operation that is immediately followed by the origin of the effect.) For example, in cutting a tree with an axe the contact between the axe and the tree is the instrumental causal condition, for the tree is cut immediately after the impact of the axe. Now suppose that efficacy or capability of producing the effect is taken to mean being a causal condition that is immediately followed by the origin of the effect. Then the reductio becomes: if the thing were not capable of producing the effect, that is, if the thing were not immediately followed by the origin of the effect, it could not have done that, that is, it could not have been immediately followed by the origin of the effect. This makes the antecedent (*āpādaka*) and the consequent (*āpādya*) of the conditional indistiguishable and, therefore, useless for the proof.

The Buddhist seeks to avoid the charge and again Udayana responds:

Vyāvṛttibhedādayamadoṣa iti cet. Na tadanupapatteḥ. Vyāvartyabhedena virodho hi tanmūlam. Sa ca na tāvanmitho vyāvartyapratikṣepāt gotvaśvatvavat tathā sati virodhādanyatarāpāye bādhāsiddhyoranyataraprasaṅgāt. Nāpi tadākṣepapratikṣepābhyām vṛkṣatvaśiṃśapātvavat parāparabhāvānabhyupagamāt. Abhyupagame vā samarthasyāpyakaraṇama-

samarthasyāpi vā karaṇam prasajyeta. Nāpi upādhibhedāt kāryatvanityatvavat tadabhāvāt. (ATV 34, 39, 41–43)

What if this is not a flaw because there is difference with respect to differentiation (*vyāvṛtti*)? No; it does not stand up upon examination. The difference [literally, opposition] due to the difference of the differentiata (*vyāvartya*) is the basis of that [difference with respect to differentiation]. That is not like the mutual exclusion of the differentiata as in the case of cowness and horseness. If it were so, since either would be negated due to opposition, the result would be either negation (*bādha*) [of the consequent] or falsity (*asiddhi*) [of the antecedent]. Nor is it like treeness and *aśoka*-ness through inclusion (*ākṣepa*) and noninclusion (*pratikṣepa*), for it is not that there is the relation of being greater and smaller. If it were so, there would have been either something that is capable of producing the effect (*samartha*) but is not an instrumental causal condition (*akaraṇa*) or something that is an instrumental causal condition but is not capable of producing the effect. Nor also is it due to difference of the associates, like that of effectness and noneternality, for there is lack of that.

Note: The traditional Buddhist theory of meaning asserts that words primarily signify by way of exclusion or differentiation from others (*anyāpoha*). For example, the word cow primarily signifies what excludes or is different from what is not a cow (*ago-vyāvṛtti*). This theory is opposed to the theories that words primarily signify (1) the individual or (2) the universal or (3) the form or (4) the relation between the individual and the universal or (5) the individual as related to the universal. Accordingly, the Buddhist claims that the antecedent and the consequent of the said conditional are distinguishable. Being incapable of producing the effect excludes all that is capable of producing the effect. On the other hand, not doing (the job) or not being the cause excludes all that does the job or all that becomes the cause.

Udayana gives the usual Nyāya response that true differentiation should be based on the difference between those that are differentiated:

1. For example, what the word *cow* excludes is different from what the word *horse* excludes. This makes sense because the differentiata—cows and horses—are different and are mutually exclusive.

2. Similarly, what the word *tree* excludes is different from what the word *aśoka* (a kind of tree having red flowers) excludes. Although all *aśokas* are trees, all trees are not *áśokas*.

3. Again, even where the two words are coextensive, the associates (*upādhi*) are different. For example, in the universe of positive reals the words *effect* (*kārya*) and *noneternal* (*anitya*) are coextensive. All positive reals that are effects are noneternal and vice versa. Still the associates of the two words are different. The word *effect* is associated with prior absence (*prāgabhāva*). An effect is nonexistent before its origin. On the other hand, the word *noneternal* is associated with destruction (*dhvaṃsa*). A noneternal (positive) thing is nonexistent after its destruction.

So it makes sense to say that there is a difference between the differentiations of the words *effect* and *noneternal*. What the word *effect* excludes are things that are not subject to origin; what the word *noneternal* excludes are things that are not subject to destruction. Thus it is feasible to interpret "all effects are noneternal" as "all those that exclude those that are not subject to origin also exclude those that are not subject to destruction."

But none of these three possibilities apply to the two sets of words under consideration, namely, incapability of producing the effect (*asāmarthya*) and not doing the job or not being the cause (*akāritva*).

1. The references of these two are not mutually exclusive as are those of the words *cow* and *horse*. If one were to claim that the references of these two are exclusive, the result would be either that the consequent would be rejected (*bādha*) or the antecedent would be false (*asiddhi*): either it would be that if something were incapable of producing the effect it could not be a noncause or it would be that if something were a noncause, it could not be incapable of producing the effect. Clearly it is impossible to accept these.

2. It is also not true that the extension of one of the two sets of words is greater than that of the other, as it is in the case of the words *tree* and *aśoka*. If such were the case, there would have been either at least one thing that is incapable of producing the effect but is an instrumental

causal condition or at least one thing that is not an instrumental causal condition but capable of producing the effect. (In the ordinary sense there are, according to the Nyāya, causal conditions that are not instruments, that is, are not immediately followed by the origin of the effect. But here capability [*sāmarthya*] has been interpreted as being an instrument [*karaṇatva*]. So if something is not an instrument, it cannot be capable either.)

3. Nor moreover is it the case that the associates (*upādhi*) of the two sets of words are different. If one were to claim that the associates are different, that should be demonstrated; but the Buddhist has not done that.

So it is not justified to claim that the differentiations (*vyāvṛtti*) of the two sets of words are different.

Could a difference be maintained merely on the grounds of terminological or cognitive difference? No, says Udayana:

> *Na ca śabdamātramupādhiḥ paryāyaśabdocchedaprasaṅgāt. Nāpi vikalpabhedaḥ svarūpakṛtasya tasya vyāvṛttibhedakatve asamarthavyāvṛtterapi bhedaprasaṅgāt. Viṣayakṛtasya tu tasya bhedakatve anyonyāśrayaprasaṅgāt. Na ca nirnimitta evāyam vyāvṛttibhedavyavahārah atiprasaṅgāt.* (ATV 43, 45)
>
> And it is not that a mere word is an associate; then there could not be equivalent words. Nor is it that there is difference [merely] of cognition (literally, construction: *vikalpa*); if that could be the basis of differentiation [merely] by nature, there would be difference even where differentiation is not in order. If it were to be the basis of differentiation through the contents, the result would be mutual dependence (*anyonyāśraya*). It is not that the usage of difference in differentiation is groundless; then there would be overcoverage.

Note: The words *asāmarthya* (incapability of producing the effect) and *akāritva* (not doing or not being the cause) are, of course, different. But that by itself does not imply that their meanings are different. If that were so, the words, say, *ghaṭa* and *kalaśa* both of which mean a pot, could not have the same meaning. Similarly, the cognition of *asāmarthya* and the cognition of *akāritva* are two different cognitions. But that by itself does not imply that their cognitive contents are different. If that were so, the cognition of, say, a triangle would have to have a different content from the cognition of a triangle taking place anytime later. If one argues that the cognitive contents are different because the cognitions are different, there would be circularity. For cognitions are differentiated on the ground that their cognitive contents are different. But now the cognitive contents are being differentiated on the ground that their cognitions are different. In brief, without a proper basis the differentiations (or meanings) cannot be said to be different. Otherwise, meanings would be different even where there is no difference.

Udayana had distinguished between two different interpretations of *sāmarthya* or efficacy: (1) being an instrument or being immediately followed by the effect, and (2) being capable by nature (*yogyatā*). He has shown that if efficacy is taken in the first sense, the Buddhist argument for momentariness is not sound. What if efficacy is interpreted in the second sense? This boiles down to having the specifier (*avacchedaka*) of causality (*kāraṇatā*), that is, as having that feature by virtue of which something becomes a causal condition. Such a causal condition is not always immediately followed by the origin of the effect, for the effect comes into being only when the sum total of causal conditions is available. For example, to make a clay pot we need clay, water, the wheel, the rod, and so on. Each one these is a necessary condition and the pot cannot be made if any one of them is missing. Thus each one of these possesses a feature by virtue of which it is a causal condition of a pot. For clay the feature may be called clayness, for the wheel, wheelness, and so on. Then clayness, wheelness, and so on, are the specifiers of causality. But none of these by itself is a sufficient condition; only their sum total is the sufficient condition. Udayana shows that the argument does not hold up in this interpretation either:

> *Nāpi dvitīyaḥ. Sa hi sahakārisākalaym vā prātisvikī vā. Na tāvadādyaḥ pakṣaḥ siddhasādhanāt parānabhyupagamena hetvasiddheśca. Yat sahakārisamavadhānavat taddhi karotyeveti ko nāma nābhyupaiti yamuddiśya sādhyate. Na ca akaraṇakāle sahakārisamavadhānavattvam asmābhirabhyupeyate yatah prasaṅgah pravarteta.* (ATV 46)

> Not also the second. Is it (1) having all the auxiliary conditions, or (2) being of the nature of each specifier of causality? But not the first, for that would involve proving

what is accepted and falsity of the sign for the reason that the opponent does not accept it. That which is attended by [all] the auxiliary conditions invariably does [the job]: Who denies this, so that the proof is offered? On the other hand, when it does not do [the job], we do not admit that [all] the auxiliary conditions are available, so that there is no room for the reductio.

Note: Suppose that efficacy is taken to mean having all the auxiliary conditions. Then the reductio would be: if it were efficacious, that is, if it were attended with all the causal conditions, it would have done the job. There is no dispute over this, Udayana points out; so no reductio is called for. On the other hand, if it does not do the job, not all of the auxiliary conditions are available. Then it would be false to say that all auxiliary conditions are available. Thus it transpires that there is no real contradiction in saying that the same thing is causally efficacious in the moment it produces the effect and not causally efficacious in the following moment. The reason why it is not causally efficacious in the following moment is that although it is still possessed of the specifier of causality and is capable by nature of being a causal condition, some auxiliary condition is missing, so that the effect is not produced. So there is no bar to agreeing with common experience (*anubhava*) and saying that the same thing continues to exist for two or more moments.

Prātisvikī to yogyatā anvayavyatirekaviṣayībhūtam bījatvam vā syāt tadavāntarajātibhedo vā sahakārivaikalyaprayuktakāryābhāvavattvam vā. (ATV 48)

Is the inherent ability to produce the effect the same as seedness (*bījatvam*), which becomes the content of the awareness of co-presence (*anvaya*) as well as co-absence (*vyatireka*), or is it a specific property subordinate to that (= *bījatva*) or is it lack of [producing] the effect due to lack of the auxiliaries?

Note: In order to prove that everything is momentary the Buddhist has offered the argument that if something has the ability to produce the effect, it produces the effect immediately. In this context the Naiyāyika has asked: What is meant by the ability to produce the effect? Is it the same as being a causal condition (*kāraṇatā*)? If so, is the latter the same as being immediately followed by the origin of the effect (*phalopadhāyakatva*) or is it inherent ability (*yogyatā*)? Udayana has previously shown that the alternative of being immediately followed by the origin of the effect does not work for the Buddhist. That leaves the second explanation of inherent ability. With reference to this Udayana has asked: Is this explicable as being attended by all the auxiliaries or is this explicable as being of the nature of each (*prātisvikī*)? Of these two althernatives Udayana has refuted the first one in the immediately preceding passage. Now he takes up the remaining alternative and offers three possible interpretations of it.

The first interpretation is that inherent ability is the same as seedness and so on. This means that that which has seedness, that is, the seed, is inherently able. The seed is a causal condition of the sapling and seedness is the specifier of the fact of being a causal condition. This is known through the observation of co-presence and co-absence of the seed and the sapling, that is, through the observation that the sapling sprouts when the seed is there and does not sprout when the seed is not there.

Udayana speaks of seedness because there is already a reference to the causal connection between the seed and the sapling in the earlier passages. In the same way there is causal connection between the thread and the cloth, the clay and the pot, and so on, and, accordingly, threadness, clayness, and so forth, too are implied in the reference to seedness. In other words, what is possessed of the specifier of the fact of being a causal condition is inherently able to produce the effect.

The second interpretation is that inherent ability is the same as a particular property (*jātibheda*) subsumed under (*avāntara*) seedness, and so on. This property is called *kurvadrūpatva*, which means roughly "being currently productive." Some Buddhists accept this additional property to account for the fact that while the seed in the field produces the sapling, the seed in a store does not. If possession of seedness and so on were the criterion of inherent ability, the seed in the store and that in the field should have both been productive. Thus what possesses this additional property is inherently able to produce the effect.

The third interpretation is that inherent ability is to be explained as not producing the effect due to the lack of auxiliaries, that is, that which produces the effect except when the auxiliaries are not available is inherently able to produce the effect. Thus that the effect is not produced once again in the moment immediately following its origin is to be explained by the lack of some auxiliary condition. In this interpretation the admission of an additional property called *kurvadrūpatva* is sought to be avoided while accounting for the fact that not all seeds will produce a sapling.

> *Na tāvad ādyah, akurvataḥ api vījajātiasya pratyakṣa-siddhatvāt tavāpi tatra avipratipratteḥ.* (ATV 49)

> Not the first, for it is known through perception that there are those which do not produce the effect and yet are of the same kind as the seed; you too do not disagree on this.

Note: The Buddhist has argued that that which is inherently able is productive and conversely that that which is not productive is not inherently able. According to the first interpretation of inherent ability this boils down to this: that which has seedness produces a sapling, and conversely, that which does not produce a sapling does not have seedness. But this is false. There is seedness in a seed that is in a store although the latter does not produce any sapling. This shows that seedness deviates from being productive of a sapling and also that not being productive of a sapling deviates from not having seedness.

> *Na dvitiyaḥ. Tasya kurvataḥ api mayānabhyupagamena dṛṣṭāntasya sādhanavikalatvāt. Ko hi nāma susthātmā pramāṇaśunyam abhyupagacchet. Sa hi na tāvat pratyakṣeṇa anubhūyate, tathānavasāyāt. Nāpyanumānena, liṅgābhāvāt. Yadi na kaśchidviśeṣah, katham tarhi kāraṇākāraṇe iti cet, ka evamāha neti. Param kim jātibhedarupaḥ sahakārilābhālābharūpu veti niyāmakam pramāṇam anusarantah na paśyamaḥ. Tathāpi yaḥ ayam sahakārimadhyamadhyāsīnaḥ akṣeparkaraṇasvabhāvo bhāvaḥ sa yadi prāgapyāsit tadā prasahya kāryam kurvaṇo gīrvāṇaśāpaśatenāpi apahastayitum na śakyata iti cet, yuktametat yadi akṣepakaraṇasvabhāvatam bhāvasya pramāṇagocarah syāt, tadeva kutaḥ siddham iti nādhigacchāmaḥ. Prasaṅgaviparyayābhyām iti cet, na, parasparāśrayaprasaṅgāt. Evam svabhāvavasiddhau tayoh pravṛttiḥ, tatpravṛttau ca evam svabhāvatvasiddhiriti.* (ATV 50)

> Not the second. Since I [= the Naiyāyika] do not admit that that which is productive possesses that [= *kurvadrūpatva*], the example [= the seed that produces a sapling] is devoid of the ground [= *kurvadrūpatva*]. Which person in

his senses would admit something that has no proof? Indeed, that is not grasped by [indeterminate] perception, for it does not become the object of [determinate] perception. It is also not inferable, for there is no probans. [Objection:] If there is no specialty (*viśeṣa*), why is it that some are productive and some are not? [Reply:] Who says that there is none? But is the explanation in terms of the particular property [= *kurvadrūpatva*] and its absence or is it in terms of the availability and nonavailability of the auxiliaries? In this regard we do not find any decisive proof even after investigation. [Objection:] If the thing that becomes immediately productive while together with the auxiliaries, already possessed this nature, it would have produced the effect by force and could not be prevented even by a hundred divine curses. [Reply:] This would have been reasonable if the property of being immediately productive were known through a proof. But we do not know how that is proved. [Objection:] The proof is by way of reasoning from justified supposition (*prasaṅga*) and reverse supposition (*viparyaya*). [Reply:] No, for then there is circularity. If this property were proved, those reasonings would have held and if those reasonings held, the property would have been proved.

Note: Udayana is offering arguments to refute the second suggestion that inherent ability is the same as having the property of being currently productive. The Buddhist has argued that whatever is inherently able is productive. With the relevant substitution this amounts to: whatever is currently productive is productive. This sounds like a truism. But it is not. Being currently productive is a newly coined property assumed by the Buddhist. Such a property is suppposedly pervaded by specifiers of causality such as seedness and so on, and different from them. The Nyāya, however, does not admit that when a causal condition happens to be immediately productive it possesses any such property. So the Buddhist claim boils down to the argument (*prasaṅga*) that whatever is possessed of the (newly coined) property of being curently productive is productive (or, applying it to the given case, whatever seed is possessed of the property of being currently productive is productive of the sapling)—a claim that is unsubstantiated in view of the Nyāya disclaimer. Similarly, the argument from reverse supposition (*viparyaya*) would boil down to that whatever is not productive is not possessed of the (newly coined) property of being currently productive (or, applying it to the given case, whatever seed is not productive of the sapling is not possessed of the [newly coined] property of being currently productive)—and this too is an unsubstantiated claim in view of the Nyāya refusal to accept the assumption of the said property.

Udayana adds that the refusal to accept this property is due to the fact that there is no evidence for it either from perception or from inference. That is, when a seed is observed to produce a sapling, no additional property is observed in this seed that is missing in another seed in a granary that is not productive of a sapling. (In the Nyāya view the production and nonproduction should be explained by the availability and otherwise of the auxiliaries.) Similarly, the existence of this property cannot also be proved through inference, for there is no suitable probans (*liṅga*) for it.

The Buddhist objects that both the seed in a field and the seed in a granary are possessed of seedness. If the possession of seedness alone sufficed for producing the sapling, both the seed in a field and the seed in a granary would have produced saplings. Since this is not so, we should infer an additional property in the seed in a field that makes it productive and also infer the lack of that property in the seed in a granary that makes it nonproductive. These inferences can be set out as an argument from justified supposition (*prasaṅga*) and an argument from reverse supposition (*viparyaya*) as indicated earlier.

Udayana replies that the facts of production and nonproduction can also be explained by the presence and absence respectively of auxiliary factors. There is no decisive ground to reject the explanation in terms of the auxiliaries and opt for the one in terms of the additional property.

The Buddhist objects that unless we infer this additional property, we cannot explain why the causal condition (the seed in our example) with the auxiliaries (i.e., the other causal conditions) produces the effect (the sapling in our example). That is, we should infer that the seed acquires this additional property when it is together with the auxiliaries like soil, water, and so on, and produces the effect. In other words, the property of being productive without any delay (*akṣepakaraṇasvabhāvatva*) serves as the probans for inferring the additional property of being currently productive (*kurvadrūpatva*). If the causal condition already had this property, it would have already produced the effect.

Udayana replies that the admission of the additional property would be in order only if there were an independent evidence for it. One could say that the arguments from justified supposition and reverse supposition provide such evidence. But this is not so. What we have is only a circular reasoning. Unless we admit the additional property, these arguments do not hold; at the same time unless these arguments hold, we cannot admit the additional property. That is, these arguments do not show why the explanation in terms of the mere presence and absence of the auxiliaries must be rejected in favor of the explanation through the additional property that is assumed to emerge when the auxiliaries are present. One can counter with equal cogency that whatever causal condition is attended by all the auxiliaries produces the effect and, reversely, that whatever causal condition does not produce the effect is not attended by the auxiliaries.

RS offers several analyses of the notion of a thing being productive without any delay (*akṣepakaraṇasvabhāvatva*). It could mean that it produces an effect at the time immediately after its origin (*svotpattyavyavahitottarasamayavṛttikāryamātrakāritvam*). However, this analysis includes the concept of origin (*utpatti*). So the question is: What is meant by origin? The latter may be analyzed as being related to the time that is not the locus of the destruction of the time to which the thing belongs (*svādhikaraṇasamayadhvaṃsānadhikaraṇasamayasambandhaḥ*). Apart from the question of adequacy of this analysis, it is, like other possible analyses of the notion of origin, very complex (*guru*). So a second analysis of a thing being productive without any delay could be that the thing does not belong to the time that precedes the time immediately preceding the time of its effect (*svakāryāvyavahitaprākkālavṛttitvam*). Then one may ask: What is meant by the time immediately preceding the time of its effect? This may be explained as the moment that is the locus (*adhikaraṇa*) of the prior absence of the moment, which in turn is the locus of the prior absence of the thing's effect (*svakāryaprāgabhāvādhikaraṇakṣaṇaprāgabhāvādhikaraṇakṣaṇa*). But that includes a reference to the notion of moment (*kṣaṇa*) which is very complex. So a third analysis of a thing being productive without any delay could be that the thing does not belong to the time that is the countercorrelative (*pratiyogin*) of the destruction that is contemporaneous with the prior absence of its effect (*svakāryaprāgabhāvasamānakālīnadhvaṃsapratiyogisamayāvṛttitvam*). If, however, an adequate and simple analysis of origin (*utpatti*) is available, the notion of being productive without any delay can be explained as being productive (or being possessed of causal operation: *vyāpāra*) at the very moment of its origin. This agrees with the Buddhist view that the thing exists for only one moment and is destroyed the moment immediately after its origin.

Syādetat, kāryajanmaiva asminnarthe pramāṇam, vilambakārisvabhāvānuvṛttau kāryanutpattiḥ sarvadā iti cet, na, vilambakārisvabhāvasya sarvadaiva akaraṇe tattvavyāghātāt. Tataśca vilambakarītyasya yāvat sahakāryasannidhānam tāvanna karotītyarthaḥ. Evam ca kāryajanma sāmagryam pramāṇayitum śakyate, na tu jātibhede. Te tu kim yathānubhavam vilambakārisvabhāvaḥ parasparapratyāsannāḥ kāryam kṛtavantaḥ kim vā yathā tvatparikalpanam kṣiprakārisvabhāvā ityatra kāryajananam ajāgarukameveti. (ATV 54–55)

[Objection:] The origin of the effect itself is the evidence for this thing [= *akṣepakaraṇasvabhāvatvam*]; if the characteristic of delayed production had continued, the effect would have never been produced. Reply: No. If delayed production meant never producing, that very nature would have been violated. Hence, delayed production means not producing until the auxiliaries are available. Thus the origin of the effect serves as evidence for [the recognition of] the sum total of causal conditions but not for the property [*kurvadrūpatvam* or *akṣepakaraṇasvabhāvatvam*] or its absence. Do these, as we find them, produce the effect later when they are all together, or do they acquire the property of producing without delay as surmised by you—in this regard the origin of the effect is certainly not an awakener [decisive evidence].

Note: The Buddhist objects that the very origin of the effect proves that the property of delayed productivity has been replaced by the property of productivity without any delay. If the former property had continued, the effect would not have been produced. Udayana replies that delayed productivity does not mean producing never; rather it means producing at a later time when all the auxiliaries are available. So the origin of the effect points to the fact that no one of many causal conditions by itself is the sufficient condition but that only the sum total of causal conditions is the sufficient condition. Such an origin does not decisively prove that there is originated a new property in the causal conditions called producing without any delay when all the causal conditions become available. No such new property is observed and the inference that there is such new property is not called for to explain the facts of origination and nonorigination of the effect. All that one needs to admit to explain the latter is that although each causal condition is necessary for the origin of the effect, none of them alone is sufficient to produce the effect, so that the production must be delayed until the sum total of each necessary causal condition is available.

In this connection BT comments that delayed productivity may be analyzed as the thing's not being productive in the moment immediately following the moment to which the thing belongs. From the Buddhist point of view there is only one moment to which the thing belongs, for the thing ceases to exist in the next moment. So if the thing is not productive in the very moment it is produced, it is not causally efficacious and, therefore, not real in the Buddhist view. This is why RS presents the Buddhist argument as the inference of the residue (*pariśeṣa*) after elimination. Either the thing is productive without any delay or it is not productive. The latter is ruled out. So the former must be accepted as the only residue and this lends support to momentariness.

Udayana, of course, rejects the second premise. Delayed productivity is not ruled out. Production must be delayed, he claims, until each necessary condition is together pointing to the idea that the totality (*sāmagrī*) alone is the sufficient condition.

> *Nāpi tṛtīyah, virodhāt. Sahakāryabhāvaprayuktakāryābhāvavāṃśca sahakārivirahe kāryavāṃśceti vyāhatam. Tasmād yad yadabhāva eva yanna karoti, tat, tatsadbhāve tatkarotyeveti syāt. Etacca sthairyasiddhereva param bījasarvasvamiti*. (ATV 57)

> Not also the third, for there is conflict. There is conflict in saying that it lacks the effect due to the lack of auxiliaries and that it has the effect due to the lack of auxiliaries. So it should be that what does not produce something because of the absence of something, produces certainly that thing because of the presence of the latter. This is certainly an excellent ground for proving permanence.

Note: Udayana explains the conflict as not having the effect due to the lack of auxiliaries and having the effect due to the lack of auxiliaries. The Buddhist has argued by way of *prasaṅga* (justified supposition) and *viparyaya* (reverse supposition) trying to prove *sāmarthya* (ability) and *asāmarthya* (lack of ability), which imply difference and that there is no continuant. If the ability is interpreted as not having the effect due to the lack of auxiliaries, what would be the formulation of the *prasaṅga*? Would it be 'what does not produce the effect due to lack of auxiliaries produces the effect then' or would it be 'what does not produce the effect due to the lack of auxiliaries produces the effect'?

The first formulation is not acceptable, for it involves the conflict. In the second formulation the antecedent (*āpādaka*) is 'not having the effect due to the lack of auxiliaries' and the consequent (*āpādya*) is 'having the effect'. Are both predicated with reference to the same time or different times? If the former, the second is equivalent to the first and involves the conflict. If the latter, the *prasaṅga* boils down to: What does not produce the effect due to the lack of auxiliaries at some time produces the effect at some other time. Then there is no overt conflict but still there is conflict with the thesis of momentariness. For what transpires is that something that fails to produce the effect at a given time due to the lack of auxiliaries, produces the effect at a different time when auxiliaries are there. This shows that the thing is a continuant and thus argues for permanence and refutes momentariness.

Udayana has said that what does not produce something because of the lack of something produces that thing with certainty because of the presence of the latter. He has used (what reads well in Sanskrit) the same pronoun 'that' (*yat*) in three places that we translate as 'what' for the first occurrence of '*yat*' and as 'something' for the second and the third occurrences. The second occurrence of '*yat*' or something signifies the effect and the third occurrence, the sum total of auxiliaries. Thus it amounts to: What does not produce the effect due to the lack of the sum total of auxiliaries certainly produces the effect when the sum total of auxiliaries is available.

Thus Udayana has disposed of a number of possible alternative explanations. Being a causal condition (*sāmarthya* or *kāraṇatā*) was distinguished as being of two types: (1) being immediately productive (*phalopadhāna*), and (2) being inherently able (*yogyatā*). The latter, again, is of two types: (1) having the sum total of auxiliaries (*sahakārisākalya*), and (2) being of the nature of each (*prātisvikī*). The last one, moreover, is of three types: (1) being the specifier of the fact of being a causal condition (*kāraṇatāvacchedakatva*), (2) being currently productive (*kurvadrūpatva*), and (3) having the absence of the effect due to the absence of auxiliaries. With the refutation of the last one in the above passage, the refutation of each of these as a ground for momentariness is complete.

Etena samarthavyavahāragocaratvam heturiti nirastam, tādṛgvyavahāragocarasyāpi bījasya aṃkurakaraṇadarśanāt.

Nāsau mukhyastatra vyavahāraḥ, tasya janananimittakatvāt, anyathā tu aniyamaprasaṅgāditi cet, kīdṛśam punarjananam mukhyasamarthavyavahāranimittam. Na tāvadkṣepakaraṇam, tasyāsiddheḥ. Niyamasya ca sahakārisākalye satyeva karaṇam karaṇamevetyevam svabhāvatvenāpi upapatteh, tataśca janananimitta evāyam vyavahāro na ca vyāptisiddhiriti. (ATV 58–59)

By this [= the argument that follows] is refuted that being the object of the usage of being able [to produce the effect] is the ground, for the seed which also is the object of such usage, is found not to produce the sapling [while in a granary]. [Objection:] There the usage is not primary, for that [the primary usage] is based on production; otherwise lack of uniformity will result. [Reply:] What kind of production is the basis of the primary use of being able? This is not being immediately productive, for that is refuted. And the uniformity is explained by way of always being productive when the sum total of auxiliaries is available [and not being productive when the said sum total is not available]. This usage, then, is based on production; but the [intended] generalization is not substantiated.

Note: The Buddhist now offers the argument that that which is the object of the usage of being able (to produce the effect) produces the effect (or that if something is the object of the usage of being able to produce the effect, it produces the effect). This is a new interpretation of the notion of *sāmarthya* or being able (to produce the effect). Earlier the notion of being able was interpreted as being immediately productive of the effect (*phalopadhāna*). Then the generalization amounted to that whatever is immediately productive of the effect is productive of the effect. Udayana had rejected it on the ground that the pervader was contained in the pervaded and was, therefore, indistinguishable. The present generalization is not open to that charge.

However, Udayana points out that this is still open to the objection that the seed and so on, too, are said to be able to produce the sapling and so forth, but the seed in a granary does not produce any sapling. So the generalization that 'whatever is the object of the usage of being able (to produce the effect) produces the effect' is false.

The Buddhist objects that the stored seed and so on are not objects of the primary usage of being able (to produce the effect), for such primary usage is restricted to what produces the effect and does not include something that does not produce the effect. So the generalization is saved if it is amended as 'whatever is the object of the primary usage of being able (to produce the effect) produces the effect'.

Udayana then explores what kind of production is the basis of the primary usage of being able (to produce the effect). Is it being productive without any delay (*akṣepakaraṇam*)? No, says Udayana, for it has been shown above that there is no evidence for the recognition of any such additional property. Indeed, it has been shown that if one tries to prove such a property through reasoning from justified supposition (*prasaṅga*) and reasoning from reverse supposition (*viparyaya*), there is circularity.

Is, then, uniformity (*niyama*) the basis of the primary usage of being able (to produce the effect)? That is, is a general rule accounting for production and nonproduction the basis? If so, the general rule can be formulated through the presence and absence of auxiliaries as well, points out Udayana. In other words, we can state a rule of uniformity as follows: Whatever produces the effect without fail whenever the sum total of auxiliaries is available and fails to produce the effect if the said sum total is not available, is the object of the primary usage of being able (to produce the effect).

If this works, both the seed in a field and the seed in a granary qualify as objects of the primary usage of being able to produce the sapling. That is, it is true of the seed in a granary as well that if it occurred with the sum total of auxiliaries it would have produced the sapling. In this crucial respect, the seed in a granary differs from a piece of stone and so on. The latter is not able to produce the sapling even if it is occurs with all the other causal conditions such as water, soil, and so on. Thus it is the possession of seedness, which is the primary basis of labeling something as being able to produce a sapling. Now, seedness is the common property of all seeds and makes them eligible for this label, and it is also that which is missing in other things so that the latter are not eligible for this label. That is, seedness is the specifier (*avacchedaka*) of the fact of seeds being a causal condition of saplings. Possession of such specifiers of causality (*kāraṇatāvacchedaka*), then, are the basis of the primary usage of something being regarded as being able to produce the effect.

This, of course, does not work for the Buddhist. What the latter needs, for the *prasaṅga* form, is the generalization that whatever becomes the object of the primary usage of being able (to produce the effect) produces the effect (or that if something is the object of the primary usage of being able [to produce the effect], it produces the effect). Similarly, what is needed for the *vyatireka* form is the generalization that whatever does not produce the effect is not the object of the primary usage of being able (to produce the effect) (or that if something does not produce the effect, it is not the object of the primary usage of being able [to produce the effect]). These generalizations are rendered false, for the seed in a granary, being possessed of seedness, remains eligible for the label of being able to produce the sapling in the primary sense although it does not produce the sapling. The seed in a field also remains eligible, for it too possesses seedness. On the other hand, a piece of stone does not become eligible, for it lacks seedness. This is why Udayana remarks at the end of the passage that the generalization (as intended by the Buddhist) is unsubstantiated.

In the above passage is the sentence *niyamasya ca sahakārisākalye satyeva karaṇam karaṇameva*. This contains two occurrences of *eva*, which means, depending on the context, "always," "without fail," and so on. Since there are two occurrences of eva, the sentence, following the standard idiom, should be analyzed, as SM, BT, RS and DT point out, into two sentences: (1) *niyamasya sahakārisākalye satyeva karaṇam* and (2) *niyamasya sahakārisākalye sati karaṇameva*. These two sentences signify respectively that the effect is produced only when the sum total of auxiliaries is available and that the effect is produced without fail when the sum total of causal conditions is available.

> *Syādetat. Etāvatāpi bhāvasya kaḥ svabhāvaḥ samarthito bhavati, na hi kṣepākṣepābhyāmanyaḥ prakāraḥ astīti cet. Na, dūṣaṇābhidhānasamaye niścayābhāvenaiva saṃdigdhāsiddhinirvāhe kathāpūrvarūpaparyavasānāt. Uttarapakṣāvasare tu saḥ api na durvacaḥ.* (ATV 62–63)

> [Objection:] What kind of nature of a thing is substantiated by this? There is after all no other alternative besides producing with delay and producing without delay. [Reply:] No. Since the flaw of uncertain probans (*saṃdigdhāsiddhi*) is established through lack of certainty in the course of the refutation, the debate resolves as before [in the refutation of the Buddhist opponent's view]. There is also no insurmountable difficulty while making one's own case.

Note: The Buddhist points out that the above refutation does not ruin his case: a thing must be either productive without any delay or productive with delay. Since the latter must be rejected, the former must be accepted; this works well for momentariness.

Udayana replies that being productive without any delay was offered by the Buddhist as the ground for momentariness. He has shown that this ground is uncertain (*saṃdigdha*), for the facts of production and nonproduction can also be explained through the availability and nonavailability of the sum total of auxiliaries. Since it has not been established with certainty that things are productive without any delay, that cannot prove that things are momentary. Thus the yield of the debate so far is that the Buddhist has failed to make his case and prove that everything is momentary. It can also be shown without a great deal of difficulty that things are nonmomentary in the course of proving one's own case.

[In this passage Udayana uses the expression '*kathāpūrvarūpa*'. *Kathā* from the context signifies a form of debate called *jalpa* in which one first refutes the opponent's view and then offers proof for one's own view. *Pūrva*, which means "before," signifies the opponent's view, which is discussed first and refuted. *Uttara*, which means "after" and is used in the last sentence, signifies one's own view, which is proved later.]

> *Tathāhi, karaṇam pratyavilamba iti kaḥ arthaḥ, kim utpatteranantaram eva karaṇam, sahakārisamavadhānānantaram eva vā. Vilamba ityapi kaḥ arthaḥ, kim yāvānna sahakārisamavadhānam tāvadakaraṇam, sarvathaiva akaraṇamiti vā. Tatra prathamacaturthayoḥ pramānābhāvadaniścaye api dvitīyatrtīyayoḥ pratyakṣam eva pramāṇam. Bījajātīyasya hi sahakārisamavadhānānantaram eva karaṇam karaṇam eva iti pratyakṣasiddham eva iti, tathā sahakārisamavadhānarahitasya akaraṇam ityapi*. (ATV 64)

> Thus what is the meaning of 'production without delay'? Is it production [by the causal condition] immediately after [its] origin or is it [production] immediately after the concatenation of auxiliaries? Also what is the meaning of '[production with] delay'? Is it not producing until there is concatenation of auxiliaries, or is it not producing under any circumstances? There while there is uncertainty over the first and the fourth due to lack of evidence, perception itself provides the evidence for the second and the third. It is certainly known from perception that what is of the same kind as the seed produces [the sapling] only after the concatenation of auxiliaries and

that it invariably produces [the sapling] after the concatenation of auxiliaries. Similarly, it is also [known from preception] that it [the seed, etc.] does not produce [the sapling, etc.] without the concatenation of auxiliaries.

Note: Udayana has shown that the Buddhist has failed to offer clear and convincing evidence to prove his case that everything is momentary. Now he offers evidence for his own case that things are permanent.

He lists four alternatives:

1. A thing always produces the effect in the very next moment after it is originated.
2. A thing always produces the effect in the very next moment after the sum total of auxiliaries is available.
3. A thing does not produce the effect until there is the sum total of auxiliaries.
4. A thing that does not produce immediately, never produces the effect.

Of these the first and the fourth are promoted by the Buddhist. Udayana points out that these are big claims that are unproven. It is not enough to show, as RS remarks, that this or that thing is immediately productive after its origin, or that this or that thing that is not immediately productive is never productive. The Buddhist has to show that this is so in every case but has failed to show that.

The second and the third alternatives are accepted by the Nyāya. The evidence for these comes from perception. We perceive that a thing like a seed produces its effect like a sapling immediately after the sum total of causal conditions such as water, soil, and so on, becomes available. We can then generalize that this is so in all cases which is a kind of perception in the Nyāya view. The crucial difference between the first alternative and the second is that while there may be some confirming examples for the first, there are also many counterexamples (e.g., a stored seed that does not produce any sapling). There are, however, no counterexamples for the second. That is, there is no known case where a causal condition occurs with each and every other causal condition but the effect is not produced. So the generalization for the second is sound, while that for the first is not. There is a similar difference between the third and the fourth alternatives. We do perceive that a thing like a seed does not produce the effect if some auxiliaries, such as water and so on, are not available. So the claim made in the third alternative has perceptual support. But the claim made in the fourth alternative goes much beyond what can be gathered from such support. There may be some cases where something that does not produce the effect immediately, never does. But this falls short of justifying that this is so in every case. For there are counterexamples (e.g., a stored seed that may produce a sapling later when appropriately planted) for such a general claim.

> *Atra ca bhavānapi na vipratipadyata eva, pramāṇasiddhatvāt, viparyaye bādhakācca. Tathāhi, yadi sahakārivirahe akurvāṇastatsamavadhāne api na kuryāt tajjātīyam akāraṇam eva syāt, samavadhānāsamavadhānayorubhayoḥ api akaraṇāt. Evam tatsamavadhānavirahe api yadi kuryāt sahakārino na kāraṇam syuḥ, tanantareṇāpi karaṇāt. Tathāca ananyathāsiddhānvayavyatirekavatām akāraṇatve kāryasya ākasmikatvaprasaṅgaḥ. Tathāca kādācitkatvavihatiriti.* (ATV 64)

> You too do not hold a different view on this, for it is backed by evidence and there is counterevidence against its denial. If a thing that does not produce the effect when auxiliaries are not available, does not produce the effect also when those [the auxiliaries] are available, then a thing of that kind is for sure not a causal condition. For it does not produce both when there is the concatenation and also when there is the lack of the concatenation. Similarly, if a thing should produce the effect when [so-called] auxiliaries are not available, those cannot be causal conditions, for there is production in spite of the absence of those. If something that is indispensably related by way of co-presence and co-absence, is not a causal condition, it follows that an effect would originate by chance. Then there is conflict with occasionality (*kādācitkatva*).

Note: Udayana offers more evidence for his own position. He explains why auxiliaries make a difference. A causal condition is able to produce the effect when all other auxiliaries are available. If something fails to produce even then, it does not qualify as a causal condition (because of deviation from universal co-presence or *anvaya-vyabhicāra*), for the effect is produced if the sum total of causal conditions is available, that is, the sum total of causal conditions is a sufficient condition. On the other hand, if something can produce the effect without the so-called auxiliaries, the latter do not count as causal conditions (because of deviation from universal co-absence or *vyatireka-vyabhicāra*), for only that without which the effect is not produced is counted as a causal condition, that is, a causal condition is a necessary condition.

SM puts one general proposition as: whichever kind is nonproductive both when the auxiliaries are available and not available is for sure not a causal condition, for instance, a piece of stone with respect to a sapling (*yajjātīyam sahakārisamavadhānāsamavadhanayoḥ akaraṇam tajjātīyam akaraṇam eva śilasakalavat*). The other general proposition is put as: that without which an effect is produced by something is not an auxiliary of that for that effect, for example, the thread with reference to a stick with which is to be produced a pot (*yatkāryam yadvyatirekeṇa yat karoti tatkārye na tasya tatsahakāritvam yathā daṇḍasya ghaṭe janayitavye tanturiti*).

Udayana remarks toward the end of the passage that if something were not a causal condition of an effect with which the former is indispensably and invariably related by way of co-presence and co-absence, that effect would, as a consequence, be a chance happening. Indispensable and invariable co-presence (i.e., directly relevant presence in the locus of the origin of the effect immediately before the origin in every case without any exception) and co-absence are the best signs of a causal connection between two admittedly distinct things. If a thing is not a causal condition in spite of such relationship, other things that are not so related cannot also be causal conditions. Then the origin of the effect must be left to chance. But this is not acceptable, for it goes against the occasional or contingent (*kādācitka*) nature of an effect. There is nothing that happens anywhere or anytime. Everything that comes into being does so on the occasion of or contingent upon certain other things. For example, food nourishes and the former is related to the latter by way of co-presence and co-absence. If, still, the former is not a causal condition of the latter, nothing else is. Then nourishment is a matter of chance. Then eating is not a necessary condition of nourishment and may be dispensed with by one who wants nourishment. But no one who seeks nourishment does that; this shows that every such person regards food as a causal condition of nourishment and does not regard nourishment as a chance happening but regards it as something contingent upon the consumption of food. Even a nonsuicidal skeptic who preaches universal doubt and rejects causation, eats without hesitation or wavering (*niṣkampa*). This shows that even such a skeptic regards food as a necessary condition of nourishment and does not practice what he preaches.

> *Evam ca dvitīyapakṣavivakṣāyām akṣepakāritvam eva bhāvasya svabhāvaḥ. Tṛtīyapakṣavivakṣāyām tu kṣepakāritvam eva bhāvasya svarūpam iti na ubhayaprakāranivṛttiriti.* (ATV 68)

> If thus the second alternative is intended to be espoused, production without delay becomes the character of a thing. If, however, the third alternative is intended, delayed production becomes the character of a thing. So it is not that both are ruled out.

Note: The first and the fourth alternatives have been refuted and the second and the third, accepted. The second alternative points to production without delay. The third alternative points to delayed production. Thus both production without delay and delayed production turn out to be characters of things as against the Buddhist claim that only production without delay is the character of a thing or that all things are immediately productive.

RS anticipates the objection that if both delayed and undelayed production are characters of things, then both characters would belong to a thing as long as that thing exists. He replies by distinguishing between three possibilities. The first is that a thing and its character are identical. The second is that a character belongs to a thing invariably as long as that thing exists. The third is that a thing and its character are different and the latter belongs to the former. He points out that the first is not accepted by the Nyāya. For example, water is cold, but water and its coldness are held to be different. The second too is not accepted by the Nyāya. For example, velocity (*vega*) is a character of a substance in motion; but velocity does not belong to that substance when it is stationary. The third is accepted by the Nyāya. But from this viewpoint a character need not belong to a thing as long as it exists. So when all the auxiliaries are available, a thing becomes immediately productive. But if all the auxiliaries are not available, a thing does not become immediately productive. There is nothing puzzling about this if it is accepted that a thing and its characters (*dharma*) are different and that the former may exist without one or more of the latter.

To summarize the main arguments so far: If something remained the same for more than one moment, it could be both productive and unproductive; but this is impossible, for nothing can have opposed characters; so nothing can remain the same for more than one moment and everything is momentary—so argues the Buddhist. Udayana replies that being productive and being unproductive are not truly opposed. To say that something is productive means that it is a causal condition (or possessed of the specifier of the fact of being a causal condition) and that it is attended by all other causal conditions. On the other hand, to say that something is unproductive means that it is a causal condition and that it is not attended by all the other causal conditions. So something could be both productive and unproductive and be permanent. The Buddhist counters by saying that being productive should mean being immediately productive or being productive without any delay and that nothing could be both immediately productive and not immediately productive. Udayana responds that being immediately productive could mean being a causal condition that is attended by all other conditions. Then there is no bar to holding that the same thing is both immediately productive and not immediately productive and is non-momentary. If, however, being immediately productive means something else that is an additional fact, the Buddhist has failed to produce sufficient evidence to show that the latter meaning is to be preferred over the former which is acceptable from the viewpoint of common experience.

From the Second Part: On the Critique of Subjective Idealism

We have seen so far a part of how Udayana has criticized the Buddhist doctrine of momentariness. We now look at how he tries to refute the Yogācāra Buddhist view that subjective conscious states alone are real. From this viewpoint nothing external is real and nothing other than consciousness exists. This goes against the Nyāya position that one's self as an immaterial substance is ontologically different from the internal states belonging to itself, other selves, or other immaterial substances as well as material substances. Udayana examines the major Buddhist arguments for a subjective idealistic view.

> With the upholder of the view that conscious states [alone are real] still awake, there is not even anything external. How can there be the self? Let him speak out upon being asked: Do you intend to say (1) that the cognizer and the cognized parts both of which are real, are identical, or (2) are not of

> different kinds, or (3) that the cognized is unreal? If the first is sought to be proved, whatever is adduced as the reason, such as being cognized together invariably or being cognized or being the revealer, the flaw is patent. (ATV 429–31)

In the Nyāya view the self is the substratum or owner of conscious states and is different from consciousness. If the Yogācāra view that conscious states alone are real is granted, the Nyāya view of the self must be rejected. That is why Udayana remarks that if the above kind of subjective idealism is granted, the self as something different from conscious states cannot exist.

Every cognition has an object. So Udayana says that within a cognition the cognizer and the cognized parts should be distinguished. One possible interpretation of the subjectivist position is that both the cognizer and the cognized are real but are nevertheless identical. If this is the intended interpretation, Udayana claims that various reasons given by the Buddhist must be flawed. What the subjectivist wants to prove is that cognition and its object are identical. The conclusion of the inference may be stated as: cognition is identical with its object. Here cognition is the inferential subject (*pakṣa*) and being identical with the object is the probandum. If the argument is sound, it would be proved that cognition is cognition and that is what the conclusion then would boil down to. Some reason would be offered to prove this conclusion and the premise will state that cognition is X. But that reason, too, would be an object of cognition. Being an object of cognition, that reason also would have to be identical with cognition. So the premise also should boil down to this: that cognition is cognition. The premise and the conclusion then become indistinguishable. Accordingly, whatever may be offered as the reason, the argument would be circular.

Now let us look at the other Buddhist reasons or signs cited by Udayana. The first is: being cognized together invariably. The implied premise is that whatever are always cognized together are identical. It may be objected that the very expression of being together implies difference, which conflicts with the thesis of identity. But it can be circumvented by interpreting the reason as 'not being the object of a cognition of which that (the other) is not the object'. The inference then becomes: cognition is nondifferent from the cognized because of not being the object of a cognition of which the cognized is not the object. The inference may also be reformulated by naming particular objects: the cognition of blue is nondifferent from the blue because of not being the object of a cognition of which the blue is not the object.

Alternatively, the blue may be made the inferential subject: the blue is nondifferent from the cognition of blue because of not being the object of a cognition of which the cognition of blue is not the object. For the argument to work it would have to be granted (in opposition to the Nyāya viewpoint) that cognition is self-revealing, that is, in the cognition of blue not only the blue but also the cognition is revealed.

The second reason is: being cognized (*grāhyatva*). The implied argument is that whatever is cognized is identical with cognition; the blue is cognized; therefore, the blue is identical with cognition.

The third reason is: being the revealer (*prakāśamānatva*). The implied argument is: whatever reveals is identical with what is revealed; cognition reveals; therefore, cognition is identical with what is revealed. While the second reason is meant for having the cognized as the inferential subject, the third reason is meant for having the cognition as the inferential subject. For the first reason—being cognized together invariably—the cognized or the cognition may alternatively be featured as the inferential subject.

But no such reason, whatever it may be, can escape, Udayana suggests, a baffling problem. Suppose there is cognition of absence of cognition. If the above arguments were sound, it would follow that cognition is the same as absence of cognition, which is absurd. For example, take the second reason. Then the argument will go as: whatever is cognized is identical with cognition; absence of cognition is cognized; therefore, absence of cognition is identical with cognition. Since the conclusion is patently false, one of the premises must be false. That absence of cognition is cognized is already supposed to be the case. So the only remaining premise, that whatever is cognized is identical with cognition, must be false. Similar remarks apply to the first reason. The first reason yields this argument: whatever does not become the object of a cognition of which that (the other) is not the object is identical with that; absence of cognition does not become the object of a cognition of which the cognition is not the object; therefore, absence of cognition is identical with cognition. Since the conclusion is false and the second premise is already accepted, the first premise must be false. Such remarks also apply, *mutatis mutandis* to the third reason and to any other reason that may be adduced.

Udayana amplifies:

> Thus we know from experience that there may be cognition of mutually opposed forms like black, white, etc.; this, then, serves for the annihilation of itself. If it has opposed characters as the contents, how can it be one and also of the nature

> of those? If it does not have them as contents, how can it of the form (*ākāra*) of those? Surely, there can be no hidden nature in what is self-revealing (*sva-saṃvedana*). (ATV 434–35)

Udayana offers an argument that cuts against both the Yogācāra, which is a Buddhist school of idealism and the Vedānta, which is a Hindu school of idealism, although he clearly has the Yogācāra as his primary target. Both the Yogācāra and the Vedānta reject the ontological difference between the character (*dharma*) and the characterized (*dharmin*) and hold that consciousness alone is real and self-revealing. But while the Yogācāra admits a plurality of states of consciousness, the Vedānta is a monistic school and regards not only the externality (*vāhyatva*) but also the plurality as empirically real and or ultimately unreal.

Udayana alludes to a cognition in which opposed characters such as black and white have become the contents. There is nothing mysterious about this: what he means is that one is sometimes aware of two or more things of different colors or of some other contrary characters. In the idealistic view cognition and its object are nondifferent. Then in the cognition of several things having contrary features, such as blue, red, and so on, the same cognition must have all these opposed characters, that is, it must be blue, red, and so on, at one and same time. That is, just as the cognition must be nondifferent from blue, it must also be nondifferent from red and so on. This can only amount to self-annihilation, for it is impossible for one and the same thing to have opposed features; so the one and the same cognition must disintegrate into many cognitions with the blue part having to be different from the red part and so on. Of course, for the criticism of the Vedānta position it is not necessary to speak of the same cognition having contrary features as its contents. Even successive cognitions of opposed natures are then equally problematic, for, from the Vedānta standpoint, one and the same consciousness would successively be of the nature (or simultaneously, as the case may be) of the opposed forms, that is, would have opposed features as contents. So if the cognized is nondifferent from the cognition and if all cognitions are nondifferent, the same cognition would have to have opposed features. The idealist cannot get away by supposing that although the opposed features are the objects, they are not revealed. If they are not revealed, they cannot be objects of the cognition either. Further, nothing can be unrevealed in a cognition that, though not in the Nyāya view, is self-revealing (in both the Yogācāra and the Vedānta views).

The Buddhist suggests an answer:

> There is fear only if such opposed natures are superimposed on external things. If they were nondifferent in spite of being so [i.e., having opposed natures], there would be the consequence that causal functions and conscious activities will overlap and also that cognition of difference would be unaccounted for. But there is no [fear] with respect to cognition. The being of cognition is not dependent on causal function. It is dependent only on manifestation [i.e., the evidence for cognition comes from that cognition itself]. No practical activity is also directed toward that [cognition]. Cognition has no causal production over and above the natural stream [of cognitions] and no pragmatist is motivated toward it. Further, since [cognition] is self-revealing, the lack of cognition of difference is a great gain. (ATV 435)

Udayana has objected that since opposed features like black and white can be the contents of the same cognition, if cognition were nondifferent from its contents, the one cognition would have to be split up into more than one cognition. The Buddhist replies that this certainly applies to external things (assuming, for the sake of argument, that there are external things). No external thing can be both blue and red. So something blue must be different from something red. Similarly, no external thing can be both a pen and a pot. A pen must be different from a pot. One external thing cannot perform the functions of another thing. For example, a pen cannot hold water like a pot. So someone looking for a pen does not look for a pot. If one were to claim that a pen is nondifferent from a pot, it may be set aside by the following reductio: if a pen and a pot were nondifferent, a pen would have performed the functions of a pot and one looking for a pen would have looked for a pot. But this is not so. Therefore, a pen and a pot are different. External things with contrary features are also cognized to be different. For all these reasons, the Buddhist says, no external thing (if there were such a thing) can be one and also have opposed features. But none of these reasons apply to cognition. Cognition does not have any causal function other than generating another cognition and keeping the stream flowing. Other things have to be causally productive in order to have their ticket to reality. But cognition reveals itself as it reveals its object and that is the only ticket to reality that it needs. It is also not something that a practically motivated person may seek to acquire for specific external needs that may be served by specific external things. So there is no call for a cognition, with two or more opposed features as its contents, to split up into more than one cognition. A cognition may very well have several opposed characters as its contents and still remain one and the same cognition. Lack of difference in spite of having opposed features is not unwelcome under these circumstances. A cognition of opposed characters such as red and blue will reveal itself as the cognition of red and blue and also reveal itself as one cognition.

Udayana replies:

> Wonderful! Do black, white, etc., give up their perennial enmity upon reaching cognition in the way a snake, a mongoose, etc., [may do so] upon reaching a peaceful hermitage or do they remain enemies inside but give up the consequences of that? Not the first. If there were lack of opposition between an affirmation and a negation which necessarily negate each other, there would be no opposition left in the universe. There can be no respite even by saying let it be so. For the said [opposed] nature cannot be set aside by any means whatsoever, opposition being verily of that constitution. And the proof of that [amounts to] the proof of difference; hence also not the second. (ATV 438)

Udayana is humorously referring to the legend of the extraordinary influence that a hermitage may have. The legend is that in a hermitage where no violence is permitted, even natural enemies such as snakes and mongooses are found to live in harmony. This may happen in either of two ways: the enemies may give up their enmity altogether or they may remain enemies inside but may suppress that and may not ever express it. Similarly, do opposed characters such as red and blue cease to be opposed when they become objects of cognition or do they remain opposed but refrain from acting in opposition?

Neither is possible, for contrary properties such as red and blue necessarily exclude each other. It is true that while blue implies the absence of red, absence of blue does not imply red, for something may be neither blue nor red but, say, yellow. So contrariety is explained in the Nyāya terminology as being mutually pervaded by the other's absence (*paraspara-abhāva-vyāpyatā*). That is, two properties are contrary if and only if the presence of either necessarily implies absence of the other. For example, in the Nyāya property-location language, wherever there is blueness there is red-absenceness and wherever there is redness there is blue-absenceness. In other words, nothing blue is red and nothing red is blue. Accordingly, Udayana points out, when two contrary characters become the contents of the same cognition, that same cognition cannot be identified with both the contents. For example, the cognition of one thing blue and another thing red cannot be the same as both blue and red. Since blue and red are contraries, if that cognition is the same as blue, it cannot possibly be the same as red or if that cognition is nondifferent from red, it cannot possibly be nondifferent from blue. It follows that the theory that cognition and its content are identical is false, for it requires identifying the same cognition with two or more contrary contents, which is impossible. The same cognition then would have to be split into two or more different cognitions, which amounts to the annihilation of that cognition. The presence of two or more opposed contents, if cognition and its content are nondifferent, is a sure ground for difference within that cognition, for nothing can be identical with two or more opposed things.

Udayana adds:

> The difference [namely, that different things have different causal functions] that was put forth to preserve the opposition in external things—let that be there. However, if the presence of opposed natures suffices with certainty to prove difference, what is the use of invoking specificity of causal functions? If not, what is the use even then? The differences of causal functions too can be there only through the presence of opposed characters. (ATV 441)

Udayana is responding to the Buddhist suggestion that the grounds for admitting differences among external things do not apply to cognition. The Buddhist position is that a cognition with two or more opposed contents need not be split up into more than one cognitions. This is because cognitions, their only function being the generation of the succeeding cognition, do not have different causal functions as different external things do (assuming that there are external things). Udayana argues that the presence of opposite characters is a sufficient ground for proving differences among external things. For example, a horse and a cow must be different, for horseness and cowness are (factually) contrary characters, that is, as a matter of fact, no horses are cows and no cows are horses. Though cows and horses do have different causal functions, the more basic ground for holding that cows and horses are different is that they have opposed characters. In particular, the differences among causal functions, too, cannot be proved without falling back on the opposed characters of the causal functions themselves. Since opposition suffices to prove difference, no appeal to difference in causal efficacy is necessary for proving difference. On the other hand, if opposition does not suffice to prove difference, no amount of appeal to differences in causal functions will suffice to prove difference, for, eventually, the differences in causal functions must be proved on the basis of opposition itself. So the Buddhist must grant that opposition suffices to prove difference and swallow the bitter pill that a cognition with opposed contents cannot be one cognition or give up opposition as a ground for difference whence monism is bound to follow.

Udayana continues with the point:

> Moreover, just as there would be the penalty for not preserving the restriction regarding causal functions in external things, so also there is the penalty for not preserving the restriction of revelation for cognitions as well. [Objection:] From where is the restriction regarding nonoverlapping of revelation, for there is revelation of opposed characters] together? [Reply:] We do not speak of non-overlapping in the sense of lack of being revealed together; [we mean] the lack of the cognition of blue as yellow and of yellow as blue. This [lack of cognition of one thing as another thing] is the ground of all opposition. (ATV 442–43)

The Buddhist has argued that if there were external things, they would have to be admitted to be different whenever the causal functions of one cannot be performed by another. If they were not admitted to be different, the price to pay would have been that we could not explain why the causal functions of one thing are not ever performed by another thing. Udayana now argues that the same consideration of different causal functions applies to cognition as well. The cognition of blue reveals blue and not yellow and the cognition of yellow reveals yellow and not blue. So the blue cognition cannot be the same as the yellow cognition. The Buddhist objects that the case in point is that of one cognition having two or more opposed contents such as blue and yellow. Since both blue and yellow are contents of the same cognition and are revealed together, the blue cognition cannot be different from the yellow cognition. Udayana replies that the difficulty is due to identifying cognition with its content. Since the said cognition has two opposed contents, it must be identified with both. Then the difference between the cognition of blue and that of yellow could not be preserved, and we could not explain why the former can only reveal blue and not yellow and the latter, only yellow and not blue. That is to say, even when only blue or only yellow is cognized, we could not explain why only the one and not the other is cognized.

From the Third Part: On Substance

We have already studied parts of Udayana's critique of the doctrines of momentariness and subjective idealism. Now we move on to consider his critique of the antisubstance position.

> [Objection:] Since a quale and a substance [literally, the owner or possessor of qualia: *guṇin*] are nondifferent, let the self be denied, for all that is left are momentary cognitions. [Reply:] There is the perception of the same thing by seeing and touching. Does this have (1) only one of the two as the content, (2) the aggregate as the content, (3) something additional as the content, (4) a form that is in disagreement with things as the content, or (5) something unreal as the content? (ATV 710)

The Nyāya view of the self is that it is a substance to which consciousness belongs as a quale and that the substance and the qualia constitute two different ontological categories (*padārtha*). So Udayana proceeds to examine and refute the Buddhist view that a substance and its qualia are nondifferent.

To challenge the Buddhist view Udayana cites the common experience of perceiving the same thing, such as a mango, by way of both seeing and touching. In the Nyāya view the mango that is both seen and touched is an additional, substantial whole over and above the qualia of color and touch. While the color and the touch are grasped respectively by the organs of seeing and touching, the mango as a substance is grasped by both these organs. This viewpoint is represented in the third of the five alternatives listed in the text above.

The other four, that is, the first two and the last two alternatives, result from a rejection of the category of substance. If there is no substance, Udayana asks for an account of what seems to be perception of the same substance by seeing and touching.

1. Is such a perception in reality the perception of color alone or of touch alone?

2. Or is it the perception of the aggregate of color and touch?
4. Or is the substance a constructed form without any objective counterpart?
5. Or, finally, is it the perception of something unreal?

The first alternative is disposed of as follows.

> But not the first. It is not that color itself is touch. Nor also that color can be grasped by the organ of touch, for then a blind person too could perceive blue, etc. It is also not reasonable that the same thing is perceived differently by a different sense organ, for that involves the consequence of being devoid of a nature of its own and of having no explanation of the exclusiveness of identity and difference. (ATV 712)

It cannot be accepted that color (or, *mutatis mutandis*, touch) is perceived by both the organs of seeing and touching, for color and touch are contrary qualia. If the difference between two contrary qualia is wiped out, Udayana observes, the very ontic status of difference and identity would be jeopardized.

Udayana next disposes of the second alternative:

> Not also the second. Is it due to (1) belonging to the same place, or (2) the same time, or (3) due to having the same effect, or (4) the same cause? It cannot be that the causal substratum serves as the same place, for their causal substrates [in the Buddhist view] are different. On the other hand, if the causal substratum were the same, that itself would be reduced to what is the bone of contention, namely, the substance. (714–15)

Udayana is exploring in what precise sense color and touch may be accepted as an aggregate. One possibility is that they are in the same place. So Udayana continues to explore in what precise sense color and touch are in the same place. Are they in the same place by virtue of inhering (*samaveta*) in the same causal substratum? No, points out Udayana. In the Buddhist view the causal substratum of color is color and that of touch is touch. So both color and touch cannot be said, from the Buddhist perspective, to be in the same place by way of having the same causal substratum. From the Nyāya point of view, of course, both color and touch have the same causal substratum. But that causal substratum is none other than the substance that the Buddhist rejects.

> It [belonging to the same place] is also not possible by virtue of having the ground as the locus. When the ground which is a particular color and the pot which too is a particular color [in the Buddhist view] are seen by the eye, it can be known that [the former] is the locus of that [the pot], for they become connected with the same cognition as being related as the locus and the located. But the touch, etc., belonging to that would be known by what source? It is not that touch, etc., are perceived by the eye. It is also not that this is the function of the organ of touch, for what is known by that is that the touch of the ground and that of the pot are related as the locus and the located. (ATV 715)

Could color and touch be known to be in the same place by way of being known to be located on the same ground? No, says again Udayana. Consider the color and the touch of a pot on a certain ground. In the Buddhist view both the ground and the pot are nothing other than color, touch, and so on. Insofar as both the ground and the pot are of the nature of color, they can both be perceived by the eye and known to be related as the locus and the located. Similarly, insofar as both the ground and the pot are of the nature of touch, they can both be perceived by the organ of touch and be known to be related as the locus and the located. Still that does not leave any room for perceiving that both color and touch are in the same place in the sense of being on the same ground. Of color and touch each is perceived by a sense organ that is incapable of perceiving the other. So from the Buddhist perspective it cannot be explained how they can both be perceived to be on the same ground or to belong to the same thing. This is not difficult to explain from the Nyāya point of view. In the Nyāya view both the ground and the pot are substances ontologically different from the qualia of color and touch. Both color and touch are perceived as belonging to the same substance that is perceivable by both the organs of seeing and touching.

Udayana continues to press on:

> It is also not that that [belonging to the same place] is possible for the two aggregates [i.e., it cannot be known that the aggregates of color and touch are in the same place], for that would involve circularity. The aggregate is inquired into only if there is co-location [i.e., only if color and touch are in the same locus]; at the same time there is inquiry into co-location if there is inquiry into the aggregate. An infinite regress too

> results, for the inquiry about what makes the ground too an aggregate cannot be terminated. (ATV 715)

Why are color and touch in the same place? Because they make an aggregate. But why are they an aggregate? Because they are in the same place. Thus circularity is inevitable. There is also an infinite regress: the ground is called an aggregate because its qualia are in the same locus. But one would also inquire about what makes that locus an aggregate and so on to infinity.

Udayana next refutes the alternative that color and touch make an aggregate by virtue of being in the same time:

> Therefore, not also by virtue of belonging to the same time, for there is no proof that they belong to the same time. Even if there were [a proof], it would involve the consequence that a donkey and a camel also make an aggregate by virtue of being in the same time: regarding the matter under consideration too there is no lack of cognition of difference. (ATV 717)

Color and touch cannot be known to be in the same time, for they are objects of different sense organs. This does not create any difficulty in the Nyāya theory, for the Nyāya admits, besides the different external sense organs each restricted to one kind of external quale, also the abiding inner sense that coordinates and supervises the activities of the external senses; but in the Buddhist theory there is neither an abiding inner sense nor an abiding self as in the Nyāya theory. Further, not any two things that are in the same time are (ordinarily) spoken of as an aggregate. For we do not (ordinarily) speak of an aggregate of a donkey and a camel. The Buddhist could say that a donkey and a camel are vastly different; hence they are not (ordinarily) considered to be an aggregate. But so too are color and touch vastly different.

Udayana next criticizes the possibility of there being an aggregate by virtue of having the same effect:

> Therefore, not also by virtue of having the same effect, for there is no one and the same effect which is to be accomplished. It is not acceptable that there is the unitary function of fetching water. For no water over and above color, etc., is admitted [by the Buddhist]. Also there is no proof that one thing is the effect of many causes. Further, the aggregate is not proved. (ATV 718)

Could color and touch be an aggregate by virtue of producing the same effect? No, says Udayana. Color produces color, touch produces touch, and these are different. The Buddhist could argue that color, touch, and so on, together make a pot, which has the function of fetching water. So fetching water, and the like, could be the common effect of color and touch. Udayana objects that from the Buddhist point of view, water too is nothing but color, touch, and so on; so water cannot be treated as one effect. Further, there is no proof that not only touch but also color is a necessary causal condition of fetching water. Since the thesis of having the same effect is unproven, the existence of the aggregate on that ground remains unproven.

Udayana now criticizes the alternative that color and touch have the same cause:

> Therefore, also not by virtue of having the same cause. If something is called an aggregate without any basis, there would be overcoverage. (ATV 719)

There is no evidence that color, touch, and so on, come from the same causal conditions. In fact, the evidence seems to point otherwise. So Udayana rejects that possibility. Udayana has already rejected three other possible explanations of why and how color and touch form an aggregate. Since no other reasonable explanation is forthcoming, the label of being an aggregate becomes baseless. But if color and touch can be called an aggregate without any basis, any collection of things may also be called an aggregate. Then the notion of an aggregate can no longer be useful in explaining why and how the same thing seems to be perceived by both the organs of seeing and touching. It is certainly not true that any two things seem to be perceived by both the organs of seeing and touching. If any two things may be called an aggregate for no reason whatsoever, merely being an aggregate surely cannot provide the requisite explanation of why and how the same thing seems to be so perceived.

> There is no dispute over the third. (ATV 719)

This is the position that what is perceived by both the organs of seeing and touching is the substance that is different from color and touch and to which both color and touch belong. Then the said perception may be accepted as true and Udayana agrees to this.

> Not also the fourth. Is this from the perspective that only conscious states are real or is this due to non-correspondence as in the case of [seeing] two moons? If the first, why the favoritism over color, etc.? (ATV 719)

This is the viewpoint that a substance is a cognitive construction (*vikalpa*). Although there are no substances, such constructions are useful for empirical and practical (*vyavahārika*) purposes and without them linguistic communication (*vyavahāra*) is hampered.

Udayana objects to this position first by saying that if substances are rejected from the perspective of subjective idealism according to which only transitory conscious states are real, there is no compelling reason to hold on to the qualia such as color as well. The Buddhist could say that the recognition of the qualia is necessary to account for the act-object distinction, that is, to distinguish the act of cognizing from the object cognized. But if the act-object distinction is real or corresponds to the nature of things, then, Udayana would insist, the recognition of the unitary substance is also necessary. The substance too is cognized and the various grounds for dismissing such cognition as false, as Udayana has already demonstrated earlier in this work, may be set aside.

> Since there are the bases of sensory connection and causal efficacy, not also the second [i.e., the cognition of substance is not false]. [Objection:] These two apply to color, etc. [Reply:] Not to these. Also why not apply to this [substance]? [Objection:] There is counterevidence. [Reply:] But neither the opposition of simultaneity and successiveness nor the opposition of red and not-red provide the counterevidence, for these have been set aside. Further, there is the case of substance in the form of momentary atoms. [Objection:] There is lack of relation [between the substance and qualia]. [Reply:] Let there be lack of relation. [Objection:] Why is then the cognition of having that[qualia]? [Reply:] Let the way out be that that is how there is origin just as for you the body has consciousness. [Objection:] Since all causal functions can be explained in terms of color, etc. , why hypostatize an additional substance? [Reply:] This leaves room for the garrulous chat that since all causal functions can be explained by that [the substance] alone, why hypostatize color, etc.? If it is said that that [qualia] are cognized [and hence should be admitted to exist], that applies equally [to substances]. (ATV 720)

Udayana argues that the cognition of a substance (such as the perception of the same thing by both seeing and touching) cannot be dismissed as false, for there is sensory connection with a substance. This cannot be explained away as sensory connection with qualia such as color: the many qualia cannot truly be perceived as one thing. Furthermore, the substance as a unitary whole has causal functions that cannot be performed by qualia either individually or collectively. For example, a pot can be used for fetching water. But a mere collection of the qualia of a pot cannot be used for fetching water. The Buddhist could object that such a substance cannot be real, for it cannot be causally efficacious either all at once or in succession. Similarly, when a thing is partly red and partly not red, how can a substance avoid being both red and not red, which is impossible? Udayana observes that these and other similar objections have already been examined and resolved. Moreover, some Buddhists admit momentary atoms. As long as they admit atoms, how can they disown substances?

The Buddhist may object that there is no satisfactory theory of how a substance is related to the qualia. From the Nyāya-Vaiśeṣika point of view the relation between a substance and the qualia is called inherence (*samavāya*). It is a relation of one-way dependence: the qualia are dependent on the substance but not vice versa. The Buddhist refuses to recognize any such relation as real. Udayana retorts that even then the substance should not be disowned. That is, the acceptance of substance is not critically dependent on the acceptance of inherence. How should we then explain such a cognition as that the pot is blue (where the quale appears to be related to the substance)? Udayana replies that in the same way in which the Buddhist explains how the body appears to be conscious. The Yogācāra Buddhist is an immaterialist. Just as the body appears to be conscious although there is no real relationship between the body and consciousness (for the Yogācāra), so also the substance appears to have qualia although there may be no real, additional, ontic relationship between substance and qualia. In other words, the substance and the qualia may, if necessary, be held to be self-related without the help of any relation that is ontologically different from the relata. Udayana also dismisses the suggestion that all causal functions of a substance may be attributed to the qualia themselves. He retorts that then it would also be permissible to attribute all causal functions of qualia to the substance. He implies that the causal functions of a substance and its qualia are different and neither can be said to perform the functions of the other. There is also no ground of preference for the qualia in that they are perceived: the substance too, Udayana claims, is perceived.

> This also serves to refute that what is cognized is unreal. (ATV 721)

This is fifth and the last alternative that what is cognized to be the same thing by both seeing and touching is something unreal like a hare's horn. Udayana disagrees. Since such a thing is both perceived and has distinctive causal functions, it cannot be unreal. On the other hand, if in spite of being perceived and having distinctive causal functions it is unreal, so also should, then, be the qualia. In other words, it is not justified to disown substance and admit qualia. A subjective idealist such as the Yogācāra may, of course, consistently disown both substance and qualia. But, Udayana seems to imply, then the Yogācāra position will look less attractive.

So Udayana has disposed of all the four alternative viewpoints that reject the substance. He has shown that what is perceived by both seeing and touching is not merely color or merely touch or the aggregate of color and touch. It is also neither a mere construction nor unreal, and there are no grounds for dismissing the awareness as false. On the other hand, there are grounds for accepting the awareness as true and admitting the existence of substance different from qualia.

> Objection: There is counterevidence [to admitting that substance is different from qualia] by way of the proof of nondifference [of substance from qualia]. Reply: What is it? If it is the rule of being [always] cognized together, it is not acceptable. The rule of being always cognized together is faulted, e.g., in the awareness of yellow shell, etc., there is cognition of the shell although there is no cognition of whiteness. (ATV 722)

The objector is of the opinion that since substance and qualia are always cognized together, they are not ontologically different. Udayana points out that the same substance and the same qualia are not always cognized together. Usually shells are perceived as white. But to a jaundiced eye (or due to some other reason) a white shell looks yellow. Since the shell is not then always cognized as white, how can it be identified with whiteness. Surely, it cannot be identified with both whiteness and yellowness, for the latter are contraries.

From the Fourth Part: On Nonapprehension

Udayana examines an argument to prove the nonexistence of the self:

> Objection: Let the nonexistence of the self be proved on the ground of not being cognized. Reply: not so. If what is meant is not being seen by any, then it is subject to doubt; if what is meant on the other hand is not being seen by oneself, then it is deviant. (ATV 739)

The above argument may be reformulated as:

> Whatever is not cognized is nonexistent.
>
> The self is not cognized.
>
> Therefore, the self is nonexistent.

Udayana asks: What precisely is meant by not being cognized? The very mention of the self does amount to some kind of awareness of it. So what may be meant is that the self is not perceived. Regarding this there are two possibilities. It may be claimed that the self is not perceived by anyone. That the self is not perceived by anyone is a premise that, Udayana argues, is questionable. He implies that it may be that the self is perceived by some (or even by all). The premise being open to doubt the conclusion that the self does not exist would also then be open to doubt. The other possibility is that the self may be claimed not to be perceived by oneself, that is, the opponent. But then the first premise would be that whatever is not perceived by oneself does not exist. This, Udayana points out, is false. There are surely things that one has never perceived. So either the premise is false or it is questionable and the argument fails.

> Objection: Not so when the qualification of being perceptible is added. Reply: No. This is not accepted [by you]. Objection: It is not a flaw since it is accepted by the other [the Nyāya]. Reply: Not so. The inference should be in accordance with one's own discipline. If the other suddenly denies this, this inference will fail. Also if perceptibility is accepted in accordance with the other's viewpoint, this [not being cognized] should be possible. But this is not possible, for it is associated with that nature, [i.e., perceptibility would imply knowability

> and the premise will again be false]. This is in a nutshell. One may elaborate analogously to the case of the [already refuted argument] that what is non-momentary is nonexistent. (ATV 739)

When something is perceptible and is not perceived (*yogyānupalabdhi*), it is taken to be nonexistent. The nonexistence of the self may be ascertained in the same way, the objector points out. Udayana replies that the objector himself does not accept the self to be perceptible; so the objection does not work. The objector adds that the self is perceived in the Nyāya view and that the argument may be understood in that light. Udayana responds that in a reductio it is permissible to have other's view as the premise but not in an inference to prove one's own position. In the latter the premise should enunciate only what one accepts to be true. Otherwise, the inference will become unsound if the other's view undergoes some sudden (perhaps injudicious) change. Further, if the objector is willing to acknowledge for the sake of argument that the self is perceptible, he should also be willing to acknowledge that the self may be cognized. But that would ruin the argument. Other objections to the above argument may be coined, Udayana adds, analogously to his refutation of the Buddhist argument for universal momentariness. He implies the following kind of objections. If the self is altogether nonexistent and unreal, not being cognized cannot be a real feature of it, for nothing unreal has any real feature. Then the premise that the self is not cognized will be false. On the other hand, if the self is conceded to be existent so that not being cognized can be a real feature of it, the conclusion that the self does not exist will be contradicted.

From the Fifth and Final Part: On the Accepted Position

> Now, what is the evidence for the existence of the self? It is perception itself, I-consciousness (*ahamiti vikalpa*) being present in all living beings. Not that this [awareness of the self] is without any objective basis or of a doubtful basis, for it is nonlinguistic and incorrigible. It is also not inferential, for even one who is not apprised of the grounds for inferring [the self] is aware of one's own self. This is also not remembrance, for that cannot be of something not already experienced. It is also not reasonable that this is a nonobjective construction (*vikalpa*) which is beginningless and which is due to begin-

> ningless craving (*vāsanā*), for that holds of constructions like blue, etc., as well. If there can be uncertainty here (i.e., about the existence of the self) by way of invoking craving, how can there be certainty regarding some other evidence, so that there can be certainty regarding constructions like blue, etc.? (ATV 743)

This is a major argument for the existence of the self and contains a number of important ideas. Udayana argues that the fundamental evidence for the existence of the self does not come from inferential proofs (as Vatsyayana has said) but from perception (*pratyakṣa*). In taking this position he is not contradicting Gotama, the founder of the Nyaya. Gotama has not explicitly said that the self is not perceived. He has offered some signs (*liṅga*) for inferring the self, as we have seen. But that does not rule out that the self is perceived. However, Vatsyayana does say explicitly that the self is not perceived, as we have noted earlier. So Udayana's apparent disagreement with Vatsyayana may be softened by interpreting Vatsyayana to mean that the difference of the self from the body, say, is not knowable by perception and that inferential proofs are necessary to show that the self is different from the body.

I-consciousness, Udayana claims, is present in all living beings and proves to each living being the reality of his or her own self. Some recent dualists seek to separate life from consciousness. They hold that although a materialistic explanation of life is possible and indeed has been provided by recent advances in biological sciences, consciousness still eludes the grasp of modern science. This is certainly not the Hindu and the Nyāya view defended by Udayana. For Udayana too being alive is different from being conscious. But being alive necessarily implies being conscious and no materialistic explanation of either can be given. For Hindu thinkers such as Udayana all living beings engage in acts of self-preservation by way of seeking out nourishment and avoiding injury. Such physiological actions of self-preservation are not purely reflexive or mere physical reactions to physical stimuli but require consciousness of one's own self even in the humblest form of life in plants and vegetables. So even the little blade of grass is aware of itself and engages in self-preservation as also do, in a much more sophisticated way, the higher animals including human beings. To each such living being the reality of its own self is self-evident and absolutely irrefutable. So there may be disagreement over the true nature of the self, and reasonings are necessary to sort that out. But to each person, in Udayana's view, the reality of its own self is guaranteed by its own, unique perception of itself.

Self-awareness, Udayana claims, is nonlinguistic (*aśābda*) and incorrigible (*apratikṣepa*). Ordinary perceptions are corrigible and contain the intrusion of language and judgment. But one's direct perception of oneself is nonlinguistic and nonjudgmental. Not that such perception involves a language that is private (as some proto-Wittgensteinians may wonder about). It does not involve any language at all (and in the Nyāya as also the Wittgensteinian views no language is private). It does not also involve relating a qualificand (*viśeṣya*) with a qualifier (*prakāra*) and is nonjudgmental. Error is possible only when a qualifer is related to a wrong qualificand. For example, the perception of a bright, glossy shell as silver is false, because the qualifier *silverness* has been wrongly attributed to a qualificand that lacks silverness. Since the direct perception of one's own self involves no such activity, such awareness is incorrigible. Needless to say, one's own perception of oneself should be distinguished from discourse about the self. The latter is certainly corrigible, as the very existence of the controversy over the self shows.

Udayana brushes aside the suggestion that self-awareness could be inferential. Inference requires signs or grounds. But no signs or grounds are involved in one's own unique and private perception of oneself. It is also not reproductive imagination. The latter is always based on a prior experience. But no prior experience is involved in one's being merely directly aware of oneself. Such self-awareness is always an immediate and original experience. Not that one cannot have remembrance of the self or offer inferential proofs of the self. Of course one can. But these do not provide the most basic evidence for the reality of the self. That comes from one's direct experience of oneself. Udayana drives home its foundational role by adding that it cannot be dismissed as a construction of a sort. If such direct self-awareness can be tainted with uncertainty, no awareness of anything whatsoever, including the vivid perceptions of qualia such as color and so on can be spared. Since all knowing is ultimately grounded in perceiving, the consequence then can only be general skepticism, agnosticism, and silence.

> Therefore, one should give up the theory of craving alone and speak of some adventitious ground [of the notion of the self as a construction if one wishes to continue to reject the reality of the self]. Is that some reliable/unreliable testimony or probans/pseudoprobans or perception/misperception? In that connection

> just as the cognition (*vikalpa*) of blue pertains to the last alternative due to the unavailability of the first and the middle alternatives, so also does the cognition of the self [i.e., the cognition of the self under consideration is perceptual and is not inferential or testimonial]. There if it is backed by perception, it has an objective basis directly. On the other hand, if it is misperception, it has an objective basis indirectly through the root. (ATV 745)

Udayana argues that the notion of the self cannot be said to be a construction based on testimony or inference. He implies that the notion under consideration is direct and immediate by comparing it to the [direct] awareness of qualia such as blue. Since the said notion is direct and immediate, it can only be perceptual. Such perception is either true or false. If true, it has directly an objective basis, for no perception is true unless what is perceived is actually where and when it is perceived. If false, it must eventually be derived from some true perception that has an objective basis. So the perception of the self cannot be devoid of an objective basis altogether. Even if the perception were false, the objective basis of it should be explored.

> Nor can it [self-awareness] be baseless simply because external perception does not apply, for then the cognition of cognition too would have to be so. There the ground is self-cognition; here also [the ground is] internal perception and there is no difference. (ATV 746)

Here the objector accepts the reality of cognitive states but not of the self. Udayana argues that both internal states like cognition and the self are objects of internal perception. So one cannot accept one and reject the other. The self is immediately perceived in the same way in which cognitive states are immediately perceived.

> Objection: The body, etc., provide the objective basis. Reply: No, for then there would be overapplication to unassociated aggregates of the body, the sense organs, and cognition. It may be said that this applies to one's own body. Then it should be spelt out what is meant by 'own'. For all, being oneself is not being the other. When that cognizes that itself, since the knower is nondifferent from the known, there should be I-consciousness. Since the pots, etc., never ever become aware of not being the other, they do not have I-consciousness. If

> such were the case, in your view too I-consciousness is transferred to the body, etc., for the knower is different from them. (ATV 747–48)

Here the objector takes a materialist position that the body and so on are the self. Udayana counters by pointing out that other bodies are not referred to as 'I'. The objector replies that only one's own body is the self. Ordinary material objects like pots are not aware of their difference from other things. That is why they do not possess I-consciousness. But each person's body is aware of its difference from other things; hence each person's body possesses I-consciousness. Udayana disagrees on the ground that the knower is not only aware of its difference from other bodies but also from its own body. The notion of the self is grounded in the notion of being different from others. Since the self is aware of its difference from its own body, the latter cannot be the self.

> [Objection:] Cognition itself is the principal [there is no self other than cognition]. [Reply:] No, for it is cognized as an act. As in 'I cut' so also in 'I cognize' the agent is cognized to be different [from cognition]. [Objection:] As in the case of the cognized blue, etc., the form of the cognition is of the cognition itself, so also the self is revealed [i.e., the self is a form of the cognition]. [Reply:] Since then the cognized and the cognition are equally useful [i.e., since the cognized is different from cognition], our purpose is served [i.e., the self is accepted to be different from cognition]. [Objection:] Let [cognition] itself alone be the stuff (*upādāna*). [Reply:] No. If that [cognition] is revealed, the form [i.e., blue, etc.] of that should also be revealed, for what has the form cannot be revealed without the form. (ATV 749–50)

Here the objector takes the position that the self and cognition are the same. Udayana replies that an act and the agent of the act must be different. So the self must be different from cognition, for the latter is an act of the former. In the cognition 'I cognize' the self is revealed to be different from and the agent of cognition, which is the act. (The Nyāya, as we know, accepts such common experience as reliable unless countermanded by reliable evidence.) The objector suggests that the self is nothing but a form of the cognition just as the objects such as blue are forms of cognition as well. (This is an idealistic position according to which cognition alone is real. Udayana has criticized it in the second part of this work.) Udayana counters that even then the self must be different from cognition, for the form of cognition must be different from cognition itself. It is only through the form (*ākāra*) that, from the objector's point of view, one cognition may be distinguished from another cognition. So the form must be different from cognition; otherwise cognitions could not be distinguished from each other. The objector next suggests that the cognition as distinct from its form should be the basis or stuff of I-consciousness. Udayana objects that then I-consciousness could never take place without the consciousness of objects such as blue and so on. Since the latter, according to the objector, are the forms of cognition, they must be revealed in the cognition including the cognition of the self. But this is not the case. Self-awareness does not necessarily involve the awareness of external things.

> Objection: The cognizer is a stream of cognition different from the stream of cognition of objects; we call that repository cognition [i.e., such cognition serves as the repository or store of the cognition of objects]. Reply: Let then the cognizer be the beginningless and the endless stuff of consciousness of objects. The question remains: Is this a flowing consciousness or the opposite of that? This has been exhaustively discussed earlier [in the first two parts]. (ATV 750)

This is the famous Yogācāra doctrine that accepts cognitions alone as real but separates I-cognition from cognition of objects. Udayana does not discuss it here, for this has been the subject of a lengthy examination in the first two parts of his work.

> What is the rational basis here [i.e., for a permanent self different from transitory internal states]? Recognition. [Objection:] If true (*tathya*), then the probans does not belong to the inferential subject (*asiddha*); if false, opposed; also circular [*aviśiṣṭa*: literally, nondifferent] and deviant (*anaikantika*). [Reply:] No. The probans has been misconstrued. Recognition alone is not the intended (probans) here. [Objection:] That the cause and the effect belong to the same stream [is the reason for] restriction to each [i.e., one can only recognize what one has experienced before]. This also is opposed [i.e., conflicts with the admission of a permanent self]. [Reply:] This too is not what is intended by us. What then? The absolute certainty that both the earlier and the later cognition

> have the same agent. If it is said that this too is accountable on the basis of being related as the cause and the effect, then it is not accepted, for that does not apply when there is the ground of permanence. Even from the standpoint of momentariness being related as cause and effect cannot be [explained as] being of the same kind and being originated by that [the cause], for that has the consequence of the teacher's cognition and the student's cognition also being so. (ATV 752)

Although perception is the fundamental evidence for the existence of the self, for the purposes of philosophical discussion the argument from recognition is offered by Udayana to prove the permanence of the self. Udayana does not explicitly state the argument in full perhaps because it was well known in his philosophical circle. It is more than likely that the argument is something like the following: the support or source or object (*ālambana*) of I-consciousness is permanent, because it is also the object of recognition. Udayana then summarizes the usual Buddhist objections to the argument from recognition. The first objection is that even if the recognition were true, it is false that the ground of I-consciousness is the object of recognition. The second objection is simply that the recognition is false. The third objection is that the premise that the basis of I-consciousness is also the object of recognition takes the conclusion about permanence for granted and so the argument is circular. The fourth objection is that recognition is not a reliable ground for permanence for it sometimes fails (as in the case of a burning fire).

Udayana replies to these objections by articulating the fuller implication of the argument from recognition. The argument boils down to that the agent of recognition must be the same as the agent of the earlier experience. The kind of recognition he has in mind is like this: I who saw the color of the pot now feel its touch. The continuity, permanence, and sameness of the agent follows because one cannot remember what has been experienced by someone else. The Buddhist raises the usual objection that continuity (and not permanence or sameness) of the stream of cognitions by virtue of the causal connection between the earlier and later states of the stream suffices to account for recognition and also why it is restricted to the person having the earlier experience. Udayana replies that this falls short of explaining why then a teacher's experience could not be remembered by the student. The teacher does influence the student's thinking and so there is causal connection between the teacher's thinking and the student's thinking. The student may very well vow to take over the teacher's mantle. Still the student can never remember the teacher's own experiences. The Buddhist could say that the teacher's stream of cognition and that of the student are not the same. But Udayana has already argued at great length (in the first two chapters) that there can be no satisfactory explanation of the sameness of the stream except by courting personal identity and permanence of the self.

Notes

1. Introduction

1. According to the standard Hindu view, one full cycle of creation called *yuga* is followed by a state of dissolution (when nothing noneternal survives) that is followed by another cycle of creation. The cyclical view is endorsed by the Nyāya. NK 117–25.

2. This account presupposes that a noneternal substance that is destroyed in the very moment of its origin is an impossibility (TSN 31).

3. *Ākāśa* is sometimes translated as ether. But the latter was introduced by some physicists as the medium of light. Since *ākāśa* is not a medium of light, we avoid this translation.

4. A specific quale (*viśeṣa-guṇa*) distinguishes a substance from other kinds of substance. For example, smell is unique to earth, in the Nyāya view, and distinguishes it from water, and so on. (I.e., a smelly water has earth in it.) A given specific quale may be imperceptible; but it may still be considered to be externally perceivable if it is of the same kind as a specific quale that is externally perceived. For example, the color of the visual organ (which is not the eyeball or the eye socket) is, in the Nyāya view, imperceptible. Still it is of the same kind as color, which is externally perceived. Hence the visual organ is 'physical' in the customary Nyāya-Vaiśeṣika sense.

5. Nothing noneternal can come into being also without God. Notably, Raghunatha Siromani (15th century) reduces God, space, time (and also *ākāśa*) to the same substance (PTN 11).

6. The inner sense is discussed in chapter 8.

7. Some Nyāya philosophers, such as Raghunatha Siromani, regard the inner sense as a physical substance (PTN 9).

8. The best available account in English is in TSD.

9. See DI, chapters 8–11.

10. In a traditional Sanskrit debate there are one or more mediators (*madhyastha*) whose decisions are binding on all parties to the debate. Such mediators may be hard to find in a contemporary set up where the cultural forces are different. If such mediators are to be searched for, one suggestion is that they should include those who are experts in both the Western and the Eastern traditions as well as those who are experts in either tradition. Regarding expertise in the Eastern tradition, there should be someone well versed in the Sanskrit oral tradition. This is specially useful if one thinks that there are some conflicts between the Western (including the contemporary) and the Sanskrit logical traditions. We do not think that there are any irresolvable conflicts, but there are some issues that may need to be thrashed out. If this is to be done in a meaningful way, the input of someone well versed in the oral tradition would be specially relevant. The study of the Sanskrit logical tradition may yield rich dividends. We have tried to show in DI (specially chapter 4) that the Nyāya conception of definition, which is looser than that of Aristotle, is more in tune with the contemporary philosophical scene. As already said, we have also tried to show in DI that the Nyāya study of induction is very advanced though some important concepts such as that of economy (*lāghava*) are only briefly covered and some others like that of nesting or meshing (*anugama*) are not treated in DI. The Sanskrit tradition seems to us to be ahead in some areas of formal logic as well and further study may bring that out.

11. See DI 43–45.

12. One may consult U. Mishra, *History of Indian Philosophy*, 2 vols. (Allahabad: Tirabhukti Publications, 1957, 1966).

2. Nyāya-Vaiśeṣika Dualism

1. For an account of the causal substratum, see BPP 102.

2. What is traditionally called the mind-body problem in Western philosophy is more appropriately described as the self-body problem in the context of our discussion. However, no harm would result if the self (*ātman*) is called the mind provided the self is carefully distinguished from the inner sense (*manas*).

3. The inner sense is discussed in chapter 8.

4. The concept of contact is discussed in BPP 518.

5. In the Nyāya-Vaiśeṣika view, the self is a pervasive substance and is automatically in contact with all measurable substances. Still an additional contact is established between a particular self and a particular body in a particular life and this accounts for individual differences.

6. An important concept in the Nyāya view of causation that we skip for lack of space is that of indispensability or relevance (*ananyathā-siddhatva*: TS 103).

7. In the Nyāya view an internal state such as desire inheres (*samavāya*) in the self, which is in a specific contact (*viśeṣasaṃyoga*) with a particular body. Hence an internal state is also located in the particular body and not located in other bodies. But a state like desire is a quale (*guṇa*) and lacks extension (*parimāṇa*) which can be attributed only to a substance (*dravya*).

8. For a brief discussion of the Nyāya view of causation and related issues, see DI 191–97.

9. Descartes was most impressed by the highly complex mechanism of water fountains (which, for example, could be triggered by walking, etc.) and other robotlike statues (such as an Aphrodite that would hide as if in shame when someone approached and a Neptune that would emerge and threaten with a trident) in the Frech royal garden and thought that animal behavior is explicable in a similar way.

3. Cognition

1. See chapter 11 for a Nyāya causal proof of the existence of God.

2. In the Nyāya view there is only one God, which is an eternal, disembodied spirit and without whose knowledge, desire, and will nothing non-eternal comes into being. However, most Indian philosophical schools deny the existence of God or deny that the existence of God is provable. On the whole, theism may be said to have a bigger following in traditional Western philosophy (before the twentieth century) than in traditional Indian philosophy. In the twentieth century there has been greater contact between Eastern and Western philosophy and (for various reasons) theism has a smaller following.

3. The identity theorist may draw a sense-reference distinction and argue that although the reference of a mental state is the same as that of a physical state, the senses are different. This is why there is an explanatory gap. But this does not explain why the explanatory gap is not eliminated with more information about brain states and mental states (as it happens in other cases of true identity statements). For the sense-reference distinction and its Nyāya analogue, see my "Some Comparisons between Frege's Logic and Navya-Nyāya Logic."

4. For the subject-predicate distinction in Western philosophy, see P. F. Strawson, *Subject and Predicate in Western Logic and Grammar*.

5. Needless to say, one is not entitled to merely assume that some epistemic distinction must be matched by some ontological hierarchy. One must make a case for it.

6. For an argument in favor of admitting indeterminate cognition, see chapter 1.

7. Gotama's definition of perception, if construed as a definition (*lakṣaṇa*), may be interpreted to target only the perception of mortals and to exclude divine perception.

8. An awareness serves as the instrument in other recognized kinds of knowing as well. According to an influential Nyāya view, awareness of similarity is the instrument of *upamāna* (which has an analogical component) and awareness of word, that of testimony.

4. Other Internal States

1. According to some, doubt may involve more than two alternatives. See BP 984.

2. The Vaiśeṣika, unlike the Nyāya, accepts only two kinds of knowing, namely, perception and inference. The Nyāya accepts these two but also adds *upamāna* (which has an analogical component) and testimony (*śabda*) as separate kinds of knowing.

3. For the distinction between determinate and indeterminate perception, see chapter 3.

4. In the Nyāya view the awareness of awareness is an after-cognition (*anuvyavasāya*) or introspection that may or may not follow a given act of cognition. This differs from the Advaita view that cognition is self-revealing (*svaprakāśa*). See chapter 13.

5. Merit or demerit are also causal conditions of indeterminate cognition and are co-inherent in the self. But they are not ordinary (*laukika*) conditions.

6. This does not rule out the possibility that something may be desirable both for oneself as well as for others.

7. This does not rule out that when the object of desire is obtained, there may be desire for more. In fact, the latter is often the case. That is why asceticism promotes the idea of elimination or eradication of desire through the realization that what appears to be useful or pleasing is not really so or the realization that what was once useful or pleasing is no longer so.

8. This is why desire plays a crucial role in the Nyāya-Vaiśeṣika case for permanence of the self. Desire shows, the Nyāya claims, that the person who had something before and the person who desires it now is the same and, therefore, a continuant (*sthāyin*).

9. Hence control and elimination of desire is important, for it helps reducing the burden of karma from the Hindu point of view.

10. The amplified explanation of different kinds of aversion is given by Sridhara in the NKD (9th century CE).

11. See Hilary Putnam, "The Nature of Mental States," in NOM 197–203; also CPM 326.

5. The Existence and Permanence of the Self

1. Kanada, the founder of the Vaiśeṣika school, also offers cognition, desire, aversion, volition, pleasure, and pain as signs of the self (VS 3.1.18, 3.2.4).

2. For the distinction between identifying and defining characters and a comparison between classical Western and Indian theories of definition, see my *Definition and Induction* (Honolulu: University of Hawaii Press, 1995), chapter 4.

3. *A Sourcebook in Indian Philosophy*, ed. S. Radhakrisnan and C. A. Moore (Princeton: Princeton University Press, 1957), 281–84. Also see SD chapter 2.

4. ATV 19.

5. *Maitrāyaṇī Upaniṣad* 7.8.

6. It may be noted that of the six signs only cognition, desire, and volition are, in the Nyāya view, possessed by God, the supreme self who does not have any pleasure, pain, or aversion but does have eternal knowledge of everything and eternal desire and volition for the origin of everything non-eternal. All the six signs apply to human and animal selves and are identifiers (*paricāyaka*) of the self in the sense that only selves have any of them. But only the three signs of cognition, desire and volition are defining marks (*lakṣaṇa*) in the narrower sense. That is, it is true that only selves have them and also that all those who have them are selves.

7. Sydney Shoemaker, *Self-Knowledge and Self-Identity* (Ithaca, N.Y.: Cornell University Press, 1963); idem, "Persons and Their Pasts," *American Philosophical Quarterly* 7: 269–85.

8. Derek Parfit, "Personal Identity," *Philosophical Review* 80 (1971): 3–27; idem, *Reasons and Persons* (Oxford: Clarendon Press, 1984).

9. David Lewis, "Survival and Identity," in A. Rorty, ed., *The Identities of Persons*, ed. A. Rorty (Berkeley: University of California Press, 1976), reprinted with postscripts in D. Lewis, *Philosophical Papers* (Oxford: Oxford University Press, 1983).

10. William James, 1890, *The Principles of Psychology*, 2 vols., (New York: Dover, 1950), chapter entitled "Stream of Thought"; William James,

1892, *Psychology: The Briefer Course*, ed. G. Alport (New York, Harper & Row, 1961), chapter entitled "Stream of Consciousness."

11. Owen Flanagan, *Consciousness Reconsidered* (Cambridge, Mass.: MIT Press, 1992), especially chapters 8 and 9.

6. Self as Substance

1. See my *The Logic of Gotama*, chapter 5.

2. For a fuller discussion, see S. Bhaduri, *Studies in Nyāya-Vaiśeṣika Metaphysics* (Poona: 1947), Bhandarkar Oriental Research Institute, especially chapter 2.

3. For a valuable discussion, see B. K. Matilal, *Perception* (Oxford: Clarendon Press, 1983), especially chapter 8.

4. Plato also speaks of the soul being conjoined with and separated from the body to account for life and death. See, for example, the *Phaedo*.

5. See my "Some Non-Syllogistic Forms in Early Nyāya Logic," in *Proceedings* of the Fifth International Congress of Logic, Philosophy and Methodology of Science, Ontario, Canada, 1975, 12:9–11, for a discussion of disjunctive syllogism in early Nyāya.

6. See Kisor Chakrabarti and Chandana Chakrabarti, "Towards Dualism: The Nyāya-Vaiśeṣika Way," *Philosophy East and West* 41 (1991): 470–91.

7. See TSD, chapter on inference for a fuller explanation of the *vyatirekin* mood. Also see my "Contraposition in European and Indian Logic," *International Philosophical Quarterly* 1989, 120–7. A brief account of the exclusion mood is given in this chapter on page 00.

8. See chapter 10, 151–52.

7. The Self and the External Sense Organs

1. This is an old view, the early version of which can be traced back to the Vedic literature (SIP 62). But it is difficult to identify the thinkers.

2. Some followers of Carvaka deny that perception is a source of knowledge in the strict sense but accept perception as the only ultimate and legitimate source of probable opinion (NDP 1:72).

3. See NK, chapter 3.

4. This does not imply that the self becomes an object of introspection. In the view of Vatsyayana, as noted earlier, the self is imperceptible.

8. The Self and the Inner Sense

1. One of the traditional Nyāya issues we skip here is whether the inner sense is atomic (*aṇu*) or not. Gotama and many other Nyāya philosophers held that the inner sense is atomic, because otherwise we cannot explain why it is unifunctional. This view is rejected by some Nyāya philosophers such as Raghunatha Siromani who do not agree that the inner sense is unifunctional. Philosophers of other Indian schools, such as the Sāṃkhya school, have also rejected the view that the inner sense is unifunctional and atomic.

What is crucial from the point of view of the Nyāya kind of dualism is that the inner sense should be distinguished from the self and held to be devoid of consciousness. This issue can be discussed without entering into the controversy over whether the inner sense is atomic. Even if it is held that two different cognitions never arise at the same time, it does not seem to be necessary to hold that the inner sense is atomic. That only one cognitive act takes place at a time may also be explained by supposing that only the strongest among the different competing impulses being sent by different external sense organs at the same time succeeds in activating the inner sense. It should then be supposed further that different external sense stimulations are of varying strengths and that two different external sense stimulations taking place at the same time are never of exactly the same strength.

In the same spirit we skip the issue whether the inner sense is a physical substance. Some Nyāya philosophers such as Raghunatha Siromani again hold that it is physical (PTN 8), while others deny that. But this is not the most important issue and the Nyāya kind of dualism can survive either way as long as it is held that the inner sense is different from the self, which alone is the substratum of consciousness.

2. Sydney Shoemaker, *The First Person Perspective* (Cambridge: Cambridge University Press, 1996), 12.

3. This may have influenced some scholars to translate *manas* as the mind (e.g. SDI 198), which may be misleading.

4. TC, chapter in introspection (*anuvyavasāya*).

5. W. G. Lycan, *Consciousness and Experience* (Cambridge, Mass.: MIT Press, 1996), 16. Lycan's view on the inner sense is not very different from that of David Armstrong: "What Is Consciousness?" in D. M. Armstrong, *The Nature of Mind and other Essays* (Ithaca, N.Y.: Cornell University Press, 1980).

6. This does not wipe out the difference between the internal and the external. The Nyāya does regard thinking as an internal activity (requiring the contact between the self and the inner sense) and external perception as in part an external activity (requiring the environmental stimulation of an external sense organ).

9. The Self and the Body

1. The motion of a stone, for example, may bring it into conjunction with another stone. The motion also disjoins the moving thing from its previous location and produces a velocity (*vega*) in it.

2. For example, sound may be produced by the conjunction of two hands while clapping and by disjoining two pieces of wood.

3. See VU 239–41. Also Plato's *Phaedo*.

4. Saul M. Kripke, *Naming and Necessity* (Cambridge, Mass.: Harvard University Press, 1980), selections in *The Nature of Mind* (NOM), ed. D. M. Rosenthal (Oxford: Oxford University Press, 1991), 236–46.

5. NOM, 165.

6. NOM, 242.

7. Descartes, *Meditations on First Philosophy*, ed. D. A. Cress (Indianapolis: Hackett), Meditation 2.

8. S. Guttenplan, ed., *A Companion to the Philosophy of Mind* (CPM) (Oxford: Blackwell, 1994), 265.

9. The doctrine of *viśeṣa* is arrived at from an application of the law of the identity of indiscernibles (BPP 63–67).

10. This is discussed in connection with *pakṣatā* (BPP 365–74). The Nyāya also holds that what is true of something under a certain specifier (*avacchedaka*) may not be true of that thing under a different specifier.

11. R. Swinburne, *The Evolution of the Soul* (Oxford: Oxford University Press, 1986). Also CPM, 265–67.

12. "Two Cartesian Arguments for the Simplicity of the Soul," *American Philosophical Quarterly* 28 (July 1991).

13. This issue has actually generated controversy in Indian philosophical circles with arguments and counterarguments flying on both sides.

14. Thomas Nagel, "What Is It Like to Be a Bat?" *Philosophical Review* 93 (October 1974): 435–50, reprinted in NOM, 422–28.

15. NOM, 425–26.

16. Frank Jackson, "What Mary Didn't Know," *The Journal of Philosophy* 93 (May 1986): 291–95, reprinted in NOM, 392–94.

17. Paul M. Churchland, *The Engine of Reason*, (Cambridge, Mass.: MIT Press, 1995), 198–99.

18. W. G. Lycan, *Consciousness and Experience*, (Cambridge, Mass.: MIT Press, 1996), 49. Also, "*privileged access* . . . is not a *problem*; it is

simply a fact, which must be explained, or at least accommodated, by any adequate theory of the mind." Ibid., 6.

19. We add a supplimentary argument adapted from Uddyotakara discussed in chapter 6: Nothing, without the immaterial self, has privileged access, for example, a stone. A living organism has privileged access. Therefore, a living organism is not without the immaterial self. This is in the *vyatirekin* form and should be analyzed accordingly as explained in the chapter 6.

20. Ibid., 49–50.

21. For a survey of the recent discussion of the physical criterion of personal identity and objections to it, see Harold W. Noonan, *Personal Identity* (London: Routledge, 1989), chapter 1.

22. John R. Searle, *The Rediscovery of the Mind* (Cambridge, Mass.: MIT Press, 1992); *Minds, Brains and Science* (Cambridge, Mass.: Harvard University Press, 1984). Some critics of Searle argue that although consciousness and semantic content may not belong to the program, these still belong to the whole system including the implementation of the program. (E.g., David J. Chalmers, *The Conscious Mind* [Oxford: Oxford University Press, 1996], chapter 9.) From the Nyāya viewpoint such attribution to the system or the implementation is objectionable. As explained earlier, the semantic content is subject to privileged access due to the fluidity of the qualificand and the qualifier as well as that of layeredness. There is nothing within the system or the implementation that accounts for this.

23. According to Searle, although mental states are nonphysical, they are nevertheless states of the physical brain. This is clearly not acceptable to the Nyāya, for in the latter view internal states belong to the immaterial self.

24. See DI, chapter 11.

25. ER, chapter 1, etc.

26. David Wiggins, *Sameness and Substance* (Cambridge, Mass.: Harvard University Press, 1980).

10. Miscellaneous Arguments

1. Strictly speaking, from the Nyāya point of view, what we mean by saying that there are no hare's horns is that no hare possesses any horn or that no horn belongs to a hare or that there is absence (*abhāva*) of the intended relationship (*sambandha*) between the hare and the horn. Each component of the complex idea of hare's horn, namely, hare, horn, possession or belonging or intended relationship, and absence is a familiar, nonempty idea; hence the denial of the existence of hare's horns is meaningful. A similar analysis will hold for other meaningful but empty terms, such as the

round square, the son of a barren mother, turtle's hair, and so on. Some of these terms are empty and contain a logical contradiction. Still in these cases also each component is a nonempty idea. For example, when we say that there are no round squares, what we mean is that there is nothing that is both square and round each component of which is an instantiated idea.

2. From the Nyāya viewpoint both the statements (1) 'the rabbit's horn is sharp' and (2) 'the rabbit's horn is not sharp' are false. Does this violate the law of excluded middle? No, if the Nyāya analysis is accepted. The first statement boils down to the compound statement that the rabbit has a horn and the horn is sharp. This compound statement is false, because the first conjunct is false and whenever a conjunct is false, the conjunction containing that conjunct must be false. Similarly, the second statement is equivalent to the compound statement that the rabbit has a horn and the horn is not sharp. This compound statement is also false for the same reason as the first. Thus the appearance of a logical paradox is avoided. See B. K. Matilal, *Epistemology, Logic and Grammar in Indian Philosophical Analysis* (The Hague: Mouton, 1971), 138–40.

What if the round square is big and not big? A similar analysis would hold. 'The round square is big' is equivalent to 'the thing is round and is square and is big' and 'the round square is not big', to 'the thing is round and square and not big'. Both these compound statements are false, because both are conjunctions and one of the conjuncts is false.

This does not suggest that a Nyāya philosopher would fail to recognize the epistemic difference between the falsity of 'the rabbit has a horn' and that of 'the thing is round and square'. In the latter the falsity can be gathered by the mind alone (*manasaiva gamyate*) but not in the former. See my "Some Remarks on Indian Theories of Truth," *Journal of Indian Philosophy* 12 (1984): 340–43.

3. Augustine argued that although I am deceived into believing many false things, I am most certain that I am. For if I am deceived, I am. For he who does not exist, cannot be deceived (*City of God* 11. 26).

Descartes argued that I can doubt everything else but my own existence. For in order to be able to doubt I must exist. Even if an all powerful, evil God deceives me into believing everything else which is false, my own existence is indubitable. For to be deceived I must exist (*Meditations on First Philosophy*, Meditation 2).

The author of the *Sāṃkhyasūtra* (6.1) argued that the self exists for there can be no proof of its nonexistence. Commenting on that, Vijnabhiksu (15th century CE) argued that the mere existence of the self is necessarily proved from the awareness that I cognize (*jānāmi*). In other words, I cannot have the awareness that I cognize something unless I exist. Hence the existence of the self is not open to dispute but only the distinction between the self and what is not the self.

4. This argument too is similar to the argument of Descartes referred to above. According to Descartes, my own existence provides the bedrock of certainty on which runs aground the ship of skepticism and on which the secure foundation of knowledge can be built.

5. The opponent, presumably a Buddhist, may here have in mind the Nyāya view that all sounds, including letter sounds, are noneternal. The Nyāya view is opposed to the Mīmāṃsā view that all sounds, including letter sounds, are eternal.

6. A similar argument has been offered by the Sāṃkhya school to prove the existence of *puruṣa* or pure consciousness as something fundamentally different from *prakṛti* or matter or the substratum of change. See chapter 12.

7. This account of darkness is rejected by many Nyāya philosophers who prefer to regard darkness as the absence of light.

11. A Proof of the Existence of God

1. *Tarkasaṃgraha-Dīpikā* (abbreviated as TSD) of Annambhatta, translation and elucidation by G. Bhattacharya (Calcutta: Progressive Publishers, 1976), 90. Annambhatta belongs to the 18th century AD. He is from South India and his work is used as an instructional text in Nyāya circles all over India. Earlier versions of Annambhatta's proof are found in Gangesa's *Tattvacintāmaṇi*, ed. K. Tarkavagisa (Calcutta: Asiatic Society, 1884–1901), chapter entitled *Īśvrānumāna* and in Udayana's *Nyāya-kusumāñjali*, ed. P. Upadhyaya and D. Sastri (Varanasi: Chowkhamba, 1957), chapter 5. Gangesa and Udayana (both great philosophers) belong respectively to the 13th century AD and the 11th century AD. K. Tarkavagisa, the editor of Gangesa's work, passed away in the first half of this century and was highly regarded all over India for his dialectical skills. All these philosophers are of the Nyāya school.

2. For a full discussion of the notions of the subject, the probans, and the probandum, see TSD, chapter on inference (*anumāna pramāṇa*), 189ff.

3. We have translated *kṣityaṅkura* as "the first product." *Kṣityaṅkura* is a compound formed out of *kṣiti* and *aṅkura*. While *kṣiti* stands for one of the four elements, namely, the earth, it is also commonly used to mean the whole world of change and the latter is the appropriate meaning in the present context. *Aṅkura* means the earliest stage of a sprout. Thus the compound literally means the first product (*prathmotpanna-kārya*).

4. TSD, 77.

5. In the face of the generalization that a new material thing always comes out of preexisting material a theist who claims that God creates matter out of nothing has the burden of proving that—a burden such a theist should

carry out independently of proving the existence of God. This by no means is an easy task.

6. TSD, 90.

7. It may be noted that the causal agent is only one kind of causal condition. The material out of which something is made, e.g., clay for a clay pot, is also a causal condition but does not obviously possess knowledge, etc. So the thesis is not that all causal conditions are conscious beings but that some are.

8. See my *Definition and Induction*, chapter 8, for reference and full discussion.

9. It may here be pointed out that the traditional Western causal arguments have sometimes been criticized on the grounds that, even if otherwise valid, the arguments would not prove a single first cause and that those arguments do not establish the present existence of the first cause. See J. J. C. Smart, "The Existence of God," in *New Essays in Philosophical Theology*, ed, A. Flew and A. C. MacIntyre (New York: Macmillan, 1955).

10. See J. L. Mackie, *Miracles of Theism* (Oxford: Clarendon Press, 1982), chapter 5. Also A. Kenny, *The Five Ways* (London: Routledge, 1969).

11. For a discussion of when an infinite regress is tolerable and when it is not, see my "The Nyaya-Vaisesika Theory of Universals," *Journal of Indian Philosophy* 3 (1975): 363–82.

12. Op cit., Chapter 5. Also Hume's *Dialogues Concerning Natural Religion*, ed. N. Kemp Smith, 2nd ed. (Edinburgh: Nelson, 1947), part IX.

13. Descartes' *Meditations on First Philosophy*, Trans. and ed. by D. A. Cress, 3rd ed. (Indianapolis: Hackett, 1993), chapter 3.

14. Ibid.

15. Plato's *Phaedo* in the *Great Dialogues of Plato*, trans. H. D. Rouse, (New York: Mentor, 1984), 82b–84c.

16. Descartes himself formulates the causal adequacy principle by saying that the cause cannot have any less reality than the effect. (*Meditations*, chapter 3) Such a formulation may avoid the objection that the effect may have new features. But then the natural questions are: (1) what precisely is meant by reality? (2) Does it make sense to say that there are different degrees of reality? (3) Can reality be a predicate?

17. Descartes has drawn the distinction between formal reality and objective reality (*Meditations*, chapter 3) which seems to imply the distinction between being an object of thought and being an object or a real in nature. It is then somewhat puzzling that he does not anticipate this objection and address it.

18. Visvanatha's *Bhasapariccheda* and *Siddhantamuktavali* with five commentaries, ed. C. S. R. Sastry, reprint ed. (Delhi: Chowkhamba Sanskrit Pratisthana, 1988), 43. Visvanatha (18th century CE) is one of the well-known Nyāya philosophers from Bengal. His work is considered to be a basic textbook and taught in Nyāya establishments all over India.

19. The point, of course, is that not only the Nyāya but also other theists like Aquinas are not in a position to reject the second premise. Other theists too hold that the first product, whatever that may be, is created by a disembodied spirit called God.

20. Ibid., 44–48.

21. See TSD 351–53 for an explanation of the subjunctive argument. Also see my *Definition and Induction*, chapter 11.

22. Jagadisa's *Avacchedakatvanirukti* with the *Manoramā* of Vamacarana, Nyāya series no. 6, Varanasi: Khelarilal, 1934, 34. Jagadisa (17th century CE) is one of the great Navya Nyāya philosophers.

23. Visvanatha's *Bhāṣāpariccheda*, 45.

24. Ibid., 46.

25. Ibid., 46.

12. The Sāṃkhya View

1. Vacaspati Misra has explained *adhyavasāya* as making the determination that I should do something (STK 334, 346). Such determination takes place after an object is grasped (*ālocana*) by a cognitive organ, the inner sense (*manas*) makes a judgment of the form 'this is that' and egoness (*ahaṃkāra*) makes the determination that I can acquire, avoid, or ignore this. This is a sense of *adhyavasāya* that presupposes egoness and the internal organ.

2. This is analogous to the neutral monism advocated by Bertrand Russell and William James. However, neither Russell nor James would accommodate *puruṣa* or pure consciousness.

3. One way out for the Sāṃkhya is to appeal to the doctrine of preexistent effect (*satkārya*) and argue that all needed processes are together potentially in the cause. But even then how can all the requisite manifestations (*abhivyakti*) of the potential processes be together is not clear.

4. *Encyclopedia of Indian Philosophies*, ed. K. H. Potter, vol. 4 (Princeton: Princeton University Press, 1987), 68.

5. See my *Logic of Gotama*, chapter 4.

13. The Advaita View

1. See my "Some Remarks on Indian Theories of Truth."

2. See chapter 12.

3. For the Nyāya defense of introspection, see TC, vol. 1, the chapter on *anuvyavasāya* or introspection.

4. For the distinction between primary and secondary meaning, see TS, the chapter on *śabda* or testimony.

14. Conclusion

1. Joseph Butler, "Of Personal Identity," reprinted in *Personal Identity*, ed. J. Perry (Berkeley: University of California Press, 1975); Thomas Reid, *Essays on the Intellectual Powers of Man*, ed. A. D. Woozley (London: Macmillan, 1941), essay III, chapters 4 and 6, reprinted in Perry, *Personal Identity*.

2. A noninherent material particle cannot be gross, although in Raghunatha's view it is minimally perceptible (PTN 8–10).

3. ER, chapters 1–3, 8–10.

4. The Nyāya would insist though that even the lowest form of animal life has minimal consciousness, which is altogether missing in a material object.

5. In the Nyāya view the process is also cyclical and not a one-time, linear process. But we have not discussed the cyclical view of time, for it is not immediately needed for our purpose and would require considerable space.

6. See J. Kim, *Supervenience and Mind* (Cambridge: Cambridge University Press, 1993).

7. Indian philosophers have traditionally shown keen interest in physiology and related studies. See STK 272–86, NSB 3.2.63–66. Further, conditioned reflexes are a relatively recent discovery in the West and early modern European philosophers such as Descartes were unaware of them. But Indian philosophers have been aware of conditioned reflexes for a long time and some yogic practices routinely involve the study and development of conditioned reflexes.

8. ER, 322–33.

9. Owen Flanagan, *The Science of the Mind*, 2nd ed. (Cambridge, Mass.: MIT Press, 1991), 21.

10. There is no evidence that there is consciousness in a frozen sperm or egg. So a Nyāya philosopher would not grant that there is consciousness there. But, from the Nyāya point of view, there cannot be absolute or ever-

lasting absence (*atyantābhāva*) of life in a frozen sperm or egg, for these have been parts (*avayava*) of some living body before and could not be produced except within a living body and, further, may be parts of a living body in future.

11. The opposite view that internal perception and self-awareness are incorrigible is familiar in the Nyāya tradition. See TC, chapter on internal perception (*anuvyavasāya*).

Selected Bibliography

Annambhatta. *Tarkasaṃgraha*, with *Dīpikā* and *Adhyāpanā* (TSN). Ed. Narayana Chandra Goswami. Calcutta: Sanskrit Pustak Bhandar, 1980.

———. *Tarkasaṃgraha*, with *Dīpikā* and *Vivṛti* (TS). Ed. Pancanana Sastri. Calcutta: Sanskrit Pustak Bhandar, 1985.

———. *Tarkasaṃgrahadīpikā* (TSD). English translation and elucidation by Gopinath Bhattacharya. Calcutta: Progressive Publishers, 1976.

Annas, Julia. *Hellenistic Philosophy of Mind*. Berkeley: University of California Press, 1992.

Aristotle. *The Complete Works of Aristotle*. Ed. Jonathan Barnes. 2 vols. Bolingen Series No. 81.2. Princeton: Princeton University Press, 1984.

Armstrong, David M. *A Materialist Theory of the Mind*. London: Routledge, 1968.

Berkeley, George. *Three Dialogues between Hylas and Philonous*. Ed. R. M. Adams. Indianapolis: Hackett, 1979.

Bhaduri, Sadananda. *Studies in Nyaya-Vaisesika Metaphysics*. Poona: Bhandarkar Oriental Research Institute, 1947.

Bhasarvajna. *Nyāyabhūṣaṇa*. Ed. Swami Yogindrananda. Benares: Saddarsana Prakasana Pratisthanam, 1968.

Bhattacharya, D. C. *History of Navya-nyaya in Mithila*. Darbhanga: Mithila Institute, 1958.

Bhattacharya, Gopikamohan. *Studies in Nyaya-Vaisesika Theism*. Calcutta: Sanskrit College, 1969.

———. *Navya-Nyāya*. Delhi: Bharatiya Vidya Prakashan, 1978.

Bhattacharya, Gopinath. *Tarkasaṃgraha-Dīpikā* of Annambhatta. English translation and exposition. Calcutta: Progressive Publishers, 1976.

Bhattacharya, S. *Gadadhara's Theory of Objectivity*. 2 vols. Delhi: Motilal Banarasidass, 1990.

Bhattacharya, Visvabandhu. *Anumānacintāmaṇi*. Calcutta: K. P. Bagchi, 1993.

Bhimacarya, Jhalkikar. *Nyāyakoṣa*. Poona: Bhandarkar Oriental Research Institute, 1978.

Block, Ned. "Troubles with Functionalism." In C. W. Savage, ed., *Perception and Cognition: Issues in the Foundations of Psychology*. Minnesota Studies in the Philosophy of Science, 9. Minneapolis: University of Minnesota Press, 1978.

———. "Functionalism (2)." In CPM, 323–32.

Borst, C. V. *The Mind-Brain Identity Theory*. London: St. Martin's Press, 1970.

Butler, J. "Of Personal Identity." First dissertation to *The Analogy of Religion*. Reprinted in J. Perry, ed., *Personal Identity*. Berkeley: University of California Press, 1975.

Cassam, Quassim, ed. *Self-Knowledge*. Oxford: Oxford University Press, 1994.

Chakrabarti, Kisor. *The Logic of Gotama*. Honolulu: University of Hawaii Press, 1978.

———. *Definition and Induction* (DI). Honolulu: University of Hawaii Press, 1995.

———. "Some Comparisons between Frege's Logic and Navya-Nyāya Logic." *Philosophy and Phenomenological Research* 36 (1976): 554–63.

———. "Some Remarks on Indian Theories of Truth." *Journal of Indian Philosophy* 12 (1984): 339–55.

———. "Contraposition in European and Indian Logic." *International Philosophical Quarterly* 29 (1989): 121–27.

———. "Towards Dualism: The Nyaya-Vaisesika Way." *Philosophy East and West* 41 (1991): 470–91 (with Chandana Chakrabarti).

———. "*Anuvyavasāya*" [Introspection]. *Encyclopedia of Indian Philosophies*. Vol. 6. Princeton: Princeton University Press, 1993, 150–55, 603–4.

———. "*Anyathākhyāti*" [Error]. *Encyclopedia of Indian Philosophies*. Vol. 6. Princeton: Princeton University Press, 1993, 100–16, 594–99.

———. "*Manoṇutva*" [Atomicity of Inner Sense]. *Encyclopedia of Indian Philosophies*. Vol. 6. Princeton: Princeton University Press, 1993, 146–50, 603.

———. "*Sannikarṣa*" [Sensory Connection]. *Encyclopedia of Indian Philosophies*. Vol. 6. Princeton: Princeton University Press, 1993, 122–25, 600.

———. "*Tarka*" [Indirect (Subjunctive) Reasoning]. *Encyclopedia of Indian Philosophies*. Vol. 6. Princeton: Princeton University Press, 1993, 183–84, 572–73, 605, 628.

———. "*Upādhi*" [Vitiators of Generalization]. *Encyclopedia of Indian Philosophies*. Vol. 6. Princeton: Princeton University Press, 1993, 187–92, 580–84, 606, 630–31.

———. "*Vyāptigrahopāya*" [Method of Generalization]. *Encyclopedia of Indian Philosophies*. Vol. 6. Princeton: Princeton University Press, 1993, 178–83, 570–72, 604–5, 628–30.

———. "*Annotated Translation of Ātmatattvaviveka*." *Journal of Indian Philosophy and Religion* 1 (1996): 148–57 and 3, (1998): 147–58.

Chalmers, David J. *The Conscious Mind*. Oxford: Oxford University Press, 1996.

Chatterjee, S. C. *The Nyāya Theory of Knowledge*. Calcutta: University of Calcutta, 2nd ed., reprint, 1965.

Churchland, Paul M. *Matter and Consciousness*. Cambridge, Mass.: MIT Press, 2nd ed., 1988.

———. *The Engine of Reason: The Seat of the Soul* (ER). Cambridge, Mass.: MIT Press, 1996.

Dasgupta, S. *A History of Indian Philosophy*. Vol. 1. Cambridge: Cambridge University Press, 1963.

Dennett, Daniel C. *Brainstorms*. Montgomery, Vt.: Bradford Books, 1978.

———. *Consciousness Explained*. Boston: Little, Brown, 1991.

Descartes, René. *Meditations*. In *Philosophical Works of Descartes*. Trans. S. Haldane and G. R. T. Ross. 2 vols. New York: Dover, 1955.

Dharmakirti. *Nyāyabindu*. Ed. Chandrasekhara Sastri. Benares: Chowkhamba, 1954.

———. *Pramāṇaviniścaya*. Ed. T. Vetter. Vol. 1. Vienna, 1966.

———. *Pramāṇavārttika*. Ed. Swami Dvarikadasa Sastri. Benares: Bauddhabharati, 1968.

Dharmarajadhvarindra. *Vedāntaparibhāṣā*, with *Vivrti*. Ed. Pancanana Sastri. Calcutta: Sanskrit Pustak Bhandar, 1969.

Eccles, J. C. and K. R. Popper. *The Self and Its Brain*. Berlin: Springer International, 1977.

Flanagan, Owen. *The Science of the Mind*. 2nd ed. Cambridge, Mass.: MIT Press, 1991.

———. *Consciousness Reconsidered*. Cambridge, Mass.: MIT Press, 1992.

Fodor, Jerry A. *Psychological Explanation*. New York: Random House, 1968.

———. *Psychosemantics*. Cambridge, Mass.: MIT Press, 1987.

——— and E. Lepore. *Holism*. Oxford: Basil Blackwell, 1992.

Foster, John. *The Immaterial Self*. London: Routledge, 1991.

Gadadhara. *Gādādharī* (GD) with *Didhiti* by Raghunatha Siromani. 2 vols. Ed. V. P. Dvivedi. Benares: Chowkhamba, 1970.

———. *Viṣayatāvāda* in *Gadadhara's Theory of Objectivity*. Vol. 2. Translation and exposition by S. Bhattacharya. Delhi: Motilal Banarasidass, 1990.

———. *Vyutpattivāda* with Śāstrārthakalā by Venimadhava Sastri. Ed. Rajanarayana Sukla. Benares: Chowkhamba, 1968.

———. *Vyutpattivāda* with *Dipika* by Sivadatta Misra. Ed. Jvalaprasada Gauda. Benares: Bharatiya Vidya Prakasan, 1973.

———. *Vyutpattivāda* with *Gūdārthatattvāloka* by Dharmadatta Jha and *Arthadīpikā* by Sasinatha Jha. Ed. Babu Misra. Darbhanga: Mithila Institute, 1977.

———. *Vyutpattivāda*. Vol. 1. Translation by V. P. Bhatta. Delhi: Eastern Book Linkers, 1990.

———. *Śaktivāda* with *Mañjuṣā* by Krsna Bhatta, Vivṛti by Madhava Bhattacharya. Ed. Damodara Goswami. Benares: Chowkhamba, 1927.

———. *Śaktivāda*. Translation and exposition by V. P. Bhatta. 2 vols. Delhi: Eastern Book Linkers, 1994 and 1995.

Gangesa Upadhyaya. *Tattvacintāmaṇi*, I (TC). Ed. K. N. Tarkavagisa. Delhi: Motilal Banarasidass, 1974.

———. *Tattvacintāmaṇi*, II, part I. Ed. N. S. R. Tatacarya. Tirupati: Kendriya Sanskrit Vidyapeetha, 1982.

Gangopadhyaya, Ashoke K. *Vivaraṇaprameyasaṃgraha* of Vidyaranya Muni. Bengali translation and exposition. Calcutta: Navabharat Publishers, 1992.

Gangopadhyaya, M. D. *Indian Atomism: History and Sources*. Calcutta: K. P. Bagchi, 1980.

Garfield, Jay L. *The Fundamental Wisdom of the Middle Way*. Translation of and commentary on Nagarjuna's *Mūlamādhyamikakārikā*. Oxford: Oxford University Press, 1995.

Gaudabrahmananda. *Gauḍabrahmānandī* (GB). Commentary on *Advaitasiddhi* (AD).

Geach, P. T. *Mental Acts*. London: Kegan Paul, 1957.

Gennaro, Rocco J. *Mind and Brain*. Indianapolis: Hackett, 1996.

Goswami, Narayana Chandra. *Tarkasaṃgrahadīpikā* of Annambhatta. Bengali translation and exposition. Calcutta: Sanskrit Pustak Bhandar, 1980.

———. *Sāṃkhyatattvakaumudī* of Vacaspati Misra. Bengali translation and exposition. Calcutta: Sanskrit Pustak Bhandar, 1982.

Gotama. *Nyāyasūtra* (NS) with *Bhāṣya* of Vatsyayana (NSB). Ed. Padmaprasada Sastri and Harirama Sukla. Benares: Chowkhamba, 1942.

———. *Nyāyasūtra*. Translation and exposition by J. R. Ballantyne. Calcutta, 1859.

———. *Nyāyasūtra* with *Bhāṣya* of Vatsyayana. Translation by Ganganath Jha. Poona: Oriental Book Agency, 1939.

———. *Nyāyasūtra* with *Bhāṣya* of Vatsyayana, *Vārttika* of Uddyotakara, *Tātparyatīkā* of Vacaspati Misra, and *Vṛtti* of Visvanatha. Vol. 1. Ed. Amarendra Tarkatirtha and Taranatha Tarkatirtha. Calcutta: Metropolitan Publishing House, 1938.

———. *Nyāyasūtra* with *Bhāṣya* of Vatsyayana, *Vārttika* of Uddyotakara, *Tātparyatīkā* of Vacaspati Misra, and *Vṛtti* of Visvanatha. Vol. 2. Ed. Amarendra Tarkatirtha and Hemanta Tarkatirtha. Calcutta: Metropolitan Publishing House, 1944.

———. *Nyāyasūtra* with *Bhāṣya* of Vatsyayana, *Vārttika* of Uddyotakara, *Tātparyatīkā* of Vacaspati Misra, and *Pariśuddhi* of Udayana. Vol. 1 (NDFC). Ed. A. L. Thakur. Darbhanga: Mithila Institute, 1967.

———. *Nyāyasūtra* with *Bhāṣya* of Vatsyayana. 5 vols. Translation and exposition by Mrinal Kanti Goagopadhyaya. Calcutta: Indian Studies.

———. *Nyāyasūtra* with *Bhāṣya* of Vatsyayana and *Prasannapadā* of Sudarsanacarya. Ed. Swami Dvarikadasa Sastri. Benares: Sudhi Prakasana, 1986.

Guha, D. C. *The Navya-Nyāya System of Logic*. 2nd ed. Delhi: Motilal Banarsidass, 1979.

Guttenplan, Samuel, ed. *A Companion to the Philosophy of Mind* (CPM). Oxford: Basil Blackwell, 1994.

Hart, W. D. *The Engine of the Soul*. Cambridge: Cambridge University Press, 1988.

Hofstadter, D. R. and D. C. Dennett. *The Mind's I*. Toronto: Bantam Books, 1988.

Hume, David. *A Treatise of Human Nature*. Ed. L. A. Selby-Bigge. Oxford: Clarendon Press, 1978.

Ingalls, D. H. H. *Materials for the Study of Navya-Nyāya Logic*. Cambridge, Mass.: Harvard University Press, 1951.

Jackson, Frank. "What Mary Didn't Know." *The Journal of Philosophy* 83 (1986): 291–95; reprinted in NOM, 392–94.

Jagadisa. *Avacchedakatvanirukti* with *Manorama* of Vamacarana. Nyāya Series no. 6, 34. Varanasi: Khelarilal.

———. *Jāgadīsī*. Benares: Chowkhamba, 1906–8.

———. *Śabdaśaktiprakāśikā* with *Kṛṣṇakāntī* by Krsnakanta Vidyavagisa and *Prabodhinī* by Ramabhadra Siddhantavagisa. Ed. Dhundiraja Sastri. Benares: Chowkhamba, 1973.

———. *Śabdaśaktiprakāśikā* with *Vivṛti*. Ed. Madhusudana Nyayacarya. 3 vols. Calcutta: Sanskrit College, 1980, 1981, and 1985.

Jayanta Bhatta. *Nyāyamañjarī* (NM). 2 vols. Ed. Suryanarayana Sukla. Benares: Chowkhamba, 1936.

Jha, Ganganatha. *Padārthadharmasaṁgraha* of Prasastapada. English translation. Varanasi: Choukhamba Orientalia, 1982.

———. *Nyāyasūtrabhāṣyavārttika*. English translation. Delhi: Motilal Banarsidass, 1984.

Kanada, *Vaiśeṣika Sūtra* (VS). Ed. Jambuvijayaji Muni. Baroda: Oriental Institute, 1961.

Kenny, Anthony. *The Five Ways*. London: Routledge, 1969.

Kripke, Saul A. *Naming and Necessity*. Cambridge, Mass.: Harvard University Press, 1972; selected passages in NOM, 236–46.

Kumarila Bhatta. *Mīmāṁsāślokavārttika* with *Nyāyaratnākara* by Parthasarathi Misra. Ed. Swami Dvarikadasa Sastri. Benares: Tara Publications, 1978.

Levine, J. "Materialism and Qualia: The Explanatory Gap." *Pacific Philosophical Quarterly* 64 (1983): 354–61.

Lewis, David. *Philosophical Papers*. Oxford: Oxford University Press, 1983.

Lockwood, Michael. *Mind, Brain and the Quantum*. Oxford: Basil Blackwell, 1989.

Lycan, W. G. *Consciousness*. Cambridge, Mass.: MIT Press, 1987.

———. "Functionalism (1)." In CPM, 317–23.

———. *Consciousness and Experience*. Cambridge, Mass.: MIT Press, 1996.

Mackie, J. L. *Miracles of Theism*. Oxford: Clarendon Press, 1982.

Madhavacarya. *Sarvadarśanasaṃgraha*. Ed. V. S. Abhyankar. Poona: Bhandarkar Oriental Research Institute, 1978.

Madhusudana Sarasvati. *Advaitasiddhi*. Ed. Anantakrshna Sastri. Bombay: Nirnayasagara Press, 1917.

Matilal, B. K. *The Navyanyāya Doctrine of Negation*. Cambridge, Mass.: Harvard University Press, 1968, including *Nañvāda* of Raghunatha Siromani.

———. *Epistemology, Logic and Grammar in Indian Philosophical Analysis*. The Hague: Mouton, 1971.

———. *Logic, Language and Reality*. Delhi: Motilal Banarsidass, 1985.

———. *Perception*. Oxford: Clarendon Press, 1986.

McGinn, Collin. *The Subjective View*. Oxford: Oxford University Press, 1983.

Mohanty, J. N. *Gangesa's Theory of Truth*. Delhi: Motilal Banarsidass, 1989.

Mukhopadhyay, Pradyot K. *Indian Realism*. Calcutta: K. P. Bagchi, 1984.

———. *The Nyāya Theory of Linguistic Performance*. Calcutta: K. P. Bagchi, 1991.

Nagarjuna. *Mūlamādhyamikakārikā*. Ed. P. L. Vaidya. Darbhanga: Mithila Institute, 1968.

Nagel, Thomas. "What Is It Like to Be a Bat." *Philosophical Review* 82 (1974): 435–50; reprinted in NOM, 422–28.

Noonan, Harold. *Personal Identity*. London: Routledge, 1989.

———, ed. *Personal Identity*. Aldershot, U.K.: Dartmouth, 1993.

Parfit, Derek. "Personal Identity." *Philosophical Review* 80 (1971): 3–27.

———. *Reasons and Persons*. Oxford: Clarendon Press, 1984.

Perry, John, ed. *Personal Identity*. Berkeley: University of California Press, 1975.

Phillips, Stephen H. *Classical Indian Metaphysics*. Chicago: Open Court, 1995.

Place, U. T. "Is Consciousness a Brain Process?" *British Journal of Psychology* 47 (1956): 44–50.

Plato. *Collected Dialogues*. Ed. E. Hamilton and H. Cairns. New York: Bolligen Foundation, 1963.

———. *Phaedo*. In the *Great Dialogues of Plato*. Translated by H. D. Rouse. New York: Mentor, 1984.

Potter, Karl H. *Padārthatattvanirūpaṇam* of Raghunatha Siromani. English translation and exposition. Cambridge, Mass.: Harvard-Yenching Institute, 1957.

———, ed. *The Encyclopedia of Indian Philosophies*. Vols. 2 and 4. Princeton: Princeton University Press, 1977, 1993.

Prabhacandra. *Prameyakamalamārtaṇḍa*. Ed. M. K. Sastri. Bombay: Nirnaya Sagar Press, 1941.

Prasastapada. *Padārthadharmasaṁgraha* with *Vyomavatī* by Vyomasivacarya, *Setu* by Padmanabha Misra. Ed. Gopinatha Kaviraja. Benares: Chowkhamba, 1930.

———. *Padārthadharmasaṁgraha* (PDS) with *Nyāyakandalī* (NKD) of Sridhara. Ed. Durgadhara Jha. Benares: Benares Sanskrit University, 1963.

Putnam, Hilary. "Minds and Machines." In *Dimensions of Mind*. Ed. S. Hook. New York: Collier Books, 1960.

———. "The Meaning of 'Meaning'." In *Language, Mind and Knowledge*. Ed. K. Gunderson. Minnesota Studies in the Philosophy of Science, 7. Minneapolis: University of Minnesota Press, 1975.

Radhakrishnan, Sarvepalli. *Indian Philosophy*. 2 vols. London: George Allen and Unwin, 9th impression, 1971.

Radhakrishnan, S. and C. A. Moore. *A Sourcebook in Indian Philosophy* (SIP). Princeton: Princeton University Press, 12th printing, 1989.

Raghunatha Siromani. *Padārthatattvanirūpaṇa*. Ed. V. P. Dvivedi. Benares: Chowkhamba, 1916.

———. *Padārthatattvanirūpaṇa*. Translation and elucidation by K. R. Potter. Cambridge, Mass.: Harvard University Press, 1967.

———. *Padārthatattvanirūpaṇa* (PTN) with *Tika* by Raghudeva Nyayalamkara. Ed. Madhusudana Nyayacarya. Calcutta: Sanskrit College, 1976.

———. *Avacchedakatvanirukti* with *Jāgadīśī* by Jagadisa and *Vivṛti* and *Manoramā* (AN) by Vamacarana Bhattacarya. Ed. Rajanarayana Sastri. Benares: Khelarilal.

———. *Tattvacintāmaṇi-anumāna-dīdhiti*. See Gadadhara, *Gādādharī*.

———. *Ātmatattvaviveka-dīdhiti*. See Udayanacarya, *Ātmatattvaviveka*.

———. *Nañvāda*. See Matilal, B. K.

———. *Ākhyātavāda* with *Vyākhyā* by Ramabhadra Sarvabhauma. Ed. Prabal Kumar Sen. Calcutta: Sanskrit Pustak Bhandar, 1979.

Reid, T. *Essays on the Intellectual Powers of Man*. Ed. A. D. Woozley. London: Macmillan, 1941.

Robinson, Howard, ed. *Objections to Physicalism*. Oxford: Clarendon Press, 1993.

Rorty, Richard. "Incorrigibility as the Mark of the Mental." *Journal of Philosophy* 67 (1970): 399–424.

Rosenberg, Jay F. *The Thinking Self*. Philadelphia: Temple University Press, 1986.

Rosenthal, D. M., ed. *The Nature of Mind* (NOM). Oxford: Oxford University Press, 1991.

Saha, Sukharanjan. *Meaning, Truth and Predication*. Calcutta: K. P. Bagchi, 1991.

Samkaracarya. *Brahmasūtrabhāṣya* with *Bhāmatī* by Vacaspati Misra, *Parimala* by Appyaya Diksita, and *Kalpataru* by Amalananda. Ed. Anantakrsna Sastri. Bombay: Tukaram Jawji, 1917.

Samkara Misra. *Upaskāra*. Calcutta: Asiatic Society, 1861.

Santaraksita. Tattvasaṃgraha with *Pañjikā* by Kamalasila. 2 vols. Ed. Swami Dvarikadasa Sastri. Benares: Bauddabharati, 1981 and 1982.

Sastri, Pancanana. *Vedāntaparibhāṣā* with *Vivṛti*. Calcutta: Sanskrit Pustak Bhandar, 1967.

———. *Bhāṣāpariccheda* with *Saṃgraha*. 3rd ed. Calcutta: Sanskrit Pustak Bhandar, 1969.

———. *Cārvākadarśanam* (CD). Calcutta: Sanskrit Pustak Bhandar, 1988.

Searle, John R. *Minds, Brains and Science*. Cambridge, Mass.: Harvard University Press, 1984.

———. *The Rediscovery of the Mind*. Cambridge, Mass.: MIT Press, 1992.

Shoemaker, Sydney. *Self-Knowledge and Self-Identity*. Ithaca, N.Y.: Cornell University Press, 1963.

———, 'Persons and their Pasts', *American Philosophical Quarterly* 7, 1970, 269–85.

———. *The First Person Perspective and Other Essays*, Cambridge University Press, Cambridge, 1996.

Shoemaker, Sydney and Richard Swinburne, eds. *Personal Identity*. Oxford: Basil Blackwell, 1984.

Smart, J. J. C. *Philosophy and Scientific Realism*. London: Routledge, 1963.

Strawson, P. F. *Individuals*. London: Methuen, 1959.

Swinburne, Richard. *The Evolution of the Self*. Oxford: Oxford University Press, 1986.

Tarkacarya, Kalipada. *Nyāyadarśanabinduh*. Benares: Benares Sanskrit University, 2021 (Śakābda).

Tarkavagisa, Phanibhusana. *Nyāyaparicaya*. Calcutta: Bangiya Jatiya Siksa Parishad, 1935.

———. *Nyāyadarśanam* (NDP). 5 vols. Calcutta: West Bengal State Book Board, 1981 (reprint, 1989), 1984, 1982, 1988, and 1989.

Udayanacarya. *Pariśuddhi* with *Prakāśa* by Vardhamana. Ed. V. P. Dvivedi and L. S. Dravid. Calcutta: Asiatic Society, 1911.

———. *Pariśuddhi*. See Gotama, A. L. Thakur edn.

———. *Kiraṇāvalī*. Ed. Sivacandra Sarvabhauma and Narendra Chandra Vedantatirtha. Calcutta: Bibliotheca Indica, 1956.

———. *Kiraṇāvalī*, I. Ed. Gaurinatha Sastri. Calcutta: U.N. Dhar, 1956.

———. *Lakṣaṇamālā*. Ed. S. Jha. Darbhanga: Mithila Institute, 1963.

———. *Nyāyapariśiṣṭa* with *Pañcikā* by Vamesvara. Ed. S. N. Srirama Desikan. Tirupati: Kendriya Sanskrit Vidyapeetha, 1976.

———. *Kiraṇāvalī*, II. Ed. Gaurinatha Sastri. Calcutta: Sanskrit Pustak Bhandar, 1978.

———. *Nyāyakusumañjali* with *Nyāyabodhanī*, *Prakāśa*, *Prakāśikā*, and *Makaranda*. Benares: Chowkhamba, 1935.

———. *Nyāyakusumañjali* with *Vistāra*. Ed. U. T. Viraraghavacarya. Tirupati: Kendriya Sanskrit Vidyapeetha, 1980.

———. *Ātmatattvaviveka* with Dīdhiti by Raghunatha Siromani, *Tīkā* by Samkara Misra, and *Tīkā* by Bhagiratha Thakkura. Ed. V. P. Dvivedi and L. S. Dravid. Calcutta: Asiatic Society, 1986.

———. *Ātmatattvaviveka* with *Tātparya* by Dinanatha Tripathi. 3 vols. Calcutta: Sanskrit College, 1984, 1989, and 1989.

Uddyotakara. *Nyāyavārttika* (NV). Ed. V. P. Dvivedi and L. S. Dravid. Benares: Chowkhamba, 1915.

Vacaspati Misra. *Nyāyavārttikatātparyatīkā* (TP). Ed. R. S. Dravid. Benares: Chowkhamba, 1925.

———. *Nyāyavārttikatātparyatīkā*. See Gotama, A. L. Thakur edn.

———. *Sāṃkhyatattvakaumudī* with *Sārabodhinī*. Ed. Sivanarayana Sastri. Bombay: P. Jawaji, 1940.

———. *Sāṃkhyatattvakaumudī* with *Adhyapanā* (STK). Ed. Narayana C. Goswami. Calcutta: Sanskrit Pustak Bhandar, 1982.

———. *Bhāmatī*. See Samkaracarya.

Vasubandhu. *Vijñaptimātratāsiddhi*. Ed. S. Levi. Paris, 1925.

———. *Abhidharmakoṣa*. Ed. Swami Dvarikadasa Sastri. Benares: Bauddhabharati, 1970, 1972.

Vattanky, John. *Gangesa's Philosophy of God*. Adyar, Madras, 1984.

Vidyaranya, Swami. *Buddhist Philosophy and Religion* (in Bengali). Calcutta: West Bengal State Book Board, 1984.

Vidyaranya Muni. *Vivaraṇaprameyasaṃgraha* with *Mīmāṃsāupakramaṇikā* and *Mādhukarī* by Ashoke Kumar Gangopadhyaya. Calcutta: Navabharat Publishers, 1992.

Visvanatha. *Bhāṣāpariccheda* with *Muktāvalīsaṁgraha* and *Vivṛti* (BPP). Ed. Pancanana Sastri. 3rd ed. Calcutta: Sanskrit Pustak Bhandar, 1969.

———. *Kārikāvalī* with autocommentary called *Muktāvalī*, *Prabhā* by Narasimha Raya, *Mañjuṣā* by Pattabhirama, *Dinakarī* by Mahadeva Bhatta, *Rāmarudrī* by Ramarudra, and *Jatīya* by Gangarama (BP). Ed. C. S. R. Sastry. Madras: Sri Balamanorama Press, 1923; reprint, Delhi: Chowkhamba, 1988.

———. *Bhāṣāpariccheda* with *Muktāvalī*. Translation and elucidation by Swami Madhavananda. 2nd ed. Calcutta: Advaita Ashram, 1954.

Wiggins, David. *Sameness and Substance*. Oxford: Basil Blackwell, 1980.

Williams, Bernard A. O. *Problems of the Self*. Cambridge: Cambridge University Press, 1973.

Yuktidīpikā (anonymous). Ed. R. C. Pandey. Delhi: Motilal Banarsidass, 1967.

Index